Rising with Roses: Monique Ruberu

A story of renewal and
lessons learned

To my amazing husband Gerard: Thank you for striving to be

the husband and father God created you to be.

You are second only to Him in my eyes.

I feel so blessed by your love, encouragement and support

Table of Contents

CHAPTER 1—MY LIFE BEFORE

I am a Roman Catholic Pro Life Ob/Gyn. But I haven't always been that way.

I was born into a Catholic family. My mother, father and grandmother have always had a very strong faith. My mother was miraculously cured from a life threatening kidney disease as a child. From that moment on, she had an unwavering love for Our Lady of

Perpetual Help. I have memories of us attending mass every Sunday and saying family rosaries often. While I was growing up my siblings and I received all of the sacraments. I attended public Catholic schools in Canada as well as a great Catholic University. While attending University of Dallas, I was blessed to sing in an a capella Latin choir named Collegium Cantorum. This choir focused on the music of the Latin Mass and sacred polyphony.

Sadly, although at times I was proud of my faith, I never truly embraced it and allowed myself to be completely nourished and dependent on our Lord until very recently. I was happy to be a "Cafeteria Catholic" picking and choosing what parts of the faith I would accept and embrace.

I always considered myself to be personally prolife. I would never have an abortion. Yet, I was very hesitant to tell others what they should do. I decided to completely ignore the possibility that contraceptives could cause abortions. I was unable to take a strong stand with regard to abortion in the case of rape and incest. Like other difficult topics pertaining to my faith I chose to simply ignore them and hope that they never affected me personally.

As the years progressed, I ultimately became a physician and then an Obstetrician/Gynecologist. In residency I was taught to address almost every GYN issue with contraceptives. It came to the point that I honestly did not know how to practice medicine without them. Although I personally chose against using them, I prescribed them time and again for my patients.

During residency I strived to be a leader among my peers. I became an active member of local and national leadership. I enjoyed the prestige and perks that accompanied participation in this group, but never truly stood up for my pro life beliefs. Instead I focused on the other projects that I was in full support of such as organizing service projects to benefit the underserved populations in our area.

Following residency, my career was progressing quite nicely. I was a respected member of the medical community. I had many patients who would share their experiences under my care and would refer friends and family to me. I was known as a practice builder and a good doctor.

After working for a few years the moment had arrived for me to prepare for the most difficult exam of my life: the Oral OB/GYN board exam. This dreaded exam strikes fear in the hearts of almost all OB/GYN physicians. As I began preparing for this exam, I also found out that I was pregnant with my third child.

Completely hormonal and stressed to the max with two small boys at home, I was not the easiest person to live with. My husband and I began arguing frequently. In my mind, these arguments were no different than any which had occurred in the past. I knew that we would fight and get over it. Sadly, the same was not true for my husband. The constant fighting led him to recede further into his own world. Pretty soon we were like two ships sailing in the night. At a moment when we should have been prioritizing God, then each other, then our children and everything else; my priorities were my exam, my children, and everything else had to take care of itself.

The contention ultimately led to my husband suggesting marital counseling. I agreed to this, but the counselor only managed to boost me up and alienate him further. The sanctity of our marriage was never discussed, nor the fact that the vows we shared were not just with one another but with Our Holy Savior. Everything ultimately hit rock bottom and we were on the brink of divorce. Things had been said and done which seemed too great to overcome. Then God stepped in.

While studying for my exam, I attended a prep course. I met a beautiful Christian doctor who had such a strong love for the Lord. Somehow we became study partners and on a nightly basis we would grill each other over the phone from Florida to Philadelphia. If it wasn't for her I don't know that I would have had the strength or peace to pass my exam. During our moments of studying we shared a lot personally. I told her about the state of my marriage and my fears. She instantly began to give me the resources that ultimately saved my marriage and changed my life. With the use of resources like Marriagetoday.com, the Love Dare, KLOVE radio and "The Divorce Remedy", I came to realize that I couldn't walk out on our marriage of 10 years.

Being a child from a divorced family myself, I saw the truth about the devastation divorce brings for children. I did not want that for my children. I had made a vow to my husband and my Lord when we married, and I wasn't going to go back on that promise. I decided to put all my energy into saving my crumbling marriage and my family.

It was a very difficult time, but God healed me and my husband. He allowed our marriage which had burned down to the ashes to be reborn. We met with our spiritual advisors and decided to begin anew with a renewal of our marital vows. Our amazing priest, Father Oliver, redid our entire wedding ceremony and blessed our marriage. It was the most beautiful and memorable day. Gerard, myself and God began our covenant again. From that moment on I was filled with a desire to repay the Lord for His kindness and love. I wanted to do something that would make Him truly proud to call me His daughter...something that I was scared to do before.

LIFE LESSON#1—NO MARRIAGE IS EASY

When I first realized that our marriage was in trouble I was mortified. I looked around and saw so many other people we knew who were in seemingly "great marriages" and we had somehow found ourselves on the brink of divorce. We were the couple who seemed so in love. We had a romantic whirlwind international romance that led to engagement and marriage.

We were a successful couple with no stress from finances. I always thought a lack of money was the thing that stressed relationships. We shared the same faith and culture. I believed we were more than compatible. Yet, somehow we found ourselves after 10 years of marriage, barely communicating and drifting farther and farther apart.

It was only after God healed me and brought us to a place of love and forgiveness that I could begin to understand just how common this situation really is. When I started speaking to my patients and friends about their relationships I realized that far too many people are in the same boat.

When we understand that we are in danger of losing the marriage, most couples reach out for counseling and support. Sadly, not all counselors are created equal. It is very important to seek someone who values the sanctity of marriage. This person must be willing to help both individuals take responsibility for the breakdown without pinning the blame on one party and pushing the couple to divorce. If at all possible, find someone who understands your faith background and will use your faith as a part of the solution. We must remember that when we marry in the church we are not just making a promise to our spouse. We are making a covenant with God and our spouse. Everything possible must be done to uphold this promise and try to heal the marriage.

Even in the most difficult situations we should not to jump to divorce. A decision can be made to separate temporarily, giving one another a chance to heal and grow. Ultimately, the goal is to rebuild the trust and commitment over time allowing the relationship to start over.

I have often noticed that the most trying period in marriage seems to be years seven through ten. During this time the fluff and sweetness of the new marriage has diminished. The husband and wife have settled into a routine of work and chores. Children have usually blessed the home by this time, but in their arrival they have changed the order of priority as well. The husband and wife who used to be only focused on each other's happiness are now focused primarily on work and the kids. They tend to spend less and less time focusing on and courting one another.

When a couple finds themselves in this position, is it hopeless? I would argue that there is always hope. How do you try to fix the situation? First and foremost, be willing to put in the work. Nobody ever tells engaged couples how much work marriage is. Marriage is HARD WORK.

When you find yourself drifting apart, one of the most important things to do is to reinstate the appropriate priority. If both husband and wife place God first, then their spouse, then the children, everything works more cohesively.

Upon waking in the morning, begin the day expressing gratitude to God for the blessings in your life. Take a moment to share your deepest needs and concerns with Him as well. Read scripture, meditate, embrace this beautiful moment of silence and ask the Holy Spirit to guide you. You will start the day off with a sense of peace and contentment.

Next, ask your spouse daily what you can do to help him or her have a better day. Try to verbalize something you appreciate about your spouse as well. Soon, you will find that your spouse will do the same for you. By prioritizing each other, the couple is strengthening and filling one another with love. When this occurs, that love pours down onto the children. Neither parent is left feeling empty and exhausted; both are supported in their daily tasks.

Children benefit immensely from witnessing the love of their parents. When children see their parents showing love and kindness to one another it gives them a sense of security and peace. When both parents are happier and content it gives them the strength to care for their children and fulfill their daily responsibilities.

Make sure you never stop dating. When couples are courting each other before marriage they can't get enough of each other. They hang on each other's words, priding themselves in knowing the likes and dislikes of each other. They go out of their way to make the other person feel loved and special. Sadly, the desire to continue this behavior often vanishes after years of marriage. The individuals continue to grow and change over the years. Likes and dislikes change just as beliefs and habits change. Shouldn't we constantly be trying to understand our partners? We can't assume that we know them now because we knew them well while we were dating.

The best way to continue learning about one another is by continuing to date in marriage. Dating doesn't mean that you have to spend a small fortune on babysitters, go out to expensive dinners, or even leave the house. It means that you should carve out a night each week where you and your spouse sit together with the TV off and phones put away for at least 1 hour. You can play games, talk, cuddle, reminisce, laugh, plan for the future, speak about your hopes and dreams, but most important... get to know each other again.

If you have small children, it is imperative that they know you are planning a weekly date night for two reasons. Firstly, they have to know not to disturb you because this is your protected time. If they need incentive, small dollar store prizes the next morning for whoever stayed in bed usually does the trick. Most importantly, if they see their parents dating each other, they will assume that dating is a normal part of married life. By setting this example you are already protecting your children's future marriages and giving them a better chance at a happier life.

Eliminate the bad stuff. Stay away from things that harm your marriage. If friends want to complain about their husbands or wives, don't feel the need to join the conversation - especially with a person of the opposite sex. Don't allow pornography of any sort into your home. When you make love you need to know that it is just both of you focusing on each other - loving and serving each other. Be very aware of the relationships you have and the boundaries that need to be set in relationships with friends of the opposite sex. Distance yourself from people who are not good for your marriage. If your friends frequent illicit bars, or participate in activities that are against your marital vows, always remember to put your spouse's feelings first – just refuse to participate. Your spouse should be second only to God in your life.

Pray for each other and serve one another. Even if you have major differences and you are the only one interested in working on the relationship, continue to show love and kindness. There is a beautiful story that always reminds me of this. An amazing woman had a major reversion to her faith. With this change her husband became pretty disgusted with her. He became unkind and uncharitable toward her. With newfound faith and closeness to the Lord, this woman kept asking God why He didn't just change her husband. In her heart, she kept feeling like the Lord was asking her to serve her husband and leave the rest to Him. After a long time of putting up with his unkindness, and continuing to take care of his needs while trying to show love to him, this woman's husband had a sudden and strong conversion.

He fell in love with his faith and everything changed.

She asked him later what had happened. He told her that

she was the cause of his conversion. He finally realized

that it would be impossible for any human being to

continue to love someone who was so unkind to them for

such a long time. That is when he realized that SHE was

not the one loving him. It was GOD loving him through

her.

Every time I think of this story it helps me to

understand the power of love and kindness in conversion.

Trying to be the vessel that Jesus uses to affect others is

such a beautiful concept. When we don't feel strong

enough or happy enough to love or be kind to our spouse

we can ask the Lord to fill us with the Holy Spirit and to

love our spouse through us.

CHAPTER 2—STEPPING OUT

I wanted to do something that was difficult for me but God honoring. About a year prior, I picked up a book from our parish lending library. It was Abby Johnson's *Unplanned.* As I devoured the pages of Abby's transformation and read about the impact of Shawn Carney and his friends from 40 Days For Life, I began to realize the importance of sidewalk counseling.

I always stayed far away from this sort of outreach for fear that I would come across as judgmental or unkind. The thought of screaming at women, or displaying pictures of aborted babies outside of abortion centers did not sit well with me. The 40 Days For Life outreach made me aware that there was a loving approach which had worked to change the heart of a Planned Parenthood director! This was a peaceful, law abiding, loving presence outside of abortion centers. The participants offered resources, support and prayer for all going through the abortion facility doors. I thought that this was quite remarkable, yet I was afraid to go there myself.

When our marriage was on the mend, and I began to search for a way to repay my Lord for His kindness, I realized that the seed planted by Abby Johnson's book was beginning to come alive. I realized that I was most afraid of praying outside of abortion centers. I decided to step out of my fear and do something for Him.

On Feb 1 2014, I woke early on one of the coldest days in Philadelphia. I had read online that people prayed at a center near Chinatown from 6:30 in the morning onwards, and I decided to join them. I remember waking at 4:30 and then 5:30 completely terrified of standing out in the cold with these unknown people. At 6:15 I arrived at the place and didn't see a soul. It was still dark outside, and the place was covered with snow. I decided to sit in my car and wait. About 15 minutes later, a young man knocked at my window. Thinking I was there for an abortion myself, he tried to offer me help. I replied that I was there to pray. He responded for me to follow him.

In the snowy cold we stood there on the sidewalk with a group of older men and prayed the rosary. After a while I felt something inside urging me to step off the sidewalk. I kept thinking, "You are an OB/GYN. You need to try to talk to these girls." I stepped off the sidewalk, grabbed a fistful of flyers, and started to reach out. "Sweetheart, can I give you some information? Please don't make this choice. We can help you." It was the saddest moment I had ever experienced. Every woman going into that building was there to end the life of her child. With tears streaming down my face, I continued to beg them to reconsider. My cheeks were frozen, and I couldn't feel my face, but I couldn't stop. The cars just kept coming, and the lives continued to march toward their end. The mothers had no idea how this decision would change their lives forever.

That day at the 777 Appletree abortion center, a young Southeast Asian couple approached the building. They didn't speak English very well, and I didn't speak their language. I pleaded with them to keep their child. Somehow the message was shared, and that day they chose life.

They got in contact with a crisis pregnancy center and they left. In my mind, naively I thought that this was a normal occurrence: People came to pray and lives were saved. But the pure joy on the faces of those present who knew how blessed we were to witness the turnaround told me that this wasn't an everyday occurrence. I knew I had to come back even if it was just for a short while.

In the midst of this morning, a gentleman named Patrick Stanton, who was leading much of the prayer and sidewalk counseling, came to me and asked, "Who are you and what do you do?" I responded that I was a pro life OB/GYN. He responded, "YOU are a prolife OB/GYN? My Pop sent you!" Ignoring the "My Pop sent you" part I said, "What's the big deal?" to which he replied, "I don't know many Prolife OB/GYN doctors. Even if I did, they haven't come out here to pray with us!" "Oh, ok" I replied. Then he said, "Well this is great!

You'll come back to pray with us right? And you can start a Gianna Center for us!"

At that time in the midst of trying to strengthen our marriage, I had made plans for my family to move to Dallas. We had family support there so Gerard and I could go away for retreats and have time to focus on our marriage. I would have my sisters and father as well as cousins for my children to grow up with. I had found a job in Dallas, located a school for the children as well as a neighborhood to live in. Everything was set except a job for my husband. I had given notice to my current job, and was working month to month at that time.

I responded, "I'd love to come back and pray with you guys, but I'm leaving for Dallas in August!" I was shocked by his response, "Whoa, whoa, whoa-- we have to pray about that!"

So I said, "I'm happy to pray about it, but I really think I'm going. We are all set. The only thing we are missing is a job for my husband"

I failed to understand the significance of the timing at that moment. I could have chosen to come on any day, but I chose to come on that day. It was the 1st day that "Pop" couldn't be there. For years and years Patrick Stanton's Father, John Patrick Stanton, was a pro-life Giant. He founded the Pro-Life Union in Philadelphia, constantly supported two crisis pregnancy homes for unwed pregnant women, helped families, mentored children, and prayed outside of abortion centers. He prayed outside of Gosnell's house of horrors before anyone even spoke of Gosnell. He was the model of peaceful, loving witness. He was unjustly jailed for 3 months because he refused to pay a fine for trespassing while sidewalk counseling. During his 3 month time, he began a prayer group within the jail and led his community from within his cell while Patrick and others carried out his jobs. John Patrick Stanton, father of 12, had passed away the night before I arrived. With a heavy heart, his eldest son Patrick had come to take his place and pray for the women and babies. That is why he said, "My Pop sent you."

I only realized the connection the following day when I was looking up more pro-life information and came across his remembrance page. I was instantly taken aback because the song associated with the page was "Danny Boy". That was **my** family song. My grandmother, Charlotte Silva, was raised by Irish nuns. She grew up singing all of the Irish tunes on stage at their concerts. She actually met my grandfather Matthew Daniel after she sang, "Danny Boy" at a concert he attended. My mother grew up singing that song, and I always sang it on stage as well. That was our family song. Something told me my recently deceased grandmother was working in cahoots with Mr. John Stanton.

Before leaving that day another pro-lifer came up to me and began a conversation. He said, "So I hear you are a pro life OB/GYN? That's great! Do you write for contraceptives?"

I responded, "Yes, I do treat patients with them for medical reasons." I saw the look of joy leave his face, and he responded, "Well you know they are abortifacients, don't you?"

I said, "I don't know what else to treat the problems with." The conversation ended shortly after, but the feeling of guilt that I was continuing to perpetuate possible abortions hit me like a ton of bricks and I felt bad.

Truthfully, when Patrick Stanton stated that I could open a Gianna center I didn't even know what that was. I had no idea that there were pro-life OB/GYNs that used natural means to solve every GYN problem that I addressed with contraceptives. They were using natural family planning to address problems and help people avoid and achieve pregnancy.

I returned home that day and spoke with my husband. I told him the story of Patrick Stanton's response to my presence at the abortion center, and that he wanted us to pray about the decision to move. I'm pretty certain that my husband would have preferred to stay in Philly anyway, so he was happy for me to pray and ask if we should stay or go. We decided that Gerard would wholeheartedly look for a job for one month. During that time I would pray, and, if God wanted us to move to Dallas, he would provide Gerard with a job offer that he couldn't refuse. I decided to do this only if my husband would give the job search his all.

During that time, I thought I would enlist all of my prayer warriors to help Gerard find a job. My family was all on board, but little did I know that Pat Stanton was working the same angle in the pro-life community. He enlisted the prayers of priests, nuns, seminarians pro-lifers; he even went on the radio and said, "I have never prayed for a man not to get a job, but I am asking all of you to pray that this doctor stays in Philadelphia." I didn't have a chance!

The following Monday morning, on my day off, Patrick Stanton found my office and dropped of a book called *The Naprotechnology Revolution*. It was an amazing book that opened my eyes to the alternative for contraceptives, Creighton Fertility Care Natural Family Planning and Naprotechnology. My interest was held by treatments for post partum depression using progesterone. The success rates were astounding with reversal of symptoms for some patients within 24 hours! Most patients treated with traditional treatments for post partum depression suffer for many weeks until the medications begin to take effect, and even then they often remain in a fog until they were weaned off. I also read about treatments for recurrent miscarriage, pre-term labor, infertility, simple ovarian cysts, PMS, abnormal bleeding, and many other problems.

As I finished the book, I realized that God had provided me with an alternative to using contraceptives. For the first time ever, I went to the drug cupboard, took out every package insert and read the mechanism of action of each and every type of contraceptive. I quickly realized that the thinning of the inner lining of the uterus either by a low dose of medication or a constant dose of progesterone served to make it difficult for implantation to take place.

I knew that life began at conception, and any interference with implantation could possibly cause the earliest abortion.

When the contraceptive fails to suppress ovulation, the earliest life -the embryo- could come into existence. When the embryo tries to implant in the thinned inner lining, it could lead to an undesired abortion. I knew at that moment that I could never prescribe contraceptives again.

I immediately decided to reach out to the Pope Paul VI Institute in Nebraska to see how I could learn to practice in this way.

LIFE LESSON#2—NATURAL SOLUTIONS

As an OB/GYN resident I was taught in a pretty typical way. Diagnosis of medical conditions occurred through a combination of history, physical exam, blood and radiologic tests. Treatments consisted of medical and surgical solutions to most problems. When it came to very common issues like abnormal uterine bleeding, endometriosis, ovarian cysts, PMS and pregnancy avoidance, the solution was often contraceptives. These contraceptives are not used to search for the underlying issue and solve it but rather to attempt to stop ovulation and effectively shut down the system, thus stopping undesired symptoms.

Many years ago in a response to the call of the Encyclical *Humanae Vitae*, a young medical student named Tom Hilgers began to search for means other than contraceptives to address the needs of women today. That calling, which was undoubtedly a gift from God for those of us that have followed, has led to an amazing, life sustaining and faith supporting science.

Beginning with an analysis of the Billings method cervical mucus charts, Dr. Hilgers soon realized that the method of family planning he and his friends were developing held the answers to many problems. With much research and hard work, Dr. Hilgers and his colleagues created a very eloquent and common sense system.

When a patient arrives at my office with a gynecologic complaint, whether it be abnormal bleeding, mood issues, pelvic pain, abnormal discharge, history of infertility, recurrent miscarriages or pre-term labor I take a full history. Following appropriate physical exam, initial baseline labs and studies the patients are advised to follow up with Fertility Care practitioners to learn how to chart their cycles. By making observations before and after visits to the toilet and before shower and bed, the patient will easily identify the main keys to charting: cervical mucus and bleeding patterns.

The cervical mucus is the highway for the sperm. Its presence and sudden absence indicates times of fertility and likely ovulation. Bleeding patterns in combination with vaginal fluid findings tell a story of their own. Often with a quick glance at a chart it is possible to diagnose anovulation, low progesterone, inadequate cervical mucus and other abnormalities. After charting for two months, patients come back to the office to analyze their charts. Utilizing the findings, we are often able to identify the likely time of ovulation and plan pre- and post-ovulation lab tests.

These lab results when compared to known normal results clearly show multiple specific hormonal deficiencies. The deficiencies are often the underlying cause of the issues we are trying to address. When the true problem is understood, it is possible to find solutions.

If a woman is lacking progesterone we supplement it back at the correct time. If a woman lacks both estrogen and progesterone we can give supplements to address that. We can give treatments to improve the quantity and quality of mucous, or to decrease too much discharge. We have treatments that significantly decrease post-partum depression and PMS in the first 24 hrs of treatment for many patients. There are treatments that help women to prevent some causes of recurrent miscarriage as well as pre-term labor.

The most amazing personal aspect of this treatment is its ability to allow me to practice my profession and my faith fully. The innate respect for life that Naprotechnology is based upon is so comforting to physicians who are trying to live their faith in all aspects of their life. Being able to quit the use of contraceptives has brought such peace. I know I am doing the very best for myself and my patients. It is a beautiful thing to know that nothing I do on a typical day in my office will necessitate a visit to confession!

CHAPTER 3—A NEW START

Getting back to the job search, my husband contacted head hunters and had several interviews on the phone. Unfortunately, he was unable to find anything that he liked. On the last day of the month, I called Pat and said, "I just wanted you to know that we are staying. Gerard didn't find a job." He responded, "I already knew that." I asked, "How did you know that?" He said, "Last night I had a dream, and my Pop told me you were going to stay."

I was a bit freaked out to say the least, but I went on to say, "Okay, if we are staying, I need you to be our family. We don't have anyone here and we need family." He chuckled and said, "No problem, I have nine kids... you can just be another one."

So we unofficially adopted the Stantons as family. They have been present for almost every birthday, had us over for dinners, invited us to march in the St Patrick's Day Parade with them and had us for family vacations at the shore. They even took care of my children after school for several months while we were transitioning from the city to the suburbs to be closer to work. I am truly blessed by my adopted Irish family.

Since I knew that we were staying, I realized that I needed to speak with administration about getting my job back. During the time that I was attempting to transition to Dallas, they had already hired a replacement for me. I arrived at my administrator's office and said, "I would like to stay, continue my part-time position, and not write any more contraceptives." She naturally looked at me like I had three heads, since the many months prior I was speaking of moving to Dallas, and the new job I had been offered. I explained that I had learned about Naprotechnology, and I wanted them to send me for the training.

She was completely shocked by my change of heart, but she shared with me that a mere year earlier, they had been searching for someone who wanted to learn Naprotechnology, and nobody was interested. Apparently John Stanton and his wife Harriet had a hand in this as well. In addition to attending daily mass and asking for people to pray that a pro-life OB/GYN would come to Jenkintown, they also reached out to administration and tried to spread information about Napro to the doctors they knew. Thus, when I reached out to the administrator with this concept, it was not completely foreign to her. God had paved the way through His servants and laid the path for my transition. Ultimately they agreed for me to stay on, continue my part-time practice, and to start a Gynecology-only practice that focused on women's health, pregnancy protection and infertility. In accepting this new role, I stepped out of prenatal care but continued to keep my obstetric skills sharp while assisting other physicians on Labor and Delivery.

Thus began the transition to natural healthcare. As God provided the guidance and path for these aspects of my life His Goodness continued to enter every aspect of my life. I began to meet on a weekly basis with a few women for a *lectio divina* prayer group. These moments of prayer and sharing were so therapeutic and such a blessing.

I started to practice in a very different way. With no contraceptives and no obstetric patients, suddenly my schedule was much clearer. I had a lot more time to really focus on each patient and speak with them about their concerns. I began to address all aspects of their lives that I felt affected their well being.

For the first time, I spent time talking to women about their relationships. I was shocked to find out that many of the women I had known for a long time were actually in a very difficult place in their marriages. I was able to share my own experiences and pass along many of the resources that I found to be healing for my husband and me.

In the past when I would review an obstetric history, I would quickly gloss over any abortions and move onto the next part of the history to be collected. I never stopped to ask the women how she was doing, or if she was aware that post abortive services existed. I was shocked at the number of people that were suffering with anxiety and depression years after the decision to have an abortion. More than that, I was shocked by how many of those people knew nothing of post-abortive resources. I began to offer these resources and love to all the women who desired them.

I really felt that I was making an impact in people's lives. I was promoting sexual integrity and natural family planning instead of contraceptives to address a myriad of issues. Many patients were so grateful to have someone who would support them in their choice to live a more natural life which aligned with their beliefs. My infertility patients were thrilled to find a new understanding of their fertility and answers to the problems they had been suffering with. Suddenly many people who had been labeled as "unexplained" infertility patients gained an understanding of issues they could address to improve their situation. Every day in my office is a blessing.

LIFE LESSON #3: SEXUAL INTEGRITY

Sexual Integrity is such an important topic, one

which should be broached in every relationship.

Decisions should be made in premarital or marital

relationships that protect the couple emotionally,

physically and spiritually.

Women need to understand that they are beautiful,

precious beings. They should be honored, revered and

protected. I completely realize that sometimes this basic notion is very difficult for women to believe. They may come from families where they didn't have a loving, strong father figure. They may never have received love and respect from anyone in their lives. They may have suffered abuse. They may have been duped by society to believe that beauty is only what one finds on a magazine cover. Yet, they are beautiful.

Every person that I have spoken to who is in a relationship prior to marriage says that their ultimate goal is to find the spouse of their dreams to love them, care for them and be with them until their dying day. They are looking for someone that will love them not only now but in the future when they may look completely different and possibly be unable to care for themselves. They are actually looking for someone who is in love with the enduring parts of them: their heart, their soul and their mind. For this reason I encourage them to look at dating as an opportunity to test out all of the possible future spouses in a safe way to find the individual who can provide this sort of enduring love.

Men and women are very different. Most men can have a physical relationship and remain emotionally detached from their partner. Women, on the other hand, become extremely attached when they share intimacy. Instantaneously, women put on rose-colored "relationship protection glasses" and cease to look for any faults that may exist in their partner. Once they have been intimate, their goal is to protect the relationship so it can grow to become something more serious. Ironically, this is even the case if the women realize that this person might not be the best. They feel like they have invested too much to let go easily.

We are all human; we all have desires and enjoy closeness. Dating should not be a race to see how quickly one can satisfy human urges for touch and affection, but rather a tool to investigate the personalities and traits of possible future spouses. We have intelligence and strength to curb these desires.

If we make a decision to save our next kiss for marriage, many beautiful things will result. First, any man that is only interested in using a girl for sexual pleasure will leave, thereby saving her from immense heart ache and possible STD exposure. Next, women will deal with the "3 monthers". These are the men who consider this to be a supreme challenge that they wish to overcome. They will be on best behavior for a few months, but then one of two things will happen. Either they will run out of patience and try to convince her to become more physically intimate, (at which time she can tell them to beat it), or they will have a conversion of heart and stick around. After these two groups of guys are dealt with, a woman will meet guys that are honestly interested in getting to know her for her mind, heart and soul. They may not be perfect, but these are the ones worth spending time getting to know.

You observe them when they are stressed, happy, sad, tired and hungry. You probe into their beliefs and thoughts on every possible controversial topic. You watch how they treat the young, the elderly, their mothers and fathers, pets, poor and wealthy. Then you can make a truly informed decision as to if this person is right for you. If you realize it won't work, you can walk away without the heartache and sadness that you gave them something you can't take back. You have effectively avoided STD's, unplanned pregnancy, possible infertility and trauma just by saving your next kiss on the lips for marriage.

One may ask, "Why can't we just not have sex, but continue to kiss?" I would argue that a kiss on the forehead, cheek or hand is fine, but a passionate kiss can so easily lead from one thing to another.

Why make life difficult? If a couple doesn't kiss in that way, they will never be tempted to do anything further.

As women we also have a responsibility to hold men to a higher standard. Many women say, "If I don't have sex I will lose him." I would argue that he is not worth holding onto. If the relationship does progress to marriage and if you are no longer able to be intimate because of illness, does that mean it is ok for him to leave you? If we treat men like dogs, they will be dogs. If we hold them to a higher standard and expect them to be gentleman, we may be pleasantly surprised to find them transforming to that.

Every adolescent girl I know dreams of a fairy tale wedding with a Cinderella kiss. They expect that the first night as a married couple will be something incredibly special and unforgettable. Sadly, when we spend our dating relationships engaging in behavior that should be reserved for marriage, the excitement and newness of these intimate moments are lost. If you have already shared a hotel room and sexual intimacy in the dating period, what makes that first night unforgettable? More likely you will fall asleep after partying the night away with your friends and drinking a bit too much. The wedding night will be a bit of a blur.

But if we have already been intimate in our relationship isn't it too late to achieve this goal? Amazingly, even couples that have been sexually intimate in the past can choose to save their next kiss on the lips for their wedding day. If they do this, their chance of attaining the "Cinderella Kiss" and the awesome wedding night are exponentially increased. It boils down to this, great marriages are built on two people who are committed to sacrificing their own wants and desires for the betterment of their spouse. In a relationship, you shouldn't want to do anything that could possibly harm your partner. Sexual intimacy when taken

out of the context of marriage can cause a lot of harm and

sadness. Sexual intimacy is **good** in the right context:

marriage. Good things are worth waiting for.

CHAPTER 4—TRUSTING AGAIN

Back to my story, after a few months of deciding to stay in Philadelphia, I began to feel a strong desire to move to the suburbs. I wanted to put an end to the 40-minute commute, have the opportunity to live closer to our new pro life friends, and have a home with a backyard for the children to play in. My hubby unfortunately was still working in the city, and he really enjoyed being near to the entertainment and cultural activities.

Once again I asked him if we could ask God to weigh in on the situation. I offered to pray for a month, and to ask the Lord to show us a sign of abundant white roses if He wanted us to move to the suburbs. I didn't just want one white rose, but an absolute abundance of roses that neither of us could question. Gerard agreed, thinking that this would end the constant nagging about my desire to move the family out of the city.

I remember the 1st week passing by. I didn't see a single white rose, and I was so saddened. I remember pleading with the Lord saying, "Really Lord? Don't you want me to move closer to the hospital? Don't you want me to be closer to the Pro-Lifers?" I researched when roses bloom in Philadelphia, and I was further disheartened when I realized that we were nowhere near the season in which roses were expected to bloom. Yet, I knew that if the Lord wanted us to move He would show us the sign.

The following week I was dropping my boys off at school. It was a very old school with a graveyard attached to the church nearby. As I glanced at the graveyard, one of the stones stood out to me. On it was written the name "Rose". Considering the era in which Rose was buried I was pretty certain that she was Caucasian. So I put her down as my first white rose.

On the way home from the school I took my usual path, and I was shocked to see that one of my neighbors put up a wreath covered with white roses (second sign).

In the following days, I was inundated with white roses. We went to visit my sister in Dallas, and all of her yellow rose bushes bloomed white (third sign).

We attended my niece's First Holy Communion, and white roses were in the girls' hair and on their outfits (fourth sign).

I went to lunch with a friend of mine and when I shared what I was doing to determine where we would be living she looked at me with amazement and said, "Monique, do you realize what my name means?" I said, "Domenica, doesn't it mean Sunday?" She laughed and said, "No! It means White Rose!!!!"(fifth sign).

I ran into a sandwich bar next door to my child's karate class because I was starving. I knew it was a sandwich shop, but I burst out laughing when I looked at the menu and realized it was called "La Rosa Blanca" (sixth sign).

Two patients came to see me with white rose tattoos and white rose earrings. (seventh and eighth signs).

My office manager put a wreath up on my office door with white roses while I was away on vacation (ninth sign).

I took a walk on one of my days off, and there were actually wild white roses blooming on the road, and several of the shop windows I passed had cards with white roses and tissue paper white roses adorning them (signs ten, eleven, twelve).

The final day of the month I was so nervous, so I thought I would stop by the church nearest to my hospital. I entered into the building; I walked straight into the church not really paying attention to anything in the foyer. I sang a Divine Mercy Chaplet, and thanked God for all of the signs He had sent. Upon exiting I was astounded to see that the foyer was full of tables promoting pro-life. There were white rose cards, key chains, and prayer cards of the little flower St Teresa in abundance adorning those tables (signs thirteen, fourteen, fifteen).

I was certain that God was guiding us again, and I shared all of the signs with my husband who agreed to allow me to begin to search for a house in the suburbs.

When I realized that a move was definitely in our future, I began the search for a school for my children. I entered Catholic Classical School into the search engine and was shocked to find Regina Coeli Academy minutes away from my place of work. When I went to visit, I was blown away by the school's dedication to teaching our Catholic faith. The children attended Mass twice weekly and had virtue formation during the other days of the school week. They studied classical literature, phonics, catechism, history, Latin, music and mathematics in addition to other subjects. They taught in the classical method of education with an emphasis on memorization in the early stages and formation of solid arguments in the latter. Everyone seemed so kind and loving; the class sizes were small and I felt that I had discovered a little bit of heaven.

Not wanting my children to miss out on even a moment of this education, I enrolled both of my sons prior to purchasing a home in the area. For the first several months of school, The Stanton family picked the boys up after school, fed them a snack, did their homework with them and looked after them until I was done work. They ate their dinner on the 40 minute commute back from the Stanton's, and ate breakfast on the 40 minute commute to the school in the morning. Pat, Wendy and their daughter Brianna wouldn't accept a dime in exchange. They weren't joking when they said they would be family. We were blessed.

LIFE LESSON#4—FINDING BLESSINGS

We are all faced with times of trial and turmoil. There are moments when we meet challenges of such enormity that we feel alone and hopeless. We are not alone. Every step of the way God is with us. When we feel that we can't walk another step, He is carrying us. Our Father never abandons us.

It is so easy to be tempted to give up and despair

at these times. Whether it is infertility, a difficult illness, a tumultuous relationship, or any other challenge, I believe it is always beneficial to know that God is not only near, but He is bringing others to love and support us.

I don't believe that He wants sadness and suffering for us, but I do believe that He wants us to turn to Him. He wants us to depend upon Him, cling to Him and rely only upon Him as the source of our strength. He loves us. Often I notice that I never feel closer to our Lord than in those times of turmoil. I pray with such fervor, seek Him in the Word and in the Sacraments and continually ask Him to be with me.

I also note that whenever I am dealing with something particularly difficult, if I offer up that discomfort or suffering for others, I find additional strength. It never fails when my head is pounding, and I offer the pain up for all the souls in purgatory, suddenly the pain doesn't seem as bad. If I am particularly concerned about something I offer it up for others who are struggling in the same way. I would urge you to bring meaning to your trials. Offer them up for others, and learn the valuable lessons so you can minister to others.

So many hardships God has walked me through have become blessings. Suffering with post-partum blues allowed me to understand how my patients feel with post-partum depression. Dealing with difficulties in marriage provided me with lessons and resources that I can share with all of my patients. It is so much easier to connect with young girls who are not choosing sexual integrity when I can explain that I dealt with the same temptations, and made mistakes as well.

For those suffering with anxiety and depression I would ask you to consider the life of Saint Mother Teresa. She lived all the days of her life asking others to smile, spread love and be grateful. However, she suffered such depth of darkness during her time of ministry in India.

Mother's response was a truly unique one. Rather than curse the darkness, and hate her sadness, she embraced it. She is said to have felt that it allowed her to experience just a small amount of the loneliness our beloved Christ suffered on the cross. All the while during these trials, she continued to light candles in the darkest places around her. It is truly far greater to light a single candle than to curse the darkness.

For those of you that are dealing with physical pain and suffering, consider the actor Jim Caviezel who played Jesus in *The Passion of The Christ*. This man was accidentally whipped, suffered with a dislocated shoulder while carrying the cross, had pneumonia with fluid in his lungs and a heart condition that required surgery at the end of the film. Finally he was struck by lightning while on the cross. He truly suffered during this time, but thought that his suffering would so benefit so many others. He wanted to suffer as Christ had suffered during the passion; he definitely received his intention. Every day he received communion and confession so that he could be as close to God as possible as he attempted to portray the story of His Passion. That movie was not done in vain. It is the one of the most viewed R-rated movies ever made. It has been the cause of many conversions, including Jim who now speaks passionately about respecting life at all stages and returning to God. Our suffering can bring us closer to God. It can help us minister to others who deal with similar trials. It can be a blessing if we allow it to be so.

CHAPTER 5—WHY NOT?

I continued to pray with Pat at the downtown Philadelphia abortion centers on my days off.

One day when we were praying outside of 12th and Locust, Pat had asked two ladies who ran a local crisis pregnancy center (Alpha Care) to join us. Karen Hess prayed with us that day, and while she watched the women entering and leaving the center she turned to me and asked, "Why don't we have a 40 Days For Life here? This abortion center kills more babies than any other in all of Pennsylvania. They have them at other places. Why haven't we had one here?" I looked at her and responded that I didn't know why. I continued to ponder her question. The following Saturday when I met Pat for our Saturday witness I went to him and said, "Pat I think we need to do a 40 Days For Life at 12th and Locust." Without a moment of pause, he responded "Ok, I guess we'll do it then."

I went home that day and began the application for the first downtown Philadelphia 40 Days For Life campaign. After sending in the application, I received a call from Steve Karlen, one of the administrators. After a brief conversation, he mentioned, "You know last year there was a gentleman who was very interested in starting a 40 Days For Life at this same location, his name was John Stanton, maybe you guys could work together."

Once again I was amazed how God was urging me to walk in the path that John Stanton had prepared. I explained that He had gone to the Lord and that I was actually teaming up with his eldest son Patrick to pull this campaign together.

The 12th and locust campaign was a very difficult one to imagine. It was located in an area which was very supportive of the abortion industry. The facility took up an entire city block. Yet, our Lord had prepared the way once again. Nearby there was a crisis pregnancy center run by the Legacy for Life Foundation. It was a beautiful welcoming place that we were able to take mothers to when they changed their mind. The volunteers at the Center were so loving and kind.

Parking in the city is always a scary thing for suburban Philadelphians. God provided free parking in a church parking lot a few blocks away.

He even placed a pro-lifer's home two doors down from Planned Parenthood. The amazingly generous owner Bill Wendt graciously allowed us to have free access to his fenced in area to store our signs, kneeler and box of resources during the vigil.

From the onset of our vigil, Pat and I made a pact to just trust in God. We felt that any presence was better than none, and if God wanted to fill the vigil He would fill it. And did He ever. In our vigil there wasn't an hour that went uncovered. Even when people dropped out because of emergencies or weather, others showed up unannounced. Thirteen women walked away from Planned Parenthood during those 40 days, and nine of them confirmed pregnancies and chose life for their babies. We had countless amazing hours of prayer and fantastic conversations with passersby and clients of the facility. We handed out a huge amount of literature that hopefully reached the people who needed it most.

We always say, we never know how many lives were saved and changed because of the 40 days witness. The willingness of the people to stand as God's vessels and be filled with His Holy Spirit is a beautiful thing. Their peaceful, loving presence changes hearts and minds.

As of May 2017, we have held six vigils at this location, and every one of them has been a phenomenal success and a blessing, thanks be to God.

This year, at the urging of the Holy Spirit, we expanded our efforts. In addition to praying at the 12th and Locust location, we began the first campaign at the privately owned abortion center near to China Town. This location also kills five thousand babies a year. It is so hard to fathom that mere blocks apart, two abortion centers exist that kill ten thousand babies each year.

Our presence there was very challenging. Yet, God continued to provide faithful prayer warriors and unique solutions to our small practical problems. We successfully stood in public witness with love and compassion for all entering both locations during the last 40 days for life campaign.

Between the vigils we have also initiated a sidewalk servants program. The purpose of this program is to train sidewalk counselors and have them present outside of these two centers covering the morning hours Monday through Saturday. The ultimate goal is to have peaceful, loving, prayerful sidewalk counselors available outside every abortion facility in Philadelphia covering every hour that they are open for service. If it is God's will, it will happen.

LIFE LESSON#5—LOVE CHANGES HEARTS

Every day in Philadelphia alone 2 babies die each hour to abortion. Over 17, 000 babies perish on a yearly basis. Sadly this is not even beginning to count the use of the unintentional abortions that occur through contraceptives. Every single one of these human beings that is conceived when the sperm, egg and soul come together is a unique, unrepeatable individual. Once that being is eliminated, there will never ever be another replica of that person.

The mothers who choose abortion, for the most part do so out of fear. They feel boxed in without adequate support. Those around them generally push them toward this decision stating that this unplanned pregnancy will jeopardize their education, their freedom and their life.

Others are forced into this decision by parents or partners who threaten them with homelessness or worse. Medical professionals often advise patients with an abnormal genetic diagnosis such as down syndrome or trisomy 18 to end the lives of their precious children.

In our country, ninety percent of babies with down syndrome are aborted. Yet, if you meet a person with down's most would agree that they are nothing less than a gift from God. They provide a sense of love and compassion that is desperately needed in our society. Each of these people can contribute so much if given the chance to do so!

A fantastic example of this is a beautiful girl named Chloe Kondrich. At the time of their pregnancy, her parents were advised to abort her because she was diagnosed with Down syndrome. Her parents opted to save her life and cover her with love and support instead. This amazing young woman, at a very young age, was the impetus for a law in Pennsylvania "Chloe's Law". This piece of legislature states that a woman given a prenatal diagnosis must also be given positive resources covering the support and help available for parents who choose to parent children with Downs. Thirteen year old Chloe is very busy. She has been on the New York Times Square billboards and speaks with famous athletes, musicians, members of the UN, and even the Vice President of our country in support of rights for the unborn. She has a book written about her and she has a very special connection to the spiritual realm. This beautiful soul is truly surrounded by angels. She brings peace and love to every person she meets.

Even in the case of lethal anomalies, most parents are unaware that the option of perinatal hospice exists. This beautiful alternative to abortion honors the child while providing complete comfort care. It allows the family the opportunity to love and support the child during his or her short life. It allows for time to grieve appropriately and find closure and peace rather than guilt and regret for abandoning or destroying a child who was placed in their care.

After the abortion is completed, these women may initially feel relief, but that relief quickly changes to regret, anxiety, and depression. They often try and ignore these thoughts and feelings. They stuff them in a deep recess of their mind, never to speak of the situation or event with anyone. Unfortunately, the memories come flooding back when abortion is a hot topic of debates or political arguments. Sometimes even when they are invited for a baby shower or a birthday of a similarly aged child they find themselves very unsettled. Some women experience recurrent nightmares. Yet, these women are rarely if ever provided with post abortive counseling. Most don't know that this option even exists. Programs such as Rachel's Vineyard, Project Rachel, Silent No More and Surrendering the Secret in Philadelphia serve these women with love. They offer peace, forgiveness and renewal. It is so unnecessary for these women to suffer in silence.

The price of abortion is not only psychological. There is evidence linking increased number of abortions to an increased risk of breast cancer. Women are also at risk of miscarriage, infertility and possible death.

When we stand outside of abortion centers, we are the last possible light of hope for this child's survival and the mother's escape from all of the problems stemming from abortion. Our job is to provide love and alternatives in this dire time. It is of utmost importance that our presence there is one of compassion and kindness. Yelling or trying to scare people away from this choice never serves to do anything but have them run away from us into the arms of the abortionist. When we are present we must respectfully offer resources. Although it is important to put on your spiritual armor, pray and be prepared for the spiritual warfare, it is vital to meet people where they are. It may not be the best time to try and convince someone to embrace religion, but it is the best time to show Christ's love for that person through love and kindness.

All signs and materials should express love. The goal of a sidewalk counselor is to have the most loving, approachable presence possible. The best sidewalk counselor is one who smiles, dresses well, speaks calmly and firmly but with love. Know that even if you feel unprepared to be there, God will give you the strength, wisdom and peace to do His work. Know the resources that are available, and the crisis pregnancy centers and hotline numbers to call for assistance.

Also know that if a mother takes the abortion pill it can be reversed. Over 300 babies have survived completely unscathed when their mothers contacted abortionpillreversal.com.

There is also help available for the workers. And Then There Were None is an amazing outreach that provides financial support, help to find another job, as well as access to a lawyer for 3 months in additional to emotional support. Hearts can change, but conversions only happen in the realm of love and respect.

CHAPTER 6--THE 41ST DAY

I informed Pat that we were planning to move to the suburbs soon after we began our preparations for the 1st 40 Days For Life vigil in the city. At that time I was living about 10 minutes away from the vigil site. His immediate response was, "I absolutely want you guys to move to Jenkintown, but you can't move until the 41st day. We need you in the city to help watch over this vigil."

I anticipated that we would find a home rather quickly since this was God's plan, but I said I would definitely be around to help.

We began looking for homes in Jenkintown; I was shocked at how long it was taking. We saw many, many homes. I was pretty certain that I would know the house straight away because it would obviously have an abundance of white roses planted outside. Yet, only one house had even a hint of white roses planted outside, and that house wasn't one that we could agree upon.

We continued our search and placed a few offers. On the first house we were outbid. The second house was sold super quickly as well. And the third house was taken off the market because of a medical illness. By this time Gerard was beginning to get a bit frustrated. We had been searching for several months, and lost on three offers. He began to question whether God was trying to steer us in another direction, but I held fast that He was preparing

the perfect place for us.

Whenever Pat met our realtor at Mass, he would

remind her that she was responsible for finding us a place

to move into by the 41st day of the vigil. She would

complain to me during our outings that he expected her to

pull a house out of her back pocket on the 41st day. But

our Lord has an amazing sense of humor.

The vigil was coming to an end and we didn't

have a house. Yet, on the 41st day our realtor called us

stating that Divine intervention had occurred. The owners

of the third house were putting it back on the market and

wanted to offer it to us. We were overjoyed and began

the process of moving ahead with the sale.

LIFE LESSON#6—GOD SIZED HOLES

Human beings are imperfect creatures. We are not meant to stand alone and be completely self sufficient. Each and every one of us has holes. We try to fill those holes with material things such as money, possessions, alcohol, cigarettes, food and drugs. Yet, we find that we are still searching for something.

Alternatively, we look to have the others around

us fill our holes. We look for people who seem supportive, funny, attractive, educated, and confident to complete us. We lean on family, friends, spouses and love interests to try and fill our holes. Sadly none of those people are perfect either. They all have their own holes and are guaranteed to disappoint at some point in the relationship.

That is when we need to realize that the only perfect being who is capable of loving us and filling our holes completely is God. He loves us when we are good or bad. He has never stopped loving us.

When we open ourselves to His love and strive to be near to Him we feel fulfilled and at peace. The holes are finally filled with Him, and suddenly we are happy by ourselves. We don't need anyone else to make us complete or content. This allows us to appreciate those we used to be dependent on differently. We no longer need them to survive, but we enjoy their company. If they say hurtful things, we are no longer affected in the same way because we are free to disengage and send them love from a distance. If they walk away, we are not devastated since everyone beside God is just a bonus.

We are finally complete with our God sized holes filled. We can let go of the dependencies, and live our lives knowing, loving and serving Him.

CHAPTER 7—WHITE ROSES

We moved into our new home that February just one year after the story began outside of 777 Appletree. I felt so blessed to have a home so near to my work and the children's school. There were train stations nearby that allowed Gerard to get back to the city with ease as well. Everything in the house was perfect. We had plenty of space and all of the bedrooms were in one area so we could be near to the children. There was a lovely kitchen, a basement for a man cave and an upstairs for a playroom. The yard was large enough, but not overwhelming. Yet I was still confused as to the lack of white roses. Since we moved in during the winter months, I half expected roses to bloom when the seasons changed, but to no avail.

Three months into our time at the house, I remember sitting with my mother for a chat in our dining room. I said to her, "You know, I love this house! Everything about it is perfect, but I'm still confused as to the lack of white roses!!" Just at that moment I looked at my dining room walls and dumbfounded I realized that the wallpaper in that room was not just gold as I had thought, it was a pattern of ALL WHITE ROSES! I burst out into laughter and said, "My sweet Lord, You have such an amazing sense of humor!"

I feel so very blessed to have a home handpicked by God as well as a beautiful pro-life community to provide friendship, love and support. I have an amazing job in which I can minister to my patients daily with love. Our children have a fantastic school where they are loved, nurtured and are growing in their faith. Most importantly, I have a redeemed relationship with My God and my husband Gerard.

I couldn't believe that in one year, God has completely transformed my life, my community and my family. I cannot begin to describe the love I have for my Lord who raised me up from the ashes and filled me with such peace. We are blessed.

LIFE LESSON #7—HIS PLAN IS THE BEST

God is not distant. He is personal, knowing and loving. He is happiest when the gravest sinners come back to Him. He is our Father, friend, strength and hope. He loves us all.

We may not understand His plan at the moment. His timing may seem so different from the timing we desire. Yet, when I look back at the way situations have unfolded, I can see clearly that His plan is always the best.

I will strive to always allow Him to lead in everything I do. I will constantly ask Him to shut the doors He doesn't want me to traverse and to fling open the ones He wants me to walk through. I ask that He brings people into my life that will draw me closer to Him.

Overall, I will trust Him completely. I will know that even though I may walk through scary situations, He is always with me.

I also must realize that even though I am striving to do His will, He loves me just as much as He loves those who persecute me. He desires their faithfulness as much as He desires mine.

I must continue to pray for those who are unkind to me, and do my best to share the light of His love in this world. If we are all willing to respond with love like His,

what a wonderful world this would be!

Marriage Resources:

Marriagetoday.com

The Love Dare by Stephen Kendrick

Maritalhealing.com (Fantastic Marriage Therapist)

The Five Love Languages by Gary Chapman

The Divorce Remedy by Michele Weiner Davis

Thedatingdivas.com

Personal Resources:

Formed.org (catholic movies, books, talks)

Girlfriendsingod.com (daily devotional for women)

K-Love Radio App for smartphones (great music)

Relevant Radio (catholic talk radio)

Thekingsmen.org (for men)

The Eucharistic Miracle of Buenos Aires (You Tube)

Saintraymond.net (Gospel Catholic Church in Philly)

Dating Resources:

Thirstingfortruth.com

chastityproject.com

Pro-Life Resources:

Unplanned by Abby Johnson

40daysforlife.com

Brilliant Souls by Stephanie Wincik

(Book about Chloe)

Jim Caviezel Testimony (You Tube)

Abortionreversal.com

Post Abortive Resources:

Rachelsvineyard.org

Surrenderingthesecret.com

Silentnomoreawareness.org

Made in the USA
San Bernardino, CA
27 January 2018

McGraw-Hill Education

Short Course for the GED® Test

McGraw-Hill Education

Short Course for the GED® Test

McGraw-Hill Education Editors

Contributor: Jouve North America

New York Chicago San Francisco Athens London Madrid
Mexico City Milan New Delhi Singapore Sydney Toronto

1 2 3 4 5 6 7 8 9 10   RHR/RHR   1 0 9 8 7 6 5 4

ISBN   978-0-07-183685-2
MHID   0-07-183685-3

e-ISBN   978-0-07-183686-9
e-MHID   0-07-183686-1

Library of Congress Control Number 2014935325

Excerpt from "Alpine Ascents: Everest Frequently Asked Questions"
reproduced by permission of Alpine Ascents International.

Excerpt from "Cycling City: Will Austin Embrace Bike Sharing?" by Erica
Pickhartz, reproduced by permission of the *Austin Post*.

Excerpt from "8 Flu Vaccination Pros and Cons You May Not Know About"
reproduced by permission of the celebrity, lifestyle, and parenting blog
"The Stir" from CaféMom.

Excerpt from *Clocks and Culture: 1300–1700* by Carlo M. Cipolla. First
published in English in 1967 by Collins, London. Copyright © 1981, 1996 by
Società editrice il Mulino, Bologna.

Excerpt from "The Coming Robot Army: Introducing America's Future
Fighting Machines" by Steve Featherstone, Copyright © 2007 by *Harper's
Magazine*. All rights reserved. Reproduced from the February issue by special
permission.

"Chapter 25" from THE GRAPES OF WRATH, by John Steinbeck, copyright
1939, renewed © 1967 by John Steinbeck. Used by permission of Viking
Penguin, a division of Penguin Group (USA) LLC.

GED® is a registered trademark of the American Council on Education (ACE)
and administered exclusively by GED Testing Service LLC under license. This
content is not endorsed or approved by ACE or GED Testing Service.

Interior design by THINK Book Works

Interior illustrations by Cenveo Publisher Services

Contents

Introducing the GED® Test

Welcome to *McGraw-Hill Education: Short Course for the GED® Test*! Congratulations on choosing the preparation guide from America's leading educational publisher. You probably know us from many of the textbooks you used in school. Now we're ready to help you take the next step—and get the high school equivalency credential you want.

Before you start your study program, this chapter will give you a brief introduction to the exam. In the following pages, you'll learn:

- The history of the GED® test and how it took its current shape
- The structure of each part of the GED® test
- How the test is scored
- Some basic test-taking strategies
- Some *dos* and *don'ts* for test days

About the GED® Test

"GED" stands for General Educational Development. The GED® test is commonly referred to as a "high-school equivalency" test because passing scores on all the test sections are usually accepted as equal to a high-school diploma.

The current version of the GED® test is a major departure from the 2002 and earlier versions. Some key difference are:

- There is no paper-and-pencil version of the test. Only a computer version is available.
- There are four, not five, test sections: Reasoning Through Language Arts, Social Studies, Science, and Mathematical Reasoning.
- The tests use new question formats that may be unfamiliar to test-takers. (But don't worry, we will get you up to speed!)
- Multiple-choice questions will have four, not five, answer options.

How Do I Register?

In 2011, more than 700,000 people took at least one of the five GED® test sections. More than 600,000 completed all five (but remember, starting in 2014, there will be only four tests). That makes it one of the most widely administered tests in the world. Luckily, that means you will probably have a lot of options about where to take the test.

The quickest way to register is to do so online at:

gedcomputer.com

Visit this website and follow the step-by-step instructions for registering and scheduling your test.

You can also register in person at an official GED® testing location. You can find the location nearest you by visiting this site:

http://www.gedtestingservice.com/testers/locate-a-testing-center

You must register and schedule your test times in advance, and the times that tests are offered vary from place to place. Each of the GED® tests is scheduled separately.

Test-taking accommodations are available for those who need them, but test-takers must get approval in advance for these accommodations. Accommodations include:

- An audio version of the test
- A private testing area
- Extended testing periods
- Additional break times
- Font size options

You must get the appropriate approval form filled out and approved. You can find the forms here:

http://www.gedtestingservice.com/testers/ accommodations-for-disability#Accommodations4

In general, you will need documentation from your doctor or your school that proves testing accommodations are recommended and necessary.

What Are the Question Formats?

Do not worry too much about the question formats. The bulk of the current version of the GED® tests is made up of multiple-choice questions, which almost everyone has experienced at one point or another. But some new question types do take some getting used to. Here is what to expect:

• **Drag-and-drop:** Drag-and-drop questions can look a variety of different ways, but what they ask you to do is use the computer mouse to select an object (it could be a word, a shape, a set of numbers, or another object) and "drag" it into a correct position in some kind of diagram. If you use a computer, you are probably familiar with the concept of "dragging" and "dropping." It is exactly what you do when you move the icon for a document from one folder to another. Look at the simple question below:

Drag and drop the words below into the correct location on the chart.

Words That Describe the Sun	Words That Do Not Describe the Sun

hot

yellow

green

large

extinct

freezing

In this case, it is clear you should drag *hot*, *yellow*, and *large* into the "Words That Describe the Sun" column and *green*, *extinct*, and *freezing* into the "Words That Do Not Describe the Sun" column. Your correct answer would look like this:

Words That Describe the Sun	Words That Do Not Describe the Sun
hot	green
yellow	extinct
large	freezing

This is the basic idea of a drag-and-drop question. You will find many more examples in the practice tests and instructional chapters of this book.

• **Hot spot:** Hot spot items appear mostly in the Mathematical Reasoning test. They require you to plot points on a graph or alter a chart or complete a similar task. Here is an example:

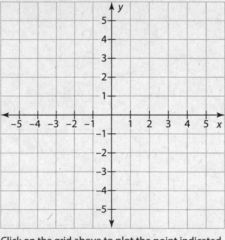

Click on the grid above to plot the point indicated by the ordered pair (1, −3).

To answer this question, you have to click with your mouse on the correct point on the graph. In this case, you would move one place over along the *x*-axis to 1, then move down the *y*-axis to −3. Your correct answer would look like this:

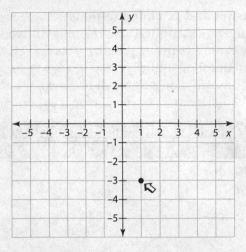

- **Fill in the blank:** This question type is familiar to most people. On the GED® tests, you will simply type in the correct answer. For example, look at this item:

  Do not forget to take (you) _____ umbrella.

  This question is testing whether you know when to use apostrophes. So your correct answer would look like this:

  Do not forget to take ____**your**____ umbrella.

  In this case no apostrophe is required because *your* is an adjective describing *umbrella*.

- **Drop-down:** In a drop-down item, you will see a blank space, usually in a reading passage. At the start of the space, you will see the word "Select ..." If you click on the space with your mouse, you will see a drop-down menu showing several answer options that could fill the blank space. This concept will be familiar to you if you often use the Internet. Many web pages have menus, and if you use your mouse to click on them, multiple options appear. Here is a simple example:

  It is raining out, so you should probably take your [Select... ▼] with you to work today.

  If you click on "Select" and the blank space, here is what you will see:

  It is raining out, so you should probably take your [Select... ▼]
  with you to work today.
  | sled |
  | horse |
  | umbrella |

  In this case, you should select *umbrella* as the best answer option.

• **Short answer and extended response:** These are two versions of the same thing: an essay question. The only difference is the length. You will see many examples in the practice tests and chapters to come. You will be asked a question and expected to answer in your own words, typing your response. The question will be based either on a passage or another set of information or on your personal experience and opinions.

The GED® Test: Test Sections and Time Limits		
Test Section	**Number of Questions**	**Time Limit**
Reasoning Through Language Arts		
Part 1: Multiple-choice	64	95 minutes
Break		10 minutes
Part 2: Essay	1 essay question	45 minutes
Mathematical Reasoning	49	90 minutes
Science	40	90 minutes
Social Studies		
Part 1: Various formats	44	65 minutes
Break		10 minutes
Part 2: Essay	1 essay question	25 minutes

The Reasoning Through Language Arts (RLA) Test

This test measures both your reading and your writing skills. You will be tested on your ability to read carefully, write clearly, and understand and use standard English grammar.

You will see multiple reading passages on this test. About 75 percent of these passages will be nonfiction. The rest will be literature. There will be no poetry selections. These items test your reading comprehension.

Your writing abilities will be assessed through short-answer and extended-response questions. Various question formats will test your understanding of standard English grammar.

You will have 140 minutes to complete the test, which will include approximately 65 questions (mostly multiple-choice).

The Mathematical Reasoning Test

The Mathematical Reasoning test is 90 minutes long and features about 49 items in a variety of formats. There is a short section on which a calculator is not allowed, but for the bulk of the test, a calculator is allowed. The calculator is available on the computer screen.

About half of the test focuses on quantitative problem solving and about half focuses on basic algebraic problem solving. There are some geometry questions as well. The test measures skills both with straightforward math problems and with hypothetical real-world situations that require you to decide how to use your problem-solving skills to arrive at the correct answer.

The Science Test

You will have 90 minutes to complete the Science test, which is about 40 questions long. About 40 percent of the test focuses on life science, about 40 percent focuses on physical science, and the remaining 20 percent focuses on Earth and space science.

The Science test features a full range of question formats.

The Social Studies Test

The Social Studies test is 90 minutes long, with one break. There is an extended-response question on the test, for which you are allowed 25 minutes. There are a total of approximately 45 questions.

Fully half of the test focuses on civics and government, so get ready to brush up on your knowledge of state and federal government and the duties of citizens. The rest of the test focuses on U.S. history, geography, and economics, with some attention to world history.

More About the Test Interface

Taking a test on a computer understandably makes many people nervous. Test-taking features you may be familiar with, such as the ability to mark skipped questions with a pencil so that you can return to them later, are not available. Scratch paper is not allowed. However, there are many features and functions of the new test that can improve the test-taking experience.

- **Built-in clock:** Keeping track of the time used to present a challenge, but the test now has a built-in clock that appears in the upper-right-hand corner of the screen.

- **Erasable note boards:** You cannot use scratch paper, but the test offers erasable note boards that work just as well as regular scratch paper. You can request one at the time of your test, and ask for another one or more if you use up all your space. You will be given an erasable marker to use, and you will deliver the note board to the test administrator after completing your test.

- **Marking skipped items:** In the past, when the GED® test was a paper-and-pencil exam, test-takers often marked skipped items on their answer sheets and returned to them as time allowed. Now the computerized GED® test allows you to mark questions as "skipped" as you proceed from one to the next. When you reach the end of the test, you can see a list of skipped items and return to them if desired.

- **Zooming and color palette:** You have the option of zooming in on text to make it easier to view, or to change the color palette of the test to improve visibility.

- **No more separate answer sheets:** One of the problems with conventional bubble-in answer sheets is that one row accidentally skipped on the answer sheet can throw off a test-taker's entire score. On the computerized GED® test, you are presented with one question on the screen at a time, and you answer directly on that screen before moving on, so there is no chance of "bubbling in" on the wrong line of an answer sheet.

How the Tests Are Scored

As computerized tests have evolved, there have been two main types: adaptive and linear. Computer-adaptive tests are designed to zero in quickly on the test-taker's ability. Test-takers get a "medium" level question first. If they answer correctly, they get a harder question. If they answer incorrectly, they get an easier question, and so on. Critics of this procedure point out that this format does not necessarily give a full picture of a test-taker's abilities because the test-taker is not able to attempt all of the questions.

A linear test is just a test with a set number of questions, all of which are available to the test-taker. The computerized GED® tests are linear, so scores are determined based on the number of correctly answered questions. All questions, however, are not weighted equally. Because of the new question types, some questions are worth more than others.

The tests are scored in their entirety by an automated scoring engine—even short-response and extended-response items will be scored by computer. Scores are reported within three hours of completion of the test.

Test-Taking Strategies

Clearly, the best preparation for the GED® tests is a solid course of study using a book like the one you have in your hands. The best path to a good score is simply knowing the material. However, no matter how hard you study, there will probably be some questions on the GED® tests that throw you for a loop. In those cases, you need to have some test-taking strategies ready.

There are a number of tried-and-true test-taking strategies that have been proven to help test-takers, particularly in solving multiple-choice questions. The GED® test still relies mainly on multiple-choice questions, so it is a good idea to keep the following strategies in mind:

- **The correct answer is staring you in the face.** Remember, the great thing about multiple-choice questions is that the correct answer is right in front of you. You just have to identify it. You do not have to retrieve it from your memory or come up with it on your own. Use this fact to your advantage.

- **Use the process of elimination.** On the GED® test, there is no penalty for wrong answers, so if you don't know the answer to a question, you have nothing to lose by guessing. And if you must guess, you can improve your chances of guessing correctly by using the process of elimination, or POE.

  Think about it this way: on the GED® test, multiple-choice items have four answer choices. If you just guess randomly, you still have a one-in-four chance of being correct. But what if you know that one of the answer choices is definitely wrong? Go ahead and eliminate that option. Now you have a one-in-three chance of guessing correctly. Your odds have just improved considerably. If you can eliminate two options, you are up to a 50 percent chance of selecting the correct answer. That's even better. Here is an example of how this works:

  Who was the first person to fly an airplane solo across the Atlantic Ocean?

  A. George Washington
  B. Orville Wright
  C. Charles Lindbergh
  D. Amelia Earhart

Let's say you are not sure of the answer. It seems clear, though, that you can eliminate George Washington as a choice. He was the first at something, of course—the first president of the United States—but airplanes were not even invented when he was alive, so he is not an option. OK, now you are down to three choices. Orville Wright might seem connected to airplanes somehow. You might remember that it was the Wright brothers who built the first airplane to successfully make a controlled, sustained flight. But neither brother flew across the Atlantic. So eliminate Orville. Now you are down to two choices. Both Charles Lindbergh and Amelia Earhart were famous pilots in the early years of aviation. But who was the first to cross the Atlantic? You have no idea? No matter. You are down to two options. Go ahead and guess. You have a 50% chance of being correct. (By the way, it was Charles Lindbergh who made the first transatlantic solo flight in 1927. Amelia Earhart became the first woman to complete a solo transatlantic flight five years later.)

- **Keep an eye on the clock, and do not get hung up.** It may be tempting to keep wrestling with a difficult question until you have it mastered, but remember that you do not have all day. You have a set amount of time, and your goal should be to at least attempt every single question on the test. If you do some quick math based on the time limits and question totals given in the previous section, you will see that the longest you should spend on any given question is about two minutes. If you have been struggling and coming up empty for five minutes, mark the question as "skipped" and move on. You probably have many questions ahead of you that you can answer correctly, so go get those points!

- **Save the last five minutes for guessing . . . and always guess!** Suppose that you have gone through every item on the test. You have returned to skipped items and applied POE and come up with an acceptable answer. If there are still a few questions that leave you completely stumped, don't sweat it. Just guess. You still have a one-in-four chance of being right on multiple-choice items. The GED® test does not penalize you for wrong answers. They simply count as zeroes. So why miss out on possible points? Pick something, even on one of the new question types. Put down some kind of answer. Never leave a question unanswered.

- **Use short, simple sentences.** On short-answer and extended-response questions, do not try to get too fancy. You can always make sure you are being grammatically correct if you keep your sentence simple and clear.

- **Use your erasable note board to outline your extended responses.** Before just starting to write an answer to an extended-response question, think for a minute or two about what you want to say, in what order, and how you intend to support your opinions or assertions. Make a quick outline. It does not have to follow a formal format. Just know where you are going with a response before you start typing.

- **Proofread your work.** Once you finish your short-answer or extended responses, read through them carefully to make sure there are no obvious mistakes.

How to Use This Book to Set Up a Study Plan

How much time you decide to devote to each subject area depends completely on your own schedule and your own level of mastery of each subject area. There is no set prescription. This book is broken into short, manageable chunks of information, so you can take it one step at a time at your own pace.

If you have a packed daily schedule with very little time to devote to studying and you find that you need a lot of review in a given area, you will probably need to give yourself plenty of time. For example, if you are a parent with a full-time job, you may find that by the time you get the children to bed, you have only enough energy for 30 minutes of studying. That's fine. Just try to do one topic a night, and give yourself at least six weeks to finish your study for each test.

On the other hand, if you want to get through your series of GED® tests as quickly as possible in order to achieve some further goal (get a certain job or promotion, apply to college, or the like) and you have several hours or more of free time every day, you could conceivably prepare yourself for one test in two weeks.

Whatever you decide, write down your plan on a calendar (how many pages per night, for example) and stick to it. It may take a lot of determination, but you can do it.

Finally, turn to family and friends for support and encouragement. What you are doing is important, hard work. You deserve plenty of praise and pats on the back.

We wish you the best of luck—on the test and beyond!

Reasoning Through Language Arts

The Reasoning Through Language Arts (RLA) Test

The Reasoning Through Language Arts (RLA) section of the GED® test measures your ability to read carefully, write clearly, and understand and use standard English grammar.

There are approximately 64 questions on the RLA test. You will have 150 minutes to complete the entire test, including 45 minutes for writing an extended response (essay) and a 10-minute break.

Many questions on the RLA test refer to reading passages. About 75 percent of these passages will be informational texts (nonfiction). The rest will be literary texts (fiction). There will not be any poetry selections. These questions test your reading comprehension ability.

Most of the RLA questions are multiple-choice with four answer choices. All of the multiple-choice questions refer to reading passages. These questions measure how well you have understood what you read.

Other RLA questions use interactive formats such as drag and drop, fill-in-the-blank, and drop-down. See "Introducing the GED Test" at the start of this book for an explanation and samples of these formats. Some of these questions will test your mastery of basic English usage and vocabulary as well as your reading comprehension skills.

Your writing abilities will be assessed through short-answer and extended-response questions. For the extended-response item, you will have 45 minutes to write a persuasive essay to explain why you think one of two reading passages makes a stronger argument than the other.

The Reasoning Through Language Arts Review

The following section of this book presents a comprehensive review of the skills that are tested on the RLA test. You will see examples of all of the kinds of passages that are included on the test, and practice exercises in every topic area.

Answers for all of the exercises in these chapters are located in the Exercise Answer Key section at the back of this book.

CHAPTER 1

Reading and Analyzing Texts

The Reasoning Through Language Arts (RLA) portion of the GED Assessment tests how well you comprehend what you read.

Reading Comprehension Skills

To be a good reader, you need to master a number of important skills. You need to be able to recognize the main idea of a text, and you should be able to locate details in the text that support that main idea. You should also be able to recognize how the different elements of a text relate to, and influence, each other. You should understand a wide range of vocabulary words, and you should also be aware of how writers choose words and use figurative language in order to convey shades of meaning.

Main Idea and Supporting Details

Everything you read, informative texts and literature, has a **subject**—what the text is about. The **main idea** of the text is different. It's the text's central focus, or the most important point the writer makes about the subject. The rest, as people say, is in the details. **Supporting details** are the information that develops or explains the main idea. They include facts, examples, and descriptions.

Writers of nonfiction texts, especially informative texts, often state the main idea directly in a **thesis statement** in the text's introduction. At other times, the main idea is **implied,** or expressed indirectly. In those situations, you need to figure it out yourself by analyzing the supporting details and determining what they have in common.

Fiction writers express their main idea as a **theme,** the story's lesson or message about life. Here are some common themes:

- Crime does not pay.
- Sacrifice brings rewards.
- Love conquers all.
- Nature is beautiful but sometimes deadly.

- Working together is more powerful than working alone.

- Never give up.

Fiction writers rarely state their themes directly. Instead they reveal them through the content of their stories. For example, they use events to shape their themes. For instance, in Jack London's story "To Build a Fire," the man's repeated, failed attempts to keep warm in the wilderness in subzero temperatures and his eventual death are events that shape the theme that nature can be deadly.

Drawing Conclusions

Determining a text's main idea or theme involves drawing conclusions. **Conclusions** are decisions based on reasoning. When reading, you reach conclusions by combining information from a text with information from your own prior knowledge and experience. In other words, you put together what you read with what you know. There are two types of conclusions: inferences and generalizations. **Inferences** are conclusions that relate specifically to the text at hand. **Generalizations** are conclusions that draw on a text to make observations about life or the world. When you determine a fictional work's theme, you are making a generalization, since you are applying what you read to understand an idea about the real world.

EXERCISE 1

Main Idea and Supporting Details

Directions: Read the passages, then choose the best answer to each of the questions that follow.

The Great Depression

The stock market crash of 1929, which occurred several months after Herbert Hoover became President of the United States, was the beginning of the Great Depression, perhaps the greatest economic calamity in U.S. history. Within a few years, by 1933, approximately 25 percent of U.S. workers were unemployed. Huge numbers of people became homeless; many lived in shantytowns that they called Hoovervilles and relied on free food given out in bread lines. Unemployment finally dipped below 10 percent in 1941.

Excerpt from *The Grapes of Wrath*

by John Steinbeck

The decay spreads over the State, and the sweet smell is a great sorrow on the land. Men who can graft the trees and make the seed fertile and big can find no way to let the hungry people eat their produce. Men who have created new fruits in the world cannot create a system whereby their fruits may be eaten. And the failure hangs over the State like a great sorrow.

The works of the roots of the vines, of the trees, must be destroyed to keep up the price, and this is the saddest, bitterest thing of all. Carloads of oranges dumped on the ground. The people came for miles to take the fruit, but this could not be. How would they buy oranges at twenty cents a dozen if they could drive out and pick them up? And men with hoses squirt kerosene on the oranges, and they are angry at the crime, angry at the people who have come to take the fruit. A million people hungry, needing the fruit—and kerosene sprayed over the golden mountains.

And the smell of rot fills the country.

1. Which statement *most* accurately states the main idea of the first passage?

   A. The Great Depression began with the 1929 stock market crash.
   B. The Great Depression was an economic catastrophe.
   C. Herbert Hoover did many things to end the Great Depression.
   D. Many lives were saved by free food distributed during the Great Depression.

2. Which detail supports the idea that Herbert Hoover was an unpopular president?

   A. The stock market crash happened after Hoover's election.
   B. Unemployment reached 25 percent in 1933.
   C. Many people were homeless.
   D. Homeless people called their shantytowns Hoovervilles.

3. What theme is expressed in the second passage?

   A. Capitalism can sometimes be an inhumane system.
   B. Hunger drives people to steal for food.
   C. People should never interfere with nature.
   D. Sacrifice brings rewards.

4. Why do the men squirt kerosene on the oranges?

   A. to cause the oranges to rot faster
   B. to keep bugs off the oranges
   C. to help burn the oranges later
   D. to stop people from eating the oranges

Answers are on page 533.

Relationships in Texts

The **plot** of a story is made up of a sequence of events. These events often unfold in **chronological order**; that is, they are arranged according to how they happen over time. Some storytellers use **flashbacks,** skipping back in time, to relate an event that happened earlier. For example, a story may flash back to a traumatic childhood encounter with a dog to explain why an adult character has a strong fear of dogs. A plot outline for this story might look something like this:

- Jess and Travis go out for a walk.

- An unleashed dog runs up to them.

- A horrified Travis recoils from the dog.

- [flashback] Young Travis is bitten by a dog.

- The dog's owner leashes the dog and apologizes.

- Jess and Travis continue their walk, though Travis is obviously shaken.

If the GED Assessment asks you to put events in order, be sure to find the proper place for flashbacks. If you were asked to put the sequence of events above *into chronological order,* you would move the flashback to the beginning of the sequence. If you were asked to show the order in which they occur in the story, you would leave the flashback where it is.

At times, you may need to make inferences about the sequence of events. In the example above, the writer might never state that Travis is afraid of dogs because of the earlier dog attack, but you can infer that this is the cause. Remember that to infer is to draw a conclusion about the text, based on what you have read and what you know. Here are some relationships you might find:

- **cause/effect**—One event in the story causes another.

   example: In *Romeo and Juliet,* Romeo crashes a party, trying to catch a glimpse of Rosaline, the object of his desire. This causes him to meet Juliet, who is also at the party. Meeting Juliet causes Romeo to fall in love with Juliet and forget his love for Rosaline. You can infer that if Romeo had not tried to see Rosaline, he might have never fallen in love with Juliet.

- **parallelism**—Events move in the same way but separately.

  example: When Juliet hears of Romeo's banishment, she reacts with forceful emotion. In the next scene, Romeo also reacts to his banishment and news of Juliet's grief with strong emotion. You can infer that both have a passionate love for each other.

- **contrast**—Events are very different.

  example: When Juliet reacts to Romeo's banishment, she is able to control her grief. Romeo, on the other hand, must be restrained by others to keep from harming himself. You can infer from this contrast that Juliet is more mature, and that Romeo is more impulsive—and that his impulsiveness may bring about much trouble later in the play.

These relationships are also seen in informative texts. For example, an article on pollution will likely include cause/effect relationships to explain where the problem started. Texts about history might use parallelism to show how two monarchs had similar rises to power. A text about weather might contrast the development of hurricanes and tornados. These relationships may be clearly outlined for you, or they may require you to make inferences about the relationships, just as you do when reading fictional works.

Influence

The GED Assessment will test your ability to recognize how different elements **influence,** or have an effect on, other elements. In an informational text, these elements include events, people, ideas, and places. Here are some examples:

- Explain how the American Frontier changed Theodore Roosevelt. (A place influences a person.)

- How did Theodore Roosevelt affect the outcome of the war in Cuba? (A person influences an event.)

- What effect did Theodore Roosevelt have on the development of conservation as a goal? (A person influences an idea.)

- How did Theodore Roosevelt influence the president who followed him in office, William Howard Taft? (A person influences another person.)

In literature, the elements that influence each other include plot, characters, theme, and setting. Here are some examples:

- How do the harsh, isolated English moors influence the theme in *Wuthering Heights*? (The setting influences the theme.)

- What effect does young Heathcliff have on Catherine? (A character influences another character.)

- How does the death of Catherine change Heathcliff? (The plot influences a character.)

EXERCISE 2

Relationships in Texts

Directions: Read the passage, then choose the best answer to each of the questions that follow.

Excerpt from *Wuthering Heights*

by Emily Brontë

I took a seat at the end of the hearthstone opposite that towards which my landlord advanced, and filled up an interval of silence by attempting to caress the canine mother, who had left her nursery, and was sneaking wolfishly to the back of my legs, her lip curled up, and her white teeth watering for a snatch. My caress provoked a long, guttural gnarl.

"You'd better let the dog alone," growled Mr. Heathcliff in unison, checking fiercer demonstrations with a punch of his foot. "She's not accustomed to be spoiled—not kept for a pet." Then, striding to a side door, he shouted again, "Joseph!"

Joseph mumbled indistinctly in the depths of the cellar, but gave no intimation of ascending; so his master dived down to him. . . . Not anxious to come in contact with their fangs, I sat still; but, imagining they would scarcely understand tacit insults, I unfortunately indulged in winking and making faces at the trio, and some turn of my physiognomy so irritated madam, that she suddenly broke into a fury and leapt on my knees. I flung her back, and hastened to interpose the table between us. This proceeding aroused the whole hive: half-a-dozen four-footed fiends, of various sizes and ages, issued from hidden dens to the common centre. I felt my heels and coat-laps peculiar subjects of assault; and parrying off the larger combatants as effectually as I could with the poker, I was constrained to demand, aloud, assistance from some of the household in re-establishing peace.

Mr. Heathcliff and his man climbed the cellar steps with vexatious phlegm: I don't think they moved one second faster than usual, though the hearth was an absolute tempest of worrying and yelping.

1. What causes the dogs to attack the narrator?

    A. He tries to pet the mother dog.
    B. He kicks the mother dog.
    C. He hits the dogs with a poker.
    D. He makes faces at the dogs.

2. In what order do the events in the excerpt occur?

   I.   The dogs attack the narrator.
   II. Heathcliff calls for Joseph.
   III. Heathcliff warns the narrator not to pet the dog.
   IV. Heathcliff leaves the room.

   A. I, II, III, IV
   B. III, II, IV, I
   C. II, IV, I, III
   D. IV, II, III, I

3. What does Heathcliff's growl reveal about his character?

   A. He feels uncomfortable around house guests.
   B. He tries to relate to the dogs on their own level.
   C. He has an animal-like nature.

Answers are on page 533.

Vocabulary: The Meaning of Words and Phrases

The GED Assessment will also test your ability to determine the meanings of words and phrases as they are used in a text. In the same text in which you determine an implied main idea, you might also be asked to define unfamiliar vocabulary. To do so, you should examine the word or phrase's **context**—the words, phrases, and sentences that surround the word. Here are some context clues you can look for when reading:

- **definition**—Familiar words or phrases define the unfamiliar word.

   example: The bat is **nocturnal,** active at night. *Nocturnal* means "active at night."

- **restatement**—The word is restated in more familiar language.

   example: Jenna is an **ovo-lacto vegetarian.** She doesn't eat meat, but she does eat dairy and egg products. *Ovo-lacto vegetarian* is "someone who doesn't eat meat but consumes dairy and egg products."

- **synonym/antonym**—Words similar or opposite in meaning provide clues about the unfamiliar word.

   example: She expected the ancient, lost manuscript to be incomplete, but when she discovered it, it was **intact.** *Intact* means "complete."

- **cause/effect**—The word shares a cause-and-effect relationship with a familiar word or phrase, one causing the other.

  example: When the riverbanks overflowed, the surrounding area was **deluged.** *Deluged* means "flooded with water."

EXERCISE 3

Vocabulary: The Meaning of Words and Phrases

Directions: Choose the best answer to each of the following questions.

1. What does the word *physiognomy* mean in this sentence?

   I unfortunately indulged in winking and making faces at the trio, and some turn of my <u>physiognomy</u> so irritated madam, that she suddenly broke into a fury and leapt on my knees.

   A. emotional state
   B. facial features
   C. life process
   D. body language

2. Read the following excerpt. Then choose the correct definition for *shantytown*.

   Huge numbers of people became homeless; many lived in shantytowns that they called Hoovervilles and relied on free food given out in bread lines.

   A. a bread line where people dependent on free food gather
   B. an area where the very poor live in crudely built homes
   C. an elite neighborhood built during the Hoover administration
   D. a farm-based encampment where immigrant laborers live

Answers are on page 533.

Word Choice, Diction, and Connotative and Figurative Meanings

Diction is the way in which words are used in writing, including word choice, with regard to correctness, clearness, or effectiveness. Writers craft their messages by carefully choosing the right words to fit the meaning they wish to convey. A good writer probably would not describe an Arctic winter as *cold*. Instead, he or she would choose a more precise word, like *frigid, intense, severe,* or *biting*. The same writer describing a Texas winter might use *brisk* or *chilly* to effectively convey that while it's not warm, it's certainly not as cold as other places. Effective writers avoid imprecise, vague words. Here's an example:

> **Vague:** Javier saw some animals chasing things outside.

> **Precise:** Javier spotted two cats chasing whirling, windblown leaves in the backyard.

The precise language paints a clearer, more effective description of the scene.

Connotations are the feelings suggested by a word in addition to the word's exact meaning. For example, *assertive* means "showing confidence." It has a positive connotation. People who stand up for themselves are called *assertive* and praised for their actions. Likewise, *insistent* and *decisive* have positive connotations for the same meaning. However, *pushy* and *overbearing,* which mean much the same thing, have negative connotations. No one likes people who are *pushy*.

Another choice writers make in diction is to express ideas indirectly, using words in imaginative ways. Instead of using literal meanings, they sometimes use **figurative language,** describing one thing in terms of another, to create a fresh, vivid image in the reader's mind. Three common kinds of figurative language are similes, metaphors, and personification.

- **simile**—the use of *like* or *as* to compare two things

    example: His heart was like a skipping child.

- **metaphor**—the use of one thing in place of another to suggest similarity

    example: The tangled kite string was a knot of snakes.

- **personification**—the attribution of human traits to non-human things

    example: The daisies smiled in the sunshine.

EXERCISE 4

Word Choice, Diction, and Connotative and Figurative Meanings

Directions: Read the passage, then choose the best answer to each of the questions that follow.

Excerpt from *Moby Dick*
by Herman Melville

You could pretty plainly tell how long each one had been ashore. This young fellow's healthy cheek is like a sun-toasted pear in hue, and would seem to smell almost as musky; he cannot have been three days landed from his Indian voyage. That man next him looks a few shades lighter; you might say a touch of satin wood is in him. In the complexion of a third still lingers a tropic tawn, but slightly bleached withal; HE doubtless has tarried whole weeks ashore. But who could show a cheek like Queequeg? which, barred with various tints, seemed like the Andes' western slope, to show forth in one array, contrasting climates, zone by zone.

1. Which definition best matches the use of the word *shades* in the paragraph?

   A. areas of darkness produced where sunlight is blocked
   B. gradations of darkness
   C. shelters from heat and glare of sunlight
   D. slight differences or variations

2. Which of the following words from the paragraph has a positive connotation?

   A. contrasting
   B. looks
   C. healthy
   D. zone

3. Which phrase is an example of a metaphor?

   A. like a sun-toasted pear
   B. to smell almost as musky
   C. a touch of satin wood is in him
   D. like the Andes' western slope

Answers are on page 533.

Text Analysis

Another skill tested by the Reasoning Through Language Arts section of the GED Assessment is your ability to analyze texts. You will closely examine several texts by looking at the texts' details and the overall structure of the texts.

Text Structures

Text structures are the organizational patterns writers use to present their ideas. They are among the style choices writers make to convey their messages and emphasize their ideas. Recognizing how a writer has organized a text can help you better focus on the text's main ideas and the relationship of ideas within the text.

Here is a list of the most common text structures and their definitions, along with the **transition words** writers often use to connect ideas and guide readers through their texts. Transition words can help you identify which type of structure a text uses.

Cause and effect

The **cause-and-effect** structure shows how one action or event (the cause) leads to another action or event (the effect).

Transition/signal words: *as a result, because, caused, consequently, if . . . then, led, since, therefore, thus*

> **EXAMPLE**
>
> During the 1930s, the southern Great Plains of the United States experienced severe dust storms caused by a combination of drought and poor farming practices. Widespread cultivation of the native grasslands destroyed the natural ground cover that anchored the topsoil and prevented erosion. As a result, when severe drought and unusually high temperatures gripped the region, much of the soil blew away. The parched land and ruined economy caused millions of people to leave the area, with many moving to California to seek work as migrant farmworkers.

Chronological Order

Chronological order, also known as time order, relates a series of events in the sequence in which they happen over time. Writers also use this text structure to show how to make or do something. Fiction writers typically use chronological order to tell their stories. Nonfiction histories and "how-to" texts also use this text structure.

Transition/signal words: *after, before, finally, first, later, last, next, now, since, then*

EXAMPLE

Before planting any large tree, be sure to contact your local utility companies to ensure that you do not dig too near buried lines, pipes, or cables. Start by digging a hole at least twice as wide and slightly less deep than the tree's root ball. Next, rough up the sides and bottom of the hole to allow root tips an easier time extending beyond the hole. Gently remove the tree from its container; then separate and straighten the roots. Next, bury the root ball in the hole, using the soil that came from the hole, not store-bought soil with amendments. Be sure the trunk of the tree is slightly above the surrounding soil. Mulch around the tree, two to three inches deep, but not touching the trunk. Finally, water the tree, about six to eight gallons of water per inch of trunk diameter, repeating weekly for the first two years.

Compare and Contrast

The **compare-and-contrast** text structure shows how topics are alike or different. Writers use two different ways to organize with this structure: block and point-by-point. In **block** structure, the writer discusses details of one topic then the details of the other. In **point-by-point** structure, the writer alternates discussing one point for the first topic, then the same point for the second topic, and so on, going back and forth between the two topics.

Transition/signal words: *also, although, both, but, however, in contrast, instead, like, nevertheless, only, on the other hand, or, similarly, too, yet*

EXAMPLE

Block

The Red Delicious apple originated in Peru and was introduced to markets in 1874. This bright red, mildly sweet, heart-shaped apple is a snacking favorite that can also be enjoyed in salads. However, it is not recommended for pies or sauces.

In contrast, the Fuji apple comes originally from Japan and was brought to market in 1962. These roughly globe-shaped apples are reddish-pink in color with a super sweet flavor. Like the Red Delicious, they are good for snacking and in salads; however, they are also tasty in pies and sauces.

Point by Point

The Red Delicious apple originated in Peru, while the Fuji apple came from Japan. The Red Delicious was introduced to markets in 1874, with the Fuji following nearly a century later in 1962. The Red Delicious is bright red, mildly sweet, and heart-shaped. In contrast, the Fuji is reddish-pink, super sweet, and roughly globe-shaped. Both apples are good for snacking or in salads, but only the Fuji is recommended for pies or sauces.

Problem and Solution

The **problem-and-solution** text structure presents a problem and explains how it was solved or can be solved. In cases where the problem has already been solved, the texts show actual solutions. Problem-and-solution structure is similar to the cause-and-effect structure. In fact, you will find some of the same signal words in both types of writing.

Transition/signal words: *because, challenge, concern, effect, hopefully, problem, since, solution, solve*

EXAMPLE

Like many people, you may love feeding birds in your yard or on the porch of your home. However, you may face the problem of feeding more squirrels than birds! Squirrels can chase away birds, eat most or all of the seeds, and even destroy feeders. Dissuading these fuzzy nuisances is a real challenge. Here are some common solutions: Squirrel-proof your feeders by putting smooth baffles above or below the feeders. Buy squirrel-proof feeders with wire cages or doors that are triggered by the squirrel's weight. Try adding cayenne pepper to the seed. Squirrels hate it, but birds do not. But above all else, do not hunt or poison the squirrels. Not only is it cruel (and in some places, illegal), but also you might unintentionally harm the birds you love.

Author's Purpose or Point of View

Writers use different text structures depending on their purpose for writing. A writer's **purpose** is the reason he or she writes. The most common purposes are to entertain, to persuade, and to inform. Writers also have **points of view,** their opinions and attitudes about their subjects. Writers don't usually declare their purposes or points of view explicitly, but you can often infer them from details in the text or details omitted.

EXAMPLE

Dmitri Shostakovich was a Russian composer who lived from 1906 to 1975. His symphonies and quartets are considered by some to be the twentieth century's greatest examples of these classical forms. He had a complex relationship with the Soviet government—honored or condemned, depending on the variable political climate.

Author's purpose: To inform readers about Dmitri Shostakovich

Author's point of view: Dmitri Shostakovich was an important composer, so readers should know about him.

Authors often use compare-and-contrast text structure to convey their points of view. In a block format, they analyze details in support of their own viewpoint, then present other points of view. Or they may analyze and compare details point-by-point. Depending on the purpose of the text, the author may devote the entire text to proving that one position is better than another, or he or she might nod to different points of view throughout the text.

EXAMPLE

While some believe Shostakovich eventually conformed to official Soviet policy, his music suggests otherwise.

EXERCISE 5

Author's Purpose or Point of View

Directions: Read the passage, then choose the best answer to each of the questions that follow.

Since 1883, the Brooklyn Bridge has been an iconic symbol of New York City, linking the boroughs of Brooklyn and Manhattan. It took 600 workers 14 years to construct the bridge at a cost of $15 million. President Chester A. Arthur and New York Governor (and future President) Grover Cleveland presided over the dedication ceremony on May 24, 1883. Fears about the bridge's safety led to a remarkable publicity stunt. To demonstrate the bridge's safety, showman P. T. Barnum paraded 21 elephants, 7 camels, and various other exotic animals from his circus across the bridge on May 17, 1884. And the bridge has stood the test of time. Today, approximately 120,000 vehicles, 4,000 pedestrians, and 3,100 cyclists cross the bridge daily.

1. Which of the following best describes the purpose of this passage?

   A. To analyze
   B. To entertain
   C. To persuade
   D. To inform

2. Which statement *best* represents the writer's point of view on the subject?

   A. The Brooklyn Bridge is vital to New York's economy.
   B. The Brooklyn Bridge must be preserved for future generations.
   C. The Brooklyn Bridge is an important part of New York's past and present.
   D. The Brooklyn Bridge required a lot of time, manpower, and money to complete.

Answers are on page 533.

Rhetorical Techniques

Rhetorical techniques are ways writers use language to convey meaning, achieve their purposes, and advance their points of view. Most often, these devices are used to persuade readers to do or believe something. Here are some common rhetorical strategies you might see on the GED RLA section.

Rhetorical Techniques		
Technique	**Definition**	**Example**
analogy	establishing a relationship between two things or ideas based on similarities	A doctor diagnoses illnesses in the same way that a detective investigates a crime. The concert was as loud as a sandblaster.
enumeration	dividing a subject into parts or details	The wonderful people, excellent museums, moderate weather, and dynamic nature make this a great city in which to live.
juxtaposition	placing two or more ideas, places, people, or actions side by side	While we eat our meals with little gratitude, others go hungry, wishing for what we have.
parallelism	using similar grammatical forms or structures to balance related ideas	Her plan was clever in conception, smart in organization, and elegant in execution. The time is not for words, but for action.
qualifying statements	adding information to make a statement less strong or show conditions under which it could be true	This restaurant has the worst service, at least in my experience. Under most conditions, iron is a solid.
repetition	repeating the same words, phrases, or sentences	Every home, every street, every neighborhood must be made safe for our citizens.

EXERCISE 6

Rhetorical Techniques

Directions: Read the following passage, and then match the excerpt to its most prominent rhetorical technique.

I would say to the House, as I said to those who have joined this government: "I have nothing to offer but blood, toil, tears and sweat." We have before us an ordeal of the most grievous kind. We have before us many, many long months of struggle and of suffering. You ask, what is our policy? I can say: It is to wage war, by sea, land and air, with all our might and with all the strength that God can give us; to wage war against a monstrous tyranny, never surpassed in the dark, lamentable catalogue of human crime. That is our policy. You ask, what is our aim? I can answer in one word: It is victory, victory at all costs, victory in spite of all terror, victory, however long and hard the road may be; for without victory, there is no survival. —Winston Churchill, 1940

_____ **1.** I have nothing to offer but blood, toil, tears and sweat

_____ **2.** long months of struggle and of suffering

_____ **3.** It is victory, victory at all costs, victory in spite of all terror

_____ **4.** however long and hard the road may be

A. enumeration

B. analogy

C. parallelism

D. repetition

Answers are on page 533.

Analyzing Arguments

The GED tests your ability to comprehend persuasive texts. A writer's **argument** consists of his or her claims and supporting evidence.

Writers present **claims,** or reasons, to defend their positions. Claims build upon one another logically. For example, to make a strong first impression, a writer might begin with his or her strongest claim. Or he or she might build up the argument, saving the best for last.

Evidence

Claims cannot be strong without support. **Evidence** is the information that proves that the claims are valid. When analyzing an argument, you should distinguish valid claims supported by evidence from claims that are unsupported. Writers have many kinds of evidence to choose from to support their claims.

Types of Evidence		
facts	statements that can be proven true	Mount Everest is the world's highest mountain.
statistics	numerical facts and data	Everest's peak is 29,035 feet above sea level.
expert opinions	quotes from authorities on the topic	Adele Pennington, who has climbed Everest twice, says, "There are far too many people going for the summit."
anecdotes	personal experiences	Having hiked to the Everest base camp, I can report that that trek alone was far more than the casual hiker should attempt.

Evaluating Evidence

To properly analyze an argument, make sure the evidence is valid and its sources are trustworthy. Ask these questions about any piece of evidence:

• Is it **relevant,** or clearly connected to the issue?

   example: Citing the population of Nepal is not relevant to the claim that too many people are climbing Mount Everest each year.

• Is it **sufficient?** Is the evidence enough to prove the claim?

   example: Stating how many people climbed Everest last year is not sufficient to prove the claim that too many people are climbing the mountain. Additional data showing how the number has increased would better support the claim and make a stronger argument.

• Is it **reliable?** Where did the evidence come from? Is the source credible, or trustworthy? Can the facts be confirmed?

   example: Statistics on Mount Everest from the National Geographic Society are more reliable than those found on a "Fun Facts" website of unknown origin.

• Is it **reasonable,** or in line with widely accepted norms?

   example: A claim that 200 people die per year on Mount Everest is not reasonable, especially when checked against the fact that a total of 248 people died there between 1921 and 2013.

Finding Logical Fallacies

Even when the evidence is valid, an argument can still suffer from **logical fallacies,** that is, poor or misleading reasoning. Keep a close watch for logical fallacies when reading persuasive texts.

Logical Fallacies		
Fallacy	Definition	Example
ad hominem	attacking the person rather than the argument	Mia Armstrong can't be our next mayor. She can hardly dress herself!
ad populum	appealing to popularity	Most people favor the new law, so it must be a good one.
circular reasoning	repeating a claim in a slightly different way, rather than supporting it	Jan's salsa should win the blue ribbon because it is the best.
false dichotomy (either/or)	claiming there are only two options when there are many	You either love New York or you hate it.
hasty generalization	drawing a conclusion based on a small sample size	My cousin, who never wears a seat belt, was in a car accident, but he was fine. So seat belts are unnecessary.
non sequitur	drawing conclusions that do not follow from the evidence	If you don't eat broccoli, then you are neglecting your body.
post hoc ergo propter hoc (false cause)	assuming that since one event follows another that the earlier event caused the later	Whenever I wash my car, it rains. If I want it to rain, all I have to do is wash my car.
red herring	introducing an irrelevant topic to draw attention away from the original issue	I know I was late for work, but Ian left early yesterday, and my boss didn't complain then.
slippery slope	declaring that if an action is taken, others will inevitably follow, with an undesired final consequence	If we allow Owens Park to be a leash-free dog area, soon all the parks will be leash free.

Fallacy	Definition	Example
straw man	misrepresenting or overstating an opponent's argument so it can be easily attacked	The city council voted to close two public elementary schools. Since they obviously do not care about education, they should be voted out of office.

Logical fallacies can stir emotions and convince many people to think or act the way the writer desires. However, careful readers can recognize fallacies and will not be swayed when solid, logical reasoning is lacking.

Considering Underlying Premises and Assumptions

The GED test may also ask you to find a writer's **underlying premises,** or unstated reasons for holding a position. Writers do not always explicitly state their claims. In these situations you can infer their claims based on evidence in the text. For example, if a writer outlines his or her ideas for cutting taxes, the underlying premise may be that the government spends too much money. When analyzing a writer's arguments, consider the underlying premises and whether the evidence presented supports them.

Assumptions are ideas that are accepted to be true without evidence. They are facts we take for granted. Assumptions are different from claims because writers do not even try to prove their assumptions; they are usually given as true. For example, it is an assumption that exercise is important to good health, or that if you drop a glass, it will break. Some assumptions are unstated. You must infer them by looking at the details and determining what facts or beliefs are behind them.

EXAMPLE

Claim: If the city builds this new youth sports complex, it will keep kids out of trouble.

Assumptions: Kids will go to the complex; kids will not get into trouble at the sports complex

When analyzing an argument, you should question whether the writer's assumptions are true. If the assumptions are false, then the writer's conclusions may be false. For example, if statistics show that troublesome kids do not go to youth sports complexes or that kids still get into trouble at sports complexes, then the unstated assumptions must be false. And if the assumptions are false, then the claim and argument may also be false.

EXERCISE 7

Analyzing Arguments

Directions: Read the passage, then choose the best answer to each of the questions that follow.

A college degree does not guarantee a better job. One-third of all college graduates work in jobs that do not require a college degree. And the federal minimum wage is not enough to live on. Many successful people never went to college or earned a degree. Ever hear of Bill Gates, Steve Jobs, or Mark Zuckerberg? Student loan debt is hard for many college graduates to pay back. The average graduate leaves college with $26,000 in debt. The U.S. Congress Joint Economic Committee states that 60% of graduates have student loan debt that is 60% of their annual income. Student debt could create a financial crisis similar to the housing bubble and crash of the late 2000s. Over 850,000 student loans, more than 15% of all loans, were in default as of 2012. That's over $1 trillion. When some of them default, the taxpayer loses. And if some default, what is to stop all of them from defaulting and leaving our economy in ruins?

1. Which statement *most* accurately represents the writer's overall position?

    A. A college education is often not worth its cost.
    B. A college education is essential to career success.
    C. A college education creates burdensome debt.
    D. A college education is a poor use of tax dollars.

2. Which sentence contains evidence that is not relevant?

    A. And the federal minimum wage is not enough to live on.
    B. Ever hear of Bill Gates, Steve Jobs, or Mark Zuckerberg?
    C. The average graduate leaves college with $26,000 in debt.
    D. Over 850,000 student loans, more than 15% of all loans, were in default as of 2012.

3. Which sentence uses the slippery slope logical fallacy?

    A. A college degree does not guarantee a better job.
    B. And federal minimum wage is not enough to live on.
    C. The average graduate leaves college with $26,000 in debt.
    D. And if some default, what is to stop all of them from defaulting . . . ?

4. Which of these is one of the writer's underlying premises?

    A. Every student takes out student loans.

    B. You don't have to go to college to be successful.

    C. Graduates employed in jobs that do not require college degrees are unhappy.

    D. People who do not go to college are more likely to be unemployed.

Answers are on page 533.

Analyzing Data

Some texts you will encounter on the RLA section of the GED test might look like they belong in the Science or Mathematical Reasoning sections because they include graphics, or visuals. Writers often use graphics to extend or clarify the information they present or to support their arguments. **Data,** or numerical information, can be more easily understood when arranged in **graphs** and **tables.** Processes and complex descriptions are often clearer when presented in **diagrams.** Here are the most common types of graphics you will see used with texts.

- **Graphs** show relationships among numbers, often comparing quantities or showing changes over time. The main types are circle, bar, and line graphs.

- **Circle graphs** (or pie charts) show the relationship of parts to the whole, often in percentages or fractions.

EXAMPLE

This circle graph below shows results from a classroom poll of favorite fruits.

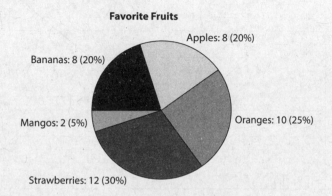

Favorite Fruits

Apples: 8 (20%)
Bananas: 8 (20%)
Mangos: 2 (5%)
Oranges: 10 (25%)
Strawberries: 12 (30%)

• **Bar graphs** use bars to represent values.

EXAMPLE

This bar graph shows the same results in a different form.

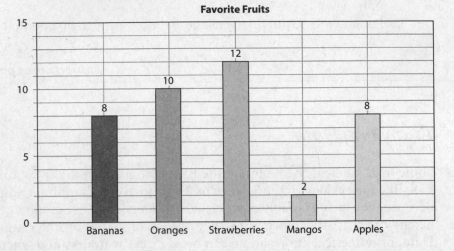

• **Line graphs** show information that is connected—for example, showing changes over time.

EXAMPLE

This line graph shows how many apples a person ate over a four-day period.

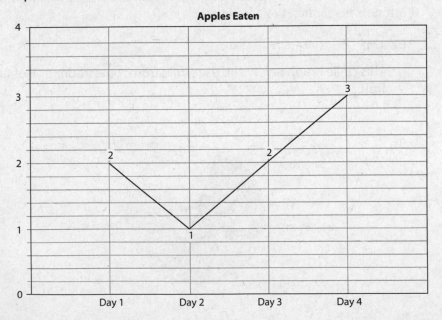

- **Tables** (or simple charts) arrange information in rows and columns. To locate information, read down the columns and across the rows.

EXAMPLE

This table shows data about medal counts at the 2014 Olympics.

2014 Winter Olympic Medal Count				
Country	Gold	Silver	Bronze	Total
Russia	13	11	9	**33**
Norway	11	5	10	**26**
Canada	10	10	5	**25**
USA	9	7	12	**28**

- **Diagrams** use simplified drawings to show what something looks like or how it works; they often use symbols such as circles and arrows.

EXAMPLE

This diagram shows the natural process known as the water cycle.

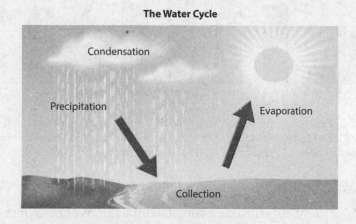

The Water Cycle

Notice that each of these graphics includes a brief but informative title. Other parts of the graphics are labeled to help readers identify and interpret information quickly and effectively.

Graphics are visual representations of information. As such, they can be evaluated like any other evidence to see if they are relevant, sufficient, reliable, and reasonable.

EXERCISE 8

Analyzing Data

Directions: Read the passages, analyze the graphics, and then answer the questions that follow.

Passage 1

Which Vital Nutrients Are Included in Fortified Cereals?

In the American diet, fortified breakfast cereals provide more iron, fiber, zinc, folic acid, and other B vitamins than any other common non-cereal breakfast item. Many fortified cereals also add certain other nutrients, such as vitamin A, thiamin, niacin, calcium, phosphorous, magnesium and/or potassium. Fortified cereals are also often combined with fortified milk, and the result is a healthful and nutrient-dense breakfast meal.

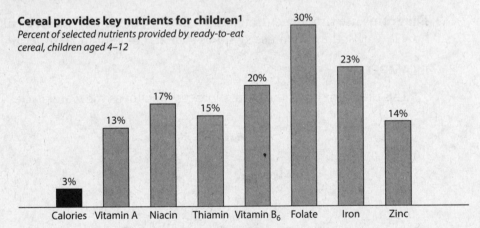

Cereal provides key nutrients for children[1]
Percent of selected nutrients provided by ready-to-eat cereal, children aged 4–12

[1] National Center for Health Statistics (NCHS). National Health and Nutrition Examination Survey Data. Hyattsville, MD: U.S. Department of Health and Human Services, Centers for Disease Control and Prevention, [2005–06] [http.cdc.gov/nchs/nhanes].

1. What relationship does the graphic have to the text?

   A. It compares breakfast cereal to other kinds of breakfast.
   B. It provides evidence that breakfast cereal is nutrient dense.
   C. It shows all the nutrients that are added to cereal when it is fortified.
   D. It explains why breakfast is the most important meal of the day.

2. Which nutrient has the highest percentage?

   A. folate
   B. vitamin A
   C. iron
   D. zinc

3. Who is the likely audience for this text?

    A. children aged 4–12
    B. the U.S. Department of Health and Human Services
    C. cereal makers
    D. parents of children aged 4–12

Passage 2

Food accounts for 15 percent of American households' expenditures

With a 15.0 percent share, food ranked third behind housing (38.4 percent) and transportation (20.5 percent) in a typical American household's 2012 expenditures. Food's share of consumer expenditures is down from 17 percent in 1984, as the share of income spent on housing, health care, and entertainment each rose slightly.

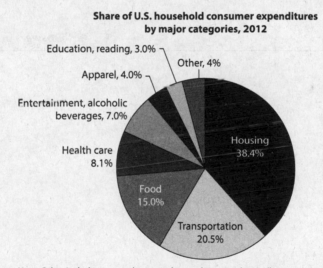

Share of U.S. household consumer expenditures by major categories, 2012

Education, reading, 3.0%
Other, 4%
Apparel, 4.0%
Entertainment, alcoholic beverages, 7.0%
Health care 8.1%
Housing 38.4%
Food 15.0%
Transportation 20.5%

Note: Other includes personal care products, tobacco, and miscellaneous expenditures.
Source: U.S. Bureau of Labor Statistics, Consumer Expenditure Survey, 2012.

4. What relationship does the graphic have to the text?

    A. It provides evidence that food was 15 percent of total household expenditures.
    B. It compares food to transportation expenditures.
    C. It shows how food expenditure relates to all other household expenditures.
    D. It proves that food's share of consumer expenditures is down.

5. Which household expenditures combined are closest to equaling the amount spent on food?

  A. health care and transportation
  B. apparel and other
  C. apparel, education, reading, and other
  D. health care, apparel, education, and reading

6. How would a circle graph showing 1984 expenditures be different from the one above?

  A. Food would be slightly smaller; housing, health care, and entertainment would each be slightly larger.
  B. Food would be slightly larger; housing, health care, and entertainment would each be slightly smaller.
  C. Food, housing, health care, and entertainment would all be slightly larger.
  D. Food, housing, health care, and entertainment would all be slightly smaller.

Answers are on page 533.

CHAPTER 2

Comparing Texts

Another way the Reasoning Through Language Arts (RLA) portion of the GED test assesses your reading comprehension is by asking you to compare texts with similar topics or themes.

Comparing Topics and Themes

Remember that everything you read has a **subject**—what the text is about. Subjects are often large and general, while **topics** are narrower aspects of the subject. For example, a general subject is "weather" with a narrower topic being "the effects of hurricanes on Atlantic states." In asking you to compare nonfiction texts, the GED test might give you two passages that discuss the same topic, such as Atlantic hurricanes, and then ask you how the passages are similar or different.

In fiction, authors often express a **theme,** the story's lesson or message about life. The GED test might give you two literary texts and ask you to identify similarities or differences in how they express their themes. For example, two texts might share the theme that love conquers all. Or they might express opposing viewpoints, one relating that love conquers all and the other showing that love often ends badly.

Comparing Literature

When the GED test presents you with two literary passages, chances are you will be called upon to compare their shared ideas or themes. The questions might focus on any one or more of the following points of comparison.

Perspective

Perspective, or **point of view,** is who tells the story. It is the vantage point of the story's narrator. The three most common perspectives are first person, third-person omniscient, and third-person limited. Pronouns can help you determine which point of view is used in a text.

- **first person**—told from a character's point of view

    pronouns: *I, me, we, us, mine, ours*

EXAMPLE

> Reader, I married him. A quiet wedding we had: he and I, the parson and clerk, were alone present. —Charlotte Brontë, *Jane Eyre*

- **third-person omniscient**—told by a narrator outside the story, who knows all the characters' thoughts and feelings

  pronouns: *he, she, him, her, his, hers, it, its, they, them, theirs*

EXAMPLE

> After this speech the two girls sat many minutes silent, each thoughtful: Fanny meditating on the different sorts of friendship in the world, Mary on something of less philosophic tendency. —Jane Austen, *Mansfield Park*

- **third-person limited**—told by a narrator outside the story, but limited to one or more characters' thoughts and feelings

  pronouns: *he, she, him, her, his, hers, it, its, they, them, theirs*

EXAMPLE

> Just to prove how happy she was, just to show the tall fellow how at home she felt, and how she despised stupid conventions, Laura took a big bite of her bread-and-butter as she stared at the little drawing. —Jane Mansfield, "The Garden Party"

Tone

Tone is the writer's attitude toward his or her subject or audience. A writer's tone can be positive (casual, tender, silly), negative (detached, disrespectful, tense), or neutral (direct, impartial, objective). The writer conveys tone through his or her choice of words and details.

EXAMPLES

> Audrey was a silly little girl, always needling others for attention. (negative)

> Audrey was a funny young lass, always delighting those around her. (positive)

> Audrey was a child who always attracted attention. (neutral)

Style

Style is the distinct way an author uses words. Authors choose which words, sentence structures, and organizational patterns to use to convey messages and emphasize ideas. Their choices often include figurative language, such as similes, metaphors, and personification. Note in the following example how the author mixes short, simple sentences with long, complex ones and uses precise—but sometimes difficult—vocabulary.

EXAMPLE

> We dug very steadily for two hours. Little was said; and our chief embarrassment lay in the yelpings of the dog, who took exceeding interest in our proceedings. He, at length, became so obstreperous that we grew fearful of his giving the alarm to some stragglers in the vicinity;—or, rather, this was the apprehension of Legrand;—for myself, I should have rejoiced at any interruption which might have enabled me to get the wanderer home. —Edgar Allan Poe, "The Gold Bug"

Purpose

Purpose is the reason an author writes. Part of every fiction writer's purpose is to entertain, and often mixed with the desire to entertain is the purpose of informing or persuading the reader.

EXAMPLES

> Tierra had read about Stonehenge, the famous prehistoric monument in western England. She could picture the huge stone monoliths, but she never thought she'd be transported in time to meet the people who built them over 5000 years ago. (entertain/inform)
>
> When Xavier visited Puerto Rico on holiday, he didn't realize that he'd fall in love with the San José Church in San Juan. Then he was informed of the threat it faced from deterioration and structural damage. He had to do something to help. (entertain/persuade)

Impact

Impact is the effect or impression the text makes on the reader. As you read the following excerpt, consider how the writer both repulses the reader with his description of the vampire Dracula and also compels the reader to keep reading, just as the narrator is drawn to touch the monster.

EXAMPLE

> It seemed as if the whole awful creature were simply gorged with blood. He lay like a filthy leech, exhausted with his repletion. I shuddered as I bent over to touch him, and every sense in me revolted at the contact; but I had to search, or I was lost. —Bram Stoker, *Dracula*

EXERCISE 1

Comparing Literature

Directions: Read the passages, then answer the questions that follow.

Passage 1

"The Sphinx in Thebes (Massachusetts)"

by Edward Plunkett, Lord Dunsany

1 There was a woman in a steel-built city who had all that money could buy; she had gold and dividends and trains and houses, and she had pets to play with, but she had no sphinx.

2 So she besought them to bring her a live sphinx; and therefore they went to the menageries, and then to the forests and the desert places, and yet could find no sphinx.

3 And she would have been content with a little lion but that one was already owned by a woman she knew; so they had to search the world again for a sphinx.

4 And still there was none.

5 But they were not men that it is easy to baffle, and at last they found a sphinx in a desert at evening watching a ruined temple whose gods she had eaten hundreds of years ago when her hunger was on her. And they cast chains on her, who was still with an ominous stillness, and took her westwards with them and brought her home.

6 And so the sphinx came to the steel-built city.

7 And the woman was very glad that she owned a sphinx: but the sphinx stared long into her eyes one day, and softly asked a riddle of the woman.

8 And the woman could not answer, and she died.

9 And the sphinx is silent again and none knows what she will do.

Passage 2

Excerpt from "The Judgment of Midas"

by Josephine Preston Peabody

1 Among the worshippers of Pan was a certain Midas, who had a strange story. Once a king of great wealth, he had chanced to befriend

Dionysus, god of the vine; and when he was asked to choose some good gift in return, he prayed that everything he touched might be turned into gold. Dionysus smiled a little when he heard this foolish prayer, but he granted it.

2   Within two days, King Midas learned the secret of that smile, and begged the god to take away the gift that was a curse. He had touched everything that belonged to him, and little joy did he have of his possessions! His palace was as yellow a home as a dandelion to a bee, but not half so sweet. Row upon row of stiff golden trees stood in his garden; they no longer knew a breeze when they heard it. When he sat down to eat, his feast turned to treasure uneatable. He learned that a king may starve, and he came to see that gold cannot replace the live, warm gifts of the Earth.

3   Kindly Dionysus took back the charm, but from that day King Midas so hated gold that he chose to live far from luxury, among the woods and fields. Even here he was not to go free from misadventure.

1. What theme is expressed in both passages?

  A. Gold cannot replace the gifts of the Earth.
  B. Be careful what you wish for.
  C. One cannot control magical beasts or gods.
  D. Death comes for all people, rich or poor.

2. From which perspective is each passage told?

  A. third-person limited; third-person omniscient
  B. first person; first person
  C. third-person omniscient; third-person omniscient
  D. third-person omniscient; first person

3. Which words best describe the tone of each passage?

  A. formal; casual
  B. worshipful; modest
  C. mocking; irreverent
  D. detached; light

4. Which answer *most likely* describes each writer's purpose in writing his or her passage?

  A. to entertain and persuade
  B. to inform and persuade
  C. to persuade only
  D. to entertain only

5. What effect do the following excerpts from the passages have on readers?

"The sphinx stared long into her eyes one day, and softly asked a riddle of the woman."

"Dionysus smiled a little when he heard this foolish prayer, but he granted it."

A. They both encourage readers to follow their dreams.
B. They both create a sense of mystery in the readers.
C. They both make the readers smile.
D. They both instill a sense of fear and horror in the readers.

Answers are on page 534.

Comparing Argumentative Passages

The GED test may also ask you to compare two argumentative texts that have the same topic but opposing claims. Remember, **claims** are the reasons that a writer holds a **position,** his or her opinion on a controversial issue. Quite often, the writer will state his or her position clearly in a thesis statement. This statement is typically found in the first paragraph of the text. Sometimes, though, the writer will not directly state his or her position. In those cases, you must infer the position by identifying the issues and looking at which side the claims support.

EXAMPLE

Claim 1: Social networking fosters relationships and helps people stay in touch.

Claim 2: Students use social networking to improve their grades.

Claim 3: Social networks are catalysts for social and political change.

Implied main idea: Social networking is a positive force in society.

To prove their claims, writers present **evidence,** information in the form of facts, statistics, expert opinions, and anecdotes.

EXAMPLE

Claim: Social networks are catalysts for social and political change.

Evidence: Social networking was a key factor in the 2011 uprising in Egypt, with protestors using Twitter and Facebook to organize demonstrations. (fact)

In America, 47% of people learn about causes through social media. (statistics)

Phillip Howard, associate professor of communication at the University of Washington, states, "Our evidence suggests that social media carried a cascade of messages about freedom and democracy across North Africa and the Middle East, and helped raise expectations for the success of political uprising." (expert opinion)

My friends' status updates reminded me that today was election day, so I made sure to vote. (anecdote)

To compare two arguments, first identify the issue. Then, determine if the writers have similar or different positions on the issue. Most often, passages on the GED test will have differing positions. To analyze how they differ, pay close attention to the evidence each writer presents. Notice which facts each writer emphasizes and which they downplay or ignore. Also look for instances in which the writers interpret evidence differently. In the following example, writers with opposite claims interpret the same evidence differently to support their claims.

EXAMPLES

Claim: Students use social networking to improve their grades.

Evidence: 50% of students use social networking sites to discuss school topics.

Claim: Students who use social networking often have lower grades.

Evidence: 50% of students do not use social networking sites to discuss school topics.

EXERCISE 2

Comparing Argumentative Passages

Directions: Read the passages, then answer the questions that follow.

Passage 1

Cell Phones Are Unsafe

1   Over 300 million Americans use cell phones regularly. Cell phone signals whiz through the air around us at amazing speeds, penetrating solid objects like buildings, cars, and even you and me. But are they safe? Simply put: No. Between cancer-causing radiation and tragic car accidents, cell phones are unsafe and should be used with caution.

2   Many peer-reviewed studies have shown a link between cell phone usage and an increased risk of brain tumors. A 2013 study of Swedish cell phone

users showed a connection between cell phone use and the development of glioma, a common type of brain tumor, and acoustic neuroma, a slow-growing, noncancerous tumor that develops on the nerve that connects the ear to the brain. Another study, done in 2009, reported that long-term cell phone use of 10 or more years correlates with a nearly double risk of developing glioma on the same side of the head where the phone is held by its user.

3   In addition, the International Agency for Research on Cancer, a division of the World Health Organization, issued a press release in 2011, announcing that they had added cell phone radiation to its list of group 2B agents—those "possibly carcinogenic to humans." A group of 31 scientists reviewed previously published studies and concluded that the radiofrequency electromagnetic fields emitted by devices like cell phones showed "limited evidence of carcinogenicity." The same RF radiation was shown in a 2012 study to possibly damage DNA and "change gene expression in brain cells," according to the *Journal of Neuro-Oncology*.

4   Some point out that other peer-reviewed studies have shown no link between cell phone usage and brain tumors. However, you should consider the credibility of the sources of those studies. According to the International EMF Collaborative, "Telecom-funded studies have been reporting highly questionable results in comparison with independent studies. Studies independent of industry consistently show there is a significant risk of brain tumors from cell phone use." In other words, the studies that have showed no link were funded by cell phone companies, making their findings suspicious.

5   Aside from causing cancer, cell phones are also unsafe in cars. Accidents are more likely when the driver is on a cell phone, even when using hands-free devices. The National Highway Traffic Safety Administration (NHTSA) has reported that 25% of all traffic crashes are the result of distracted driving, including the use of cell phones. In 2012, 3,328 people were killed and an estimated 421,000 people were injured in distraction-affected crashes. People talking on cell phones are as dangerous as drunk drivers. Researchers at the University of Utah found that drivers talking on cell phones show an impairment equal to drivers with a 0.08% blood alcohol content. Hands-free calling and texting are also unsafe since drivers' mental distraction is the real issue. According to the AAA Foundation for Traffic Safety, "as mental workload and distractions increase, reaction time slows, brain function is compromised, and drivers scan the road less and miss visual clues." Many state legislatures have recognized this problem and have enacted laws prohibiting cell phone use by drivers. Twelve states ban all drivers from using hand-held cell phones, while thirty-seven states forbid their use by novice drivers. Forty-two states ban all drivers from text messaging. Still,

we all know that passing laws and enforcing them are different beasts. We commonly see drivers talking or texting on their phones—even in school zones—as long as no police patrol cars are in sight.

6   Cell phone users should, by all means, follow the Food and Drug Administration's (FDA) and FCC's suggestions for cell phone usage by using cell phones only for shorter conversations or those situations in which landline phones are unavailable. They also recommend using hands-free devices, to keep distance between the user's head and the cell phone antenna—the source of RF energy. Additionally, drivers should avoid talking and texting at all times, including the use of hands-free devices. Let a passenger take and make your calls, or pull over. The life you save may be your own.

Passage 2

Cell Phones Are Safe

1   Cell phones are everywhere. If you don't have one in your pocket, chances are pretty high that someone within arm's reach does. They have revolutionized communication, yet some people seek to curb their usage, based on misinformation. Cell phones are perfectly safe.

2   Many of the concerns about cell phone usage are based on the fact that cell phones use radiofrequency (RF) radiation. When people see or hear the word "radiation," their minds automatically spin to "cancer." However, the worries are unfounded. Unlike ionizing radiation from X-rays and ultraviolet light, which can damage DNA and cause cancer, the radiation from cell phones is non-ionizing and doesn't have enough energy to cause cancer. The same RF radiation is also used by radios, televisions, laptops, tablets, and cordless home phones. Some people worry about the thermal radiation—you and I know it better as "heat"—put out by cell phones and its effect on the brain. Don't fret. The Federal Communications Commission (FCC) regulates how much thermal radiation cell phones are permitted to emit. In fact, the amount of heating caused by cell phones is, according to the University of Pittsburgh's Eric Swanson, "about one one-thousandth as much as the brain heating caused by wearing a hat."

3   Additionally, many peer-reviewed studies have found no link between cell phone use and brain tumors. The *British Medical Journal* published the results of a 2011 study of more than 350,000 Danish cell phone users and concluded that "there was no association between tumors of the central nervous system or brain and long term (10 years +) use of mobile phones." In the same year, the *Journal of the National Cancer Institute* reported that there was no evidence of causation between cell phone usage and brain tumors among children and adolescents. In fact, some studies have actually shown a decreased risk of certain brain tumors; for example, a 2005 Danish

study found a "decreased odds ratio" for developing glioma or meningioma types of brain tumors.

4   But what about all those other studies that have shown links between cell phone use and brain tumors? In response to those concerns, the U.S. Food and Drug Administration has posted this statement on their website: "While some researchers have reported biological changes associated with RF energy, these studies have failed to be replicated. The majority of studies published have failed to show an association between exposure to radiofrequency from a cell phone and health problems."

5   Still, we all know that talking on a cell phone while driving is terribly unsafe, right? Not so! According to the CATO Institute, a nonpartisan libertarian think tank, other distractions, such as eating, drinking, fiddling with the radio, and talking to passengers, are responsible for more accidents than cell phone use. In fact, cell phone usage factors into less than 1% of all accidents. As for that 1%, a 2005 press release by Lincoln University states that "it was the conversation, not the technology that was to blame . . . cell phone conversations consume a great deal of attention and produce considerable interference, [but] drivers can learn to control the situation by learning to emphasize safe driving."

6   So, next time you read or hear about the dangers of cell phone usage, take it with a grain of salt. Don't worry about RF radiation frying your brain. And if you need to make a call while driving, keep your eyes on the road and your mind focused, and all should be fine.

1. On which fact do both passages agree?

   A. Cell phones emit RF radiation.
   B. X-rays are more dangerous than cell phones.
   C. RF radiation causes glioma.
   D. 25% of all accidents are caused by distracted drivers.

2. Which evidence in passage 1 contradicts the claim in passage 2 that "many peer-reviewed studies have found no link between cell phone use and brain tumors"?

   A. Long-term cell phone use of ten or more years correlates with a nearly double risk of developing glioma on the same side of the head where the phone is held by its user.
   B. The International Agency for Research on Cancer . . . added cell phone radiation to its list of group 2B agents—those "possibly carcinogenic to humans."
   C. "Studies independent of industry consistently show there is a significant risk of brain tumors from cell phone use."
   D. "The majority of studies published have failed to show an association between exposure to radiofrequency from a cell phone and health problems."

3. Which sentence from passage 2 refutes the claim made in passage 1 that "many peer-reviewed studies have shown a link between cell phone usage and an increased risk of brain tumors"?

   A. They have revolutionized communication, yet some people seek to curb their usage based on misinformation.
   B. But what about all those other studies that have shown links between cell phone use and brain tumors?
   C. "While some researchers have reported biological changes associated with RF energy, these studies have failed to be replicated."
   D. In fact, cell phone usage factors into less than 1% of all accidents.

4. Which evidence from passage 2 best agrees with the following evidence from passage 1?

   According to the AAA Foundation for Traffic Safety, "as mental workload and distractions increase, reaction time slows, brain function is compromised, and drivers scan the road less and miss visual clues."

   A. Cell phone usage factors into less than 1% of all accidents.
   B. Other distractions, such as eating, drinking, fiddling with the radio, and talking to passengers, are responsible for more accidents than cell phone use.
   C. "It was the conversation, not the technology that was to blame."
   D. "Cell phone conversations consume a great deal of attention and produce considerable interference."

Answers are on page 534.

Comparing Across Genres and Forms

The GED test may also ask you to compare texts across genres. A **genre** is a category, or type, of writing. The categories are often characterized by style, form, and content. Two major genres are **fiction,** which describes imaginary events and people, and **nonfiction,** which describes real events and people. Those major genres can be divided into other subgenres as well.

Common Genres	
Fiction	**Nonfiction**
dramas	biographies and autobiographies
fables and folktales	essays
novels	histories
short stories	media articles (newspaper, magazine, online)

Additionally, nonfiction can be delivered in different **formats,** for example, feature articles, online FAQs and fact sheets, blogs, and tables and timelines. The GED test may ask you to compare a novel excerpt with a blog posting, a short folk tale with a historical article, or a biography with a timeline.

The two texts will typically have related ideas or themes. Unlike argumentative texts, the texts will not take two positions on a topic. Instead, they will present ideas and information in different ways. Some ideas and information will be similar, while others will be different. To compare the texts, you should evaluate both their similarities and their differences using several criteria:

- **Scope**—How much of the topic is covered by each text? Is the area covered by one text broader or narrower than the other?

- **Purpose**—Why is each author writing? Does he or she want to inform, persuade, entertain, or a mix?

- **Emphasis**—Where does each writer focus his or her attention?

- **Audience**—Who does each writer think will read his or her work?

- **Impact**—What effect or impression does each text have on the reader?

In addition to comparing texts, the GED test may ask you to synthesize details from both texts. When you **synthesize** details, you combine information from both texts to draw your own conclusions about how the two texts relate to each other.

EXAMPLES

Novel excerpt: Offenders against the revenue laws, and defaulters to excise or customs who had incurred fines which they were unable to pay, were supposed to be incarcerated behind an iron-plated door closing up a second prison, consisting of a strong cell or two, and a blind alley some yard and a half wide, which formed the mysterious termination of the very limited skittle-ground in which the Marshalsea debtors bowled down their troubles. —Charles Dickens, *Little Dorrit*

Informative text: In 1822, Charles Dickens's family moved to London from Portsmouth. His father, John, was imprisoned for debt in 1824, spending six months in the Marshalsea Prison. At that time, young Charles, age 12, began working full-time to support his family.

Synthesis and conclusion: Charles Dickens's experience contributed to his knowledge of Marshalsea Prison and the realities faced by debtors in London, which he wrote about later.

It seems likely that Dickens's description of Marshalsea Prison was based on information he had gained from his father's imprisonment and that experience influenced his writing.

EXERCISE 3

Comparing Across Genres and Forms

Directions: Read the passages, then answer the questions that follow.

Passage 1

Excerpt from *The First High Climb*

by George Herbert Leigh Mallory

1   About the other dangers it is necessary to say more, because they must vitally affect the organization of any attempt to climb the mountain. Everyone will remember how Morshead's collapse compromised our plan of descent. . . . The causes of this collapse are obscure; his heart was not affected; possibly it was due to want of liquid food. At starting from the North Col Morshead seemed fitter than any one; his failure was a complete surprise to all of us; and in view of it I think a party of the future should reckon that some such experience may happen to any one of them. At a high altitude even the strongest might suffer this loss of muscular power; and he will not recover up there. The danger in such a case can hardly be overestimated; all calculations of time will be upset, and the awful fate of a night out, perhaps above 27,000 feet, will be hanging over the party. . . .

2   It is not too much to assert that all dangers through faults in climbing are immensely greater on Mount Everest than, for instance, on Mont Blanc or the Matterhorn.

3   The sum of all these dangers is increased to an extent that cannot be overemphasized by unfavourable weather. A party with one man [unable to climb], a party who have passed that indefinite line beyond which mere weakness becomes a danger, . . . or finding fresh snow on the steep slope below the North Col; men in such circumstances are in gravest peril when the wind blows on Mount Everest. It is when we view our problem as a whole, in the light of the weather experienced this year, that we should be least inclined to optimism. Apart from any consideration of the monsoon's date, and that of 1922 was admittedly early, the conditions before it came were not encouraging. The weather . . . presented us with a dilemma; either we might have a taste of the monsoon and the threat of snow in the air—it will be remembered that snow fell while we were encamped at 25,000 feet— or we should have that bitter enemy, the north-west wind, the wind that drove us to camp a thousand feet lower than we intended. . . .

4   Perhaps it is not impossible for men to reach the summit of Mount Everest, in spite of wind and weather; but unless the weather can mend the

habit we observed this year, or grant a long respite, their chances of reaching it and getting down in safety are all too small. . . .

Passage 2

Excerpt from "Alpine Ascents: Everest Frequently Asked Questions"

1   Below please find some additional information that may be helpful. The most relevant information can be found on our Everest web pages and upon registration, and each climber receives a detailed information package.

2   **What is the skill level of this climb?**
Climbers should have a well-proven track record of high altitude climbs. Denali, Cho-Oyu, or 8000-meter peaks are most relevant. Most climbers begin with our mountaineering school and then climb more challenging peaks, taking on greater altitude. Training courses and climbs on Rainier, Ecuador Volcanoes and Denali are the most common path. We are happy to email our "From Mountaineering School to Everest" brief and work with you individually.

3   **What is the physical conditioning level needed for this climb?**
Climbers must be in excellent physical condition. This is a long expedition requiring patience, stamina, mental fortitude, and strong willpower. Summit day can be 20 hours long.

4   **Any tips on how a climber can maximize their chances of success?**
Along with the required climbing skills, review cardio training on the Everest training page. We strongly recommend following the advice of our guides to acclimatize properly.

5   **Who is the guiding team composed of? (How many guides? Climber to guide ratio?)**
Your expedition leader will be one of our Professional Mountain Guides. We are well known for our expert guides and climber-to-guide ratio and invite you to read our "Why Climb Everest with Us" page.

6   **What is the best season to climb/which dates will have the most chance for success?**
The best time to climb Everest is in the spring, April–May.

7   **Will I be sharing a tent or lodging with other climbers?**
During the trek we will be lodging in teahouses. Climbers will either be sharing a teahouse room or may have a private room. In Base Camp each climber will have their own tent. Above BC, in camps I–IV, climbers will be sharing tents.

8   **How much will my pack weigh?**
During the trek, team members will only be carrying gear and supplies for the day. At no point do we carry camping gear or equipment for overnight during the trek. Daypacks will weigh no more than 20 lbs. Above BC, on the climb, we will typically be carrying packs that weigh 20–30 lbs.

9   **What gear will I need?**
Please review the gear list.

10   **Any further advice on gear and using your gear list?**
While all items are required, there may be times when some of the items on the gear list may not be used (such as warm weather or changing conditions). The gear lists are created by the guides to assist in having climbers be prepared to summit in any conditions. We look to work with each climber individually.

1. What is the *primary* scope of each passage?

   A. Passage 1 discusses the collapse of the mountaineer Morshead; Passage 2 gives statistics about Mount Everest.
   B. Passage 1 discusses the dangers encountered on an early attempt to climb Mount Everest; Passage 2 answers questions about Everest Expeditions.
   C. Passage 1 discusses problems caused by bad weather on Mount Everest; Passage 2 discusses the physical condition needed to climb Mount Everest.
   D. Passage 1 explains that people should not climb Mount Everest; Passage 2 gives rules for climbing Mount Everest.

2. What is the *main* reason each writer probably created his or her text?

   A. to inform readers of how Mallory's expedition reached the summit of Mount Everest; to convince readers that Alpine Ascents expeditions are the safest
   B. to entertain readers with a thrilling adventure story; to provide information for readers about gear needed to climb Mount Everest
   C. to persuade readers not to climb Mount Everest; to persuade readers to climb Mount Everest
   D. to inform readers of the dangers encountered while climbing Mount Everest; to provide information for readers interested in climbing Mount Everest

3. Who is the likely intended audience for each passage?

   A. skilled mountain climbers; general readers
   B. skilled mountain climbers; skilled mountain climbers
   C. general readers; skilled mountain climbers
   D. general readers; general readers

4. With which statement in the FAQ page would George Mallory *most* strongly agree?

    A. Climbers must be in excellent physical condition.

    B. The best time to climb Everest is in the spring, April–May.

    C. During the trek, team members will only be carrying gear and supplies for the day.

    D. The gear lists are created by the guides to assist in having climbers be prepared to summit in any conditions.

5. What can you infer about when the passages were written?

    A. Both passages were written before the first successful attempt to reach the summit of Mount Everest.

    B. Passage 1 was written before the first successful attempt to reach the summit of Mount Everest; passage 2 was written soon after the first successful attempt.

    C. Passage 1 was written before the first successful attempt to reach the summit of Mount Everest; passage 2 was written many years after the first successful attempt.

    D. Both passages were written after the first successful attempt to reach the summit of Mount Everest.

Answers are on page 534.

CHAPTER 3

Writing Extended Responses

The GED Assessment asks you to demonstrate your ability to read closely, write clearly, and use the conventions of standard written English correctly. To test all three skills, the Reasoning Through Language Arts section includes one 45-minute **Extended Response (ER)** item.

Extended Response Questions

The Extended Response question requires you to analyze one or more source texts, each 650 words or less. Then you will create a writing sample in response to a prompt. The writing prompt will generally ask you to analyze a point of view presented in the text(s). To do so, you will need to analyze the text(s) and draw conclusions about the topic. The prompt will then ask you if you think the given point of view is supported by the evidence presented (or if two contrasting points of view are given, you will be asked which one is better supported). To answer the prompt, you will need to develop an argument. An **argument** is a set of reasons for or against a particular idea. You will also need to support your argument with evidence from the source text(s) and from your own background information. Your argument must be persuasive enough to convince readers that your ideas are correct.

Extended Response Format

You will read the ER source text or texts and respond to the writing prompt online. The item format will be a split screen. The source text(s) will appear on the left side of the screen. Longer texts are tabbed by page, so you can easily page through them. On the right side of the screen are the directions, the prompt, and the area in which you type your response.

Guidelines

You will be given guidelines to help you remember all the elements that go into a well-written response. Here is a simplified version:

Extended Response Answer Guidelines for Reasoning Through Language Arts

You will have at least (but no more than) <u>45 minutes</u> to complete this task. Do not rush. Read the passage(s) and the prompt. Then think carefully about what you want to say. Outline the points you wish to make before you begin writing. Draft your response. Be sure to leave time to review your work and revise it as necessary.

As you read the passage(s), pay close attention to the author's argument. What claims is the author making? What assumptions is the argument based on? What supporting evidence is presented, and how credible is it? What strategies does the author use to present and support his or her ideas?

When you write your response, make sure to

- ☐ decide which argument presented in the passage(s) is better supported by evidence
- ☐ tell why you think that argument is the better-supported one (remember that it doesn't have to be the one you personally agree with)
- ☐ support your ideas with evidence from the passage(s)
- ☐ state your main points clearly and completely
- ☐ organize your main points in a logical structure and support them with details from the passage
- ☐ keep your audience in mind and choose language that is appropriate
- ☐ use transition words and phrases to link your ideas
- ☐ choose words that express your thoughts clearly
- ☐ vary the sentence structure to improve the style of your writing
- ☐ when you are finished drafting your response, take the time to re-read it and correct any errors of grammar, usage, or mechanics

Scoring

Your Extended Response writing sample will be scored across three traits.

Trait 1 Creation of Arguments and Use of Evidence

This score measures how well you analyze arguments and gather evidence from the source texts in support of your own position.

Trait 2 **Development of Ideas and Organizational Structure**
This score measures how well you develop and organize your writing.

Trait 3 **Clarity and Command of Standard English Conventions**
This score measures how well you demonstrate fluency with conventions of standard American English.

Materials

Instead of scratch paper, your testing center will provide you with an 8.5 × 14–inch erasable noteboard. This board can be used with an erasable marker. For test security, scratch paper is not allowed.

Finding the Main Idea in the Source Text

Your writing sample is scored in part on how well you understand the Extended Response source text or texts. To start, make sure you understand the main idea of each text. The **main idea,** also called the **thesis,** is the central focus of the passage. Think of it as the text's most important idea.

An ER source text may focus on one **position,** or side, of a controversial **issue.** In that case, the main idea would be subjective, showing the writer's **position,** his or her opinion, on the issue. For example, the text might say, "Everyone should get an annual flu vaccination." A second text arguing a different position might say, "Annual flu vaccinations are unnecessary."

Another type of Extended Response source text provides an overview of an issue, presenting both positions. In these cases, the main idea is objective, not favoring one side or the other. For example, the main idea might be "there are convincing arguments both for and against annual flu vaccinations."

EXERCISE 1

Finding the Main Idea of the Source Text

Directions: Read the passages, then answer the questions that follow.

Passage 1

The legal driving age varies from country to country. In many countries the minimum driving age is 18 years. In the United States, however, most states issue restricted or full licenses at 16 years of age, with some issuing learner permits to drivers as young as 14. The United States should standardize the minimum driving age across all states, and that age should be raised to 18.

Passage 2

Young drivers have more accidents than older drivers. This is a fact. However, calls to raise the minimum driving age to 18 years are misguided. Younger drivers have more accidents because they are inexperienced, not because of how old they are. If the minimum age is raised to 18, then 18-year-olds—still inexperienced drivers—will have more accidents.

1. Which sentence in passage 1 states the main idea of the passage?

    A. The legal driving age varies from country to country.
    B. In many countries the minimum driving age is 18 years.
    C. In the United States, however, most states issue restricted or full licenses at 16 years of age, with some issuing learner permits to drivers as young as 14.
    D. The United States should standardize the minimum driving age across all states, and that age should be raised to 18.

2. Which statement reflects the position of the writer in passage 2?

    A. The United States should raise the minimum driving age to 18.
    B. More serious accidents are caused by younger drivers than older drivers.
    C. Minimum driving ages in the United States should not be raised.
    D. Younger drivers lack the mental and physical qualifications to drive.

Answers are on page 534.

Making Inferences

Sometimes writers do not state their ideas directly. In these cases, you need to make an **inference,** a conclusion based on information in the text and your own prior knowledge and experience.

EXAMPLE

Statement: One research study that strongly supports annual flu vaccinations was funded by a pharmaceutical company that makes the vaccine.

Inference: The study's findings may not be trustworthy, since its sponsor has a financial stake in the results.

EXERCISE 2

Making Inferences

Directions: Read the passages, then answer the questions that follow.

Passage 1

Wild animals should not be kept in zoos. Removing animals from their natural habitats for public entertainment is wrong. Once in zoos, animals suffer needlessly. Their enclosures are often vastly smaller than their natural habitats, causing them terrible psychological distress.

Passage 2

Zoos are perfectly acceptable. Modern zoos emphasize education, not entertainment. They encourage visitors to learn about the animals and their natural habitats and to take an active role in habitat conservation. Zoos also save endangered species through breeding programs.

1. What inference can you draw from passage 1?

   A. Zoos treat animals cruelly because they care only about profit.
   B. Wild animals should live free, not in captivity.
   C. Wild animals in zoos often display self-destructive behaviors.
   D. Most people visit zoos to be entertained, not informed.

2. With which statement is the writer of passage 2 most likely to agree?

   A. People who go to zoos are more likely to care about wild animals than those who do not.
   B. Most modern zoos are not at all entertaining.
   C. Captive breeding programs should be undertaken only in nature reserves, not zoos.
   D. People can learn more about wild animals in books, videos, or online than they ever could at a zoo.

Answers are on page 534.

Identifying Arguments and Evidence

Once you know the main idea of the text(s), you can begin to analyze the arguments and gather evidence. An **argument** is a reason or set of reasons for or against something. A writer who supports annual flu vaccinations might present the argument that flu vaccines save lives. An argument against flu vaccinations might be that flu vaccines are not entirely effective. **Evidence** supports a writer's arguments. In most cases, writers state a **claim,** or assertion that some particular fact is true. Then they give evidence to support that claim. Another way to think about this relationship is by using the following formula:

Claims + Evidence = Argument

Evidence comes in many forms:

- **facts**—statements that can be proven true

    example: Flu is caused by a virus.

- **statistics**—numerical facts and data

    example: Approximately 36,000 people die from flu-related causes each year in the United States.

- **expert opinions**—quotes from authorities on the topic

    example: The Centers for Disease Control and Prevention recommends yearly flu vaccinations.

- **anecdotes**—personal experiences

    example: My cousin did not get the flu vaccine this year, and she got very ill.

As you might guess, anecdotes are not the strongest type of evidence. However, they do provide real-world examples that create a personal connection for readers, a way for them to relate to the topic. Look for all types of evidence in an ER source text, but be wary of any claims that are supported only by anecdotes.

EXERCISE 3

Identifying Arguments and Evidence

Directions: Read the passage, then answer the questions that follow.

Biofuels are the future! These energy sources come from living sources, such as trees and crops. Unlike fossil fuels—gas, oil, and coal—biofuels like ethanol and biodiesel are renewable. Biofuels can help the United States cut dependency on foreign energy. President George W. Bush was right when he said, "America is addicted to oil, which is often imported from unstable parts of the world." Currently the United States buys most of its oil from unstable and hostile nations, such as Iran, Argentina, and Nigeria. Roughly 22% of our oil comes from Africa, 22% from the Middle East, and 19% from Latin America. Instability in those regions leads to higher gas prices. According to the U.S. Department of Agriculture, 30% of the U.S. energy needs could be met with biomass grown at home and processed in U.S. facilities. A reduced dependence on foreign energy supplies would strengthen national security and protect military service members. My older sister served in Iraq and Afghanistan, protecting dangerous fuel convoys. She now suffers from post-traumatic stress disorder (PTSD). Other soldiers have suffered serious injury and death in the Middle East to keep oil delivery routes open.

1. Which sentence states the main claim of the passage?

    A. These energy sources come from living sources, such as trees and crops.
    B. Biofuels can help the United States cut dependency on foreign energy.
    C. According to the U.S. Department of Agriculture, 30% of the U.S. energy needs could be met with biomass grown at home and processed in U.S. facilities.
    D. A reduced dependence on foreign energy supplies would strengthen national security and protect military service members.

2. Which sentence from the passage contains an expert opinion?

    A. Biofuels are the future!
    B. President George W. Bush was right when he said, "America is addicted to oil, which is often imported from unstable parts of the world."
    C. Roughly 22% of our oil comes from Africa, 22% from the Middle East, and 19% from Latin America.
    D. My older sister served in Iraq and Afghanistan, serving to protect dangerous fuel convoys.

3. Which sentence from the passage contains an anecdote?

    A. Biofuels are the future!
    B. President George W. Bush was right when he said, "America is addicted to oil, which is often imported from unstable parts of the world."
    C. Roughly 22% of our oil comes from Africa, 22% from the Middle East, and 19% from Latin America.
    D. My older sister served in Iraq and Afghanistan, serving to protect dangerous fuel convoys.

4. Which sentence from the passage contains statistics?

    A. Biofuels are the future!

    B. President George W. Bush was right when he said, "America is addicted to oil, which is often imported from unstable parts of the world."

    C. Roughly 22% of our oil comes from Africa, 22% from the Middle East, and 19% from Latin America.

    D. My older sister served in Iraq and Afghanistan, serving to protect dangerous fuel convoys.

Answers are on page 534.

Evaluating Evidence

Part of analyzing an argument is evaluating its evidence. Does the evidence provide good support for the claims made? Check the evidence given in the source text(s) for these factors:

- **specific**—Is it exact, precise information?

  example: Saying that flu vaccines are not very effective is not specific; saying that in 2011, one study said that flu vaccines were only about 59 percent effective is specific.

- **relevant**—Is it connected to the issue?

  example: Facts about how many people are hospitalized with the flu each year are relevant to a discussion of the annual flu vaccinations; facts about how many people are hospitalized with broken arms are not.

- **reliable**—Is it trustworthy? Is the source of the evidence an expert? Can the facts be confirmed?

  example: The expert opinion of a physician from a well-known hospital is reliable; opinions from a first-year medical student are not as reliable.

- **reasonable**—Is it in line with widely accepted norms? For example, is scientific data derived via appropriate use of the scientific method (such as clinical studies)?

  example: Saying that about 36,000 U.S. citizens die each year from the flu is in line with most expert estimates; saying that millions of Americans die each year from the flu is not—and is not reasonable.

Not all evidence has to meet all four of these factors, but if it meets only one or two, then you might be justified in being unconvinced.

EXERCISE 4

Evaluating Evidence

Directions: Read the passage, then answer the questions that follow.

Advertising is a powerful marketing tool. Ads saturate our lives, with the average person encountering many messages per day. One study showed that children are unable to engage advertising critically; thus, advertising aimed directly at them should be banned. The fast-food industry spends over $100 billion annually on advertising aimed at children. Bad eating habits developed in childhood often become lifelong problems. Watching TV instead of playing outside also contributes to poor health in children.

1. Which sentence from the passage contains a statistic that might not be accurate and that suggests an unreasonable argument?

   A. Ads saturate our lives, with the average person encountering many messages per day.
   B. One study showed that children are unable to engage advertising critically; thus, advertising aimed directly at them should be banned.
   C. The fast-food industry spends over $100 billion annually on advertising aimed at children.
   D. Watching TV instead of playing outside also contributes to poor health in children.

2. Which sentence from the passage uses information that is not adequately specific?

   A. Ads saturate our lives, with the average person encountering many messages per day.
   B. One study showed that children are unable to engage advertising critically; thus, advertising aimed directly at them should be banned.
   C. The fast-food industry spends over $100 billion annually on advertising aimed at children.
   D. Watching TV instead of playing outside also contributes to poor health in children.

3. Which sentence from the passage uses an unreliable source?

   A. Ads saturate our lives, with the average person encountering many messages per day.
   B. One study showed that children are unable to engage advertising critically; thus, advertising aimed directly at them should be banned.
   C. The fast-food industry spends over $100 billion annually on advertising aimed at children.
   D. Watching TV instead of playing outside also contributes to poor health in children.

4. Which sentence from the passage presents evidence that is not relevant?

    A. Ads saturate our lives, with the average person encountering many messages per day.

    B. One study showed that children are unable to engage advertising critically; thus, advertising aimed directly at them should be banned.

    C. The fast-food industry spends over $100 billion annually on advertising aimed at children.

    D. Watching TV instead of playing outside also contributes to poor health in children.

Answers are on page 534.

Highlighting as You Read

As you read the source text or texts, be sure to use the on-screen highlighter. The highlighter tool has a variety of different colors you can use to mark up the source text(s). One good use of the tool is to mark a writer's claims in one color and evidence in another color. Or you may want to assign each type of evidence a different color.

Sample Stimulus Passage

Here is a sample Extended Response source text.

8 Flu Vaccination Pros and Cons You May Not Know About

1   Every year you probably ask yourself the same thing: Should I get a **flu shot** this year, or should I pass it by?

2   It's understandable that you might feel uncertain. There's a lot of **confusing information** floating around out there about flu **vaccines**, which are available either as a shot or as a nasal spray. For instance, a recent study indicated that flu vaccines offer you only "moderate protection" from catching **this season's flu**. That's hardly inspiring. On the other hand, "moderate protection" is better than no protection at all, right?

3   What should you do? The CDC recommends that everyone over the age of six months receive the flu vaccine each year, unless you are allergic to the vaccine. But even still, there's no one-size-fits-all answer.

4   Here are a few **flu shot pros and cons** to consider as you weigh what's right for you:

PROS

5   **Flu shots can be life-saving:** In the United States alone, more than 200,000 people are hospitalized for the flu every year, and about 36,000 die from causes related to the flu. The prevention a flu vaccine provides could literally save your life.

6   **Flu shots don't cause the flu:** Yes, it's true that flu vaccines contain strains of the flu virus itself, but flu shots are made with a totally inactivated form of the virus. The nasal-spray flu vaccine is made with a severely weakened form of it. Neither type of flu vaccine puts you at risk of catching the flu.

7   **Flu shots are safer than you might think:** For a long time, many parents were concerned that a preservative that had been used in vaccines, **thimerosal**, was linked to autism in children. Studies have shown **no link** between vaccines that contain thimerosal and autism—and the study that originally sparked concern has been discredited and withdrawn. What's more, nowadays, most flu vaccines given to children in the United States do not contain thimerosal, and adults can request **thimerosal-free vaccines** as well.

8   **Flu shots are easy to get:** These days, you don't have to make a special trip to the doctor to get a flu shot. Many pharmacies will give you a shot— without an appointment, in a jiffy, and for a very reasonable fee.

CONS

9   **Flu shots may not be safe for some people:** If you are allergic to eggs, flu shots, which are cultivated inside of chicken eggs, may put you at risk. Be sure to consult your doctor.

10   **Flu shots can have minor side effects:** Some people develop symptoms like soreness, redness, or swelling where the shot was given; low-grade fever; or aches. These are usually pretty mild and no cause for concern, and resolve within a day or two.

11   **Flu shots aren't a one-shot deal:** Because flu viruses change each year, the vaccines are reformulated annually to keep up. To make sure you're protected, you have to get vaccinated again every year during flu season, which generally lasts from October to May. Health experts generally recommend getting it sooner (like before December) rather than later.

12   **Flu shots aren't 100 percent effective:** A recent study found that flu shots were only about 59 percent effective in healthy adults. Your annual flu shot may protect you from this season's most dominant strains of flu, but unfortunately, it won't protect you from all the other bugs that might be floating around out there.

After weighing the pros and cons, do you plan to get a flu shot this year?

PROMPT

The article presents arguments from both sides of the debate regarding annual flu shots.

To respond, analyze both positions presented in the article to determine which one is best supported. Use relevant and specific evidence from the article to support your response.

Type your response on your computer. You should expect to spend up to 45 minutes planning, drafting, and editing your response.

Organizing Your Response

After reading the source text(s) but before you begin writing, take time to plan your response. You may feel the need to hurry, but your response will be better if you plan and organize before writing. Whether you create an informal plan or outline, be sure to organize your main points in a logical order so that your response flows logically.

If you use an outline, consider following a pattern similar to this:

I. Introduction (1 paragraph)

Identify issue.
State which position is better supported.

II. Body (2–3 paragraphs)

Analyze strongest/weakest arguments.
Evaluate evidence from text(s).

III. Conclusion (1 paragraph)

Summary
Provide final thoughts.

You can use the erasable noteboard to briefly outline your response, or you can key in an outline to follow (but be sure to overwrite it or delete it before you finish).

Writing Your Response
Supporting Your Ideas

Remember, your writing sample is scored in part on how well you develop your ideas and organize your response. Follow your plan or outline. Defend your ideas with evidence from the source text(s). Try not to merely cut-and-paste text directly from the source text(s). Put the ideas into your own words, using direct quotations only when the source text writer has expressed an idea in an especially good way.

Your primary evidence will come from the source text(s); however, you may sparingly include additional evidence from your own prior knowledge or experience to support or attack claims made in the source text(s). For example, if an argument against annual flu vaccinations is that the vaccinations hurt and may frighten small children, you might point out, if the text does not already, that painless nasal-spray flu vaccines are also available.

Considering Audience and Purpose

Keep your audience and purpose in mind as you write.

Your **audience** is the readers of your writing sample. You can't know who exactly will read your response. Assume that your audience will know something—but not everything—about the issue. Remember, though, that a reader may already hold an opinion on the issue and may not agree with you. So be sure to respectfully address the position with which you disagree.

Your **purpose** is the primary reason you are writing your sample. Of course, everyone knows you are writing because the GED Assessment requires it. Think beyond that, though, and consider *why* the GED requires it. The Extended Response portion tests you to see how well you can

- analyze arguments
- develop and organize your ideas
- use Standard English

Your purpose, then, is to show through your writing how well you can do these three tasks. Keep them in mind as you write.

Maintaining Coherence

To ensure your response is **coherent,** or logical and well-organized, use transition words and phrases to show how your ideas are connected. Here is a list of common transitions.

- **to add:** also, and, besides, in addition, likewise, next, similarly, too
- **to contrast ideas:** although, but, however, in contrast, instead, nevertheless, on the other hand, or, still, yet
- **to show importance:** first, last, mainly, then, most/least important
- **to clarify:** in other words, to put it another way, that is

- **to emphasize:** above all, especially, in fact, more importantly, naturally, obviously
- **to summarize or conclude:** at last, consequently, eventually, finally, in conclusion/summary, lastly, so, summing up, therefore, thus, to conclude

Sample Response

Here is a sample response to the source text "8 Flu Vaccination Pros and Cons You May Not Know About," including a sample outline. Keep in mind as you read that this is a first unedited draft.

SAMPLE OUTLINE

I. Introduction

Issue: Flu vaccinations, pro and con

The "pro" position is better supported.

II. Body

Strongest arguments for:

Claim: Flu vaccinations can be lifesaving.

Evidence: 200,000 people hospitalized & 36,000 deaths annually (statistics)

Evaluate: Evidence is specific, relevant, and reasonable. Include source of information to show reliability.

Claim: Flu vaccinations are safer than you think.

Evidence: no link between thimerosal and autism (fact)

Evaluate: Evidence is specific and relevant. No source of information to prove reliability

Strongest argument against:

Claim: Flu vaccinations aren't 100 percent effective.

Evidence: only 59 percent effective in healthy adults (statistic)

Evaluate: Evidence is specific and relevant. No source of information to prove reliability. Not strong evidence, though. 59 percent is better than nothing.

III. Conclusion

Summary

Final thought: You should get a flu vaccination.

SAMPLE RESPONSE

The article "8 Flu Vaccination Pros and Cons You May Not Know About" clearly presents both sides to the issue of annual flu vaccines. While the writer presents both arguments in an unbiased, objective way, I believe that the position in favor of the vaccine is better supported.

The Centers for Disease Control (CDC) recommend annual flu vaccines every year for everyone six month or older. The CDC is worried about public health. Their expert opinion on the issue should be paid attention to. The article does not merely take the CDC's advice, but gives good reasons for us to listen. The best claim that the article makes is that flu vaccinations save lives. Many of us have had the flu and might think it's no big deal. You get sick, you stay home from work or school for a few days, you are resting while watching a few of your favorite movies and napping. Your back to normal in no time. That is the best case. More than 200,000 people are hospitalized each year for the flu and over 36,000 die each year in the United States alone. These statistics make a very good case that taking that vaccine can save lives. They are specific and relevant to the issue. It would be nice to see where the statistics come from.

Another good point that the article makes in favor of annual flu vaccinations is that the vaccine is safe. In the past, parents have worried about the connection between vaccines and autism. The cause of their concern was a study in which thimerosal, a preservative used in making vaccines, was shown to have possibly caused autism in children. However, as the article points out, that study has been discredited. Additional studies have shown no link between thimerosal and autism. Furthermore, most vaccines given to kids in the U.S. no longer use thimerosal. These facts should really help to alleviate parents' fears about giving the vaccine to their children. Any parent who is still concerned could easily confirm these facts and research the issue further. Of course, as the article argues, the flu vaccine is not safe for people with egg allergies, since the vaccinations are cultivated in eggs. For these people, an adverse reaction could be more dangerous than the flu itself! However, these are rare cases and should not influence the decision of the average person whether or not to get the vaccine. People with egg allergies should talk to their doctors about their options, and the rest of us should not worry about the vaccine's safety.

Nevertheless, a valid argument against annual flu vaccinations is that the vaccine is not 100 percent effective. The actual number in one year was closer to 60 percent effectiveness for healthy adults. In other words, about 40 percent of people who got the flu vaccination that year could get the flu or some other flu-like virus. Each year's flu vaccine contains inactive forms of the top flu strains. It does not contain all strains. This evidence is specific and relevant to the argument; yet it seems weak when you consider how many people are hospitalized and die from the flu each year. I will take my chances with a 60 percent success rate rather than worry about being one of the 40 percent! 60 percent coverage still beats zero percent coverage any day.

In conclusion, the position supporting annual flu vaccinations proves its argument better with convincing claims and stronger evidence that the vaccine is both lifesaving and safe. The article ends with this question: "After weighing the pros and cons, do you plan to get a flu vaccination this year?" The logical answer is a resounding "Yes!"

Editing Your Response

Leave time to edit your response. First, make sure the essay is well organized and coherent. Do you need to reorder any paragraphs or ideas? Drag and drop or cut and paste paragraphs, sentences, or words to create the best flow of ideas. Be sure to reread the edited parts to ensure that they make sense. You may need to add transitional words or phrases to create the best fit. Check your sentences for variety. Avoid overuse of the basic subject + verb sentence pattern, which can make your writing seem repetitive and dull. Try beginning some sentences with introductory words, phrases, or clauses.

EXAMPLE

Before: The Center for Disease Control (CDC) recommends annual flu vaccines . . .

After: As the article indicates, the Center for Disease Control (CDC) recommends annual flu vaccines . . .

Another way to vary sentence structures is to combine shorter sentences.

EXAMPLE

Before: Each year's flu vaccine contains inactive forms of the top flu strains. It does not contain all strains.

After: Each year's flu vaccine contains inactive forms of the top flu strains, but it does not contain all strains.

Once you are satisfied with the organization of your response, read it through again, from the beginning to the end, correcting errors in spelling, capitalization, and punctuation. Scorers do not expect perfect grammar, usage, and mechanics, but too many errors can muddle the clarity and coherence of your ideas.

Here is an edited paragraph from the sample response. The words in italics were added by the writer during the editing process.

*As the article indicates, t*he Center for Disease Control (CDC) recommends annual flu vaccines every year for everyone six months or older. ~~The CDC is worried about~~ *The CDC is concerned with* public health, *and their* expert ~~opinion~~ *advice* on the issue should be ~~paid attention to~~ *followed. However, t*he article does not merely *expect us to* take the CDC's advice, but gives good reasons for us to listen. The best claim that the article makes is that flu vaccinations save lives. Many of us have had the flu and might think it's no big deal. You get sick, you stay home from work or school for a few days, *and* you ~~are~~ resting while watching a few of your favorite movies and napping. ~~Your~~ *You're* back to normal in no time. *However, t*hat is the best case. *Each year, m*ore than 200,000 people are hospitalized ~~each year for the flu~~ and over 36,000 die *from the flu* ~~each year~~ in the United States alone. These statistics make a very good case that ~~taking that~~ *the* vaccine ~~can~~ save*s* lives. *Although it would be nice to see where these statistics come from, t*hey are specific and relevant to the issue *and could be easily checked against other sources.*

For more on editing for grammar and usage, see Chapter 4. For more on editing for capitalization and punctuation, see Chapter 5.

How Your Response Will Be Graded

Remember, your writing sample will be scored across three traits.

Trait 1   **Creation of Arguments and Use of Evidence**

Trait 2   **Development of Ideas and Organizational Structure**

Trait 3   **Clarity and Command of Standard English Conventions**

Your response is scored one trait at a time. The following is a simplified version of the scoring rubrics that the graders will use to score your response.

Score	Description
Trait 1: Creation of Arguments and Use of Evidence	
2	• Creates an argument based on the source text(s), with a purpose that relates to the prompt • Supports the argument with evidence from the source text(s) • Analyzes issues and/or evaluates arguments in the source texts (e.g., identifies claims that are not supported, makes reasonable inferences about underlying assumptions, identifies unsound reasoning, evaluates source credibility, etc.)

(continued)

Score	Description
1	• Creates an argument that has some relation to the prompt • Supports the argument with some evidence from the source text(s) • Makes some attempt to analyze issues and/or evaluate arguments in the source texts
0	• May try to create an argument OR response lacks any relation to the prompt • Presents little or no evidence from the source text(s) • Makes very little attempt to analyze issues and/or evaluate arguments in the source texts; may show little or no understanding of given argument(s)
Trait 2: Development of Ideas and Organizational Structure	
2	• Presents well-developed, generally logical ideas; elaborates on most ideas • Organizes ideas in a sensible sequence; clearly links main points and details • Structures the response to clearly convey the message and purpose; makes use of transition words • Uses a formal style and appropriate tone showing awareness of the audience • Chooses words that express ideas clearly
1	• Presents ideas in a way that indicates vague or simplistic reasoning; elaborates on only some ideas • Sequence of ideas has some logic, but connections between main ideas and details may be poor or missing. • Organization of ideas may be inconsistent or not fully effective at conveying the argument; few transition words are used • Style and tone may be inconsistent or not always appropriate for the audience or purpose of the response • May sometimes misuse words and/or choose words that do not make the meaning clear.
0	• Develops ideas without consistency or logic; offers little or no elaboration on main ideas • Organization of ideas is unclear or shows no logic; details may be missing or unrelated to the main idea • Creates an organizational structure that is ineffective or cannot be followed; does not use transition words or uses them inappropriately • Uses an inappropriate style and/or tone and shows little or no awareness of the audience • May frequently misuse words, overuse slang, repeat ideas, or express ideas unclearly

Score	Description
	Trait 3: Clarity and Command of Standard English Conventions
2	• Uses largely correct sentence structure in regard to the following: ○ Sentence structure varies within a paragraph or paragraphs ○ Subordination, coordination, and parallelism are used correctly ○ Wordiness and awkwardness are avoided ○ Transitional words are used as appropriate ○ There are no run-on sentences, fused sentences, and sentence fragments • Applies standard English conventions competently in regard to the following: ○ Frequently confused words and homonyms, including contractions ○ Subject-verb agreement ○ Pronoun usage, including pronoun-antecedent agreement, unclear pronoun references, and pronoun case ○ Placement of modifiers and correct word order ○ Capitalization ○ Use of apostrophes with possessive nouns ○ Punctuation • May make some errors in usage and mechanics, but these do not interfere with meaning overall
1	• Uses inconsistent sentence structure; may include some repetitive or awkward sentences that interfere with clarity; control over sentence structure and fluency is inconsistent • Control of standard English grammar and punctuation is inconsistent • May make frequent errors in usage and mechanics that occasionally interfere with meaning
0	• Sentence structure is consistently flawed and may obscure meaning; control over sentence structure and fluency is minimal • Control of standard English grammar and punctuation is minimal • Makes severe and frequent errors in usage and mechanics that interfere with meaning OR • Response is insufficient to demonstrate level of mastery over usage and mechanics

Non-scorable responses

• Response contains only text copied from source texts or prompt

• Response shows no evidence that test-taker has read the prompt or is off-topic

- Response is incomprehensible
- Response is not in English
- Response has not been attempted (blank)

EXERCISE 5

Writing an Extended Response

Source Text

Cycling City: Will Austin Embrace Bike Sharing?

by Erick Pickhartz

1   Let's say you want to ride a bike only once in a while, sometimes to get to work but other times just for fun. You don't want to deal with maintenance, but you want to be able to enjoy the air and exercise at your convenience. That just might become a reality.

2   The City of Austin has tossed around the idea of funding a bike share program for a couple years, but officials are still weighing pros and cons. Bike sharing would work much like the Car2Go car-sharing program, in which a membership is required but rides are unlimited. City staff already participate in their own bike sharing program. If approved, the program would take about two years to get up and running—or shall we say, rolling.

3   As a step in the deciding process, the State Capitol housed a B-Cycle demo Monday with examples of the bikes used in the program, as well as the kiosks where users would pick up and drop off their wheels.

PROS

4   Bike sharing programs stand to make major decreases in carbon emissions and overall car pollution in a city, state, and country that's beginning to see the side effects of overcrowding. Cringe-worthy gas prices are certainly a motivator. Traffic in Austin is enough to drive the most mellow of the Austin weirdos batty. Even local actor Matthew McConaughey would find something to complain about with the streets crowded with gas guzzlers. And he played Wooderson!

5   We're a cycling city, and our reputation as a forward-thinking, environmentally conscious town leads most to assume something like

this is inevitable. San Antonio established its own B-Cycle program, and Austin should show the rest of the country that we care about these types of things, too.

6   The bikes are easy to ride. They may be slightly heavier than what you would find at Mellow Johnny's [Bike Shop], but anybody who's halfway competent on two wheels will have no trouble riding a B-Cycle. Promoting cycle commuting should be a priority of a bike share program, and getting even more Austinites onto a bike can only help things.

7   Other pros: Cycling is an easy way to make friends ("Meet me at the kiosk on Sixth and Congress [Avenue]!"); bike sharing could get novices excited about the idea of commuting by bicycle; riding a bike instantly makes you more attractive to the opposite sex, as long as you wear deodorant.

CONS

8   Sure, it makes sense to be centrally-located if you're a bike sharing station, but some of the best parts of Austin cycling involve getting out of downtown and enjoying the more scenic rides and commutes available in the surrounding area (think North or East Austin bike routes, or the Veloway). If you want to grab a bike for a reason other than a short ride to work and back, you may not see a use for a membership.

9   Money, money and money. Setting up B-Cycles here in town would cost the City of Austin $1.8 million, not to mention around $225,000 a year in operating costs. Um, aren't we trying to recover from a recession? Aren't all city budgets being slashed and burned? Don't deficit figures make your eyes bug out? We can always apply for grants, but that doesn't always work smoothly or swiftly. There are likely a thousand other proposed uses for that much moola, and those uses are just as good (if not better) than a bike sharing program. It doesn't take a genius to think of some: schools are threatening to close, parks need care and attention, people can't afford the homes they live in, unemployment still lingers, etc., etc., etc.

10   Weather can mess with any bike ride. If you tie yourself into a bike share membership and don't have another reliable mode of transportation, rain or sleet could completely ruin your efforts. And of course, there's nothing fun about riding a bike to work on a 100 degree August day. And there's nothing fun about sitting next to the guy who rode to work on a 100 degree day.

11   Other cons: People, especially Americans, don't like to share; the Austin bicycling facilities and infrastructure still need work; it's far less safe to ride a bike than cruise 40 miles per hour down Congress in a metal box.

PROMPT

The article presents arguments from both sides of the bike-sharing debate.

To respond, analyze both positions presented in the article to determine which one is best supported. Use relevant and specific evidence from the article to support your response.

Type your response on your own computer. You should expect to spend up to 45 minutes planning, drafting, and editing your response.

CHAPTER 4

Editing for Conventions of Standard English: Grammar and Usage

Some questions on the GED Assessment test your ability to use Standard English grammar and usage.

Grammar and Usage

Grammar refers to the parts of speech and parts of sentences and paragraphs, as well as how they function together to communicate. *Usage* refers to how the parts of speech and parts of sentences are employed—correctly or incorrectly, effectively or ineffectively—in writing and speech.

Parts of Speech

In English grammar, different parts of speech have different functions in sentences.

Part of Speech	Examples
noun: names a person, place, thing, or idea	Eleanor Roosevelt, Uncle Louis, butterfly, Mississippi River, courage, book
pronoun: refers to a noun, or to a person, place, thing, or idea	I, you, he, her, it, that, this, one, something, which, themselves
verb: expresses action or state of being	run, think, do, weigh, taste, is, be, had gone, was swimming
adjective: modifies a noun or pronoun; tells *what kind* or *which one*	*(The adjective is boldfaced.)* **green** car, **silly** child, **serious** student, **Spanish** architecture, **Texan** landscape

(continued)

Part of Speech	Examples
adverb: modifies a verb, adjective, or adverb and tells *where, when, how, to what extent*	soon, happily, never, thoroughly, quite, too, hurriedly
preposition: relates one noun or pronoun, called the object of the preposition, to another word	*(The preposition is boldfaced.)* the one **in** the car, the flight **beyond** the moon, the season **before** autumn, ran **past** the curb, focused **on** the goal
conjunction: joins words or word groups	and, but, or, nor, for, so, yet, either . . . or, if, although, while
interjection: expresses emotion	wow, oh, yikes, ah, oops

EXERCISE 1

Parts of Speech

Directions: Answer the following questions.

1. Identify the noun in the following sentence: We are going there after we cross the river.

2. Identify all of the pronouns in the following sentence: Is that the book he requested?

3. What part of speech is the boldfaced word in the following sentence? He is sitting **under** an oak tree. _____

4. What part of speech is the boldfaced word in the following sentence? Connor **quickly** cut the wires. _____

Answers are on page 535.

Parts of a Paragraph

Paragraphs are made of sentences. Sentences are made of phrases and clauses. Phrases and clauses are made of words. To understand most English grammar, it is important to be able to recognize phrases, clauses, and sentences.

Parts of a Paragraph	Examples
phrase: a word group that does not include both a subject and its verb and that functions as a grammatical unit such as a noun or adjective	*(The phrase is boldfaced.)* character **in a book** [the phrase acts as an adjective modifying *book*] **the large black umbrella** that is open [the phrase acts as a noun] Nicole **will be singing** [the phrase is a verb] walking **away from him** [the phrase acts as an adverb modifying *walking*]
clause: a word group that includes both a subject and a verb	the dog barks when the dog barks are you well whether he is staying here tomorrow
sentence: a word group that includes at least one clause and any number of phrases and that expresses a complete thought	The dog barks. When the dog barks, I let him in. Are you well? I'll ask whether he is staying here tomorrow.

EXERCISE 2

Parts of a Paragraph

Directions: Categorize each boldfaced word group as a phrase or a clause.

1. The chicken **on my porch** has ruddy feathers. _____

2. The tree **we planted yesterday** needs to be watered. _____

3. The clouds covered the sun **all morning long**. _____

4. **I delivered the books** to the librarian after I ate lunch. _____

Answers are on page 535.

Coordination, Subordination, and Parallelism

When you create sentences, paragraphs, and lists, you often join words and word groups. You use coordination and subordination to help the audience understand the relationships between ideas and between words.

Coordination

Coordination refers to the use of coordinating conjunctions (*and, but, for, nor, or, so, yet*) or other grammatical elements to join words, phrases, and clauses that are of similar importance and that are expressed in similar grammatical terms.

EXAMPLES

The red, white, **and** blue decorations are for July 4. [*And* joins three adjectives.]

Which came first: the chicken **or** the egg? [*Or* joins two noun phrases.]

Eliana hurried to the corner, **but** she missed the bus. [*But* joins two clauses.]

Three or more coordinate items in a series are separated by commas:

EXAMPLES

The **red, white,** and **blue** decorations are for July 4. [Commas separate three adjectives.]

There is glitter **on the table, in her hair, under my nails,** and even **on the cat.** [Commas separate four prepositional phrases.]

I registered for the class, and **I bought the textbook,** but **I haven't met the instructor.** [Commas separate three clauses.]

The final comma in a series is known as the **serial comma.** Sometimes that comma is omitted, but using it helps make your writing clear and logical.

When you use a coordinating conjunction to join two independent clauses, place a comma before the conjunction:

EXAMPLES

Stella is going to Kentucky this summer**, and** Pete will go with her.

Did Marc finish building the console**, or** does it need more work?

However, when a coordinating conjunction joins two parts of a compound verb, no comma is needed between them:

EXAMPLES

Stella is going to Kentucky this summer **and** returning to Texas in the fall.

Did Marc finish building the console **or** setting the gauges?

EXERCISE 3

Coordination

Directions: Answer the following questions.

1. Choose the sentence that shows the correct punctuation:

   A. Should I go to the store for black beans or just use the chick peas?
   B. Should I go to the store for black beans, or just use the chick peas?

2. Choose the answer that shows the correct punctuation:

   A. The rice is already cooking but I need to wash and chop the vegetables.
   B. The rice is already cooking, but I need to wash and chop the vegetables.

3. Choose the answer that shows the correct punctuation:

   A. I am studying the Civil War, the Great Depression and, the Dust Bowl.
   B. I am studying the Civil War, the Great Depression, and the Dust Bowl.

Answers are on page 535.

Subordination

Subordination refers to the use of a connector such as a relative pronoun (for example, *that, which, who,* or *whom*) or a subordinating conjunction (for example, *when, because, while, since, if, although, where*) to show the relationship between ideas or grammatical elements of unequal importance.

EXAMPLES

The instructor **who teaches in room 102** won an award last week. [The boldface subordinate clause, introduced by the relative pronoun *who*, expresses an idea that is of less importance—is subordinate to—the main clause.]

At the laundromat, **while I waited for the laundry to dry,** I worked on my essay. [The boldface subordinate clause is introduced by the subordinating conjunction *while*.]

Although we were early, there were not many seats left. [The boldface subordinate clause is introduced by the subordinating conjunction *although*.]

There are different kinds of **subordinate clauses.** Some are set off by commas and some are not, depending on the kind of information in the clause.

- An **adjective clause** modifies, or describes, a noun or pronoun.

- An **adverb clause** modifies, or describes, a verb, adjective, or other adverb.

- A **noun clause** acts as a noun in a sentence.

An adjective clause may be **essential** to the meaning of the sentence (that is, restrictive) or **nonessential** (nonrestrictive). Essential clauses ARE NOT set off by commas. Nonessential clauses ARE set off by commas.

EXAMPLES

The cat **that lives next door** is named Banjo. [The clause, which modifies the noun *cat*, contains information that is essential to the basic meaning of the sentence.]

That orange tabby, **which lives next door,** is named Banjo. [The clause, which modifies the noun *tabby*, adds "extra" information that the reader does not need in order to understand the basic meaning of the sentence.]

Do you know the person **who left this phone here**? [The clause, which modifies *person*, is essential to the basic meaning of the sentence.]

Do you know someone named Emily McCall, **who left this phone here**? [The clause, which modifies *Emily McCall*, adds "extra" information that the reader does not need in order to understand the basic meaning of the sentence.]

An **adverb clause,** which modifies a verb, adjective, or other adverb and tells *when, where, how, under what condition,* or *to what extent,* is followed by a comma when it begins a sentence. It is usually not set off by commas when it appears in the middle or at the end of a sentence.

EXAMPLES

When you get to the corner, you should turn left.

You should turn left **when you get to the corner.**

If you are hungry, we can go have lunch.

We can go have lunch **if you are hungry.**

A **noun clause,** which acts as a noun in a sentence, is usually not set off by commas, unless a single-word noun in its place would be set off by commas.

EXAMPLES

I asked **whoever was standing there** the way to the library.

The subject of the talk is **how students can apply for college loans.**

The next person who is ready, **whoever finishes the forms first,** can go next.

EXERCISE 4

Subordination

Directions: Answer the following questions.

1. Choose the sentence that shows the correct punctuation:

   A. When you listen to that song, what do you think about?
   B. When you listen to that song what do you think about?

2. Choose the answer that shows the correct punctuation:

   A. The first-place runner, who is Josh Grossman, will receive a medal at the ceremony.
   B. The first-place runner who is Josh Grossman will receive a medal at the ceremony.

3. Choose the answer that shows the correct punctuation:

   A. The Dust Bowl which was an ecological disaster occurred in the 1930s.
   B. The Dust Bowl, which was an ecological disaster, occurred in the 1930s.

Answers are on page 535.

Parallelism

For clarity and impact, similar (coordinate) items should be expressed in similar grammatical terms. When you use the same grammatical form for similar ideas, you create **parallel form,** or **parallelism.**

EXAMPLES

The list of readings includes **poems, plays,** and **novels**. [three nouns]

The Mullaneys are known **for their musical abilities** and **for their restless tendencies.** [two prepositional phrases]

I wanted to go to the show, Eliot wanted to go to the show, Marisa wanted to go to the show, yet we all stayed home and watched TV. [three clauses]

Bulleted and numbered lists should be in parallel form:

Not Parallel	Parallel
Please remember	Please remember to
• to turn off the lights • unplug the power strip • your phone charger	• turn off the lights • unplug the power strip • take your phone charger

EXERCISE 5

Parallelism

Directions: Answer the following questions.

1. Choose the sentence that shows correct parallelism:

   A. I like reading, writing, and to run.
   B. I like reading, writing, and running.

2. Revise this sentence to create correct parallelism:

   The gems were prized for their value, for their rarity, and because they were beautiful.

   _____

   _____

3. Make the bulleted items parallel:

   • How to draft   _____

   • Revising   _____

   • Editing   _____

   • Proofreading   _____

   • Publication   _____

Answers are on page 535.

Writing Clearly and Concisely

Using Specific and Concrete Words

When you are speaking or writing, avoid vague, nonspecific words. Use concrete, specific ones when possible.

Nonspecific: The guy said that when he was around, I should give him some stuff.

Specific: The lab director said that when he was in his office, I should give him the application and a list of references.

Nonspecific: There are several things in the piece that could be discussed.

Specific: The magazine article includes several ideas for discussion.

Writing Concisely

Think of writing as a machine with many parts (words), which performs a specific task. Just as machines should not have extra parts and pieces cluttering the works, writing should contain only the words it needs. When you are writing and revising, use only the words you need to make your point. Use repetition rarely and thoughtfully. Also, prefer short words and expressions to long ones.

EXAMPLES

Wordy: It is this writer's opinion that over the course of time each and every person will locate a pathway to greater understanding, judgment, and intelligence.

Better: I believe that everyone eventually finds a path to wisdom.

Many common wordy expressions can be replaced with single words.

Wordy	Better
in order to	to
due to the fact that	because
each and every	every
similar to	like
is able to	can
despite the fact that	although

EXERCISE 6

Writing Clearly and Concisely

Directions: Choose the *best* answer to each of the following questions.

1. What is the *best* way to revise the following sentence for clarity and conciseness?

   We cannot find a way to accommodate your request for reservations at the present time.

   A. We cannot make reservations for you now.
   B. We are unable to accommodate you with reservations.
   C. We cannot request reservations at present.
   D. We cannot now help you with your request for reservations.

2. What is the *best* way to revise the following sentence for clarity and conciseness?

   The book was written by the author Jonah West in order to communicate his amazing, remarkable narrative.

   A. The book, which tells an amazing, remarkable story, was written by Jonah West.
   B. Jonah West tells his amazing, remarkable story in the book he wrote.
   C. Jonah West wrote the book to tell his remarkable story.
   D. The book is written by the author Jonah West.

Answers are on page 535.

Using Transitions

Use conjunctive adverbs and transitional expressions to make your writing clearer and your logic easier to follow. **Conjunctive adverbs** are adverbs that conjoin, or connect, clauses and sentences and show how those clauses and sentences are related. **Transitional expressions** are word groups that do the same.

Common Conjunctive Adverbs		
additionally	finally	nonetheless
also	however	otherwise
anyway	instead	still
besides	meanwhile	then
consequently	nevertheless	therefore
eventually	next	thus

Common Transitional Expressions	
after all	for instance
as a result	in addition
at any rate	in fact
by the way	in other words
even so	on the contrary
for example	on the other hand

Conjunctive adverbs and transitional expressions can be used between sentences to show a relationship between the ideas expressed. Use a comma to set off the transition:

EXAMPLES

> I was hoping to go camping this weekend. **However,** I have too much work to do. **In addition,** the forecast is for rain.

Conjunctive adverbs and transitional expressions can also be used to join independent clauses that are separated by a semicolon. Use a comma to set off the transition:

EXAMPLES

> I was hoping to go camping this weekend**; however,** I have too much work to do.

> I plan to review several chapters**; in fact,** I will go over the first half of the book.

EXERCISE 7

Using Transitions

Directions: Choose the answer option that shows the *best* revision, with a logical transitional expression or conjunctive adverb and correct punctuation.

1. Roger missed Austin the whole time he lived in Chicago; he decided to move back to Austin.

    A. Roger missed Austin the whole time he lived in Chicago; however, he decided to move back to Austin.
    B. Roger missed Austin the whole time he lived in Chicago, thus, he decided to move back to Austin.
    C. Roger missed Austin the whole time he lived in Chicago. He decided to move back to Austin.
    D. Roger missed Austin the whole time he lived in Chicago; eventually, he decided to move back to Austin.

2. The hiking trails and waterfall were spectacular. The campground was dirty and unpleasant.

    A. The hiking trails and waterfall were spectacular. In fact, the campground was dirty and unpleasant.
    B. The hiking trails and waterfall were spectacular, on the contrary, the campground was dirty and unpleasant.
    C. The hiking trails and waterfall were spectacular. However, the campground was dirty and unpleasant.
    D. The hiking trails and waterfall were spectacular. Furthermore, the campground was dirty and unpleasant.

3. A summer of drought withered the crops; flash floods in the fall washed away the topsoil.

    A. A summer of drought withered the crops; additionally, flash floods in the fall washed away the topsoil.
    B. A summer of drought withered the crops; in other words, flash floods in the fall washed away the topsoil.
    C. A summer of drought withered the crops, next, flash floods in the fall washed away the topsoil.
    D. A summer of drought withered the crops, then; flash floods in the fall washed away the topsoil.

4. Taylor, Logan, and Emma are running late. Their project will not be finished by the deadline.

    A. Taylor, Logan, and Emma are running late. As a result, their project will not be finished by the deadline.

    B. Taylor, Logan, and Emma are running late. Besides, their project will not be finished by the deadline.

    C. Taylor, Logan, and Emma are running late. Even so, their project will not be finished by the deadline.

    D. Taylor, Logan, and Emma are running late, in fact, their project will not be finished by the deadline.

Answers are on page 535.

Subject-Verb Agreement and Pronoun-Antecedent Agreement

A word that refers to one person, place, thing, or idea is usually **singular.** A word that refers to more than one is usually **plural.** Singular subjects take singular verbs, and plural subjects take plural verbs. Similarly, singular pronouns should be used to refer to singular persons, places, things, and ideas, while plural pronouns should be used to refer to plural ones.

EXAMPLES

Frank leaves early on Tuesdays to get to **his** job on time. [*Frank* is singular and takes a singular verb. A singular pronoun is used to refer to him.]

Daniel and Bryan leave early on Tuesdays to get to **their** jobs on time. [*Daniel and Bryan* is plural and takes a plural verb. A plural pronoun is used to refer to them.]

In some situations, it is easy to make errors in subject-verb agreement or in pronoun-antecedent agreement. Let's look at situations that may be confusing.

Intervening Words and Phrases

Sometimes a verb or pronoun is not immediately next to the word it needs to agree with. Words that intervene, or come between, a subject and verb or a pronoun and its antecedent do not change the need for agreement.

EXAMPLES

That **topic**, along with many others, **is** on the agenda; **it** will be discussed after the break. [The subject, *topic*, agrees with its verb, *is*, and the pronoun *it*. The intervening phrase does not make it plural.]

One of the senators **raises her** hand to make an objection. [The subject, *one*, agrees with its verb, *raises*, and the pronoun *her*.]

Both **keys** to the gate on the other side of the stadium **are** missing from **their** assigned hooks. [The subject, *keys*, agrees with its verb, *are*, and the pronoun *their*.]

Collective Nouns

Some nouns that are singular in form refer to a group of persons, animals, or things. A collective noun is singular when it refers to the group as a unit but is plural when it refers to the individual, separate members of the group.

Common Collective Nouns		
army	committee	jury
assembly	crowd	public
audience	family	staff
band	flock	swarm
class	group	team
club	herd	troop

EXAMPLES

The jury **is** deadlocked on one charge; **it** may not be able to resolve the question.

The jury **are arguing** among **themselves** about one charge.

The **group** of tourists **leaves** whenever **its** bus arrives.

The **group** of tourists **have scattered**, with some of **them** going to uptown landmarks and some going downtown.

Compound Subjects

A compound subject that names one person, place, thing, or idea is singular and takes a singular verb or pronoun. A compound subject that names more than one is plural and takes a plural verb or pronoun.

SINGULAR

The first **paragraph or** the last **one states** the preliminary findings in **its** topic sentence. [Singular subjects joined by *or* take a singular verb and pronoun.]

My next-door **neighbor and** best **friend** is Lucinda. [*Neighbor* and *friend* name the same singular person.]

PLURAL

The first **paragraph and** the last **one state** the preliminary findings in **their** topic sentences. [Singular subjects joined by *and* take a plural verb and plural pronoun.]

My next-door **neighbor and** my best **friend are coming** over later to pick up **their** books. [*Neighbor* and *friend* name two people and take a plural verb and plural pronoun.]

EXERCISE 8

Subject-Verb Agreement and Pronoun-Antecedent Agreement

Directions: Answer the following questions.

1. Identify the option that shows correct subject-verb agreement:

   A. Carina, along with her two classmates, are studying the Civil War.
   B. Carina, along with her two classmates, is studying the Civil War.

2. Identify the option that shows correct subject-verb agreement:

   A. The crowd shows approval by applauding loudly and long.
   B. The crowd show approval by applauding loudly and long.

3. Identify the option that shows correct subject-verb agreement:

   A. This unit or the one to the left of the landings has been upgraded.
   B. This unit or the one to the left of the landings have been upgraded.

4. Identify the option that shows correct pronoun-antecedent agreement:

   A. One of the rarest birds in these canyons will build its nest nearby.
   B. One of the rarest birds in these canyons will build their nest nearby.

5. Identify the option that shows correct pronoun-antecedent agreement:

   A. The flock will fly away if someone makes a noise that disturbs them.
   B. The flock will fly away if someone makes a noise that disturbs it.

6. Identify the option that shows correct pronoun-antecedent agreement:

   A. Several feathers and one eggshell took their place on my windowsill.
   B. Several feathers and one eggshell took its place on my windowsill.

Answers are on page 535.

Pronoun Case

Pronouns take different forms, called **case forms,** depending on how they are used. Pronouns that are used as subjects are in **nominative (or subject) case.** Pronouns that are objects (those that receive the action of a verb or are objects of a preposition) are in **objective case.** Pronouns that show possession are in **possessive case.**

Nominative (Subject) Case	Objective Case	Possessive Case
I, we	me, us	my, mine, our, ours
you	you	your, yours
he, she, it, they	him, her, it, them	his, her, hers, its, their, theirs

Use the correct case for pronouns when you are writing and speaking.

EXAMPLES

She and **I** drove. [Nominative-case pronouns function as the subject of *drove.*]

I said that **he** and **I** would leave. [Nominative-case pronouns function as the subject of *would leave.*]

Aunt Clara gave **her** and **me** a ride. [Objective-case pronouns function as objects of the verb *gave.*]

My car and **her** car are parked. [Possessive pronouns show ownership.]

Be careful to use the correct case when using pronouns in compound constructions.

Nominative: Will **Tony** and **she** [not *Tony and her*] drive?

Nominative: Natalie and **they** [not *Natalie and them*] meet tomorrow morning.

Objective: Aunt Clara offered **Sasha** and **me** [not *Sasha and I*] a ride.

Objective: What will Diego say to **Don** and **me** [not *Don and I*]?

If you have trouble deciding which case form to use in a compound construction, try saying the sentence with just one part of the compound at a time.

> **Nominative:** Will ~~Tony and~~ **she** [not *her*] drive?

> **Nominative:** ~~Natalie and~~ **they** [not *them*] meet tomorrow morning.

> **Objective:** Aunt Clara offered ~~Sasha and~~ **me** [not *I*] a ride.

> **Objective:** What will Diego say to ~~Don and~~ **me** [not *I*]?

EXERCISE 9

Pronoun Case

Directions: Choose the *best* answer to each of the following questions.

1. Identify the option that shows correct pronoun case:

    A. Stella and him are heading to the studio.
    B. Stella and he are heading to the studio.

2. Identify the option that shows correct pronoun case:

    A. The award was given to Justin and me.
    B. The award was given to Justin and I.

3. Identify the option that shows correct pronoun case:

    A. Give Jacqui and he a hand moving the easel, please.
    B. Give Jacqui and him a hand moving the easel, please.

Answers are on page 536.

Pronoun Reference

To prevent ambiguity and misunderstanding, a pronoun should refer clearly to its antecedent.

> **Unclear:** After Sara gave Bella the invoices, she became worried. [Who became worried?]

> **Clear:** Sara became worried after she gave Bella the invoices.

Sometimes you may need to revise or reword a sentence to correct an unclear pronoun reference.

Unclear: We saw bats, spiders, a snake, and a scorpion. It frightened the children. [Did one animal in particular frighten the children, or did seeing all of the animals frighten them?]

Clear: Seeing bats, spiders, a snake, and a scorpion frightened the children.

Unclear: We spent the day working at the art kiosk, but we didn't sell any. [It's not clear what *any* refers to.]

Clear: We spent the day working at the art kiosk, but we didn't sell any paintings.

EXERCISE 10

Pronoun Reference

Directions: Choose the *best* revision of each ambiguous or unclear pronoun reference.

1. After he recommended ordering new parts, Jorge and Jon talked about the purchase order.

   A. Jorge and Jon talked about the purchase order after he recommended ordering new parts.
   B. After Jorge recommended ordering new parts, he and Jon talked about the purchase order.

2. Michael wants to build a new coop, but Ben wants to repair the old one. It's a surprise to me.

   A. Michael wants to build a new coop, but Ben wants to repair the old one. Which is a surprise to me.
   B. Michael wants to build a new coop. I'm surprised to know that Ben wants to repair the old one.

Answers are on page 536.

Using Modifiers Correctly

A **modifier** is a word or word group that makes the meaning of another word or word group more specific. **Adjectives** modify nouns and pronouns. **Adverbs** modify verbs, adjectives, and other adverbs. Both phrases and clauses can act as adjectives or adverbs. In your writing and speaking, make sure that it is clear which words or word groups your adjectives and adverbs modify.

Unclear: We almost ate all the rolls.

Clear: We ate almost all the rolls.

Unclear: We will to go to the movie that's reviewed in today's paper tomorrow.

Clear: Tomorrow we will go to the movie that's reviewed in today's paper.

Unclear: I will watch all the movies that Charlie Chaplin made over winter vacation.

Clear: Over winter vacation, I will watch all the movies that Charlie Chaplin made.

Unclear: After rotting on a shelf in the pantry for a week, my brother found two old tomatoes.

Clear: My brother found two old tomatoes after they had been rotting on a shelf in the pantry for a week.

EXERCISE 11

Using Modifiers Correctly

Directions: Choose the *best* revision of each sentence.

1. Viewing the footage, a new theory developed.

    A. Viewing the footage, they developed a new theory.
    B. They developed a new theory viewing the footage.

2. We found an alternative water source using the map.

    A. We found an alternative water source, which was using the map.
    B. Using the map, we found an alternative water source.

3. After spending a long time trying to decide, I chose the book that you had recommended eventually.

    A. After spending a long time trying to decide, I eventually chose the book that you had recommended.
    B. After spending a long time trying to decide, I chose the book that you had eventually recommended.

4. Completely worn out, home and bed were a welcome sight to the traveler.

    A. Completely worn out, the traveler welcomed the sight of home and bed.
    B. The traveler welcomed the sight of home and bed, completely worn out.

Answers are on page 536.

Nonstandard and Informal Usage: Frequently Confused Words

Standard English is language that is regarded as grammatically correct; it is considered acceptable in both formal and informal contexts. **Formal Standard English** is grammatically correct language that is appropriate in situations such as speeches, job applications, and academic writing. **Informal Standard English** includes language that is grammatically correct but casual in tone. **Nonstandard English** does not follow generally accepted language conventions.

STANDARD ENGLISH

Formal: The security lapse was an issue of serious concern.

Informal: The security lapse was a freaky problem. [*Freaky* is too casual for formal use.]

Nonstandard English: The security lapse caused alot of troubel. [*Alot* and *troubel* are incorrect.]

In academic writing and on the GED Assessment, you should use Formal Standard English. Here are some nonstandard usages that you should avoid, as well as some words that are often confused.

accept/except: *Accept* means "to receive" (*I accept your offer*). *Except* can be a verb meaning "to leave out" (*He was excepted from the rule*) or a preposition meaning "excluding" (*Everyone except Cami was late*).

affect/effect: *Affect* is a verb meaning "to influence" or "to change" (*The criticism affected her attitude.*) *Effect* is most often used as a noun meaning "result" (*The effect of the criticism was a change in attitude*). It is occasionally used as a verb meaning "to bring about" (*The committee effected long-overdue reform.*)

all right/alright: *Alright* is a nonstandard form, or misspelling, of *all right,* which means "satisfactory" or "yes."

a lot/alot: *Alot* is a nonstandard form, or misspelling, of *a lot,* which means "a great deal."

between/among: Use *between* when referring to only two items *(The supervisor and employee discussed it between themselves).* Use *among* when referring to more than two *(The supervisors and their employees discussed it among themselves).*

bring/take: *Bring* means "to come with something" *(When you come to my house, please bring my phone). Take* means "to go with something" *(Take your phone with you when you go).*

don't/doesn't: *Don't* is the contraction of *do not. Doesn't* is the contraction of *does not.* Use *doesn't,* not *don't,* with singular subjects except *I* and *you (He doesn't know yet; it doesn't matter).*

farther/further: *Farther* is used to express physical distance *(Let's drive farther). Further* is used to express metaphorical distance or an extension of time or degree *(Let's see if we can explore this idea further).*

fewer/less: Use *fewer,* which refers to a number, "how many," with items that can be counted *(There are fewer eggs in the nest).* Use *less,* which refers to an amount, "how much," to modify a singular noun or non-count noun *(There is less pie in the dish).*

imply/infer: *Imply* means "to suggest" *(Her remarks imply that I am mistaken). Infer* means "to interpret" or "to draw a conclusion" *(I infer from your remarks that you think I'm mistaken).*

its/it's: *Its* is a possessive pronoun meaning "belonging to it" *(The dog is in its kennel). It's* is a contraction of *it is (It's in the kennel).*

literally: *Literally* means "actually" or "in a strict sense," but it is often misused to mean the opposite.

supposed to/used to: In the past tense, both expressions have a *–d* on the end *(She was supposed* [not *suppose] to clock in. She used* [not *use] to remember to do so).*

than/then: *Than* is a subordinating conjunction used in comparisons. *Then* is an adverb telling *when. (I like avocados more than you do. Let's go to the restaurant and then order guacamole.)*

their/there/they're: *Their* is a possessive pronoun meaning "belonging to them." *There* is an adverb pointing out a place or an expletive used to begin a sentence. *They're* is a contraction of *they are. (They're* looking for *their* cat, which is over *there.)*

try and/try to: *Try to* is considered standard; *try and* is not. *(Try to open the stuck door, please.)*

well/good: *Good* is an adjective and should not be used to modify an action verb. *Well* is sometimes an adjective meaning "in good health" and sometimes an adverb meaning "capably" or "satisfactorily." *(It is good that you are feeling well and that you did well on your test.)*

your/you're: *Your* is a possessive pronoun meaning "belonging to you." *You're* is a contraction of *you are.* *(You're about to reach your goal.)*

EXERCISE 12

Nonstandard and Informal Usage: Frequently Confused Words

Directions: Identify all of the sentences containing nonstandard usage. Then, revise each of those sentences to correct the nonstandard usage.

A. That is alot of mulch.

_____

B. Try and turn the knob.

_____

C. It is all right with me if you borrow a rake.

_____

D. I have fewer than ten binder clips.

_____

E. Your going to win the race!

_____

F. Please except my apology.

_____

G. It's getting late.

_____

H. How will that effect you?

_____

I. Divide the dessert between the four of you.

_____

J. Please take this with you when you go.

_____

K. It don't matter to Connor.

_____

L. He did good on that assessment.

_____

M. I'd like to extend the deadline further.

_____

N. I imply from the results that I misunderstood the directions.

_____

O. Marti saw they're lost cat hiding in the bushes.

_____

P. She was literally catapulted to fame.

_____

Q. Am I supposed to know the answer?

_____

R. I like swimming more then hiking.

_____

Answers are on page 536.

CHAPTER 5

Editing for Conventions of Standard English: Capitalization and Punctuation

Mechanics

Some questions on the GED Assessment test your ability to use Standard English mechanics—that is, capitalization and punctuation. *Capitalization* refers to the use of capital and lowercase letters to make specific, conventional distinctions in meaning. *Punctuation* refers to the use of periods, commas, question marks, semicolons, apostrophes, and the like, to clarify meaning.

Capitalization

In English, capital letters are conventionally used to designate certain kinds of words and certain functions in sentences and titles. This chapter reviews many conventions governing the use of capital letters.

Proper Nouns and Proper Adjectives

A **common noun** names a nonspecific, or general, member of a group of persons, places, things, or ideas. Common nouns are usually NOT capitalized. A **proper noun** names a specific, particular person, place, thing, or idea. Proper nouns are usually capitalized. **Proper adjectives** are modifiers that are formed from proper nouns; they are usually capitalized.

Common Noun	Proper Noun	Proper Adjective
person	William Shakespeare	**Shakespearean** language
place	New Orleans	**New Orleanian** cuisine
idea	Naturalism	**Naturalistic** plot

Here are specific kinds of proper nouns and proper adjectives that should be capitalized.

Type of Name	Examples
Names of Persons and Animals	Lao Tzu, Ms. Peggy Ramirez, E. M. Forster, Aunt Shirley, Grandpa, Lassie, Nemo
Geographical Names	Travis County, Tallahassee, New York, the Western Hemisphere, Iran, Mount Rainier, Lake Louise, Pedernales Falls State Park, Route 66, Twenty-first Street, Painted Desert
Organizations and Institutions	New Orleans Saints, National Football League, Southside General Hospital, Department of Labor
Peoples, Religions, Holy Writings, Deities	Zulu, Norse, Christian, Hinduism, New Testament, Yahweh, Zeus
Businesses and Brand Names of Business Products	Acme Widget Co., Acme widgets *[Note that the common name of the product itself is not capitalized.]*
Specific Buildings, Structures, Monuments, Memorials, Awards	Saenger Theater, Cochiti Dam, Golden Gate Bridge, Statue of Liberty, Washington Monument, Vietnam Veterans Memorial, Presidential Medal of Freedom
Person's Title *[when part of a name]*	Ms. Washington, Captain Sparrow, Senator Watson *[but* a captain of a ship, the senator from Texas]
Titles and Subtitles	*Riddley Walker, Anger: Wisdom for Cooling the Flames, Star Wars: A New Hope,* "The Waste Land"

Notice that when such words are used generically—that is, when they do not refer to a particular individual or specific thing—they are common nouns and should be lowercased.

EXAMPLES

I want to visit **a lake,** so let's go to **Lake Pontchartrain.**

Let's introduce **Uncle Louis** to your **aunt** and **uncle.**

How many **theaters** are in Cincinnati, and have you been to the **Emery Theatre?**

Also use a capital letter at the beginning of each sentence and for the pronoun *I.*

EXAMPLES

The movie was bittersweet; I enjoyed most of it.

When do I need to turn in my application?

EXERCISE 1

Capitalization

Directions: Identify each word that should be capitalized.

1. my cats are named banjo and chimmy.

2. Have you ever been to the lincoln memorial in washington, d.c.?

3. The restaurant we are going to with ranjan and abby is on webberville road.

4. Ask aunt retha if this book is from acme bookstore or from the library.

5. For school, i am reading a book titled *greek mythology: classic myths.*

6. Is buddhism older than hinduism?

Answers are on page 537.

Writing Correct Sentences

To communicate well, it is important to know how to write complete, correct sentences. A **complete sentence** includes at least one **subject** (usually a noun or pronoun that tells who or what is performing an action or being something) and at least one **verb** (a word that tells what the subject is doing or being), and it expresses a complete thought.

EXAMPLES

I spoke. [*I* is the subject, and *spoke* is the verb. Notice that a complete sentence can be quite short, as long as it includes a subject and a verb and expresses a complete thought.]

The U.S. is in North America. [*United States* is the subject, and *is* is the verb.]

Are Jonah and Zeb leaving for Canada soon? [The subject is *Jonah and Zeb*, and the verb is *are leaving*.]

When Katherine was at the theater, she saw Hank and Ken. [This sentence contains two clauses, each with a subject and verb: *Katherine was* and *she saw*.]

Sentence Errors

Common sentence construction errors include run-on sentences and fragments. A **run-on sentence,** or **fused sentence,** is made up of two or more complete sentences run together as if they were one sentence, with no punctuation or only a comma between them.

> **RUN-ON:** The chapter is twenty-one pages, the pretest takes up another five pages.

> **CORRECTED:** The chapter is twenty-one pages. **T**he pretest takes up another five pages.

> **CORRECTED:** The chapter is twenty-one pages**, and** the pretest takes up another five pages.

A **fragment** is a word group that is missing a subject or a verb (or both) or that does not express a complete thought.

> **FRAGMENT:** The chapter is twenty-one pages. **While the pretest takes up another five pages.** [The fragment is a dependent clause. Although it contains a subject (*pretest*) and a verb (*takes*), it does not express a complete thought.]

> **CORRECTED:** The chapter is twenty-one pages**, while** the pretest takes up another five pages.

> **CORRECTED:** The chapter is twenty-one pages. **T**he pretest takes up another five pages.

> **FRAGMENT:** The stripes are black and white. **Or perhaps gray and white.** [The fragment is missing a subject and a verb. It should be joined to the sentence before it.]

> **CORRECTED:** The stripes are black and white **or** perhaps gray and white.

EXERCISE 2

Writing Correct Sentences

Directions: Identify each of the following word groups as a correct sentence, a run-on, or a fragment. If it is a run-on (fused sentence) or a fragment, revise it to make it a complete, correct sentence.

1. That puppy belongs to Mr. Ewing.

2. Because we will be late.

_____

3. I saw that movie, it was good.

_____

4. The light turned green we turned left.

_____

5. Where are the leftover desserts?

_____

6. Whenever you decide to get your plane ticket.

_____

Answers are on page 537.

End Marks

End marks help show the difference between kinds of sentences. In academic writing and most Standard Formal English, you will mostly use periods. Use question marks for questions. Use exclamation points—very sparingly—to show strong emotion.

EXAMPLES

That is my blue notebook. [This basic declarative sentence ends with a period.]

Is that my blue notebook? [This interrogative sentence—a question—ends with a question mark.]

Hey! That's my blue notebook! [An exclamation point is used to show strong feeling.]

Periods are also used to create abbreviations.

INITIALS: W. E. B. Du Bois, Ida B. Wells

TITLES: Mr. Rogers, Ms. Reyes, Dr. Caroline Skiles, Gen. Mullaney, Prof. Rothenberg

GEOGRAPHICAL TERMS: London, U.K.; Houston, Tex.; St. Charles Ave.

TIMES: 6:00 A.M., 2:00 P.M., 163 B.C., A.D. 26

MEASUREMENTS: Most units of measurement are written without periods, but do use a period with *in.*, the abbreviation for *inch,* to avoid confusing it with the word *in.*

EXERCISE 3

End Marks

Directions: Add periods, question marks, and exclamation points to correctly punctuate the following sentences.

1. Are you really getting up at 4:00 A M

2. The vegetable garden needs to be watered

3. Ms Carter asked all the students to line up in the front hall

4. The artifact is from 12 B C or perhaps A D 34

5. Watch out for that falling anvil

Answers are on page 537.

Commas in Series and Sentences

Commas are used to separate, or set off, grammatical or logical elements. Use commas to separate **items in a series:**

EXAMPLES

The team includes Madison, Josh, Latoya, and Chen. [Commas separate four nouns.]

We looked under the benches, on the shelves, and in the cabinets before we found the markers. [Commas separate three prepositional phrases.]

I said that I had the assignment, that I was running late, and that I needed an extension. [Commas separate three dependent clauses.]

Note: Do not use a comma before the first item or after the last item.

A few style authorities omit the comma between the last two items in the series (known as the **serial comma** or Oxford comma). However, most style authorities recommend using the serial comma for the sake of logic and consistency.

UNCLEAR: In his speech, he thanked his parents, Prince Charles and Nelson Mandela. [The sentence can be misread as identifying someone's parents as Prince Charles and Nelson Mandela. It also can be read as saying that Prince Charles' last name is Mandela.]

CLEAR: In his speech, he thanked his parents, Prince Charles, and Nelson Mandela. [The speaker is clearly thanking four different people.]

Most of the time, use commas to separate two or more **adjectives before a noun.**

EXAMPLE: The cookbook is full of delightful, simple, delicious recipes.

Use a comma before a coordinating conjunction that joins two **independent clauses in a compound sentence.**

EXAMPLES

Ben will be tutoring Miles, and Dylan will be working with Martha.

I was hoping to leave early, yet I didn't focus on tasks that had to be done first.

You do not need a comma between parts of a **compound verb.**

COMPOUND SENTENCE: The cat hid under our house, and it wouldn't come out.

COMPOUND VERB: The cat hid under our house and wouldn't come out. [No comma is needed before *and,* which joins *hid* and *wouldn't come.*]

EXERCISE 4

Commas in Series and Sentences

Directions: Add commas as needed to correctly punctuate the following sentences.

1. The recipe calls for peas carrots and potatoes.

2. Paint was everywhere: on the sofa in the carpet and even under the bookshelves.

3. Kirk wrote the script last winter and Madge directed the play this season.

4. That is a kind thoughtful gesture and I really appreciate it.

5. Well Annie illustrated the book but did not write it.

Answers are on page 537.

Commas with Nonessential Elements

Use a comma to set off **nonessential elements**. If a word group can be deleted from the sentence without changing the basic meaning of the sentence, it is nonessential, or nonrestrictive.

ESSENTIAL CLAUSE: The college gave a scholarship to the student **who wrote the best essay.** [The clause is essential to the basic meaning of the sentence, so no comma sets it off.]

NONESSENTIAL CLAUSE: The college gave a scholarship to Marvin Jackson, **who wrote the best essay.** [The clause adds "extra" information to the sentence but is not necessary to the sentence's basic meaning. Therefore, it is set off with a comma.]

ESSENTIAL PARTICIPIAL PHRASE: The lines **quoted in the article** are about human achievement. [The phrase identifies *which* lines and is necessary to the sentence's basic meaning.]

NONESSENTIAL PARTICIPIAL PHRASE: Lines 3–12, **quoted in the article,** are about human achievement. [The phrase is not necessary to the sentence's basic meaning—we know which lines are about human achievement even without the phrase.]

ESSENTIAL APPOSITIVE: My cousin **Ahmed** will be traveling next week. [The speaker has more than one cousin; the appositive identifies *which* cousin.]

NONESSENTIAL APPOSITIVE: My husband, **Ahmed,** will be traveling next week. [The speaker has only one husband; the appositive is not necessary to the sentence's basic meaning.]

EXERCISE 5

Commas with Nonessential Elements

Directions: Add commas as needed to correctly punctuate the following sentences. If a sentence is correct as is, write *C*.

1. Andy's son Sly is an only child.

2. The movie *The Fall* which I recommended the other night is available at the library.

3. The man practicing on the trapeze is the aerialist that I told you about.

4. Leaving in a hurry Miranda forgot to put the dog in its crate and bring in the mail.

Answers are on page 537.

Commas with Introductory Elements

Use a comma to set off **introductory elements.**

YES/NO or MILD INTERJECTION: No, I don't think so. **Well,** I suppose so.

NONESSENTIAL PARTICIPLE: Whistling, the boy strolled to the corner.

NONESSENTIAL PARTICIPIAL PHRASE: Whistling a cheerful tune, the boy strolled to the corner.

ADVERB CLAUSE: As he whistled a cheerful tune, he strolled to the corner.

EXERCISE 6

Commas with Introductory Elements

Directions: Add commas as needed to correctly punctuate the following sentences.

1. Yes I'd love to share a salad with you.

2. If you are online will you please check tonight's weather forecast?

3. Hurrying toward the finish line the runner experienced a burst of energy.

4. Startled the chihuahua began barking madly.

Answers are on page 538.

Semicolons

Semicolons are used to **punctuate compound sentences** not joined by a coordinating conjunction and to separate, or set off, **items in a series** when one or more of the items contain commas.

EXAMPLES

> The deadline is coming up quickly; we should finishing filling out the applications. [The semicolon joins two independent clauses.]

> The deadline is still three months away; however, we should fill out the applications early. [The semicolon joins two independent clauses.]

> The destinations are Austin, Texas; New Orleans, Louisiana; and Des Moines, Iowa. [Semicolons separate three items that contain commas.]

EXERCISE 7

Semicolons

Directions: Add commas and semicolons as needed to correctly punctuate the following sentences.

1. The itinerary includes three cities: Houston Texas Washington D.C. and Gainesville Florida.

2. The weather on the island will be cold the team should pack very warm clothes.

3. Robyn volunteers weekly at the homeless shelter also she is raising money to help a local family who lost their home in a fire.

4. I like studying insects however I still don't like live cockroaches.

Answers are on page 538.

Apostrophes

Apostrophes are used to show possession, to form contractions, and to form a few plurals.

> **POSSESSION, SINGULAR NOUNS:** that boy's bicycle; one goat's hoofprint; Joe Jackson's shoes [Add an apostrophe and s to show possession of a singular noun.]

> **POSSESSION, PLURAL NOUNS:** those boys' bicycles; two goats' hoofprints; the Jacksons' house [Add an apostrophe after the s to show possession of a plural noun.]

Do not use an apostrophe with possessive pronouns.

> **INCORRECT:** The car is their's. Is that her's? What is it's license number?

> **CORRECT:** The car is **theirs**. Is that **hers**? What is **its** license number?

Use apostrophes to stand for omitted letters or numbers in **contractions**.

I am	you are	let us	here is	has not	cannot	1980s	you will
I'm	you're	let's	here's	hasn't	can't	'80s	you'll

Most of the time, it is incorrect to use apostrophes to form plurals. However, there are a few cases where doing so helps prevent misreading and is correct. Use an apostrophe to form the **plurals of lowercase letters, some capital letters, numbers, symbols, and words referred to as words.**

> **EXAMPLES**
>
> How many *a*'s are in your last name?
>
> There are two *I*'s and two *2*'s in the password.
>
> How many *um*'s did you count?

Do not use apostrophes to form the plurals of ordinary nouns.

> **INCORRECT:** four Sunday's in a row; three owls' in the tree; hot dog's for sale

> **CORRECT:** four **Sundays** in a row; three **owls** in the tree; **hot dogs** for sale

EXERCISE 8

Apostrophes

Directions: Add apostrophes as needed to correctly punctuate the following
sentences.

1. Sarahs new bike lock, which she cant find, is green.

2. All four teams medals are in that box, but the ribbons in the other box
   have to be returned.

3. The ribbons have extra *os* in the city name.

4. Its unclear to me whether the *60s* was an unusually turbulent decade or
   whether its hype is overblown.

5. Theyre coming over to look for something of theirs that they left behind
   on Monday.

Answers are on page 538.

Other Punctuation

Here are other punctuation marks and their uses.

colon	:	introduces a list or a concluding explanation
quotation marks	" "	indicate exact words someone said
dash	—	marks an abrupt shift in thought
hyphen	-	separates syllables for line breaks or separates parts of some compound words
parentheses	( )	enclose information that is not necessary to a sentence's meaning
ellipsis	…	shows where words have been omitted or shows someone's voice trailing off

EXERCISE 9

Review of Capitalization and Punctuation

Directions: Add capital letters and punctuation as needed to correct the following sentences.

1. wheres the charger for your new phone

2. Well i dont know if theyre ready to go however ana definitely is.

3. Shivering in the icy drizzle we looked forward to building a cozy warm fire at our new home at 1230 hearthstone street.

4. The bees butterflies and birds all seem to enjoy those two beautiful trumpet vines which cedric planted last year

5. if you could go anywhere would you go see the grand canyon the brooklyn bridge or hoover dam today

Answers are on page 538.

Mathematical Reasoning

The Mathematical Reasoning Test

The Mathematical Reasoning section of the GED® test measures your ability to use reasoning and mathematics knowledge to make calculations and solve problems. About half of the test focuses on quantitative problem solving, and about half focuses on basic algebraic problem solving. There are some geometry questions as well.

There are approximately 50 questions on the Mathematical Reasoning test. You will have 90 minutes to complete the entire test. There is a short section on which a calculator is not allowed, but for the bulk of the test, a calculator is allowed. The calculator is available on the computer screen.

Some of the test questions simply ask you to make calculations. Others describe real-life situations that you must decide how to solve using mathematics. Many questions are based on graphs or diagrams.

Most of the Mathematical Reasoning questions are multiple-choice with four answer choices. Other questions ask you to indicate a point on a graph, write your answer in a box, select an answer from a drop-down menu, or "drag" an answer into the correct position in a math expression or equation. See "Introducing the GED Test" at the start of this book for an explanation and samples of these formats.

The Mathematical Reasoning Review

The following section of this book presents a comprehensive review of the skills that are tested on the Mathematical Reasoning test. The chapters cover all of the mathematics topics that appear on the test, and there are practice exercises in every topic area.

Answers for all of the exercises in these chapters are located in the Exercise Answer Key section at the back of this book.

CHAPTER 1

Integers

Whole Numbers and Integers

The Number Line

A **number line** is a convenient way to visualize numbers. On a horizontal line, a point on the left end of the line is marked and assigned the number 0, and additional points are marked off to the right of 0, equal distances apart, and assigned consecutive whole numbers. An arrowhead on the right end of the line signifies that the line and the numbers are understood to continue on, even though they aren't drawn.

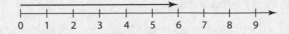

There are two common ways of designating a specific number on a number line. The simpler method places a dot or tick mark on the number line at the number's location.

EXAMPLE

Plot 6 on the number line.

The other method places an arrow above the number line, with the tail of the arrow at 0 and the head of the arrow above the number.

EXAMPLE

Plot 6 on the number line.

When larger numbers are plotted, a different scale may be needed.

EXAMPLE

Plot 40 on the number line.

When there are several numbers to be plotted, the scale may be omitted if the numbers are labeled.

A different scale may call for using an estimation of the location of a point.

EXAMPLE

Plot 535 on the number line.

When there are several numbers to be plotted, the scale may be omitted if the numbers are labeled.

EXAMPLE

Plot 20, 239, 511, and 700 on the number line.

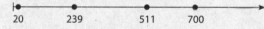

EXERCISE 1

The Number Line

Directions: Plot 39 and 65 on the number line.

Answer is on page 539.

Signed Numbers

The number line can be extended to the left of 0. The adjectives *positive* and *negative* distinguish numbers to the right of 0 from numbers to the left of 0. **Positive numbers** are the numbers to the right of 0; **negative numbers** are the numbers to the left of 0. A subtraction sign is written in front of a negative number to indicate that it is negative. A positive number may have an addition sign written in front of it, if desired, to emphasize that it is positive. Negative two is written –2, and positive two may be written +2 or 2, most commonly 2.

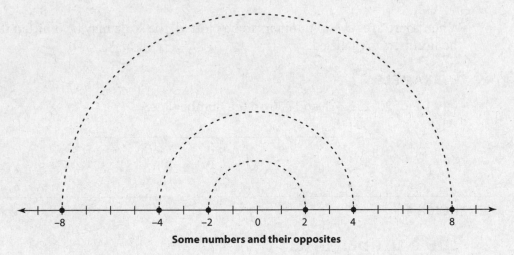

Negative numbers are used for quantities below zero. Depths underwater or cold temperatures are examples: 20 feet below the water's surface or 20 degrees below zero can both be represented by –20. Negative numbers are also used when a quantity gets smaller: if a car's speed changes from 60 mph to 50 mph, the change in speed is –10 mph. Numbers like 2 and –2, which differ only in sign, are said to be **opposites** of each other and are the same distance from 0 but on different sides of 0.

Some numbers and their opposites

A subtraction sign is also used to signify the opposite of a number. The opposite of –2 is –(–2), which is the same as +2. Note that –0 = 0. That is, 0 is its own opposite. Collectively, all the whole numbers together with their opposites and 0 are called **integers**.

EXERCISE 2

Signed Numbers

Directions: Answer the following questions.

1. Plot –4 with an arrow, and plot –7 with a dot.

2. Express each of the following quantities with a negative number.

  A. A debt of 20 dollars.
  B. A change in length from 30 inches to 22 inches.

3. A. What is the opposite of 5?   B. What is the opposite of –10?

Answers are on page 539.

Order

Given two distinct numbers, one number is either less than or greater than the other. The number line can be used to determine order, and the **inequality** symbols < and > are used to express the order. Geometrically, the symbol < **means "lies farther to the left on the number line"** and the symbol > **means "lies farther to the right on the number line."** Given the number line below, you can write two statements.

Because 215 is to the left of 784, you can write 215 < 784, and because 784 is to the right of 215, you can also write 784 > 215. You can write two such statements for any two distinct numbers on the number line.

When comparing two negative numbers, it might seem that the order is turned around. The statement –7 < –3 may not seem right until the relative position of the numbers is properly considered: since –7 is to the left of –3, –7 < –3. It is important to remember that the symbols < and > have nothing to do with the distance of a number from 0, but are used to make a statement about relative position of the two numbers on the number line. Also, every negative number is to the left of every positive number, so even a statement like –999,999 < 1 is a true statement.

There are two other inequality symbols that are common in mathematics. They are ≤ and ≥. Each is a combination of < or > and an equal sign. These symbols are used extensively in algebra; they will be discussed further in other chapters.

Absolute Value

Sometimes the distance of a number from zero is more important than on which side of 0 the number lies. Two vertical bars surrounding the number are used to designate the distance of the number from zero, or the **absolute**

value of the number. |–3| = 3, and also |3| = 3, because distance is a positive quantity. Absolute value can also be used to find the distance between any two numbers on the number line. This distance is always the absolute value of the difference of the numbers.

EXERCISE 3

Order and Absolute Value

Directions: Answer the following questions.

1. Place the correct symbol, < or >, between the two numbers.

   A. 423 _____ 425   B. –34 _____ –37   C. –6 _____ 4   D. 0 _____ –50

2. Find A. |–44| B. |12| C. –|11| D. –|–72|

Answers are on page 539.

Operations on Signed Numbers

Signed numbers may be added, subtracted, multiplied, and divided. The number line can be used to illustrate the rules for some of these operations.

Adding Signed Numbers

The geometric meaning of addition can be illustrated by head-to-tail arrows on the number line. The addition problem 5 + 3 = 8 is modeled on the number line below. The tail of the arrow representing the number coming after the addition sign is placed at the head of the arrow representing the number coming before the addition sign. The result is the same as a single arrow representing the sum.

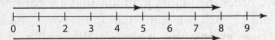

The sum –5 + (–3) can be found the same way: place the tail of an arrow representing –3 at the head of an arrow representing –5. The result is the same as an arrow representing –8.

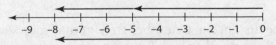

When modeling addition of numbers with different signs, the arrows would overlap if they were put head-to-tail because the arrow representing the negative number points to the left and the arrow representing the negative number points to the right. A slight offset can help make the illustration clearer. The addition 5 + (–3) is represented on the following number line. Adding –3 to 5 has the effect of moving 3 units to the left, so 5 + (–3) = 2.

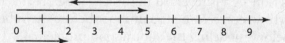

If the larger number were negative, as in the addition –5 + 3, the arrows would still point in opposite directions. From the diagram, –5 + 3 = –2.

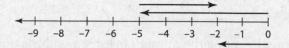

Computing 3 + 5 will give the same result as 5 + 3. There are only two computations that need to be performed to get any of the four sums obtained: either addition, to get 8 or –8, or subtraction, to get 2 or –2. When addition is used, the numbers added have the same sign, and the sum shares that sign. When subtraction is used, the difference shares the sign of the "longer" number—that is, the number with the larger absolute value. Thus, here is the general rule for adding two signed numbers:

To add two numbers with the same sign, add their absolute values and use the sign of the numbers added. To add two numbers with different signs, subtract their absolute values and use the sign of the number with the larger absolute value.

EXAMPLES

–8 + 3 = –5	9 + (–3) = 6	–2 + (–5) = –7
–5 + 7 = 2	–6 + (–2) = –8	4 + (–9) = –5

EXERCISE 4

Adding Signed Numbers

Directions: Solve the following items.

1. –23 + 17   2. 13 + (–20)   3. –11 + (–16)

4. 21 + (–15)   5. –14 + 18   6. –26 + (–13)

Answers are on page 539.

Subtracting Signed Numbers

Like addition, subtraction has a geometric interpretation, and it is very nearly the same as the geometric interpretation of addition. The only difference is that the arrow that represents the number that comes after the subtraction sign is reversed in direction before it is placed head-to-tail with the arrow representing the number before the subtraction sign. In the diagram below, modeling the subtraction problem $4 - 1 = 3$, notice how the arrow representing 1 points to the left instead of the right. This is a consequence of the subtraction operation.

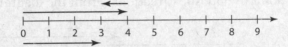

The arrow representing the number before the subtraction symbol is not reversed. Changing the direction of the arrow amounts to changing the sign of the number. Putting it head-to-tail with the other arrow signifies addition. Thus, here is the general rule for subtracting two signed numbers:

To subtract two signed numbers, change the sign of the number after the subtraction symbol and use the above rules for adding two signed numbers.

EXAMPLES

$-6 - 2 = -6 + (-2) = -8$ $6 - (-3) = 6 + 3 = 9$

$-2 - (-5) = -2 + 5 = 3$ $2 - (-7) = 2 + 7 = 9$

$-9 - (-7) = -9 + 7 = -2$ $4 - 9 = 4 + (-9) = -5$

$-3 - 4 = -3 + (-4) = -7$ $6 - 5 = 6 + (-5) = 1$

The distance between -5 and 3 is $|-5 - 3| = |-5 + (-3)| = |-8| = 8$.

The distance between -5 and -3 is $|-5 - (-3)| = |-5 + 3| = |-2| = 2$.

EXERCISE 5

Subtracting Signed Numbers

Directions: Solve the following items.

1. $42 - (-13)$ 2. $-53 - (-21)$ 3. $15 - 37$ 4. $-19 - 35$

5. $-44 - 23$ 6. $-17 - (-25)$ 7. $14 - (-36)$ 8. $31 - 22$

9. Find the distance between -4 and 11.

10. Find the distance between -7 and -2.

Answers are on page 539.

Multiplying and Dividing Signed Numbers

The rules for signs of products and quotients are identical: **The product or quotient of two numbers with the same sign is positive; the product or quotient of two numbers with different signs is negative.** There is no consideration for the size of the two numbers, only whether the signs are or aren't the same.

EXAMPLES

$-7(-8) = 56$ $6(-5) = -30$ $-4(5) = -20$

$32 \div (-4) = -8$ $-45 \div 9 = -5$ $-18 \div (-3) = -6$

EXERCISE 6

Multiplying and Dividing Signed Numbers

Directions: Solve the following items.

1. $-2(-6)$ **2.** $-5(3)$ **3.** $8(-5)$ **4.** $-3(-7)$

5. $-15 \div (-3)$ **6.** $-28 \div 7$ **7.** $6 \div (-2)$ **8.** $-36 \div (-9)$

Answers are on page 540.

The Coordinate Plane

The coordinate plane is formed by crossing two number lines at right angles where they are both equal to 0, so that one of the number lines is vertical, with positive values extending upward, while the other number line, which we have been using in this chapter, is horizontal, with positive values extending to the right. The horizontal number line is called the *x*-**axis,** and the vertical number line is called the *y*-**axis**.

Locations in the coordinate plane are identified by **ordered pairs**, two numbers enclosed in a pair of parentheses. In the plane that follows, point A has coordinates (6, 2), while point B has coordinates (2, 6). These are distinct points, so points A and B illustrate that the order of the two numbers in an ordered pair is important.

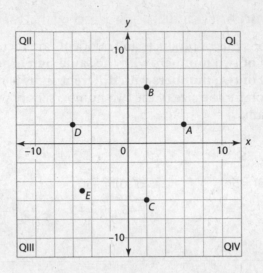

The Coordinate Plane

Directions: Find the coordinates of the given points using the plane above.

1. C   **2.** D   **3.** E

Answers are on page 540.

Quadrants and Coordinates

Zero, where the axes cross, is called the **origin** and has coordinates (0, 0). The axes divide the plane into four regions called **quadrants**, referred to as the first, second, third, and fourth quadrants, starting in the upper right quadrant and proceeding counterclockwise. Note that when two points have the same x-value but opposite y-values, the points are reflections of each other in the x-axis. Likewise, when two points have the same y-value but opposite x-values, the points are reflections of each other in the y-axis.

EXERCISE 8

Quadrants and Coordinates

1. In the preceding diagram, which pairs of points are reflections of each other, and in which coordinate axis?

2. In which quadrant do each the following pairs of conditions apply?

   A. *x*-values positive, *y*-values negative
   B. *x*-values negative, $y < 0$
   C. $x > 0, y > 0$
   D. $x < 0$, *y*-values positive

Answers are on page 540.

Multiples

A list of all of the multiples of a number is made by multiplying the number by 1, then multiplying the same number by 2, then multiplying the same number by 3, and so on.

EXAMPLE

List the multiples of 7.

Multiples of 7: $1 \cdot 7, 2 \cdot 7, 3 \cdot 7, 4 \cdot 7, 5 \cdot 7, 6 \cdot 7, 7 \cdot 7, \ldots$

Simplified, this is 7, 14, 21, 28, 35, 42, 49, . . .

Note that the list of multiples of a number never comes to an end.

Common Multiples

The **common multiples** of two or more numbers are the numbers that occur in all of the lists of multiples of the numbers in question. To find common multiples, list the multiples of the individual numbers and select the numbers that are in each list.

EXAMPLE

Find the common multiples of 5 and 7.

The multiples of 5: 5, 10, 15, 20, 25, 30, 35, 40, 45, 50, 55, 60, 65, 70, . . .

The multiples of 7: 7, 14, 21, 28, 35, 42, 49, 56, 63, 70, 77, 84, 91, 98, . . .

The common multiples of 5 and 7: 35, 70, 105, 140, . . .

The common multiples of more than two numbers may be found.

EXAMPLE

Find the common multiples of 4, 6, and 9.

The multiples of 4: 4, 8, 12, 16, 20, 24, 28, 32, 36, 40, 44, 48, 52, 56, 60, 64, 68, 72, 76, 80, . . .

The multiples of 6: 6, 12, 18, 24, 30, 36, 42, 48, 54, 60, 66, 72, 78, 84, . . .

The multiples of 9: 9, 18, 27, 36, 45, 54, 63, 72, 81, 90, 99, . . .

The common multiples of 4, 6, and 9: 36, 72, 108, . . .

Note that, like the list of multiples of a number, the list of common multiples of two or more numbers never comes to an end.

Least Common Multiple

The **least common multiple** of two or more numbers is the smallest number that occurs in the list of common multiples of the numbers. Referring to the above examples, the least common multiple of 5 and 7 is 35, and the least common multiple of 4, 6, and 9 is 36.

EXAMPLE

Find the least common multiple of 20 and 30.

Multiples of 20: 20, 40, 60, 80, 100, . . .

Multiples of 30: 30, 60, 90, 120, . . .

Common multiples: 60, 120, . . .

Least common multiple: 60

EXERCISE 9

Multiples

Directions: Answer the following questions.

1. Find the multiples of 9.

Find the common multiples of the following:

2. 10 and 15   **3.** 6, 8, and 10

Find the least common multiple of the following:

4. 10 and 12   **5.** 6, 8, and 9

Answers are on page 540.

Factors

The list of **factors** of a number is a list containing all of the number's divisors that leave a remainder of 0.

EXAMPLE

The factors of 12 are 1, 2, 3, 4, 6, and 12.

The list of factors of a number will always include 1 and the number itself. To find the factors of a number, divide the number by successive whole numbers until repetition begins.

EXAMPLE

Find all of the factors of 18.

$18 \div 1 = 18$ (no remainder)

$18 \div 2 = 9$ (no remainder)

$18 \div 3 = 6$ (no remainder)

$18 \div 4$ leaves a remainder

$18 \div 5$ leaves a remainder

$18 \div 6 = 3$: Repetition begins here.

The factors of 18 are the divisors that left no remainder and the corresponding quotients: 1, 2, 3, 6, 9, and 18.

Divisibility Tests

There are some easy-to-use tests that can help determine whether a number is divisible by 2, 3, 4, 5, 6, 9, or 10.

A number is divisible by	if
2	the units digit (final digit) is 0, 2, 4, 6, or 8
3	the sum of the digits is divisible by 3
4	the last two digits are divisible by 4
5	the units digit is 0 or 5
6	it is divisible by both 2 and 3
9	the sum of the digits is divisible by 9
10	the units digit is 0
12	it is divisible by both 3 and 4
15	it is divisible by both 3 and 5
20	it is divisible by both 4 and 5

Common Factors

The **common factors** of two or more numbers are the numbers that occur in all of the lists of factors of the numbers in question.

EXAMPLE

Find the common factors of 12 and 18.

The factors of 12 are 1, 2, 3, 4, 6, and 12.

The factors of 18 are 1, 2, 3, 6, 9, and 18.

The common factors of 12 and 18 are 1, 2, 3, and 6.

EXAMPLE

Find the common factors of 15 and 20.

The factors of 15 are 1, 3, 5, and 15.

The factors of 20 are 1, 2, 4, 5, 10, and 20.

The common factors of 15 and 20 are 1 and 5.

Greatest Common Factor

The **greatest common factor** of two or more numbers is the largest number that occurs in the list of common factors of the numbers. From the preceding examples, you can see that the greatest common factor of 12 and 18 is 6, and the greatest common factor of 15 and 20 is 5.

EXERCISE 10

Factors

Directions: Answer the following questions.

1. List the factors of 32.

List the common factors of the following:

2. 20 and 30   **3.** 24, 32, and 36

Find the greatest common factor of the following:

4. 24 and 36   **5.** 40, 50, and 60

Answers are on page 540.

Division by Zero

Division by zero is not allowed in mathematics. To understand why, consider the connection between division and multiplication. The multiplication sentence $12 = 3 \cdot 4$ can be written as the division sentence $12 \div 3 = 4$. Suppose for a moment that division by zero were possible, and the result was a whole number. Then a division sentence might be $12 \div 0 = \#$. What multiplication sentence corresponds to this? It would be $12 = 0 \cdot \#$, but this would mean that the product of any number and 0 would not be 0! This contradicts what you know about multiplying by 0.

CHAPTER 2

Exponents and Properties of Numbers

Exponents, Roots, and Number Properties

Exponents

Multiplication can be regarded as a notational shorthand for repeated addition of the same number. For example, the repeated addition $5 + 5 + 5$ may be written $3 \cdot 5$. In a like manner, repeated multiplication of the same number has a notational shorthand called **exponentiation**. A repeated multiplication such as $5 \cdot 5 \cdot 5$ is written 5^3 and is read "five raised to the power of three," or "five raised to the third power," or "five to the third." The superscript, 3 in the example, is called an **exponent** or a **power**, and the number to which it is attached, 5 in the example, is called a **base**. Unlike the factors in a multiplication statement, the exponent and base are not interchangeable: $5^3 = 5 \cdot 5 \cdot 5 = 125$, while $3^5 = 3 \cdot 3 \cdot 3 \cdot 3 \cdot 3 = 243$. Note that the exponent tells how many equal bases are being multiplied, not how many multiplications are performed. When an exponential expression is written as repeated multiplication of the same base, the number of multiplication symbols is one less than the exponent. In the formal definition that follows, letters called variables are used to represent numbers, so that the definition can be said to hold for the widest range of values possible.

> **Definition:** If x is any number and n is any positive integer, then
>
> $$x^n = \underbrace{x \cdot x \cdot x \cdot \cdots \cdot x,}_{n \text{ factors}}$$
>
> where the repeated factor x is understood to occur n times on the right side of the equal sign.

The three dots, called an ellipsis, are meant to indicate that an established pattern continues as shown. They are needed in the definition because you do not have a specific value for the exponent and so you cannot write a specific number of factors. Variables are also used to state properties in arithmetic and algebra in as general a form as possible.

EXAMPLE

In 9^7, which number is the base and which is the exponent?

The base is 9 and the exponent is 7.

EXAMPLES

Write with an exponent: **1.** $2 \cdot 2 \cdot 2 \cdot 2 \cdot 2 \cdot 2$ **2.** $7 \cdot 7 \cdot 7 \cdot 7$

1. 2^6 **2.** 7^4

EXAMPLES

Write as repeated multiplication: **1.** 16^3 **2.** 9^{12}

1. $16 \cdot 16 \cdot 16$ **2.** $9 \cdot 9 \cdot 9 \cdot 9 \cdot 9 \cdot 9 \cdot 9 \cdot 9 \cdot 9 \cdot 9 \cdot 9 \cdot 9$

EXAMPLES

Compute: **1.** 6^2 **2.** 2^4

1. $6^2 = 6 \cdot 6 = 36$ **2.** $2^4 = 2 \cdot 2 \cdot 2 \cdot 2 = 4 \cdot 4 = 16$

EXERCISE 1

Exponents

Directions: Answer the following questions.

1. Identify the base and the exponent in the expression 24^{73}.

2. Write with an exponent:

   A. $2 \cdot 2 \cdot 2 \cdot 2 \cdot 2 \cdot 2$ **B.** $5 \cdot 5 \cdot 5 \cdot 5 \cdot 5 \cdot 5 \cdot 5 \cdot 5$

3. Write as repeated multiplication: **A.** 6^4 **B.** 7^{10}

4. Compute: **A.** 4^5 **B.** 7^3

Answers are on page 540.

Exponents—Special Cases

There are a few instances of exponential expressions that deserve special mention. When the exponent is 2, as in 5^2, the exponential expression is often read as "the square of five" or "five squared." Likewise, an exponent of 3, in an expression such as 5^3, is often read "the cube of five" or "five cubed." There are no special ways to read other exponents.

Exponents of 1 or 0

When the exponent is 1, the value of the entire exponential expression is the same as the base; that is, $5^1 = 5$, $0^1 = 0$, $3^1 = 3$, and so on. When the exponent is 0 and the base is not 0, the value of the entire exponential expression is 1. This might be better understood when you look at the patterns on both sides of a partial list of powers of 2:

$$2^5 = 2 \cdot 2 \cdot 2 \cdot 2 \cdot 2 = 32$$
$$2^4 = 2 \cdot 2 \cdot 2 \cdot 2 = 16$$
$$2^3 = 2 \cdot 2 \cdot 2 = 8$$
$$2^2 = 2 \cdot 2 = 4$$
$$2^1 = 2 = 2$$
$$2^0 = 1$$

The pattern on the left is that the exponent gets smaller by 1 in each successive line, from 5 to 0. The pattern on the right is that the numbers are half of the number on the previous line; half of 32 is 16, half of 16 is 8, half of 8 is 4, half of 4 is 2, and finally, half of 2 is 1, so $2^0 = 1$. If a different base were to be used, such as 3, the fraction would be a third instead of a half, so $3^0 = 1$; with a base of 5, the fraction would be a fifth, so $5^0 = 1$.

$$3^5 = 3 \cdot 3 \cdot 3 \cdot 3 \cdot 3 = 243 \qquad 5^5 = 5 \cdot 5 \cdot 5 \cdot 5 \cdot 5 = 312!$$
$$3^4 = 3 \cdot 3 \cdot 3 \cdot 3 = 81 \qquad 5^4 = 5 \cdot 5 \cdot 5 \cdot 5 = 625$$
$$3^3 = 3 \cdot 3 \cdot 3 = 27 \qquad 5^3 = 5 \cdot 5 \cdot 5 = 125$$
$$3^2 = 3 \cdot 3 = 9 \qquad 5^2 = 5 \cdot 5 = 25$$
$$3^1 = 3 = 3 \qquad 5^1 = 5 = 5$$
$$3^0 = 1 \qquad 5^0 = 1$$

The previous discussion about powers equal to 1 or 0 prompts the following definitions:

Definition: if x is any number, then $x^1 = x$.

Definition: if x is any non-zero number, $x^0 = 1$.

Bases of 0 or 1

The last two special cases to be considered are bases that are equal to 0 or 1. Both special cases are consequences of the multiplication properties of these numbers.

Multiplication Property of 0: for any number x, $0 \cdot x = 0$.

Multiplication Property of 1: for any number x, $1 \cdot x = x$.

What is 0^4? $0^4 = 0 \cdot 0 \cdot 0 \cdot 0 = 0$. What if the exponent were a different number? There would be a different number of 0s multiplied, but the result would still be 0. How about 1^6? $1^6 = 1 \cdot 1 \cdot 1 \cdot 1 \cdot 1 \cdot 1 = 1$. If the exponent were a different number, there would be a different number of 1s multiplied, but the result would still be 1.

If n is any number, then $1^n = 1$.

If n is any positive number, then $0^n = 0$.

You may have noticed that the value of 0^0 is not addressed in the previous discussion. In higher mathematics, the occurrence of 0^0 requires special attention. When it does occur, it could have a value of 0 or 1 or some other number. For the purposes of arithmetic, the expression is left undefined.

0^0 is undefined.

EXAMPLES

Evaluate each of the following:

1. 6^0 **2.** 9^1 **3.** 1^4 **4.** 0^7 **5.** 0^0

1. $6^0 = 1$ **2.** $9^1 = 9$ **3.** $1^4 = 1$ **4.** $0^7 = 0$

5. 0^0 is undefined

Powers of 10

Another special case arises when considering powers of 10. Notice the pattern in the list:

$$10^0 = 1$$
$$10^1 = 10$$
$$10^2 = 100$$
$$10^3 = 1,000$$
$$10^4 = 10,000$$
$$10^5 = 100,000$$

Any of those powers of 10 may be verified by expanding the exponential expression into repeated multiplication of the appropriate number of 10s and carrying out the multiplication. For example, $10^3 = 10 \cdot 10 \cdot 10 = 100 \cdot 10 = 1,000$. The pattern that makes this a special case is that no computation is necessary to evaluate a power of 10. Instead, write a 1 followed by a number of 0s specified by the exponent. 10^3 is a 1 followed by three 0s.

EXAMPLES

Evaluate:

1. 10^{10} **2.** 10^{14}

1. $10^{10} = 10,000,000,000$ **2.** $10^{14} = 100,000,000,000,000$

EXAMPLES

Write with an exponent:

1. 1,000,000,000,000   **2.** 10,000,000

1. 10^{12} **2.** 10^7

EXERCISE 2

Exponents—Special Cases

Directions: Evaluate each of the following:

1. 1^{17} **2.** 0^{10} **3.** 0^0 **4.** 3^1 **5.** 7^0 **6.** 10^{11} **7.** 10^9

Write with an exponent:

8. 1,000,000   **9.** 10,000,000,000,000

Answers are on page 541.

Negative Bases

Bases can often be negative numbers, which will affect the sign of the product of an exponential expression. How the sign comes out is a consequence of the rule for multiplying signed numbers. Since the product of two negative numbers is positive, and since positive signs are usually not explicitly written, an expression like $(-2)^4$ can be evaluated by considering pairs of negative signs "canceling out": $(-2)^4 = (-2)(-2)(-2)(-2) = 4 \cdot 4 = 16$. Likewise, in $(-2)^5$ pairs of negative signs would cancel out, but there would be a negative sign left over: $(-2)^5 = (-2)(-2)(-2)(-2)(-2) = 4 \cdot 4(-2) = 16(-2) = -32$. In short, **a negative number raised to an even power comes out positive, while a negative number raised to an odd power comes out negative**.

> If n is even, then $(-1)^n = +1$.
>
> If n is odd, then $(-1)^n = -1$.

Be careful about the position of the negative sign. In the expression -2^4, the base is positive, and after evaluation of 2^4, the sign is to be changed. Compare $-2^4 = -(2 \cdot 2 \cdot 2 \cdot 2) = -16$ with $(-2)^4 = (-2)(-2)(-2)(-2) = +16$.

EXAMPLES

Evaluate:

1. $(-3)^2$	**2.** $(-4)^3$	**3.** -7^2	**4.** $-(-2)^3$	**5.** $-(-1)^4$
1. 9	**2.** −64	**3.** −49	**4.** 8	**5.** −1

EXERCISE 3

Negative Bases

Directions: Evaluate each of the following:

1. -6^3	**2.** $-(-1)^{11}$	**3.** $(-5)^2$	**4.** $-(-2)^6$	**5.** $(-2)^7$

Answers are on page 541.

Roots and Radicals

Square Roots

Exponents equal to 2 were previously mentioned as a special case. An exponent of 2 is often read "squared," as in 3^2 = "three squared." You can also say that the square of 3 is 9. Conversely, **square roots** allow you to go the other way, as in "the square root of 9 is 3," written as a **radical expression**, $\sqrt{9} = 3$. The symbol that looks like a division symbol with a hook, $\sqrt{}$, is called a **radical sign,** and the number beneath it, 9, is called a **radicand**. Likewise, $\sqrt{25} = 5$, because $5^2 = 25$, and $\sqrt{196} = 14$, because $14^2 = 196$.

> **Definition:** a is the **square root** of a positive number x if $a^2 = x$. You write
>
> $$a = \sqrt{x}.$$

The requirement that x be positive in the definition exists because of the rule for multiplying two negative numbers. You can't say that $\sqrt{-4} = -2$, because $(-2)^2 = 4$, not -4. The square roots of negative numbers generally remain undefined.

Most numbers aren't perfect squares and don't have whole-number square roots. In those cases you have a choice of either settling for a decimal approximation or a simplified exact equivalence. For instance, 12 is not a perfect square, but it lies between the consecutive perfect squares 9 and 16. $9 < 12 < 16$, so $\sqrt{9} < \sqrt{12} < \sqrt{16}$, or $3 < \sqrt{12} < 4$, so $\sqrt{12}$ is between 3 and 4. Next, compute $3.5^2 = 12.25$. Since that is larger than 12, you can refine the estimate by replacing 4 with 3.5: $3 < \sqrt{12} < 3.5$. Continuing in this manner you can approximate $\sqrt{12}$ to any number of decimal places you desire. An alternative depends on a multiplication property of square roots:

$$\text{For positive } a \text{ and } b, \sqrt{ab} = \sqrt{a}\sqrt{b}.$$

So $\sqrt{12} = \sqrt{4 \cdot 3} = \sqrt{4}\sqrt{3} = 2\sqrt{3}$ is a simplified, but exact, equivalence. The idea is to write the radicand as the product of a perfect square and another whole number. There may be more than one perfect square factor, in which case they may be extracted all at once or a few at a time. For example, $\sqrt{72} = \sqrt{36 \cdot 2} = \sqrt{36}\sqrt{2} = 6\sqrt{2}$, extracting squares all at once, or $\sqrt{72} = \sqrt{4 \cdot 18} = \sqrt{4}\sqrt{18} = 2\sqrt{18} = 2\sqrt{9 \cdot 2} = 2\sqrt{9}\sqrt{2} = 2 \cdot 3\sqrt{2} = 6\sqrt{2}$, extracting squares one at a time.

Cube Roots

Just as squares lead to square roots, cubes lead to cube roots. Since $2^3 = 8$, the cube root of 8 is 2, or $\sqrt[3]{8} = 2$. The small number 3 in the radical sign is called the **index** and is used to distinguish roots. The index for square roots is understood to be 2.

> **Definition:** a is the **cube root** of a number x if $a^3 = x$. You write
>
> $$a = \sqrt[3]{x}\,.$$

The restriction that x be positive is not needed with cube roots as it is with square roots. $\sqrt[3]{-8} = -2$ because $(-2)^3 = -8$.

Simplification of cube roots proceeds in a manner like that for square roots, by use of a multiplication property of cube roots similar to that for square roots:

$$\text{For all } a \text{ and } b,\ \sqrt[3]{ab} = \sqrt[3]{a}\sqrt[3]{b}.$$

To use this property to simplify cube roots, a should be a perfect cube so that perfect cube factors are extracted instead of perfect square factors. For instance, $\sqrt[3]{72} = \sqrt[3]{8 \cdot 9} = \sqrt[3]{8} \cdot \sqrt[3]{9} = 2\sqrt[3]{9}$. As with square roots, the perfect cube factors can be extracted one at a time or all at once, as seen in the next example.

EXAMPLE

$$\sqrt[3]{2000} = \sqrt[3]{1000 \cdot 2} = \sqrt[3]{1000}\sqrt[3]{2} = 10\sqrt[3]{2}$$

$$\text{Alternately, } \sqrt[3]{2000} = \sqrt[3]{8 \cdot 250} = \sqrt[3]{8}\sqrt[3]{250} = 2\sqrt[3]{250}$$
$$= 2\sqrt[3]{125 \cdot 2} = 2\sqrt[3]{125}\sqrt[3]{2} = 2 \cdot 5\sqrt[3]{2} = 10\sqrt[3]{2}$$

Radicals don't stop with square roots and cube roots. There are fourth roots, fifth roots, ninth roots, twelfth roots, etc. In general, any positive whole number can be the index of a radical.

> **Definition:** For a positive whole number n, a is the **nth root** of a number x if $a^n = x$. You write
>
> $$a = \sqrt[n]{x}.$$

The GED test doesn't go beyond square roots and cube roots.

Roots and Radicals

Directions: Evaluate the following:

1. $\sqrt{64}$ 2. $\sqrt{225}$ 3. $\sqrt{-49}$ 4. $\sqrt[3]{125}$ 5. $\sqrt[3]{-27}$

Simplify the following:

6. $\sqrt{24}$ 7. $\sqrt{45}$ 8. $\sqrt{162}$ 9. $\sqrt[3]{81}$ 10. $\sqrt[3]{432}$

Answers are on page 541.

Properties of Numbers

There are several properties of numbers that you may use when performing calculations. These properties involve only addition and multiplication; there are no equivalent properties for subtraction and division.

Commutative Properties

What is the difference between $5 + 7$ and $7 + 5$? They are the same, as can be seen by carrying out the additions. The **Commutative Property of Addition** says this is always the case, no matter what two numbers are being added. Likewise, the **Commutative Property of Multiplication** says that similar statements for multiplication are also true. For instance, $9 \cdot 4 = 4 \cdot 9$, as can be seen by carrying out the multiplications.

Commutative Property of Addition: For any numbers a and b,
$$a + b = b + a$$

Commutative Property of Multiplication: For any numbers a and b,
$$ab = ba$$

Note: Multiplication symbols are often not used with variables. The expression "xy" means "x times y."

Associative Properties

When adding three numbers, which two numbers should be added first? The **Associative Property of Addition** says that, for example, $4 + (6 + 2) = (4 + 6) + 2$. For this reason, such a problem is usually written without grouping symbols indicating which addition to find first, as in $4 + 6 + 2$. The Associative Property of Addition makes it possible to write the addition of several numbers without multiple pairs of grouping symbols instructing how the additions have to be carried out. Without this property, an addition like $8 + 2 + 7 + 1 + 9 + 3 + 5$ might need to be written as $(((((8 + 2) + 7) + 1) + 9) + 3) + 5$. Taken together, the Associative and Commutative Properties for Addition allow the computation to be carried out by regrouping the numbers in any manner that is convenient, so that the total might even be worked out in your head. The 8 and 2 could be grouped together, as could the 9 and 1, and the 7 and 3. That gives 30, with 5 left over, so the total of 35 could be found in your head.

There is also an **Associative Property of Multiplication**, which says that, for example, $4 \cdot (6 \cdot 2) = (4 \cdot 6) \cdot 2$. For this reason, this multiplication is normally written $4 \cdot 6 \cdot 2$. The Associative Property of Multiplication has advantages for computation similar to those of the property for addition. It disposes of the need for multiple pairs of grouping symbols when there are several numbers being multiplied, and together with the commutative property of multiplication, allows for the possibility of efficient mental calculations.

> **Associative Property of Addition:** For any numbers a, b, and c,
>
> $$a + (b + c) = (a + b) + c = a + b + c$$

> **Associative Property of Multiplication:** For any numbers a, b, and c,
>
> $$a(bc) = (ab)c = abc$$

The Distributive Property

A property that involves both operations, addition and multiplication, is the **Distributive Property**. An example of this property is $10(3 + 6) = 10 \cdot 3 + 10 \cdot 6$. Again, this can be verified by carrying out the calculations. Follow the proper order of operations to get $10 \cdot 9 = 30 + 60$, and then $90 = 90$. The most common use of the Distributive Property is with variables, so that variable expressions may be rewritten when the order of operations cannot be followed.

> **The Distributive Property:** For any numbers a, b, and c,
>
> $$a(b + c) = ab + ac$$

There are actually an infinite number of Distributive Properties, one with subtraction instead of addition, one with three terms inside the grouping symbols instead of two, one with three terms including both addition and subtraction, one with four terms inside, one with the factor on the right, etc. A plain-language translation captures them all: Multiply the quantity on the outside of the grouping symbols by each of the quantities on the inside of the grouping symbols.

EXAMPLES

$7(6 - 2) = 42 - 14$ $-5(2 - 7 + 6) = -10 + 35 - 30$

$4(7 + 5 - 2) = 28 + 20 - 8$ $(5 + 7 - 2)3 = 15 + 21 - 6$

The Transitive Properties

Another property provides a means to combine two or more statements into a single statement. The Transitive Property of Equality is used when two different expressions are both equal to a common third quantity, as in $7 + 2 = 9$, and $9 = 3^2$, so $7 + 2 = 3^2$. It might be said that the Transitive Property "cuts out the middleman," the middleman being the number 9 in the example. The Transitive Property is not often used in ordinary arithmetic, but it is very handy for finding new connections in other areas of mathematics. There are also Transitive Properties for each of the different inequality symbols that are used in mathematics. These Transitive Properties also "cut out the middleman." For instance, $-7 < 0$ and $0 < 5$, so $-7 < 5$

The Transitive Property of Equality: For any numbers a, b, and c,

if $a = b$ and $b = c$, then $a = c$.

The Transitive Property of Inequality: For any numbers a, b, and c,

if $a < b$ and $b < c$, then $a < c$.

(There are three more transitive properties of inequality, one that uses the inequality symbol > instead of <, one that uses ≤, and one that uses ≥.)

If there is more than one "middleman" involved, they can all be "cut out" at once with what amounts to repeated use of the appropriate Transitive Property: if $x < a + b$ and $a + b < c$ and $c < 3$ and $3 < w$, then $x < w$. The type of symbol, whether it is =, <, >, ≤, or ≥, must be the same in each statement. Any occurrence of more than one type of symbol prohibits use of the Transitive Property.

EXAMPLES

If $x > 2$ and $2 > -1$, then $x > -1$.

If $2 \le p$ and $p \le z$, then $2 \le z$.

If $s \ge 11$ and $11 \ge t$, then $s \ge t$.

EXERCISE 5

Properties of Numbers

Directions: Answer each of the following questions.

Which is a use of a Commutative Property? Which is a use of an Associative Property?

1. $(4 \cdot 7) \cdot 3 = 4 \cdot (7 \cdot 3)$ **2.** $9 + 2 = 2 + 9$

Use the Distributive Property to write each statement as a sum or difference.

3. $7(5 - 2)$ **4.** $(2 + 6)9$ **5.** $3(8 + 1 + 5)$

Use the Transitive Property to write a single statement.

6. $x = 5$ and $5 = a$ **7.** $6 \le v$ and $v \le x$

8. $2 = d$ and $d = r$ and $r = y$ **9.** $p > q$ and $q > 7$ and $7 > a$

Answers are on page 541.

Properties of Exponents

The Product Rule

Work with exponents is made easier through the use of properties of exponents. The first of these addresses products of expressions with equal bases, as in $3^7 \cdot 3^5$. Expanding each factor as repeated multiplication of 3 gives $(3 \cdot 3 \cdot 3 \cdot 3 \cdot 3 \cdot 3 \cdot 3)(3 \cdot 3 \cdot 3 \cdot 3 \cdot 3)$. Because of the associative and commutative properties of multiplication, this is the same as $3 \cdot 3 \cdot 3 \cdot 3 \cdot 3 \cdot 3 \cdot 3 \cdot 3 \cdot 3 \cdot 3 \cdot 3 \cdot 3$, and writing this with an exponent gives 3^{12}. What's the shortcut? How can 3^{12} be produced from $3^7 \cdot 3^5$ without going through all of the expanding and rewriting in between? It looks like the only thing that needs to be done is to add the exponents, but does that make sense? Considering what happened in the expanding and rewriting steps, where 7 factors and 5 factors were combined to get a total of 12 factors, it seems to make perfect sense. This is the basis for the first property of exponents.

> **The Product Rule:** For any positive numbers a, m, and n,
> $$a^m \cdot a^n = a^{m+n}$$

This property applies to more than two factors, as long as the bases are equal.

EXAMPLES

$$5^8 \cdot 5^4 \cdot 5^2 = 5^{14} \qquad x^3 \cdot x^7 = x^{10} \qquad 7^p \cdot 7^q = 7^{p+q}$$

$$13^3 \cdot 13^4 \cdot 13 \cdot 13^2 = 13^{10} \qquad 2^5 \cdot 11^3 \text{ can't be rewritten}$$

The Factor Rule

Another property that applies to multiplication allows an exponent to be shared among the factors of a number. It also relies on the associative and commutative properties of multiplication. For example, $21^5 = (3 \cdot 7)^5 = (3 \cdot 7)(3 \cdot 7)(3 \cdot 7)(3 \cdot 7)(3 \cdot 7) = (3 \cdot 3 \cdot 3 \cdot 3 \cdot 3)(7 \cdot 7 \cdot 7 \cdot 7 \cdot 7) = 3^5 \cdot 7^5$. The shortcut is to directly apply the exponent to each of the factors.

> **The Factor Rule:** For any positive numbers a, b, and n,
> $$(ab)^n = a^n b^n$$

Like the previous property, this could be applied to more than two factors, as in $30^8 = (2 \cdot 3 \cdot 5)^8 = 2^8 \cdot 3^8 \cdot 5^8$.

EXAMPLES

$$6^4 = (2 \cdot 3)^4 = 2^4 \cdot 3^4 \qquad\qquad 15^7 = 3^7 \cdot 5^7$$

$$70^{12} = 2^{12} \cdot 5^{12} \cdot 7^{12} \qquad\qquad (10x)^6 = 2^6 \cdot 5^6 \cdot x^6$$

Both of the properties might be needed.

EXAMPLES

$$15^4 \cdot 21^2 = 3^4 \cdot 5^4 \cdot 3^2 \cdot 7^2 = 3^6 \cdot 5^4 \cdot 7^2 \quad (2x)^5 (3x)^4 = 2^5 \cdot 3^4 x^9$$

$$6^3 \cdot 10^2 \cdot 15^6 = 2^3 \cdot 3^3 \cdot 2^2 \cdot 5^2 \cdot 3^6 \cdot 5^6 = 2^5 \cdot 3^9 \cdot 5^8$$

EXERCISE 6

The Product Rule and the Factor Rule

Directions: Use the Product Rule to rewrite the following.

1. $2^3 \cdot 2^8$ **2.** $10^x \cdot 10^3$ **3.** $7^3 \cdot 3^7$ **4.** $x^3 \cdot x^2$ **5.** $4^6 \cdot 4^3 \cdot 4^5$

Use the Factor Rule to rewrite the following.

6. 14^3 **7.** $(5x)^4$ **8.** 10^8 **9.** $(21a)^5$ **10.** $(11xy)^9$

Use the Product Rule and the Factor Rule to rewrite the following.

11. $10^6 \cdot 15^4$ **12.** $6^x \cdot 10^y$ **13.** $(5x)^3 (2x)^6$ **14.** $35^3 \cdot 15^2 \cdot 21^5$

Answers are on page 541.

The Quotient Rule

The Product Rule says that multiplying like bases is done by adding exponents. The Quotient Rule says that dividing like bases is done by subtracting exponents. This rule is helpful when reducing fractions to terms. In an expression such as $\dfrac{2^7}{2^4}$ there are more factors lowest than are necessary to specify the value of the number. After expanding each of the exponents into $\dfrac{2 \cdot 2 \cdot 2 \cdot 2 \cdot 2 \cdot 2 \cdot 2}{2 \cdot 2 \cdot 2 \cdot 2}$, there is the opportunity to remove common factors a pair at a time, one factor from the numerator with one from the denominator.

$$\frac{2 \cdot 2 \cdot 2 \cdot 2 \cdot 2 \cdot 2 \cdot 2}{2 \cdot 2 \cdot 2 \cdot 2} = \frac{2 \cdot 2 \cdot 2 \cdot 2 \cdot 2 \cdot 2}{2 \cdot 2 \cdot 2} = \frac{2 \cdot 2 \cdot 2 \cdot 2 \cdot 2}{2 \cdot 2} = \frac{2 \cdot 2 \cdot 2 \cdot 2}{2}$$

$$= \frac{2 \cdot 2 \cdot 2}{1} = \frac{2^3}{1}.$$

The last fraction is the same as 2^3, and after writing 2^3, the shortcut from $\dfrac{2^7}{2^4}$ seems to be to subtract the exponents. This makes sense because you need to know how many factors are left over after all the cancelling has been done. Take care to leave the factors in the proper location. If the original fraction had been $\dfrac{2^4}{2^7}$, the exponents could still be expanded and the common factors could still be canceled, but the extra factors would remain in the denominator since there were more factors there to begin with.

$$\frac{2 \cdot 2 \cdot 2 \cdot 2}{2 \cdot 2 \cdot 2 \cdot 2 \cdot 2 \cdot 2 \cdot 2} = \frac{2 \cdot 2 \cdot 2}{2 \cdot 2 \cdot 2 \cdot 2 \cdot 2 \cdot 2} = \frac{2 \cdot 2}{2 \cdot 2 \cdot 2 \cdot 2 \cdot 2} = \frac{2}{2 \cdot 2 \cdot 2 \cdot 2}$$

$$= \frac{1}{2 \cdot 2 \cdot 2} = \frac{1}{2^3}.$$

The shortcut is still subtracting the exponents, but the last fraction, $\frac{1}{2^3}$, cannot be written without the fraction bar. Because there could be more factors on top or on bottom of a fraction, the Quotient Rule comes in two parts.

> **The Quotient Rule:** For any positive numbers a, m, and n,
>
> $$\frac{a^m}{a^n} = a^{m-n} \text{ when } m > n$$
>
> $$\frac{a^m}{a^n} = \frac{1}{a^{n-m}} \text{ when } n > m$$

When the exponent on top is larger ($m > n$), subtract the exponent on bottom from the exponent on top, and put the result in the numerator of a fraction. If there are no factors remaining in the denominator, write as a whole number to a power. When the exponent on bottom is larger ($n > m$), subtract the exponent on top from the exponent on bottom and put the result in the denominator of a fraction. When the exponents are equal, all of the factors involved cancel, leaving 1s behind.

EXAMPLES

$$\frac{5^9}{5^3} = 5^6 \qquad \frac{8^5}{8^{12}} = \frac{1}{8^7} \qquad \frac{a^5}{a^2} = a^3 \qquad \frac{x^{10}}{x^{14}} = \frac{1}{x^4}$$

Both parts of the rule may be used together.

EXAMPLES

$$\frac{2^7 3^4}{2^2 3^6} = \frac{2^5}{3^2} \qquad \frac{5^4 8^7}{5^3 8^7} = 5 \qquad \frac{3^3 x^7}{3^9 x^3} = \frac{x^4}{3^6} \qquad \frac{x^5 y^4}{x^5 y^8} = \frac{1}{y^4}$$

EXERCISE 7

The Quotient Rule

Directions: Rewrite the following using the Quotient Rule.

1. $\dfrac{5^8}{5^2}$ 2. $\dfrac{8^4}{8^6}$ 3. $\dfrac{x^7}{x^3}$ 4. $\dfrac{3^9 a^6}{3^5 a^8}$ 5. $\dfrac{n^2 x^8}{n^4 x^5}$

Answers are on page 542.

The Fraction Rule

The rule for multiplying fractions says that all numerators are multiplied together and all denominators are multiplied together. This leads to a shortcut for raising a fraction to a power.

$$\left(\frac{2}{3}\right)^4 = \left(\frac{2}{3}\right)\left(\frac{2}{3}\right)\left(\frac{2}{3}\right)\left(\frac{2}{3}\right) = \frac{2\cdot2\cdot2\cdot2}{3\cdot3\cdot3\cdot3} = \frac{2^4}{3^4}$$

It looks like the shortcut is to raise both the numerator and the denominator to the power to which the fraction is raised. And in fact, this is what the Fraction Rule says.

The Fraction Rule: For any positive numbers a, b, and n,

$$\left(\frac{a}{b}\right)^n = \frac{a^n}{b^n}$$

EXAMPLES

$$\left(\frac{5}{7}\right)^6 = \frac{5^6}{7^6} \qquad \left(\frac{x}{4}\right)^9 = \frac{x^9}{4^9} \qquad \left(\frac{4}{9}\right)^n = \frac{4^n}{9^n} \qquad \left(2\frac{1}{3}\right)^3 = \left(\frac{7}{3}\right)^3 = \frac{7^3}{3^3}$$

The Power Rule

In an expression like $\left(7^3\right)^2$, a number is raised to a power twice in succession. A shortcut can be found by expanding the outer exponent, and then using the Product Rule. $\left(7^3\right)^2 = 7^3 \cdot 7^3 = 7^6$. The operation used to get a 6 from a 2 and a 3 is multiplication, so when a number is raised to a power twice in succession, a simplified form can be written by multiplying the powers. This is the Power rule.

The Power Rule: For any positive numbers a, m, and n,
$$(a^m)^n = a^{mn}$$

EXAMPLES

$$\left(3^5\right)^7 = 3^{35} \qquad \left(5^n\right)^4 = 5^{4n} \qquad \left(x^6\right)^2 = x^{12} \qquad \left(s^8\right)^p = s^{8p}$$

EXERCISE 8

The Power Rule

Directions: Use the Power Rule to evaluate the following items.

1. $\left(2^3\right)^4$ **2.** $\left(x^2\right)^3$ **3.** $\left(3^4\right)^r$ **4.** $\left(7^a\right)^5$ **5.** $\left(x^n\right)^3$

Answers are on page 542.

EXERCISE 9

Exponent Rules

Directions: Use the exponent rules to evaluate the following items.

1. $\left(x^4\right)^2\left(x^3\right)^5$ **2.** $\left(\dfrac{3^5}{5^3}\right)^4$ **3.** $\left(3x^7\right)^2$ **4.** $\left(\dfrac{2x}{7y}\right)^3$

5. $\left(2x^3\right)^5\left(2x^4\right)^2$ **6.** $\left(p^5q^2\right)^3$ **7.** $\dfrac{\left(r^3\right)^5}{\left(r^7\right)^4}$ **8.** $\dfrac{\left(a^3x^5\right)^3}{\left(b^2y^6\right)^2}$

Answers are on page 542.

Negative Exponents

The definition of *exponent* requires that an exponent be a positive whole number. The Quotient Rule comes in two parts, with conditions that help determine which part to use. Ignoring those conditions leads to a way to attach meaning to negative exponents. If someone wasn't paying close attention to the conditions and applied the first part of the rule to the quotient $\dfrac{3^5}{3^7}$, the result would be $3^{5-7} = 3^{-2}$. The calculations were performed correctly, but what does an exponent of –2 mean? It can't specify the number of bases being multiplied, because that can only be a positive number. Correctly applying the second part of the rule produces $\dfrac{1}{3^{7-5}} = \dfrac{1}{3^2}$.

It appears that $\dfrac{3^5}{3^7} = 3^{-2}$, but also that $\dfrac{3^5}{3^7} = \dfrac{1}{3^2}$, so by the transitive property of equality, maybe $3^{-2} = \dfrac{1}{3^2}$. In fact, discussions like this can lead you to the following definition.

Definition: If x is any non-zero number and n is a positive whole number, then

$$x^{-n} = \frac{1}{x^n}$$

A combination of this definition, the Fraction Rule, and the rule for dividing fractions provides an efficient way to handle a fraction raised to a negative power: invert the fraction and change the sign of the exponent:

$$\left(\frac{x}{y}\right)^{-n} = \frac{x^{-n}}{y^{-n}} = \frac{\frac{1}{x^n}}{\frac{1}{y^n}} = \frac{1}{x^n} \cdot \frac{y^n}{1} = \frac{y^n}{x^n} = \left(\frac{y}{x}\right)^n, \text{ so that } \left(\frac{x}{y}\right)^{-n} = \left(\frac{y}{x}\right)^n.$$

The definition of a negative exponent allows you to ignore the second part of the Quotient Rule as well as both of its conditions. Here is the revised Quotient Rule:

The Quotient Rule (revised): For any positive numbers a, m, and n,

$$\frac{a^m}{a^n} = a^{m-n}$$

If an exponent comes out negative when you are using this form of the Quotient Rule, use the definition of a negative exponent and put the factor in the denominator, changing the sign of the exponent. In practice, the original Quotient Rule is still used, but when in doubt, the revised Quotient Rule takes precedence.

Note

Some textbooks include the following as part of the definition of a negative exponent:

$$\frac{1}{x^{-n}} = x^n$$

Mathematically, it isn't necessary to include this in the definition, but knowing about it can help when simplifying certain expressions containing negative exponents. Together, the definition and the statement above suggest that factors with negative exponents can be moved across a fraction bar, changing the sign of the exponent to compensate. Because of this, an efficient way to handle a fraction raised to a negative power is to invert the fraction and change the sign of the exponent:

$$\left(\frac{x}{y}\right)^{-n} = \frac{x^{-n}}{y^{-n}} = \frac{\frac{1}{x^n}}{\frac{1}{y^n}} = \frac{1}{x^n} \cdot \frac{y^n}{1} = \frac{y^n}{x^n} = \left(\frac{y}{x}\right)^n, \text{ so that } \left(\frac{x}{y}\right)^{-n} = \left(\frac{y}{x}\right)^n.$$

EXAMPLES

$$\frac{9^7}{9^{13}} = 9^{7-13} = 9^{-6} = \frac{1}{9^6}, \text{ or } \frac{9^7}{9^{13}} = \frac{1}{9^{13-7}} = \frac{1}{9^6} \qquad \frac{2^6 x^7}{2^9 x^5} = 2^{-3} x^2 = \frac{x^2}{2^3}$$

$$\left(\frac{2}{x}\right)^{-3} = \frac{2^{-3}}{x^{-3}} = \frac{x^3}{2^3}, \text{ or } \left(\frac{2}{x}\right)^{-3} = \left(\frac{x}{2}\right)^3 = \frac{x^3}{2^3} \qquad \left(\frac{a}{4}\right)^{-8} = \frac{4^8}{a^8} \qquad \frac{a^{-5} x^8}{b^2 y^{-3}} = \frac{x^8 y^3}{a^5 b^2}$$

EXERCISE 10

Negative Exponents

Directions: Rewrite the following with positive exponents

1. 7^{-4}

2. $\frac{1}{3^{-5}}$

3. $\left(\frac{5}{3}\right)^{-2}$

4. $\frac{b^{-3}}{b^{-7}}$

5. $\frac{5a^{-6}}{6b^{-5}}$

6. $\left(\frac{8}{p}\right)^{-4}$

7. $\frac{m^4 p^{-3}}{n^2 q^{-7}}$

8. $\frac{7^{-2} t^{-4}}{7^{-6} t^{-1}}$

9. $\left(\frac{u}{v}\right)^{-7}$

10. $\left(\frac{p^{-3}}{q^{-5}}\right)^{-1}$

Answers are on page 542.

Fractional Exponents

The range of values that an exponent can take was extended from only non-negative integers to all integers by creative use of the Quotient Rule, namely by briefly disregarding the conditions that were attached to its first part. The range of allowable values for exponents can be further extended by using the Power Rule, again by briefly disregarding a condition. This time the extension includes fractions.

The simplest fraction that you can use for an exponent is $\frac{1}{2}$. What meaning can be attached to $x^{\frac{1}{2}}$? The definition at the beginning of this section doesn't apply, since the exponent isn't a whole number. You want whatever meaning you assign to the expression to conform to the properties of exponents already in use, so that a whole new set of rules isn't needed. After much thought and a flash of inspiration, a mathematician long ago realized that he would want to be able to use the Power Rule to

write $\left(x^{\frac{1}{2}}\right)^2 = x^{\frac{1}{2}\cdot 2}$. Since $\frac{1}{2}\cdot 2 = 1$, $x^{\frac{1}{2}\cdot 2} = x^1$, and since $x^1 = x$,

the Transitive Property of Equality gives you $\left(x^{\frac{1}{2}}\right)^2 = x$. You have seen

this before: something is squared and the result is x. This is the definition of a

square root, so you can conclude that $x^{\frac{1}{2}} = \sqrt{x}$. This leads to the following result:

> If n is a positive whole number and x is positive,
> $$x^{\frac{1}{n}} = \sqrt[n]{x}$$

Numerators of fractions aren't restricted to only the value 1, so more

thought is needed to give meaning to exponents like $\frac{7}{2}$ or $\frac{3}{5}$. Fortunately,

the hard work has already been done. Since $\frac{3}{5} = \frac{1}{5}\cdot 3$, you can use the

Power Rule again to handle a case like $x^{\frac{3}{5}}$:

$$x^{\frac{3}{5}} = x^{\frac{1}{5}\cdot 3} = \left(x^{\frac{1}{3}}\right)^5 = \sqrt[3]{x}^{\,5}$$

So you have your final definition of a fractional exponent.

> **Definition:** If m and n are positive whole numbers and x is positive,
> $$x^{\frac{m}{n}} = \sqrt[n]{x}^{\,m}$$

What if you had written $\frac{3}{5} = 3\cdot\frac{1}{5}$? You might have come up with a slightly

different definition: $x^{\frac{m}{n}} = x^{m\cdot\frac{1}{n}} = \left(x^m\right)^{\frac{1}{n}} = \sqrt[n]{x^m}$. The difference is that here

the base is raised to the power first and then the radical is applied, whereas in the definition the radical is applied first followed by the exponent. The good news is that as long as the fractional exponent is in lowest terms, the two expressions are equivalent:

If $\frac{m}{n}$ is in lowest terms, then $\sqrt[n]{x^m} = \sqrt[n]{x}^m$.

EXAMPLES

Rewrite with a radical.

$$31^{\frac{1}{2}} = \sqrt{31} \qquad 15^{-\frac{1}{2}} = \frac{1}{\sqrt{15}} \qquad 4^{\frac{1}{3}} = \sqrt[3]{4} \qquad 11^{-\frac{1}{3}} = \frac{1}{\sqrt[3]{11}} \qquad (ab)^{\frac{1}{2}} = \sqrt{ab}$$

Rewrite with a fractional exponent.

$$\sqrt{6} = 6^{\frac{1}{2}} \qquad \sqrt[3]{21} = 21^{\frac{1}{3}} \qquad \frac{1}{\sqrt{35}} = 35^{-\frac{1}{2}} \qquad \frac{1}{\sqrt[3]{47}} = 47^{-\frac{1}{3}}$$

$$\frac{1}{\sqrt[3]{x}} = x^{-\frac{1}{3}}$$

Evaluate.

$$25^{-\frac{1}{2}} = \frac{1}{\sqrt{25}} = \frac{1}{5} \qquad 125^{\frac{1}{3}} = \sqrt[3]{125} = 5 \qquad 216^{-\frac{1}{3}} = \frac{1}{\sqrt[3]{216}} = \frac{1}{6}$$

EXERCISE 11

Fractional Exponents

Directions: Rewrite with a radical.

1. $7^{\frac{1}{2}}$ **2.** $5^{\frac{1}{3}}$ **3.** $2^{-\frac{1}{2}}$ **4.** $9^{-\frac{1}{3}}$ **5.** $x^{\frac{2}{3}}$

Rewrite with a fractional exponent.

6. $\sqrt[3]{10}$ **7.** $\frac{1}{\sqrt{3}}$ **8.** $\frac{1}{\sqrt[3]{4}}$ **9.** $\sqrt{6}$ **10.** $\frac{1}{\sqrt{x}}$

Evaluate the following.

11. $49^{\frac{1}{2}}$ **12.** $121^{-\frac{1}{2}}$ **13.** $27^{\frac{1}{3}}$ **14.** $8^{-\frac{1}{3}}$ **15.** $\sqrt[3]{64}$

Answers are on page 542.

CHAPTER 3

Fractions

Fractions and Mixed Numbers

Fractions are one of three common ways to express parts of a whole. The other two are decimals and percents.

Fractions have two parts. On the bottom is a **denominator**, which shows how many pieces of a whole there are. On the top is a **numerator**, which shows how many of those pieces you have. The following fraction says you have 3 pieces of something that is split into 16 equal portions.

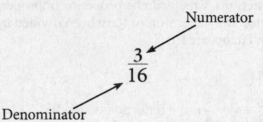

When the denominator and numerator are equal, the fraction equals 1.

$$\frac{16}{16} = 1.$$

Proper fractions have numerators less than their denominators. A proper fraction's value is less than 1.

EXAMPLES

$$\frac{1}{4} \quad \frac{4}{5} \quad \frac{13}{16}$$

Improper fractions have numerators equal to or larger than their denominators. An improper fraction's value is greater than or equal to 1.

EXAMPLES

$$\frac{5}{3} \quad \frac{14}{5} \quad \frac{30}{4}$$

Like fractions have the same denominator but different numerators.

> ### EXAMPLES
>
> $$\frac{5}{7} \quad \frac{6}{7} \quad \frac{30}{7}$$

Equivalent fractions share equal values, but have different denominators.

> ### EXAMPLES
>
> $$\frac{1}{2} \quad \frac{5}{10} \quad \frac{8}{16}$$

Mixed numbers are made of a whole number followed by a fraction.

> ### EXAMPLES
>
> $$1\frac{1}{2} \quad 7\frac{5}{8} \quad 6\frac{2}{3}$$

Reduced fractions, which can be proper or improper, are fractions in which the numerator and denominator have been divided by common factors until no common factors are left.

> ### EXAMPLE
>
> $$\frac{6}{8} = \frac{3}{4} \quad [\frac{3}{4} \text{ is the reduced fraction.}]$$

EXERCISE 1

Fractions and Mixed Numbers

Directions: Match the description to the item by placing the correct letter in the blank. Each definition is used twice.

A. Proper fraction   **B.** Improper fraction
C. Mixed number   **D.** Proper fraction

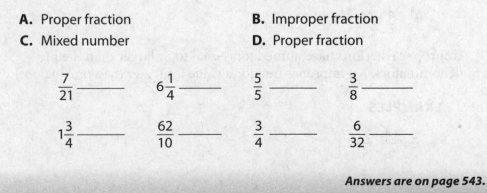

$\frac{7}{21}$ _____ $6\frac{1}{4}$ _____ $\frac{5}{5}$ _____ $\frac{3}{8}$ _____

$1\frac{3}{4}$ _____ $\frac{62}{10}$ _____ $\frac{3}{4}$ _____ $\frac{6}{32}$ _____

Answers are on page 543.

Reducing Fractions and Converting Between Fractions and Mixed Numbers

Reducing Fractions

To reduce fractions, divide the numerator and denominator by a common factor. Some trickier fractions may take several divisions to reduce completely.

> **EXAMPLE**
>
> Reduce $\frac{8}{32}$.
>
> $\frac{8}{32} = \frac{4}{16} = \frac{2}{8} = \frac{1}{4}$ The reduction was done in three rounds of division
>
> by 2. You could also reduce the fraction in one step by using a factor of 8.

Converting Fractions

Converting a fraction changes the denominator without changing the fraction's value. Multiply the numerator and denominator by a number that gives the desired denominator.

> **EXAMPLE**
>
> Convert $\frac{4}{5}$ to an equivalent fraction with the denominator 30.
>
> To go from a denominator of 5 to a denominator of 30, multiply numerator and denominator by 6.
>
> $\frac{4}{5} \times \frac{6}{6} = \frac{24}{30}$

Converting Mixed Numbers to Improper Fractions

You may need to change mixed numbers to improper fractions. Multiply the fraction's denominator by the whole number. Then add that product to the original numerator and place the sum over the denominator.

> **EXAMPLE**
>
> Convert $3\frac{3}{8}$ to an improper fraction.
>
> Multiply the whole number by the denominator: $3 \times 8 = 24$.
>
> Add the product to the numerator: $24 + 3 = 27$.
>
> The improper fraction is $\frac{27}{3}$.

Converting Improper Fractions to Mixed Numbers

At other times you need to convert an improper fraction to a mixed number. Start with the improper fraction. Divide the denominator by the numerator.

Reserve the whole number while the remainder becomes the numerator of the fraction.

EXAMPLE

Convert $\frac{17}{3}$ to a mixed number.

Divide $3\overline{)17} = 5r2 = 5\frac{2}{3}$

EXERCISE 2

Reducing Fractions and Converting Between Fractions and Mixed Numbers

Directions: Reduce the following fractions to lowest terms.

1. $\frac{5}{10}$

2. $\frac{17}{51}$

Convert the fractions to equivalent fractions with the denominator specified.

3. $\frac{1}{2} = \frac{}{24}$

4. $\frac{3}{16} = \frac{}{48}$

Convert the mixed number to an improper fraction.

5. $1\frac{3}{8} =$

6. $2\frac{4}{5} =$

Convert the improper fraction to a mixed number.

7. $\frac{15}{3}$

8. $\frac{18}{5}$

Answers are on page 543.

Adding and Subtracting Fractions and Mixed Numbers

When Fraction Denominators Are Equal

To **add**, add the numerators but leave the denominator the same. Reduce or convert to a mixed number as needed.

EXAMPLE

Add $\frac{1}{5} + \frac{3}{5} + \frac{4}{5}$.

Adding across the top [1 + 3 + 4 = 8] gives $\frac{1}{5} + \frac{3}{5} + \frac{4}{5} = \frac{8}{5}$, an improper

fraction. Converting the fraction to a mixed number gives $\frac{8}{5} = 1\frac{3}{5}$.

To **subtract**, subtract numerators as indicated. Reduce as necessary.

EXAMPLE

Subtract $\frac{8}{15} - \frac{5}{15}$.

Subtracting across the top and reducing the answer gives this:

$$\frac{8}{15} - \frac{5}{15} = \frac{3}{15} = \frac{1}{5}$$

When Fraction Denominators Are Different

With different, or unlike, denominators, you need to convert to equivalent fractions before doing the operations. You need a **common denominator**, a denominator into which each original denominator divides evenly. The **lowest common denominator** is the smallest number that works, but there are countless more numbers that are common denominators. One of the simplest ways to find a useful common denominator is by multiplying the denominators together.

EXAMPLE

Add $\frac{1}{2} + \frac{2}{3} + \frac{4}{5}$.

$2 \times 3 \times 5 = 30$

Use 30 as the common denominator because all of the denominators divide into 30 without remainders. (Try the divisions yourself just to be sure.) Convert each fraction to an equivalent with a denominator of 30.

$$\frac{1}{2} \times \frac{15}{15} = \frac{15}{30}$$

$$\frac{2}{3} \times \frac{10}{10} = \frac{20}{30}$$

$$\frac{4}{5} \times \frac{6}{6} = \frac{24}{30}$$

Adding numerators (15 + 20 + 24) gives $\frac{59}{30}$, which reduces to $1\frac{29}{30}$.

EXAMPLE

Subtract $\frac{3}{8} - \frac{1}{5}$.

The lowest common denominator is 8×5, or 40. Convert fractions and subtract.

$$\frac{3}{8} \times \frac{5}{5} = \frac{15}{40}$$

$$\frac{1}{5} \times \frac{8}{8} = \frac{8}{40}$$

$$\frac{15}{40} - \frac{8}{40} = \frac{7}{40}$$

When Mixed-Number Denominators Are Equal

For mixed numbers, calculate the fractions and the whole numbers separately. To **add** mixed numbers when the denominators are the same, add the fractions and convert to mixed numbers as needed.

EXAMPLE

Add $1\frac{3}{4} + 2\frac{3}{4}$.

Add the whole numbers and fractions separately.

$$1\frac{3}{4}$$

$$+2\frac{3}{4}$$

$$3\frac{6}{4}$$

But $\frac{6}{4}$ is an improper fraction, so it is converted to a mixed number

and added to the whole: $3 + 1\frac{1}{2} = 4\frac{1}{2}$

Subtracting is done the same way unless the fraction being subtracted is larger than the original. Then you must borrow from the whole number to be able to subtract.

EXAMPLE

Subtract $3\frac{1}{4} - 1\frac{3}{4}$.

You cannot subtract $\frac{3}{4}$ from $\frac{1}{4}$. So borrow one, in the form of $\frac{4}{4}$, from

the whole number. $3\frac{1}{4}$ now becomes $2\frac{1}{4} + \frac{4}{4} = 2\frac{5}{4}$, and you can subtract.

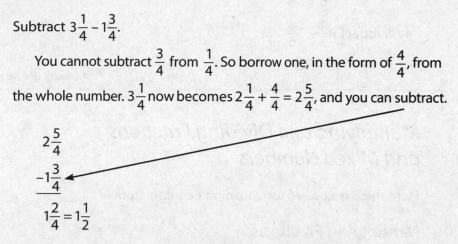

$$2\frac{5}{4}$$
$$-1\frac{3}{4}$$
$$\overline{1\frac{2}{4} = 1\frac{1}{2}}$$

When Mixed-Number Denominators Are Different

These problems are like the ones above, except that you must first convert all the fractions to like fractions.

EXAMPLE

Add $3\frac{1}{4} + 2\frac{4}{5}$.

Using a common denominator of 20,

$$3\frac{1}{4} = 3\frac{5}{20}$$
$$2\frac{4}{5} = +2\frac{16}{20}$$
$$\overline{5\frac{21}{20} = 5 + 1\frac{1}{20} = 6\frac{1}{20}}$$

EXERCISE 3

Adding and Subtracting Fractions and Mixed Numbers

Directions: Perform the indicated operations. Reduce all answers to lowest terms and mixed numbers.

1. Add $3\frac{3}{4} + 6\frac{3}{4}$

2. Add $7\frac{5}{8} + 4\frac{3}{5}$

3. Subtract $7\frac{1}{6} - 4\frac{5}{6}$

4. Subtract $8\frac{1}{3} - 3\frac{4}{5}$

Answers are on page 544.

Multiplying and Dividing Fractions and Mixed Numbers

Here there is no need for common denominators.

Multiplying Fractions

Multiply across the top and across the bottom. Reduce as needed.
WARNING: If you multiply proper fractions and get an improper fraction as the product, you have made a mistake.

EXAMPLE

Multiply $\frac{3}{5} \times \frac{1}{6}$.

$$3 \times 1 = 3$$
$$5 \times 6 = 30$$

$$\frac{3}{5} \times \frac{1}{6} = \frac{3}{30} = \frac{1}{10}$$

Dividing Fractions

Take the reciprocal of (flip over) the second fraction (divisor), and multiply.

EXAMPLE

Divide $\frac{3}{5} \div \frac{1}{2}$.

Flipping over the divisor fraction, $\frac{3}{5} \times \frac{2}{1} = \frac{6}{5} = 1\frac{1}{5}$

NOTE: Unlike multiplication of fractions, dividing proper fractions can result in products that are improper fractions.

Multiplying and Dividing Mixed Numbers

There are a couple of ways to multiply and divide mixed numbers. Most people find it easiest to convert mixed numbers to improper fractions, multiply or divide, and then convert the answer back to a mixed number.

EXAMPLE

Multiply $3\frac{3}{8} \times 6\frac{3}{4}$.

Converting to improper fractions and multiplying:

$$3\frac{3}{8} = \frac{27}{8}$$

$$6\frac{3}{4} = \frac{27}{4}$$

$$\frac{27}{8} \times \frac{27}{4} = \frac{729}{32} = 22\frac{25}{32}$$

EXAMPLE

Divide $3\frac{3}{8} \div 6\frac{3}{4}$.

$$\frac{27}{8} \div \frac{27}{4} = \frac{27}{8} \times \frac{4}{27} = \frac{108}{216} = \frac{1}{2}$$

Note the reciprocal of the second fraction in the multiplication.

Reducing While Multiplying and Dividing

Some problems can be made much simpler by reducing fractions as you multiply or divide. To do this, reduce denominators and numerators even if they appear in different fractions.

EXAMPLE

Divide $3\frac{3}{8} \div 6\frac{3}{4}$.

$$\frac{27}{8} \div \frac{27}{4} = \frac{\cancel{27}}{\cancel{8}_2} \times \frac{\cancel{4}^1}{\cancel{27}}$$

Note that there is a 27 in the numerator and in the denominator. These cancel each other out, leaving a 1. The 4 and 8 both have a factor of 4 and may be reduced. The answer becomes $\frac{1}{2}$.

EXERCISE 4

Multiplying and Dividing Fractions and Mixed Numbers

Directions: Do the indicated operations. You may reduce while calculating if you wish.

1. $\dfrac{1}{8} \times \dfrac{3}{32}$

2. $1\dfrac{3}{5} \div 2\dfrac{2}{3}$

3. $1\dfrac{3}{4} \div \dfrac{3}{5}$

Answers are on page 544.

Working Problems with Fractions

In all problems it is good to remember that the word "of" generally means that you should multiply.

EXAMPLE

Sandy stacked $\dfrac{1}{3}$ **of** a pile of 1125 bricks. How many bricks did he stack?

$$\dfrac{1}{3} \times 1125 = \dfrac{1}{3} \times \dfrac{1125}{1} = \dfrac{1125}{3} = 375 \text{ bricks}$$

Some problems, such as those giving you today's situation and asking about the past, require division of fractions.

EXAMPLE

Today Leena did 48 reps of her exercise in fitness class.

This is $1\dfrac{1}{3}$ times as many as she did two days ago. How many reps did she do two days ago?

To solve, divide 48 by $1\dfrac{1}{3}$. First convert $1\dfrac{1}{3}$ into an improper fraction:

$1\dfrac{1}{3} = \dfrac{4}{3}$. This is the divisor, so flip it (take its reciprocal) and multiply.

$$48 \times \dfrac{3}{4} = \dfrac{48}{1} \times \dfrac{3}{4} = 36 \text{ reps.}$$

EXERCISE 5

Working Problems with Fractions

Directions: Solve the following problems.

1. Saul finished $\frac{1}{4}$ of the 56 questions he had for homework. How many questions were left to do?

2. Last year the booster club sold 125 Christmas trees. This year it sold $1\frac{3}{5}$ times as many. How many trees did they sell this year?

3. $2\frac{3}{4}$ is exactly $\frac{1}{2}$ of the original number. What is the original number?

Answers are on page 544.

CHAPTER 4

Decimals

Decimals are closely related to fractions in that they are also used when talking about parts of a whole. Unlike fractions, though, which allow any value in the denominator, decimals essentially represent fractions whose denominators are powers of 10.

Place Values in Decimals

If you think about it, it is quite amazing that, unlike the Romans and other earlier cultures, we can express any number from the size of the universe down to the sizes of particles that make up the atom, using just ten symbols: 1, 2, 3, 4, 5, 6, 7, 8, 9, and 0. This is possible because our numbering system is positional in nature. Not only does each symbol have a meaning, but its position within a larger number also has a meaning.

1,000	100	10	1	.	$\frac{1}{10}$	$\frac{1}{100}$	$\frac{1}{1000}$	$\frac{1}{10000}$
Thousands	Hundreds	Tens	Units (ones)	Decimal point	tenths	hundredths	thousandths	ten-thousandths

EXAMPLES

A. What is the place value of the underlined digit in 437.60<u>5</u>?

The underlined digit, *5*, is in the thousandths place and stands for 5 thousandths.

B. What is the value of the digit underlined in 3.<u>7</u>02?

The underlined *7* is in the tenths place and represents 7 tenths.

C. What is the value of the underlined digit in 127.2<u>0</u>7?

The underlined digit is a zero in the hundredths place. It is a placeholder and carries no value in itself.

EXERCISE 1

Place Values in Decimals

Directions: Give the place value for the underlined digits in the following numbers.

1. 127.9<u>8</u>7   **2.** 32.<u>7</u>09   **3.** 11.95<u>3</u>

Answers are on page 544.

Rounding

Often you are asked to round a number to a given number of decimal places. To round a number, first identify the place of the last digit to be reported. If you are asked to round to two decimal places, count right from the decimal place to the second digit. Draw a line under it so you do not lose your place. Now look at the next digit to the right. If this digit is 5 or greater, round up by adding 1 to the underlined digit. If it is 4 or less, round down by leaving the underlined digit alone. Drop all digits that are to the right of the specified place.

EXAMPLES

A. Round 21.4356 to two decimal places.

Underline the second decimal place: 21.4<u>3</u>56.

Now look at the digit to the right. It is 5, so you add 1 to the 3 and report 21.44.

B. Round 123.4538 to two decimal places.

Underline the second decimal place: 123.4<u>5</u>38. The digit to the right is less than 5, so you leave everything to the left alone and report 123.45

EXERCISE 2

Rounding

Directions: Round to the required number of decimal places.

1. 167.925 to two decimal places

2. 0.0034 to three decimal places

3. 6.78925 to four decimal places

4. 123.456 to the nearest whole number

Answers are on page 544.

Adding and Subtracting Decimal Numbers

The four arithmetic operations of addition, subtraction, multiplication, and division are carried out with decimal numbers in much the same way as they are with whole numbers, with extra consideration for the decimal point. When adding and subtracting decimal numbers, line up the decimal points and perform the operation. Any "missing" places can be replaced with zeros. In adding, doing so is only for neatness, but in subtraction, doing so is necessary when you are subtracting numbers with different numbers of decimal places.

EXAMPLES

A. Add 143.25, 1.007, and 3.451.

143.250 ← Note the zero added for neatness.

1.007

+   3.451

147.708

B. Subtract 34.709 from 42.5.

42.500 ← Note added zeros.

– 34.709

7.791

EXERCISE 3

Adding and Subtracting Decimal Numbers

Directions: Perform the following operations without a calculator.

1. Add: 12.34 + 1.0095 + 14.56 + 234.567

2. Add: 0.005 + 0.0067 + 0.034 + 0.0001

3. Subtract: 123.45 – 2.387

4. Subtract: 0.00345 – 0.00023

Answers are on page 545.

Multiplying Decimal Numbers

When multiplying decimal numbers, multiply in exactly the same fashion as when multiplying whole numbers. There is no need to line up decimal points. The challenge in decimal multiplication is where to place the decimal in the answer. The rule for this is straightforward: **the product must contain the same total number of decimal places as the two original numbers**. If you are multiplying a three-decimal-place number by a two-decimal-place number, the answer will have five decimal places.

EXAMPLE

Multiply 2.343 by 1.75.

2.343	three decimal places
× 1.75	two decimal places
4.10025	five decimal places in the answer

EXERCISE 4

Multiplying Decimal Numbers

Directions: Give the number of decimal places in the following products.

1. 67.975 × 87.12

2. 49.988 × 187.973

3. 44.5567 × 11.876

4. 0.003 × 0.00456

Answers are on page 545.

Multiplying by a Power of 10

Decimal multiplication is easiest when one of the factors is a power of 10. In this case, the product has the same sequence of digits as the other factor, but the decimal is moved to the right by the same number of digits as either the number of zeros in the power of 10 or the number expressed by the power itself.

EXAMPLES

$54.882 \times 100 = 5488.2$ $0.687223 \times 10^4 = 6872.23$

$36.97 \times 10^6 = 36{,}970{,}000$ $2.5 \times 100{,}000 = 250{,}000$

Dividing Decimal Numbers

Decimal division differs from whole-number division in that a remainder isn't obtained. Instead, the division process continues until a desired degree of precision is reached or the division terminates itself.

You cannot divide decimal numbers as they stand; you have to change them a bit. You must multiply the **divisor** (the number doing the dividing) and the **dividend** (the number being divided) by the same power of ten so that the divisor is a whole number. Many teachers call this "moving the decimal."

EXAMPLE

Divide 27.75 by 1.5.

You can do the division as a fraction or begin by using long division. As a fraction, you have $\frac{27.75}{1.5}$. If you multiply both the divisor and the dividend by 10, you get $\frac{277.5}{15}$, which you can express as $15\overline{)277.5}$ with quotient 18.5.

(18.5 is the answer.) Starting with long division, you do the same thing, but it looks different. You start with $1.5\overline{)27.75}$ and then move the decimal in both numbers one place to the right to get $15\overline{)277.5}$ with quotient 18.5. You can look at this as sliding the decimal in each number to the right by the same number of places until the divisor is a whole number.

EXAMPLE

Divide 342.45 by 0.05.

Starting with $0.05\overline{)342.45}$, slide both decimals two places to the right to make the divisor, 0.05, into a simple 5. You get $5\overline{)34245}$ with quotient 6849.

Once the last digit in the dividend is brought down in the division process, the process doesn't stop with a remainder unless the last subtraction step in the division process has a difference of zero. Otherwise, it continues by bringing down zeros from the dividend. This works because every whole number can be treated as a decimal number whose decimal part consists of as many zeros as is needed: 3 = 3.0000. Often, the division does not terminate by itself or goes on for a long time, and a decision must be made to stop the process and round off the answer. With a problem involving dollar values, rounding is usually done in the hundredths place, or to the nearest cent. Other times, there may be other criteria to help determine where to round.

EXAMPLE

Compute 0.001571 ÷ 0.0004 to the nearest hundredth.

After writing $0.0004\overline{)0.001571}$, you shift the decimal point four places to the right: $4\overline{)15.71}$. Carrying out the division gives $4\overline{)15.71}$ with quotient 3.92. If you are going to round to the hundredths place, you need to know the digit in the thousandths place. Bring down a zero and go through the division process one more time: $4\overline{)15.710}$ with quotient 3.927. The 7 tells you to round up, so the properly rounded quotient is 3.93.

EXERCISE 5

Dividing Decimal Numbers

Directions: Perform the following operations without a calculator.

1. Divide 234 by 0.003.

2. Divide 0.0075 by 1.5.

3. Divide 11.35 by 5.

4. Divide 8.64 ÷ 2.01 to the nearest tenth.

5. Compute 0.352 ÷ 0.3 to the nearest thousandth.

6. Find the quotient 463.7 ÷ 0.055 to the nearest ten.

Answers are on page 545.

Dividing by Powers of 10

When the divisor is a power of 10, the quotient will have the same sequence of digits as the dividend, with the decimal point shifted to the left. The number of places shifted is the same as the number of zeros in the power of 10 or is the power itself.

EXAMPLES

$5547.336 \div 10^3 = 5.547336$ $5789.35 \div 100 = 57.8935$

$3.21 \div 10{,}000 = 0.000321$ $65.332 \div 10^6 = 0.000065332$

Converting Between Fractions and Decimals

Fractions to Decimals

To convert a fraction to a decimal, divide the numerator (upper number) by the denominator (lower number) and report the decimal rounded to the appropriate number of decimal places.

EXAMPLES

Convert to a decimal. If necessary, round to the nearest ten-thousandth.

A. $\frac{3}{4}$

B. $\frac{11}{7}$

$4)\overline{3.00}$ = 0.75 so $\frac{3}{4} = 0.75$

$7)\overline{11.00000}$ = 1.57142 so $\frac{11}{7} \approx 1.5714$

Decimals to Fractions

To convert a decimal number to a fraction, drop the decimal point. Use the sequence of digits as the numerator of a fraction. The denominator of the fraction is a 1 followed by as many zeros as there are decimal places in the original number. Reduce to simplest form if needed. The only prime numbers that will divide the denominator are 2 and 5, so don't bother trying to cancel any numbers that have other prime factors.

EXAMPLES

A. Convert 0.725 to a fraction and reduce it to lowest terms.

There are three decimal places in the number, so you write

$\frac{725}{1000} = \frac{29}{40}$

B. Convert 0.0345 to a fraction and reduce it.

It has four decimal places, so there are four zeros in the denominator: $\frac{345}{10000} = \frac{69}{2000}$

C. Convert 1.25 to a fraction and reduce it.

It has two decimal places, so there are two zeros in the denominator: $\frac{125}{100} = \frac{5}{4}$

EXERCISE 6

Converting Between Fractions and Decimals

Directions: Fill in the missing values below without using a calculator.

	Decimal	Fraction
1.	0.002	
2.		$\frac{3}{16}$
3.		$\frac{4}{15}$
4.	2.375	

Answers are on page 545.

Scientific Notation

In order to write very large or very small numbers without long strings of zeros, mathematicians use **scientific notation**. In scientific notation, all numbers, large or small, are reduced to a decimal number with one non-zero digit to the left of the decimal point. The number in this form is called the **significand** or **mantissa**.

To get this number, the decimal in the original number must be moved either right or left. The number of places the decimal is moved is called the exponent, or **order of magnitude**, and is expressed as a power of 10 in the form 10^n. Scientists and engineers often refer to the order of magnitude as simply **magnitude**. The exponent n is related to the number of places the decimal is shifted. If the original number is greater than 1, n is positive, and if the original number is less than 1, n is negative.

EXAMPLES

A. Express 1,123,697 in scientific notation.

To get one non-zero digit to the left of the decimal, you must shift the decimal six places to the left. The mantissa becomes 1.123697, and the exponent is +6. The number is expressed as 1.123697×10^6 in scientific notation.

B. Express 0.000234 in scientific notation.

Move the decimal four places right to get 2.34. The number is written 2.34×10^{-4}, with a negative magnitude because the number is less than 1.

To convert a number in scientific notation to a number in standard notation, reverse the procedure.

EXAMPLES

A. Convert 3.792×10^8 to standard notation.

You start with 3.792 and move the decimal eight places to the right. Add some zeros to keep your place: 3.7920000000. Doing that, you get 379200000, or 379,200,000.

B. Convert 1.795×10^{-4} to standard notation.

Again, you need to add some zeros so you can move the decimal, but here you add them to the left side: 000001.795. Then, moving the decimal four places left, you get 0.0001795.

Confusion sometimes occurs when deciding which direction makes the exponent positive or negative. Remember: if the original number if less than 1, the exponent is negative. And if the exponent is negative, the resulting number must be less than 1. Also, numbers larger than 1 have positive exponents, and positive exponents yield numbers bigger than 1. Move the decimal accordingly.

EXERCISE 7

Scientific Notation

Directions: Provide the missing items below.

	Scientific Notation	Number
1.	6.02×10^5	
2.		1145.25
3.	5×10^{-4}	
4.		17

Answers are on page 545.

Operations in Scientific Notation

You can do calculations on numbers in scientific notation without the need to change them into standard notation first.

Adding in Scientific Notation

Usually, numbers in scientific notation are added only when they have the same or almost the same order of magnitude. For example, you would probably not add

$$1.5 \times 10^2 + 3.25 \times 10^{-6}$$

That's adding 150 + 0.00000325, which isn't a calculation you would often be called upon to make.

Adding numbers in scientific notation is based on this form of the Distributive Property: $ac + bc = (a + b)c$. This tells you that to add two numbers in scientific notation, you add the mantissas and keep the same power of 10.

$$6 \times 10^{-7} + 3 \times 10^{-7} = (6 + 3) \times 10^{-7} = 9 \times 10^{-7}$$

When adding two or more numbers in scientific notation, there may be two separate adjustments that need to be made. First, the numbers may need adjusting so that they have the same magnitude. Once the magnitudes are equal, you keep the magnitude unchanged and add the mantissas. Second, the answer may have to be adjusted to fit scientific notation. Let's look at the difficulty with answers first.

EXAMPLE

Add $3.75 \times 10^6 + 7.29 \times 10^6$.

$$3.75 \times 10^6$$
$$+ \ 7.29 \times 10^6$$
$$11.04 \times 10^6$$

The magnitudes are equal, so you add mantissas. But the answer does not look like good scientific notation because there are too many digits to the left of the decimal point. To fix this, write the mantissa so that only one digit is to the left of the decimal point, and combine the powers of 10 using the Product Rule from the properties of exponents: $11.04 \times 10^6 = (1.104 \times 10^1) \times 10^6 = 1.104 \times 10^7$.

The next kind of adjustment is necessary *before* adding if the magnitudes are not equal.

EXAMPLE

Add $1.02 \times 10^4 + 6.06 \times 10^6$.

You cannot add the two numbers right away because they have different magnitudes. First, change 1.02×10^4 to 0.0102×10^6 by moving the decimal point two places left and adding 2 to the magnitude. Now add the mantissas, getting $0.0102 \times 10^6 + 6.06 \times 10^6 = 6.0702 \times 10^6$

Subtracting in Scientific Notation

Subtraction also relies on a form of the Distributive Property: $ac - bc = (a - b)c$.

$$5 \times 10^9 - 2 \times 10^9 = (5 - 2) \times 10^9 = 3 \times 10^9$$

As with addition, you often face the same issue of matching the magnitudes.

EXAMPLE

Subtract $1.025 \times 10^{12} - 3.0 \times 10^9$.

Change 3.0×10^9 to 0.003×10^{12}. Note that making the magnitude bigger compensates for making the mantissa smaller. The answer then comes by subtracting the mantissas:

$$1.025 \times 10^{12} - 0.003 \times 10^{12} = (1.025 - 0.003) \times 10^{12} = 1.022 \times 10^{12}.$$

When subtracting, the mantissa may drop below 1 (as it sometimes exceeded 10 in addition). If this happens, you will need to adjust the answer.

EXAMPLE

$4.16 \times 10^3 - 3.85 \times 10^3 = (4.16 - 3.85) \times 10^3 = 0.31 \times 10^3$. The answer isn't in scientific notation, but changing the mantissa to scientific notation and combining the magnitudes provides the proper form:

$$0.31 \times 10^3 = (3.1 \times 10^{-1}) \times 10^3 = 3.1 \times 10^2.$$

Multiplying in Scientific Notation

When multiplying or dividing numbers in scientific notation, you do not need to match magnitudes as you do in adding and subtracting. The magnitudes are exponents and as such are subject to the properties of exponents. A multiplication such as $(4 \times 10^{-3}) \times (2 \times 10^5)$ is really a problem involving the multiplication of four numbers. Applying the Associative and Commutative Properties of Multiplication several times, the multiplication can be written $(4 \times 2) \times (10^{-3} \times 10^5) = 8 \times 10^{-3+5} = 8 \times 10^2$;

the Product Rule of exponents is used on the magnitudes. When multiplying two numbers in scientific notation, multiply the mantissas and then *add* the magnitudes. Adjust the answer if needed to match scientific notation.

EXAMPLE

Multiply $(6.35 \times 10^7) \times (9.67 \times 10^5)$.

You multiply the mantissas and *add* the magnitudes:

$(6.35 \times 10^7) \times (9.67 \times 10^5) = (6.35 \times 9.67) \times (10^7 \times 10^5) = 61.40 \times 10^{12}$

But this requires an adjustment because it is not good scientific notation. Write the mantissa in scientific notation and combine magnitudes:

$61.4 \times 10^{12} = (61.4 \times 10^1) \times 10^{12} = 6.14 \times 10^{13}$.

Dividing in Scientific Notation

Division is much the same as multiplication. Divide the mantissas and *subtract* the magnitudes. To see why, you need to employ the notion of division that is used when dividing fractions. Just as dividing by 2 is the same as multiplying by $\frac{1}{2}$, dividing by 2×10^4 is the same as multiplying by $\frac{1}{2 \times 10^4}$, which is the same as $\frac{1}{2} \times \frac{1}{10^4}$. So the division problem $(8 \times 10^6) \div (2 \times 10^4)$ can be rewritten in terms of multiplication as

$\left(\frac{8}{1} \times \frac{10^6}{1} \right) \times \left(\frac{1}{2} \times \frac{1}{10^4} \right)$ Again, using the Associative and Commutative

Properties of Multiplication as above, you can write $\left(\frac{8}{1} \times \frac{1}{2} \right) \times \left(\frac{10^6}{1} \times \frac{1}{10^4} \right)$,

which is the same as $\frac{8}{2} \times \frac{10^6}{10^4}$, or 4×10^2. To state it in a shorter way,

$(8 \times 10^6) \div (2 \times 10^4) = (8 \div 2) \times (10^6 \div 10^4) = 4 \times 10^{6-4} = 4 \times 10^2$

In other words, divide the mantissas and subtract the magnitudes. If the mantissa is less than 1, you will need to adjust the answer.

EXAMPLE

Divide $(6.75 \times 10^{-8}) \div (2.5 \times 10^{-2})$.

Dividing the mantissas gives 2.7, and subtracting the magnitudes gives $-8 - (-2) = -8 + 2 = -6$.

$(6.75 \times 10^{-8}) \div (2.5 \times 10^{-2}) = (6.75 \div 2.5) \times (10^{-8} \div 10^{-2})$

$= 2.7 \times 10^{-8 - (-2)}$

$= 2.7 \times 10^{-6}$

Operations in Scientific Notation

Directions: Perform the indicated operations.

1. Add: $3.5 \times 10^5 + 7.20 \times 10^6$

2. Subtract: $1.23 \times 10^8 - 3.17 \times 10^7$

3. Multiply: $(4.75 \times 10^{11}) \times (3.95 \times 10^5)$

4. Divide: $(5.00 \times 10^4) \div (7.50 \times 10^{10})$

Answers are on page 545.

CHAPTER 5

Ratios, Rates, and Proportions

Ratios, rates, and proportions are used in mathematics and the real world when dealing with several quantities that come in relative sizes.

Ratios

A **ratio** is used to compare measurements of quantities with the same units. It is written with the word *to*, with a colon (:), or as a fraction. For example, the quantities 3 miles and 7 miles can be compared as a ratio by writing $\frac{3 \text{ miles}}{7 \text{ miles}} = \frac{3}{7}$, 3:7, or 3 to 7. All three are read the same way, "three to seven." When writing ratios in any form, the common units are not written because they cancel, as can be seen in the fraction. The fraction form of a ratio is also justification for canceling common factors from the quantities.

EXAMPLE

Compare 20 hours and 25 hours as a ratio in lowest terms.

$$\frac{20 \text{ hours}}{25 \text{ hours}} = \frac{4}{5}, \text{ or 4:5, or 4 to 5}$$

Ratios are most commonly written as a fraction or with a colon. Because a fraction has only two locations in which to place quantities, the numerator and the denominator, the colon has the advantage of being useful when comparing more than two quantities. The comparison of 3 miles, 7 miles, and 11 miles can't be written as a fraction but can be written with a colon as 3:7:11.

EXAMPLE

Compare 6 honeydews, 15 honeydews, 12 honeydews, and 9 honeydews as a ratio in lowest terms.

Canceling the common factor of 3, the ratio is 2:5:4:3.

EXERCISE 1

Ratios

Directions: Write each comparison in lowest terms as a fraction and with a colon.

1. 30 feet and 24 feet

2. 8 people and 2 people

Write each comparison in lowest terms.

3. 28 cars, 35 cars, and 14 cars

4. 8 m, 40 m, 4 m, and 20 m

Answers are on page 545.

Rates

Whereas ratios compare quantities that are expressed in the same units, **rates** are used to compare quantities expressed in different units. When writing rates as fractions, the units do not cancel because they aren't common, but common numerical factors are still canceled.

EXAMPLE

Compare 98 miles and 4 hours using a fraction and a colon.

$$\frac{98 \text{ miles}}{4 \text{ hours}} = \frac{49 \text{ miles}}{2 \text{ hours}}; 49 \text{ miles}:2 \text{ hours}$$

EXERCISE 2

Rates

Directions: Write each rate in lowest terms as a fraction and with a colon.

1. 400 cashews and 35 people

2. $144 and 20 minutes

Answers are on page 545.

Unit Rates

A unit rate is used when the second quantity is one unit. Unit rates are almost always written as fractions, and the fraction bar is read "per." In everyday life, you often use abbreviations for the units, and the numerical part of the fraction is written separately from the units.

EXAMPLES

You can write each comparison as a unit rate.

700 miles and 10 hours:

$$\frac{700 \text{ miles}}{10 \text{ hours}} = \frac{70 \text{ miles}}{1 \text{ hour}} = 70\frac{\text{miles}}{\text{hour}} = 70 \text{ mph}$$

$60 and 5 books:

$$\frac{\$60}{5 \text{ books}} = \frac{\$12}{\text{book}} = \$12 \text{ per book}$$

When the denominator doesn't reduce to one unit, you can use division to obtain the numerical part of the unit rate. Depending on how the unit rate is used, either mixed numbers or decimal numbers are appropriate for the numerical part of the unit rate.

EXAMPLES

You can write each comparison as a unit rate.

65 feet and 15 seconds:

$$\frac{65 \text{ feet}}{15 \text{ seconds}} = \frac{13 \text{ feet}}{3 \text{ seconds}} = 4\frac{1}{3} \text{ feet per second}$$

23 pounds and 4 boxes:

$$\frac{23 \text{ pounds}}{4 \text{ boxes}} = 5.75 \text{ lb./box}$$

EXERCISE 3

Unit Rates

Directions: Write the following as unit rates.

1. Compare 560 houses and 14 blocks as a unit rate.

2. Compare 91 mice and 26 cages as a unit rate with a mixed number.

3. Write 213 rooms and 6 floors as a unit rate with a decimal number.

Answers are on page 546.

Using Unit Rates

Unit rates are often used to find total quantities, using different versions of this equation:

total quantity = unit rate × number of items.

Here are some examples with different names for the parts of the equation:

distance = rate of speed × time

earnings = hourly wage × hours worked

total cost = unit cost × number of items bought

EXAMPLES

A train traveling at 45 mph for 6 hours will cover a distance of 45 × 6 = 270 miles.

A worker earning $12.58 per hour will earn $12.58 × 40 = $503.20 in a 40-hour workweek.

$3\frac{3}{4}$ pounds of organic tomatoes at $2.00 per pound have a total cost of $3\frac{3}{4} \times 2 = \$7.50$.

EXERCISE 4

Using Unit Rates

Directions: Use the given unit rates to find total values.

1. 22 students per classroom in a school with 30 classrooms

2. 5 buckets of strawberries at $3.99 per bucket

3. 12 dump trucks containing 3.5 tons of sand per truck

4. driving at 70 miles per hour for 4 hours

5. 16 boxes of nails with 80 nails per box

6. 25 hours at $8.22 per hour

7. 120 square feet of wall per gallon of paint, $5\frac{1}{3}$ gallons of paint

8. 24 hours per day for 7 days

Answers are on page 546.

Proportions

A **proportion** is a comparison between two ratios or rates. A proportion may be written with fractions or colons or may be written out in words. When using fractions, a proportion looks like a statement of equality of two fractions: $\frac{26}{39} = \frac{50}{75}$. When written with colons, a double colon takes the place of the equal sign: 26:39::50:75. In both cases, the proportion is read and written as "26 is to 39 as 50 is to 75." When using colons, either proportion may have more than two components, as in 3:4:5::6:8:10, and when using either form, there may be more than two proportions to be compared, as in $\frac{5}{8} = \frac{10}{16} = \frac{15}{24}$.

When proportions are used to solve problems, one of the quantities is unknown and you usually need to find the value of the unknown quantity. One method of solving a proportion uses a double number line. Suppose that a recipe that serves 4 calls for 7 ounces of grated cheddar, but the cook is preparing for a catering job where 60 people are to be served. How much cheddar will be needed? A proportion can be used to express the relationship between people and cheese in the recipe and for the banquet if an unknown is used to represent the amount of cheddar needed for the larger batch. If n is the number of ounces used, then a proportion that represents the relative sizes of the quantities is 7:4::n:60. To use a double number line to determine the value of n, start by drawing two parallel number lines with the known ratio:

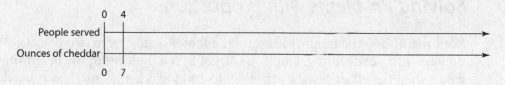

Continue marking off successively larger numbers of people by counting by fours until the desired number of people is reached:

Next, count by sevens until the matching number of people is reached:

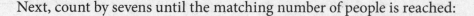

The number of ounces of cheese needed for the banquet is 105 ounces.

This problem could also be solved by using a table.

people	4	8	12	16	20	24	28	...	60
ounces of cheddar	7	14	21	28	35	42	49	...	105

The idea behind using the table is similar to using the double number line. Multiples of quantities are counted off until the desired goal is reached.

EXERCISE 5

Proportions

Directions: Use a double number line or a table to solve the following problem.

A computer hard drive with a capacity of 150 GB costs $40. Assuming cost and capacity are proportional, what would be the cost of a hard drive with a capacity of 750 GB?

The answer is on page 546.

Solving Problems with Proportions

Both methods—the number line and the table—suffer from two defects: they are time-consuming, and if the target isn't a multiple of the beginning value, then the effort saved by the easy technique is lost. A method is needed that is more efficient and that always works.

Test for Proportionality

$a:b::c:d$ if and only if $ad = bc$

In terms of fractions,

$$\frac{a}{b} = \frac{c}{d} \text{ if and only if } ad = bc$$

The fraction form of the test is where the term *cross-multiply* comes from. The method that can always be used to solve proportions is a slight modification of the test. Write the proportion as an equality between fractions, with the unknown quantity in the numerator of one of the fractions. For the banquet example, write $\frac{7}{4} = \frac{n}{60}$. Next, multiply both sides of the equal sign by the number in the denominator beneath the variable:

$$\frac{60}{1} \cdot \frac{7}{4} = \frac{n}{60} \cdot \frac{60}{1}$$

On the side of the equation with the variable, the numbers cancel each other to leave the variable isolated. On the other side, carry out the indicated operations and simplify.

$$\frac{15}{1} \cdot \frac{7}{1} = n$$
$$105 = n$$

This process doesn't depend on the target values being multiples of the starting values.

EXAMPLE

A quarry sells 9 tons of rock aggregate for $550. How much aggregate can a landscaper buy for $1200?

Assuming the landscaper buys the aggregate at the same unit rate, the proportion $\frac{9}{550} = \frac{n}{1200}$ applies. Multiply both sides of the equation by 1200 to isolate the variable:

$$\frac{1200}{1} \cdot \frac{9}{550} = \frac{n}{1200} \cdot \frac{1200}{1}$$
$$\frac{24}{1} \cdot \frac{9}{11} = n$$
$$\frac{216}{11} = n$$
$$19.64 = n$$

$1200 buys 19.64 tons of aggregate.

EXERCISE 6

Solving Problems with Proportions

Directions: Solve the following problems.

1. Three diesel engines can pull a train 0.85 miles long. How long of a train can be pulled by 5 diesel engines?

2. A gardener uses 8 pounds of plant food for a garden that covers 36 square feet of ground. How much ground would 22 pounds of plant food cover?

3. On a purchase of $132, the sales tax is $10.89. At the same tax rate, what would be the sales tax on a $77 purchase?

Answers are on page 546.

CHAPTER 6

Percents

The key to percents is buried in the name. *Percent* is short for the Latin phrase *per centum,* which literally means "by the hundred" and signifies division by 100. This division is accomplished by moving a decimal point two places to the left, in the case of decimal numbers, or by multiplying by $\frac{1}{100}$, in the case of fractions.

Converting Between Percents and Decimals

Percentages need to be converted to decimal numbers or fractions for calculations. Remembering the definition of *percent* will help you.

Converting Percents to Decimals

To convert a percent to a decimal, drop the percentage sign and divide by 100, moving the decimal two places to the left.

EXAMPLES

Convert the following percentages to their decimal equivalents.

1. 50%

Take *50%,* drop the percent sign, and assume the decimal point is at the right end. Move the decimal point two places left. 50% → 0.50

2. 37.5%

Drop the percent sign, and move the decimal point two places to the left. 37.5% → 0.375

Converting Decimals to Percents

To convert a decimal to a percent, multiply by 100%. This is accomplished by moving the decimal point two places to the right and attaching a percent sign.

EXAMPLES

Convert the decimals to percentages.

1. 0.75

Move the decimal point two places right and attach a percent sign. 0.75 → 75%

2. 1.35

Even though this is a number greater than 1, you do not change your procedure. Move the decimal point two places to the right and attach a percent sign. 1.35 → 135%

What you have been doing by moving the decimal is multiplying and dividing by 100. Rather than remember a rule as to how to move the decimal point, think about the result you are looking for. Percents are always larger than the decimal numbers they represent. If you are trying to convert a decimal to a percent and move the decimal point to the left, you get a smaller number. That does *not* correspond to what you already know and should alert you to the error. Moving the decimal point to the right gives a bigger number, assuring you that that is the correct way to convert a decimal to a percent. When converting a percent to a decimal, just the opposite is true: you want a smaller number, so you move the decimal point left. Keep these ideas in mind and you will immediately recognize an error if you make one.

EXERCISE 1

Converting Between Percents and Decimals

Directions: Convert the percentages to equivalent decimal numbers.

1. 45%   **2.** 127%   **3.** 0.25%

Convert the decimal numbers to equivalent percentages.

4. 0.17   **5.** 2.45   **6.** 0.085

Answers are on page 546.

Converting Between Percents and Fractions

Converting Percents to Fractions

To convert a percent to a fraction, drop the percent sign, multiply by $\frac{1}{100}$, and reduce. You may need to multiply top and bottom by a power of 10 to remove decimals, as shown in the following example.

EXAMPLE

Convert 47.2% to a fraction.

You drop the percent sign and multiply by $\frac{1}{100}$, but you must also multiply the numerator and denominator by 10 to remove the decimal. You then reduce the fraction.

$$\frac{47.2}{1}\cdot\frac{1}{100} = \frac{47.2}{100} = \frac{47.2}{100}\times\frac{10}{10} = \frac{472}{1000} = \frac{59}{125}$$

Converting Fractions to Percents

To convert a fraction to a percent, multiply the fraction by $\frac{100}{1}$, simplify, and attach a percent sign.

EXAMPLE

Convert the fraction $\frac{7}{16}$ to a percent.

$$\frac{7}{16}\cdot\frac{100}{1} = \frac{7}{4}\cdot\frac{25}{1} = \frac{175}{4} = 43\frac{3}{4}, \text{ so } \frac{7}{16} = 43\frac{3}{4}\%.$$

EXAMPLE

Convert $2\frac{3}{8}$ to a percent.

First change the mixed number to an improper fraction: $2\frac{3}{8} = \frac{19}{8}$.

Then change the improper fraction to a percent:

$$\frac{19}{8}\cdot\frac{100}{1} = \frac{19}{2}\cdot\frac{25}{1} = \frac{475}{2} = 237\frac{1}{2}, \text{ so } 2\frac{3}{8} = 237\frac{1}{2}\%.$$

EXERCISE 2

Converting Between Percents and Fractions

Directions: Convert the fraction to a percent.

1. $\frac{4}{5}$ 2. $\frac{36}{125}$ 3. $99\frac{44}{100}$

Convert the percent to a fraction.

4. 72%   5. 827%   6. 0.055%

Answers are on page 547.

Basic Percentage Questions

When asked to find a percentage of something, remember that the word *of* tells you to multiply and the word *is* shows where to put the equal sign. You can use the clues to set up an equation that, when solved, will lead to the correct answer. When setting up the equation, convert the percent to a decimal or fraction equivalent.

> ### EXAMPLE
>
> What is 17% of 135?
>
> Using x to represent the answer, this question can be translated to $x = 0.17 \cdot 135$. Carry out the indicated multiplication: $0.17 \cdot 135 = 22.95$, so 22.95 is 17% of 135.

> ### EXAMPLE
>
> 55 is 11% of what number?
>
> Changing 11% to a decimal and using x as a placeholder for the unknown number, the problem translates directly to $55 = 0.11 \cdot x$. Solve this equation by dividing both sides by 0.11: $\dfrac{55}{0.11} = \dfrac{0.11x}{0.11}$. Carrying out the division on the left side and canceling the common factors on the right side gives $500 = x$, so 55 is 11% of 500.

When the percent is the quantity to be found, solving the equation produces a fraction or decimal equivalent to the percent. This needs to be converted to a percent using one of the procedures above.

> ### EXAMPLE
>
> What percent of 700 is 35?
>
> The equation is $x \cdot 700 = 35$. Dividing both sides of the equation by 700 gives $\dfrac{x \cdot 700}{700} = \dfrac{35}{700}$. Canceling the common factors and reducing the fraction gives $x = \dfrac{1}{20}$. The question asked for a percent, so convert $\dfrac{1}{20}$ to a percent by multiplying by $\dfrac{100}{1}$ and attaching a percent sign: $\dfrac{1}{20} \cdot \dfrac{100}{1} = 5$. The answer is 5%.

EXERCISE 3

Basic Percentage Questions

Directions: Answer the following questions.

1. What percent of 55 does 11 represent?

2. 17% of 355 is what number?

3. 45% of what number is 15?

4. Sondra has paid off 22.5% of her $15,000 school loan. How much does she still need to pay?

Answers are on page 547.

Percent Increase and Decrease

Often increases and decreases are quoted in percentages. Statements like, "With only 20 incidents this year, violent crime in town has decreased by 31% since last year" and "That stock is selling at $45 per share, and that's a 25% increase in the last week!" are not unusual.

But perhaps either statement brings a question to mind. What was the number of violent incidents last year? What did the stock sell for last week? In either case, you must remember that the increase or decrease is in relation to the *original* amount.

Percent Decrease Problems

If a figure is said to be a decrease, then it represents less than 100% of the original. You can subtract the decrease from 100% to get the present figure. If a certain item is selling for 55% off (a decrease of 55% from the original price), then the new price is only 45% of the original price (100% – 55% = 45%). Knowing this, you can divide the new price by 0.45 to get the original price.

EXAMPLE

The mayor of a small town states, "With only 20 incidents this year, violent crime in town is down by 31% since last year." What was the number of violent crimes last year?

From the statement, you can say that this year's figure, 20 violent crimes, is 69% of last year's number (100% − 31% = 69%). You can then translate the sentence into an equation with x representing last year's figure: $20 = 0.69x$. Dividing both sides of this equation by 0.69, you get $\frac{20}{0.69} = x$. The division comes out to about 28.99, or rounded to the nearest whole number, 29. There were 29 violent crimes last year.

Percent Increase Problems

If there is an increase, you can say that the present number is more than 100% of the original. If a store raises its prices by 10%, you will now pay 110% of the old price.

EXAMPLE

A stock is selling today for $45 a share, which is a 25% increase over last week's price. What did a share cost last week?

Today's price is 125% of the old price, or if you let x be the old price, $45 = 1.25x$. Dividing both sides by 1.25 gives $\frac{45}{1.25} = x$, and carrying out the division results in $36 = x$. The price of the stock was $36 last week.

Multiple Increases and Decreases

A particularly tricky problem is one in which a figure increases or decreases over two separate periods or increases during one period and decreases the next, or the other way around. These kinds of problems must be worked one step at a time. You cannot simply add or subtract percents from the original figure, though it might be tempting to do so, because that figure will have changed from one period to the next.

EXAMPLE

Rivera Plumbing had sales of $327,000 this year, which is an increase of 20% over last year's sales figures. Last year's sales were a 30% increase over those of the year before. What were the sales figures for last year and the year before?

This year's sales figure of $327,000 is 120% of last year's figure, so you can write $327,000 = 1.20x$, where x is last year's sales. Solving, $x = \frac{327,000}{1.20} = 272,500$ for last year's sales number. That figure, $272,500, is 130% of the sales for the year before that. Again, you can write an equation, $272,500 = 1.30x$ with x representing the sales number for the year before. Solving, $x = \dfrac{272{,}500}{1.3} = 209{,}615$ to the nearest dollar.

The figures for the three years are: $209,615, $272,500, and $327,000.

EXERCISE 4

Percent Increase and Decrease

Directions: Solve the following problems.

1. Tourism at a resort is up 4% from last year's count of 3000 visitors. How many visitors are there this year?

2. At the beginning of summer, a reservoir held 50,000 acre-feet of water. At the end of summer, the reservoir was down to 37,200 acre-feet. What percent decrease does this represent?

3. A book is on sale for $12.99, which is 35% off the regular price. What is the regular price?

4. A small town experienced a population boom of 30% to 117 residents. What was the population of the town before the boom?

5. Jenny got a raise in her hourly wage from $9.85 to $10.44 per hour. What percent increase is this?

6. Mikey decides he is watching too much TV. He cuts his weekly viewing time back by 20% in the first week. Not happy with the results, he cuts back an additional 25% in the second week. He is happy with his final weekly total of 18 hours. How much TV was Mikey watching each week before he started cutting back?

7. Genya transplants a flower from a flowerpot into her flower garden. The flower gains 45% in height in the first month and another 30% in the second month, at which time it is 24.5 inches tall. How tall was the flower when it was transplanted?

8. The Sanderson family has a gross income of $52,000. Because Ms. Sanderson received a raise, this is a 5% increase over last year. However, last year's income was a 10% decrease from the year before because Mr. Sanderson's hours at work were cut back. What was the family income two years ago, rounded to the nearest dollar?

Answers are on page 547.

CHAPTER 7

Probability and Statistics

Probability

In the modern world, probability has uses that range from calculating insurance premiums to deciding how often a particular auto part or even an entire car will fail. The study of probability can get very complex; this chapter covers the basics that you need to know.

The **probability** of an event (something happening) is defined as the number of desirable outcomes divided by the number of possible outcomes. Another way to look at it is "wins divided by tries."

For example, if you flip a fair coin, the probability of getting heads is the number of ways to get heads, 1, divided by the number of possible results, 2 (heads or tails). The probability is $\frac{1}{2}$, 50%, or 0.5, depending upon how you want to write it. Probabilities can be written as fractions, decimals, or percents. The total of the probabilities for all the results always adds up to 100%, or 1.

EXAMPLE

There are 3 black and 5 yellow puppies in a litter of Labs. Picking at random, what is the probability of selecting a black Lab?

A "win" is picking a black Lab. There are 3 black puppies out of 8, so the probability is $\frac{3}{8} = 0.375 = 37.5\%$

EXERCISE 1

Probability

Directions: Answer the following question.

Given a standard 52-card deck, what is the probability of picking the given card(s) below on the first try?

A. a face card (jack, queen, or king)
B. an ace
C. the ace of hearts

Answers are on page 547.

Solving Problems Using Probability

The most common probability problems deal with selection: picking numbered balls out of a bowl (as in the lottery), selecting groups of people from a crowd, getting a certain dice throw, or picking a card or series of cards from a deck of 52.

The problems usually differ in whether the probabilities change with each try. If you are selecting colored balls from a jar with 5 red and 5 yellow balls and don't put balls back once they are picked, the more red balls you pick, the more likely the next pick will be a yellow ball. However, if you put the balls back so that all balls are in the bowl for every pick, the probabilities stay the same.

In some of these situations, you add probabilities. Other times, you multiply them.

Probabilities of Repeated Events

Take a fair coin. What is the probability of throwing two heads one after the other? Going back to the definition of probability, there are four possible outcomes: HH, HT, TH, TT. Only one of these, HH, is what you want. The probability of two heads is 1 out of 4, or $\frac{1}{4}$. You can also say the probability of a head on the first throw is $\frac{1}{2}$. On the second throw, it is also $\frac{1}{2}$. The throws are **independent**: the outcome of the first throw doesn't affect the outcome of the second throw. When outcomes are independent, probabilities are multiplied. To compute the probability of getting two heads, multiply $\frac{1}{2}$ times $\frac{1}{2}$ to get $\frac{1}{4}$, the same as the previous result.

EXAMPLE

What is the probability of throwing 3 heads in 3 tries?

Every time you flip the coin, the probability of a head is the same, $\frac{1}{2}$.

The probability of getting three heads in three flips is: $\frac{1}{2} \times \frac{1}{2} \times \frac{1}{2} = \frac{1}{8}$.

EXERCISE 2

Probabilities of Repeated Events

Directions: Answer the following question.

What is the probability of rolling 3 consecutive 3's with a fair die?

The answer is on page 547.

Mutually Exclusive Events

When two events cannot both possibly occur, they are said to be **mutually exclusive**. The probabilities for mutually exclusive events may be added. In the example of throwing a coin twice, there are four possible events, but only two, HT and TH, in which you get a single head. Each of those two has a probability of $\frac{1}{4}$. However, those two events cannot *both* occur. To answer the question "What is the probability of getting one head in two throws?" you add the probabilities: $\frac{1}{4} + \frac{1}{4} = \frac{1}{2}$, a result easily verified by applying the definition of probability: 2 desired events out of 4 possible events gives a probability of $\frac{2}{4} = \frac{1}{2}$.

Probabililty Trees

In some cases, figuring out the different results and probabilities is more complex. In situations like these, you can use a probability tree to map things out. Trees, such as those used in business to evaluate risk and reward of certain actions, can get very complex. However, all trees are basically the same.

For example, let's use a tree to figure the probabilities of the genders of children in a family with three children. The actual probability of a boy being born is 0.512 and that of a girl is 0.488. The first child may be a boy or a girl. You plot that like this:

The second birth leads to another set of possibilities, boy or girl, which is plotted as follows:

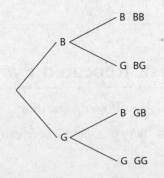

Finally, the third child comes along, and the tree looks like this:

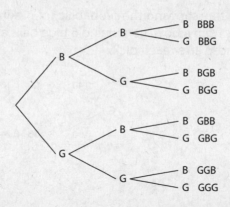

Possible gender combinations are found by following the paths on the tree. Putting the probabilities on each branch helps you to calculate the probability of each outcome. Gender determination is independent from one birth to another, so the probability for each combination is found by multiplying. For the track highlighted, GBG, the probability is 0.488 × 0.512 × 0.488 = 0.122.

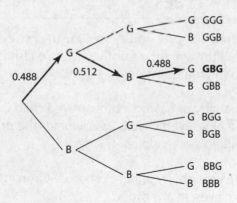

This chart shows the probabilities worked out, using these data.

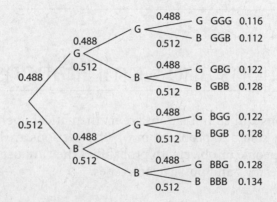

EXAMPLE

Here is a tree showing the probability of picking different combinations of 2 balls from a bowl containing 6 blue balls and 4 green balls. The balls are replaced after each pick.

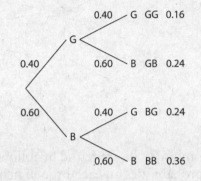

EXERCISE 3

Probability Trees

Directions: Draw the probability tree for the eye color possibilities, blue and brown, for a family with two children. Then answer the following questions.

1. If the probability of having a brown-eyed child is 75% and the probability of having a blue-eyed child is 25%, what is the probability of each possible pair of children's eye colors?

2. What is the probability of having two children, one with blue eyes and one with brown eyes, in any order?

Answers are on page 547.

Permutations and Combinations

Permutations and combinations are mathematical operations that are particularly suited to problems in which selections are being made from a group of people or objects. In probability they are used for counting the number of events and possible outcomes.

Factorials

Permutations and combinations both rely on the concept of the **factorial.** The factorial multiplies all the numbers from a given number down to 1. For example, 5! is read "five factorial," and 5! = 5 × 4 × 3 × 2 × 1 = 120. For purposes of calculation, 1! and 0! are both defined as 1.

EXAMPLE

Evaluate six factorial (6!).

6! = 6 × 5 × 4 × 3 × 2 × 1 = 720

EXERCISE 4

Factorials

Directions: Evaluate the following:

1. 3!

2. 6!

3. 10!

Answers are on page 548.

Problems Using Permutations and Combinations

Permutations are used when the order in which items are arranged is important. Otherwise, a **combination** is used.

Let's take a basketball coach at a very small high school. Only five students come out for basketball tryouts. There is only one combination (selection of five students) that will form the team—all five. But when the coach looks at which student to play at which position, there are a greater number of permutations (arrangements) to consider.

The number of possible combinations of r items (or ways to select r items) from a pool of n objects where order is unimportant (that is, where A, B, C is considered the same as B, C, A or C, B, A) is mathematically given as

$$_nC_r = \frac{n!}{(n-r)!r!}$$

Take the basketball coach just described. The coach must pick a team of 5 ($r = 5$) from a pool of five players, ($n = 5$), so

$$_5C_5 = \frac{5!}{(5-5)!5!} = \frac{5!}{(0)!5!} = \frac{5!}{(1)5!} = 1,$$

which you already know. (The coach can choose only one combination: all five of the students trying out.)

However, the five students can be assigned to different positions in several different ways; that is, as A, B, C, D, E or as B, C, D, E, A, and so on. The number of possible player arrangements is the permutation and is mathematically given as

$$_nP_r = \frac{n!}{(n-r)!}$$

The coach still has $n = 5$ and $r = 5$ but now the position played counts. Thus,

$$_5P_5 = \frac{5!}{(5-5)!} = \frac{5!}{(0)!} = \frac{5!}{1} = 5 \times 4 \times 3 \times 2 \times 1 = 120 \text{ different arrangements.}$$

EXAMPLE

A bride gets to play her choice of 3 out of 7 songs during the wedding ceremony. How many ways can she select them if the order in which they are played does not matter?

Order or arrangement does not matter here, so the calculation is a combination.

($r = 3$) and ($n = 7$), so

$$_7C_3 = \frac{7!}{(7-3)!3!} = \frac{7 \times 6 \times 5 \times 4 \times 3 \times 2 \times 1}{(4 \times 3 \times 2 \times 1)(3 \times 2 \times 1)} = 35 \text{ different programs.}$$

If the bride considers the order in which to play the selections, she can use a permutation formula to calculate how many possible arrangements there are:

$$_7P_3 = \frac{7!}{(7-3)!} = \frac{7!}{4!} = \frac{7 \times 6 \times 5 \times 4 \times 3 \times 2 \times 1}{4 \times 3 \times 2 \times 1} = 7 \times 6 \times 5 = 210$$

separate ways to arrange the selections.

As a way to decide when to use which calculation, remember that the permutation always provides more possibilities than the combination. Anything in a problem that increases the possibilities, such as asking different people to take different jobs on a committee, requires a permutation. A mixed salad is a combination, because the order in which ingredients are put in the bowl does not matter. What we call a combination lock might more accurately be called a "permutation lock" because the order in which you dial the numbers matters.

EXERCISE 5

Problems Using Permutations and Combinations

Directions: Solve the following problems.

1. A dress designer needs to select a group of 5 different shades of cloth from 7 available for a client's outfit. How many different groups of 5 shades can be chosen?

2. After selecting the group of 5, the designer learns that the client wants only 3 different shades in the dress, one each for the top, skirt, and belt. Assuming all combinations of the 3 shades will work, how many arrangements does the designer have to choose from?

Answers are on page 548.

Statistics: Mean, Median, and Mode

Statistics is the study and analysis of data usually in an effort to answer questions. For example, the predictions one sees before elections or a politician's approval ratings after the election rely on statistics. Statistics can be expressed as ratios, percents, or fractions.

In order to analyze and describe data, statisticians use a wide range of calculations and come up with a variety of descriptive measurements. Three of these are the **mean**, **median**, and **mode**.

Mean

The **mean** is an average. There are actually two kinds of mean. One is used when all the data values have equal importance, or weight. Called the *arithmetic mean*, this is simply an average. Add the data together and divide by the number of data points to calculate an average. If you look at 25 service stations and average the price of one gallon of gasoline, you would be finding the arithmetic mean.

The second type of mean is called the **weighted mean**, or weighted average. This is used when different data have different importance, or weight. You are probably familiar with such a mean: a grade point average, or GPA, is a weighted mean. For a weighted mean, you multiply the data times its weight, total the products, and divide by the total of the weights. Look at the following example.

EXAMPLE

For this semester, Saied has the grades shown in the chart. If an A is worth 4 points, a B is worth 3, a C is worth 2, and a D is worth 1 point, what is his GPA?

Course	Credit Hours	Letter Grade	Points	Hours x Points
English	3	B	3	9
Math	3	C	2	6
Science	4	B	3	12
History	3	A	4	12
Physical Ed	1	D	1	1
TOTALS	14 hours			40

$$\frac{40}{14} = 2.86$$

In business, the same process is used in calculating the value of inventory when different amounts of merchandise are bought at different prices and then mixed together.

Median

Another measure is the **median**. Just like the median on a highway, which splits the highway into two equal parts, the **median** is the value right in the middle. It divides the data into two sets with the same number of items in each. If you have an even number of data points, the median is halfway between the two center points as shown.

EXAMPLE

Find the median of the distribution 6, 7, 3, 4, 9, 11, 2, 0, 20.

First, arrange the data in order: 0, 2, 3, 4, 6, 7, 9, 11, 20. Count from each end to find the middle value. That value is the 6. There are four values less than 6 and four more than 6.

EXAMPLE

Find the median of the distribution: 7, 9, 10, 3, 4, 2.

Put the numbers in order: 2, 3, 4, 7, 9, 10.

Count from each end. The median falls between 4 and 7. Use the average of the two points. Average 4 and 7 to get a median of $5\frac{1}{2}$.

Mode

The last measure is the **mode**. The mode is that data value that is seen most often in the data set. Data sets can have no mode (all values appear only once), one mode, or two or more modes.

EXAMPLE

What is the mode of the set 2, 3, 6, 7, 7, 9, 1, 8?

The most seen data value is 7. It is the mode.

EXERCISE 6

Statistics: Mean, Median, and Mode

Directions: Solve the following problems.

1. For the given distribution, find the mean, median, and mode(s).

Student Number	Shoe Size (in cm)
1	30.0
2	27.5
3	32.0
4	27.5
5	26.0
6	34.0
7	25.0

2. Ari's Rapid Oil Change and Garage bought oil filters on the dates shown below. What is the weighted average cost of the filters?

Date	Number of Filters	Price per Filter
1 January	25	$2.50
15 January	15	$2.75
21 January	10	$3.00
5 February	15	$2.50
12 February	15	$2.00
Totals		

Answers are on page 548.

CHAPTER 8
Geometry

In this section, you will study several mathematical formulas. The ones you need to memorize for the GED test are underlined. Formulas that are not underlined are provided when you take the GED test.

Geometry Basics

Perimeter is expressed in singular units of length, such as inches or centimeters, and is represented by the symbol p.

Area is expressed in square units, such as square feet, and is represented by A.

Volume is expressed in cubic units, such as cubic yards, and is represented by V.

The **radius**, r, is the distance from the center of a circle to its edge and is one-half the diameter of the circle.

Slant height, represented by the symbol ℓ, is measured perpendicular to an edge of the base *on the outside of a three-dimensional body.* It is not necessarily perpendicular to the base itself.

Height, h, is the distance from the base of a body to its top, measured perpendicular to the base.

Slant Height and Actual Height

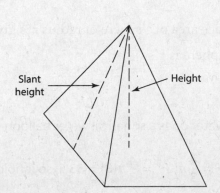
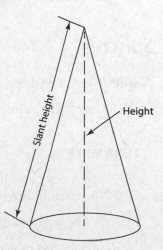

Circles and Spheres

The number π (pi)

Formulas for circles, spheres, cones, cylinders, and other round objects often have the number π in them. This number has an infinite decimal expansion, but the values 3.14, 3.142, 3.14159, or $\frac{22}{7}$ may be used as approximations. Many calculators, including the on-screen calculator you will use on the GED test, have a button with this value already programmed in.

Circles

The perimeter of a circle, the distance around it, is given a special name: **circumference**. For a circle with radius r, the circumference is given by $C = 2\pi r$. You may have learned this as $C = \pi d$, where d is the diameter. Just remember that diameter $d = 2r$.

The **area of a circle** of radius r is given by $A = \pi r^2$ and is expressed in square units such as square inches.

EXAMPLE

A circular ring for showing horses at the county fairgrounds needs to be fenced, and then wood shavings need to be carted in and spread over the ring's surface. If the ring has a 30-foot radius, how much fencing is needed, and what is the area to be covered in shavings?

The fence must go around the circumference, so $C = 2\pi r = 2\pi(30) = 189$ feet, rounded to the next whole foot. The area to be covered in shavings is $A = \pi r^2 = \pi(30)^2 = 2828$ square feet, to the next whole square foot.

Spheres

A **sphere** is a round ball. The surface area of a sphere of radius r is given by $SA = 4\pi r^2$. The volume of the sphere is $V = \frac{4}{3}\pi r^3$.

EXAMPLE

How many cubic inches of water does a spherical water balloon with a 2-inch radius hold?

The volume of water is $V = \frac{4}{3}\pi(2)^3 = \frac{4}{3}\pi(8) = 33.5$, so it holds 33.5 cubic inches of water.

EXERCISE 1

Circles and Spheres

Directions: Answer the following questions.

1. A circular doughnut shop under construction is to have an area of 1810 square feet. What will the radius of the building be?

2. The shop described in Question 1 is to have a domed roof that is a hemisphere: one half of a sphere. How many square feet of roofing will be needed to cover the roof? (Hint: Check the answer to Question 1 to get the correct value for the radius of the building and dome.)

Answers are on page 549.

Squares, Cubes, Rectangles, and Rectangular Prisms

Squares

The perimeter is the distance around something. Squares have four equal sides, so for a square of side s, the perimeter is $p = 4s$. The area of a square with side s is $A = s^2$—hence the term "squared" for anything to the second power.

Cubes

A cube is a three-dimensional object whose edges are equal and that has six square sides. The surface area of a cube of edge s is $SA = 6s^2$. The volume of a cube is $V = s^3$ cubic units. This is why anything to the third power is said to be "cubed."

EXERCISE 2

Cubes

Directions: Answer the following questions.

Sam creates a box in the shape of a cube 15 cm on an edge.

1. What is its volume?

2. If the box has no top, what is the surface area of the outsides of the cube?

Answers are on page 549.

Rectangles

A rectangle has four sides made up of parallel pairs of equal length, at right angles to one another. The perimeter of a rectangle l units long and w units wide is $p = 2l + 2w$. The area of that same rectangle is $A = lw$.

Rectangular Prisms

A **rectangular prism** has six sides, like a cube, but not all the sides are squares—some or all are rectangles. Think of a shoe box. The surface area for a rectangular prism of length l, width w, and height h is $A = 2lw + 2hl + 2hw$. The volume of a rectangular prism is $V = lwh$, which is the same as multiplying the area of the base, $B = lw$, times the height, h, to get $V = Bh$.

Triangles, Pyramids, Cones, and Cylinders

Triangles

A triangle has three sides, and the sum of its internal angles is 180°. The perimeter of a triangle is the sum of all three sides. You get the perimeter by adding the sides: $p = a + b + c$, where a, b, and c are the lengths of the sides of the triangle. If the triangle is a right triangle (one that has a 90° angle), you may need to remember the Pythagorean theorem: $a^2 + b^2 = c^2$. In this equation a and b are the lengths of the two shorter sides, and c is the length of the longest side, called the **hypotenuse**. The area of a triangle is $A = \frac{1}{2}bh$, where b is the length of the base and h is the height of the triangle. This works for all triangles regardless of shape.

EXAMPLE

Find the area of the following triangle.

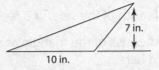

Here the base is 10 inches and the height is 7 inches. This works even when the height measurement is outside the triangle. Using the equation for area,

$$A = \frac{1}{2}bh = \frac{1}{2}10 \times 7 = \frac{1}{2} \times 70 = 35 \text{ square inches}$$

EXERCISE 3

Triangles

Directions: Answer the following question.

1. Three triangular harbor signs of base $b = 12$ feet and height $h = 12$ feet need to be painted. How many square feet will the paint need to cover?

The answer is on page 549.

Pyramids

A regular **pyramid** is a three-dimensional body with a square base and four triangular sides that meet at a point above the center of the base.

The surface area of a pyramid is $A = \frac{1}{2}pl + B$ where p is the perimeter of the base, l is the slant height, and B is the area of the base. The area of the base is $B = l \times w$ and may require a calculation all its own. A pyramid's volume is simpler, just $V = \frac{1}{3}Bh$ where B is the area of the base and h is the height of the pyramid (*not* the slant height). The height is the vertical distance between the base and the peak of the pyramid. If you are given the slant height instead, you must calculate the true height. You can use the Pythagorean theorem to make that calculation.

EXAMPLE

Given a regular pyramid with a square base 6 feet on a side and slant height of 5 feet, calculate the volume.

You need to calculate the true height of the pyramid. The height is measured from the center of the base, so you have a triangle whose base is $\frac{1}{2}$ the length of the side, or 3 feet. The slant height of 5 feet forms the hypotenuse of the triangle as shown on the side view of the pyramid shown here.

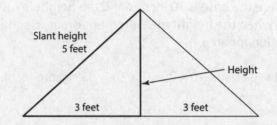

Slant height
5 feet

Height

3 feet   3 feet

By the Pythagorean theorem:

$$h^2 + 3^2 = 5^2$$

$$h = \sqrt{5^2 - 3^2} = \sqrt{25 - 9} = \sqrt{16} = 4$$

Knowing that the true height is 4, you can apply the formula $V = \frac{1}{3}Bh$ where the area of the base is $B = 6^2 = 36$.

$$V = \frac{1}{3}(36)(4) = 48 \text{ cubic feet.}$$

EXERCISE 4

Pyramids

Directions: Answer the following question.

1. According to one source, the Great Pyramid in Egypt has a base 756 feet on a side and a slant height of 480 feet. What is the volume of the pyramid in cubic feet?

The answer is on page 549.

Cones

A cone is a three-dimensional figure with a circular base and a triangular cross-section, just like an ice-cream cone. The surface area of a cone is $A = \pi rl + \pi r^2$ where l is the slant height of the cone and r the radius of the base. If the base is not counted, the area is $A = \pi rl$. The volume of the cone is $V = \frac{1}{3} Bh$ or $V = \frac{1}{3} \pi r^2 h$, since πr^2 is the area of the base.

EXAMPLE

Not counting the base, what is the surface area of a cone of slant height 5 feet if the radius of the base is 2 feet?

The area of the cone without the base is $A = \pi rl$. Substituting the cone's dimensions, you get

$A = \pi rl = \pi(2)(5) = 10\pi = 31.4$ square feet of area.

EXERCISE 5

Cones

Directions: Answer the following question.

1. What is the total surface area and volume of a cone whose base is 11 cm in diameter and whose slant height is 17 cm? Include the area of the base.

The answer is on page 549.

Cylinders

A cylinder is shaped like an ordinary metal can. It has straight sides and circular ends. For a cylinder of height h, with ends of radius r, the surface area is $A = 2\pi r^2 + 2\pi rh = 2\pi r(r + h)$, and the volume is $V = \pi r^2 h$.

EXAMPLE

If you look back at the county fair's show ring, 30 feet in radius, its area was 2828 square feet. If the shavings must be spread to a depth of 8 inches, how many cubic feet of shavings are needed?

Looking at the volume of shavings as a wide, flat cylinder, the volume is area multiplied by height. Because 8 inches is only part of a foot, the height (depth) of the cylinder is $\frac{8}{12}$.

$$V = \pi r^2 \times \frac{8}{12} = 2828 \times \frac{8}{12} = 1886 \text{ cubic feet of shavings}$$

EXERCISE 6

Cylinders

Directions: Answer the following questions.

1. What is the surface area of a tuna fish can that measures 1.25 inches in height and has a diameter of 3.5 inches?

2. What is the volume of the tuna fish can?

Answers are on page 550.

Other Geometric Shapes

Hexagons

Regular hexagons are really six equilateral triangles put together in a circular arrangement. The area of a regular hexagon can be found if the length of a side s is known, using this formula:

$$A = \frac{3\sqrt{3}s^2}{2} = \left(\frac{3}{2}\sqrt{3}\right)s^2$$

If you know the apothem, a, the distance from the center of the hexagon perpendicular to one side, the formula becomes

$A = 3sa$

EXERCISE 7

Hexagons

Directions: Answer the following question.

1. What is the difference in area between a circle with a radius of 6 units and a regular hexagon with a side of 6 units?

The answer is on page 550.

Pentagons

For a regular pentagon—that is, one whose sides are equal—the area is $A = \frac{5}{2}sa$ where s is the length of a side and a is the apothem.

Other Polygons and Prisms

All right prisms, that is, three-dimensional bodies whose sides are perpendicular to their bases (ends), have the same formula for their volumes: the area of the base times the height of the prism, $V = Bh$. The base may be a square, rectangle, hexagon, triangle, circle, or another plane figure. Finding the area of the base may present the only challenge in questions requiring you to calculate the volume of polygons and prisms.

Complex Bodies

Many seemingly complex bodies can be broken down to simpler forms and each part calculated separately. For example, a medical pill (capsule) is a cylinder with half a sphere on each end. If a manufacturer needs to calculate the volume of a capsule, it is a simpler matter than you might think.

EXAMPLE

A fancy gift box has the shape of a rectangular prism with a square base at the bottom and a pyramid on the top. The rectangular prism of the box measures 6 inches long, and its base is 4 inches on a side. The pyramid has a slant height of $3\frac{1}{2}$ inches. What are the surface area and volume of the box?

The surface area of a rectangular prism is $A = 2lw + 2hl + 2hw$. But because the base is a square, the area of the sides is $A = 4sh$. When you add the area of one end, it becomes $A = 4sh + s^2$ plus the surface area of the pyramid at the other end without the base of the pyramid.

The pyramid's surface area is $A = \frac{1}{2}pl$, with $p = 4s = 4(4) = 16$.

Combining these two areas, the total area is $A = 4sh + s^2 + \frac{1}{2}pl$. Substituting numbers,

$$A = 4(4)(6) + 4^2 + \frac{1}{2}(16)\left(3\frac{1}{2}\right) = 4(24) + 16 + \frac{1}{2}(56) = 96 + 16 + 28 = 140$$

The area is 140 square inches. The volume of the rectangular prism is $V = lwh = 4 \times 4 \times 6 = 96$ cubic inches. The volume of the pyramid is $V = \frac{1}{3}Bh$ with $B = s^2 = 4^2 = 16$. You have the slant height, but you need the true height. You can use the Pythagorean theorem to find the true height. You have a triangle with hypotenuse of $3\frac{1}{2}$ and base 2, (half the side of the base of the pyramid), so

$$h^2 + 2^2 = 3.5^2$$
$$h^2 + 4 = 12.25$$
$$h^2 = 8.25$$
$$h = 2.87$$

The Pythagorean theorem gives you a true height of 2.87 inches. The volume of the pyramid is $V = \frac{1}{3} \times 16 \times 2.87 = 15.3$ cubic inches. The total volume is $96 + 15.3 = 111.3$ cubic inches.

EXERCISE 8

Complex Bodies

Directions: Answer the following question.

1. A pharmaceutical capsule (pill) is 0.75 cm across and has a length of 1.25 cm, not counting the two half-sphere ends. What is the volume of the capsule?

The answer is on page 550.

CHAPTER 9

Polynomials and Rational Expressions

Polynomial Basics

Polynomials are mathematical expressions made up of individual **terms**. Terms are separated from each other by arithmetic signs and can be made up of several parts, as shown below. Not all parts appear in every term.

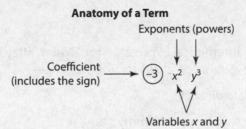

Anatomy of a Term

EXAMPLE

List the *terms* in $15x^4 - 3x^3y^4 + 15y^4$.

Terms are separated by plus or minus signs. There are three terms: $15x^4$, $-3x^3y^4$, and $15y^4$.

Writing Polynomials

Most of the time, polynomials are written in **descending order**. The term with the greatest exponent goes first, and the rest follow in order of decreasing exponents.

EXAMPLE

Rewrite the polynomial $x^2 + 5x^3 - 3x^5 - 4 + 2x$ in descending order:

$$-3x^5 + 5x^3 + x^2 + 2x - 4$$

The largest exponent is 5, so the term $-3x^5$ is first, followed by $5x^3$ and so on. The exponent in $2x$ is 1 because $2x = 2x^1$, and the constant, without a variable part, is always last.

Because mathematics is a language that tells about how things act in the real world, you can translate situations from words to mathematical statements. Of course, any good translator needs a glossary, and one appears below. In the lists, the most commonly used terms are boldfaced and underlined.

Plus sign: Add, plus, **sum**, **total**, increased by, increase

Minus sign: subtract, minus, **difference**, fewer, decreased by, decrease

Multiplication sign: product, times, **of**, multiplied by, multiples

Division sign: quotient, divided, **per**, split into, parts of

Equal sign: equals, **is**, are, totals, results

When reading a sentence and creating a mathematical expression, rely on the glossary and replace terms with correct symbols.

EXAMPLE

Write a mathematical expression for "Today, Suzy is twice Tommy's age," using S for Suzi's age and T for Tommy's age.

Translate directly:

Today, Suzi is twice Tommy's age.

$S = 2$ times T or $S = 2T$

EXAMPLE

Write, "seven less than the square of one more than a number" as a polynomial expression in x.

One more than a number is $x + 1$. The square of that is $(x + 1)^2$, and 7 less than that is $(x + 1)^2 - 7$.

EXERCISE 1

Writing Polynomials

Directions: Write the following as polynomials in terms of x.

1. Six less than the cube of a number.

2. Four more than twice a number.

3. The square of three less than a number.

4. Two more than the cube of a number.

5. Twice the cube of one more than a number.

Answers are on page 550.

Evaluating Polynomials

Since polynomials include variables, it is important to be able to evaluate polynomials when you have known values for the variables. To do this, replace each variable with the known value. Then evaluate the polynomial following the order of operations and other rules of calculation. Let's look at a purely mathematical example and then a real-life one.

EXAMPLE

If $k = x^2yz^3$, what is k if $x = 2$, $y = 12$, and $z = 15$?

Substituting the given values into the expression,
$k = x^2yz^3 = 2^2 \cdot 12 \cdot 15^3 = 4 \cdot 12 \cdot 3375 = 162,000$

EXAMPLE

Simple interest on a loan is given by $A = P(1 + ni)$, where A is the amount owed, P is the principal (the amount loaned), n is the time in years, and i is the annual interest rate as a decimal. If Mr. Jones loans $10,000 to his nephew for college, to be paid back in full over 10 years with a simple interest rate of 2.0% per year, how much should Mr. Jones get back at the end of that time?

Here, $P = \$10,000$; $n = 10$ years, $i = 0.02$. Substituting,

$A = P(1 + ni)$

$ = 10,000(1 + 10 \cdot 0.02)$

$ = 10,000(1 + 0.20)$

$ = 10,000(1.20)$

$ = 12,000$

Mr. Jones will get back $12,000.

EXERCISE 2

Evaluating Polynomials

Directions: Read the passage, then answer the questions.

The height of a rocket above the ground in meters is given by $h = -4.9t^2 + v_i t$ where t is the time since launch and v_i is the launch velocity.

1. If a toy rocket has a launch velocity of 75 meters per second, how high is it after 5 seconds?

2. How high is the toy rocket after 15 seconds?

Answers are on page 550.

Operations with Polynomials

Polynomials can be added, subtracted, multiplied, and divided. To perform these operations with polynomials, follow the steps outlined in this section.

Adding Polynomials

In polynomials, you can combine **like terms.** Like terms have the same variables to the same power. All x^2 terms are like, regardless of coefficient. For example, $3x^2, -2x^2$, and $7\frac{1}{5}x^2$ are like terms. All constants are like terms. Like terms are combined by adding their coefficients. For instance, $9x^2 - 6x^2 + 2x^2 = 5x^2$, since $9 + (-6) + 2 = 5$.

To add polynomials, combine like terms. For organization, arrange each polynomial in descending order. Write out the first polynomial, putting a "null term" (a zero coefficient) as a placeholder for any missing power of the variable. Next, arrange the second polynomial below, aligning like terms vertically. Then add columns.

EXAMPLE

Add $(x^4 + 2x - 2x^2 + 5) + (2x + x^3)$.

Arrange both polynomials in descending order. You might notice some missing terms in the first polynomial, places where there are no terms with the expected exponent. Place terms with zero coefficients in the polynomial as placeholders. Doing that, you get $x^4 + 0x^3 - 2x^2 + 2x + 5$ for the first polynomial.

Now add, making sure you are adding like terms. Notice there are also some missing terms in the second polynomial. Be careful to line things up correctly or to insert placeholders.

$$
\begin{array}{r}
x^4 + 0x^3 - 2x^2 + 2x + 5 \\
+ \quad\ \ x^3 + 0x^2 + 2x + 0 \\
\hline
x^4 + x^3 - 2x^2 + 4x + 5
\end{array}
$$

Subtracting Polynomials

When subtracting polynomials, write the two polynomials in descending order with all signs *as given*. Next, change all the signs of the bottom polynomial, the one that is being subtracted. Then add the two polynomials.

EXAMPLE

Subtract $\left(3x^3 + 2x^4 - 2x - 4\right) - \left(5x^3 + 7x - 3 + 5x^2\right)$.

Arranging the two polynomials in descending order, including placeholder terms, you get

$$
\begin{array}{r}
2x^4 + 3x^3 + 0x^2 - 2x - 4 \\
- \quad\quad (5x^3 + 5x^2 + 7x - 3) \\
\hline
\end{array}
$$

Next, change all the signs in the polynomial being subtracted, and add.

$$
\begin{array}{r}
2x^4 + 3x^3 + 0x^2 - 2x - 4 \\
+ \quad\quad -5x^3 - 5x^2 - 7x + 3 \\
\hline
2x^4 - 2x^3 - 5x^2 - 9x - 1
\end{array}
$$

EXERCISE 3

Adding and Subtracting Polynomials

Directions: Add or subtract, as indicated.

1. $(4x^2 + 7x - 2) + (x^2 - 3x + 3)$

2. $(2x^3 + 5x + 8) + (-3x^3 + 4x^2 - 4)$

3. $(3x^3 + x^2 + 3x + 1) - (x^3 + 2x^2 + 3x - 5)$

4. $(7x^4 + 4x^2 - 5x + 11) - (3x^4 - 6x^3 + 4x^2 + 5x)$

Answers are on page 550.

Multiplying Polynomials

Multiplying Polynomials by Constants

When multiplying a polynomial by a constant, you apply the Distributive Property. According to this property, you can multiply every term inside the parentheses by the constant outside.

> **EXAMPLE**
>
> Multiply $7(4x^3 - 2x^2 + 12x - 7)$.
>
> Using the Distributive Property, multiply each term in the parentheses by 7: $(7)(4x^3) + (7)(-2x^2) + (7)(12x) + (7)(-7) = 28x^3 - 14x^2 + 84x - 49$.

Multiplying Monomials

Monomials are polynomials with only one term. Looking at how to multiply these can help you understand some more complex multiplications. To multiply monomials, first multiply the coefficients. Then, multiply the variable parts, following the rules of exponents. Remember, these rules state that when you multiply variables, you add exponents.

> **EXAMPLE**
>
> Multiply $3x^2 \cdot x^5 \cdot 2x^9$.
>
> Multiply the coefficients: $3 \cdot 1 \cdot 2 = 6$. Then, multiply the variables by following the Product Rule from the laws of exponents: $x^2 \cdot x^5 \cdot x^9 = x^{2+5+9} = x^{16}$. The coefficient of the answer is the product of the coefficients. The final product is $6x^{16}$.

Multiplying a Monomial and a Polynomial

Use the Distributive Property to do this.

> **EXAMPLE**
>
> Multiply $6x(4x + 5)$.
>
> Distribute the monomial according to the Distributive Property. $6x(4x) + 6x(5)$. Multiplying each term as a monomial times a monomial, you get $24x^2 + 30x$.

Multiplying Two Polynomials

Multiplying two polynomials is a further extension of this process, using the Distributive Property.

EXAMPLE

Multiply $(2x + 7)(x^2 - 3x - 9)$.

Applying the Distributive Property, distribute each of the two terms in the first parentheses to get $2x(x^2 - 3x - 9) + 7(x^2 - 3x - 9)$. Again applying the Distributive Property, each term expands to $2x(x^2) - 2x(3x) - 2x(9) + 7x^2 - 7(3x) - 7(9)$

Multiplying each pair of terms, you get
$2x^3 - 6x^2 - 18x + 7x^2 - 21x - 63$

Collect like terms to get $2x^3 + x^2 - 39x - 63$.

Thus, the product of two polynomials is found by multiplying every term in one polynomial by every term in the other polynomial, then combining like terms. Each multiplication is a monomial times a monomial. The large problem of polynomial multiplication is transformed into a series of smaller problems, all of which are handled by simple rules: multiply coefficients and add exponents.

Multiplying Two Binomials

In mathematics, multiplying two binomials occurs so often that people came up with a quick way of getting the right answer, called FOIL. This is a mnemonic. A **mnemonic** is a memory trick you can use to remember complex things easily. Here each letter of FOIL stands for a separate multiplication. The letters stand for First, Outside, Inside, Last. This refers to pairs of terms in the two binomials. In order, you multiply the **first** term of each binomial. Next, you multiply the terms on the **outsides** of the problem. You now multiply the terms on the **inside** of the problem. Finally, you multiply the **last** terms in each binomial.

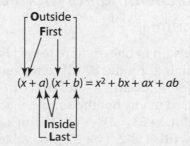

EXAMPLE

Multiply $(2x + 5)(x - 7)$.

Following FOIL, multiply the **first** terms in each binomial:

$(\underline{x} + 5)(\underline{x} - 7)$ x^2

Next, multiply the **outside** terms:

$$(\underline{x}+5)(x-\underline{7}) \qquad x^2 - 7x$$

Now multiply the **inside** terms:

$$(x+\underline{5})(\underline{x}-7) \qquad x^2 - 7x + 5x$$

Then, multiply the **last** terms:

$$(x+\underline{5})(x-\underline{7}) \qquad x^2 - 7x + 5x - 35$$

Collect like terms, and you get

$$(x+5)(x-7) = x^2 - 2x - 35$$

Notice that FOIL always puts the two terms you need to collect right next to each other.

EXERCISE 4

Multiplying Polynomials

Directions: Find each product.

1. $-5x^3 \cdot 3x^4$ **2.** $4(x^2 - 5x + 3)$ **3.** $3x^2(2x - 7)$

4. $-2x^4(3x^2 - 2x + 7)$ **5.** $(x + 3)(x - 7)$ **6.** $(2x - 5)(3x + 2)$

7. $(2x + 3)(x^2 - 3x + 5)$ **8.** $\left(6x^2 - 4x - 4\right)\left(x^2 - 8x - 1\right)$

Answers are on page 550.

Factoring and Dividing Polynomials

Factoring Polynomials

A polynomial is the sum of one or more terms. Factoring is a technique used to rewrite polynomials as products. All factoring is based on the Distributive Property, but it is not necessarily useful to try to see how the Distributive Property is being used in any but the simplest factoring problems. Consider the multiplication $2x(x + 3) = 2x^2 + 6x$. Factoring takes the sum $2x^2 + 6x$ and finds a way to write it as $2x(x + 3)$, if possible. Look at each term of $2x^2 + 6x$. Separating out the factors of each term, you get

$$\underline{2} \cdot \underline{x} \cdot x + 3 \cdot \underline{2} \cdot \underline{x}$$

You see that each term has as factors both 2 and x. To factor, write the common factors $2x$ and then write what remains from each term inside a pair of parentheses, $(x + 3)$. This is referred to as factoring out the greatest common factor (GCF) and is always the priority in a factoring problem.

EXAMPLE

Factor $3x^2y + 21xy^3 - 6xy$.

Each coefficient is a multiple of the number 3, so you can factor that out and get $3(x^2y + 7xy^3 - 2xy)$. You are not finished; each term has at least one x. Factoring out this x gives you $3x(xy + 7y^3 - 2y)$. Last, factor out y, which is present in each term, to get $3xy(x + 7y^2 - 2)$.

It is not necessary to go through all these separate steps if you can identify the greatest common factor immediately. Here, the greatest common factor is $3xy$. In general, the GCF will include the greatest common factor of the coefficients and each variable raised to the lowest power to which it is raised in the polynomial being factored. Also, be aware that factoring out a negative quantity will change the signs of each term inside the parentheses. This fact can come in especially handy when factoring trinomials.

Dividing Polynomials

Sometimes factoring can help divide polynomials.

EXAMPLE

Divide $\dfrac{7x^2y^2 + 21xy^3}{14xy^2}$.

Factor the numerator: $\dfrac{7x^2y^2 + 21xy^3}{14xy^2} = \dfrac{7xy^2(x + 3y)}{14xy^2}$. Now you can

reduce the fraction by canceling to get $\dfrac{x + 3y}{2}$.

EXERCISE 5

Factoring and Dividing Polynomials

Directions: Factor each of the following.

1. $15a^2b + 5ab^2 - 20ab$ **2.** $-14x^6 - 21x^4 + 7x^3$

Divide each of the following.

3. $\dfrac{15a^2b + 5ab^2}{10ab}$ **4.** $\dfrac{8x^3y^5}{12x^2y^3 + 16x^2y^2}$ **5.** $\dfrac{14p^5q^2 - 21p^4q^5}{6p^4q^3 - 9p^3q^6}$

Answers are on page 551.

Factoring Trinomials

Trinomials are polynomials with three terms. In many cases, you can write a trinomial as the product of a pair of binomials. The multiplication aid FOIL is important when factoring trinomials. Multiply two binomials using FOIL.

$$(x + 7)(x + 5) = x^2 + 12x + 35$$

The answer, $x^2 + 12x + 35$, is in the form of $ax^2 + bx + c$, where a and b are the coefficients of the first two terms and c is the last term. That is, $a = 1$, $b = 12$, and $c = 35$. Notice that the last term, c, comes from multiplying the last numbers in the binomials, 7 and 5. The sign of c tells you about the signs of the 7 and the 5.

If **c is positive**, the last terms have the **same** signs. You have either $(x + \quad)(x + \quad)$ or $(x - \quad)(x - \quad)$.

If **c is negative**, the last terms have **different** signs. You have either $(x + \quad)(x - \quad)$ or $(x - \quad)(x + \quad)$.

You can use other information from the trinomial to help decide which of these possibilities is correct.

If **c is positive**, the outer and inner terms from FOIL combine to produce the middle term bx. If c is positive and b is positive, both binomials have plus signs.

$(x + \quad)(x + \quad)$

If **b is negative**, the two binomials have minus signs.

$(x - \quad)(x - \quad)$

In **either case**, you will add factors of c to get b.

It may be helpful to refer to cases like the ones here.

CASE I: The trinomial is $x^2 + bx + c$ (**b is positive**). The signs in the binomials are plusses: $(x + \quad)(x + \quad)$

CASE II: The trinomial is $x^2 - bx + c$ (**b is negative**). The signs in the binomials are minuses: $(x - \quad)(x - \quad)$

EXAMPLE

Factor $x^2 + 4x + 4$.

The c is positive, and the b is, too. This is CASE I and will factor as

$(x + \quad)(x + \quad)$

You need to pick factors of the last term, 4, that add up to 4 to get the coefficient of the middle term.

The factors of four are either 4 and 1 or 2 and 2.

2 and 2 add up to 4, so the factoring is $(x + 2)(x + 2)$. Because the factors are equal, this should be written $(x + 2)^2$.

You can check the answer by using FOIL to multiply the two binomials.

EXAMPLE

Factor $x^2 - 5x + 4$.

The positive last term tell you that the signs are the same. The negative middle coefficient tells you that the signs are negative (CASE II). But you still add factors of 4 to get 5. And $4 + 1 = 5$, so the completed factoring is

$(x - 4)(x - 1)$

EXERCISE 6

Factoring Trinomials

Directions: Factor each of the following.

1. $x^2 + 5x + 4$ **2.** $x^2 - 5x + 4$ **3.** $x^2 - 3x + 2$

4. $x^2 + 3x + 2$ **5.** $x^2 - 6x + 8$ **6.** $x^2 + 12x + 20$

Answers are on page 551.

Factoring Trinomials When c Is Negative

If **c is negative**, the signs of the last factors are opposite (one is positive and one is negative). You subtract factors of the last term, c, to get the middle coefficient, b. This is the third case in the flowchart on page 211:

CASE III: The trinomial is $x^2 \pm bx - c$ (**b has either sign**). The signs in the binomials are different: $(x + \quad)(x - \quad)$ or $(x - \quad)(x + \quad)$.

EXAMPLE

Factor $x^2 + 4x - 12$.

The negative last term means the binomials include different signs, so you need factors of 12 that differ by 4.

Factors of 12 are   12 and 1

                6 and 2

                4 and 3

6 and 2 differ by 4, which is the middle coefficient. The possibilities are

$(x - 6)(x + 2)$ and $(x + 6)(x - 2)$.

The middle term of the trinomial is positive, so the outer and inner terms from FOIL have to combine to give $4x$. Try both possible answers: $2x - 6x = -4x$ isn't the term you want, but $-2x + 6x = +4x$ is. The factored trinomial is $(x + 6)(x - 2)$.

EXAMPLE

Factor $x^2 - 3x - 10$.

The negative last term means the binomials include different signs, so you need factors of 10 that differ by 3.

Factors of 10 are   10 and 1

                5 and 2

5 and 2 differ by 3, which is the middle coefficient. The possibilities are

$(x - 2)(x + 5)$ and $(x + 2)(x - 5)$.

The middle term of the trinomial is positive, so the outer and inner terms from FOIL have to combine to give $-3x$. Try both possible answers: $5x - 2x = +3x$ isn't correct, but $-5x + 2x = -3x$ is. The factored trinomial is $(x + 2)(x - 5)$.

Here is a flowchart based on these ideas.

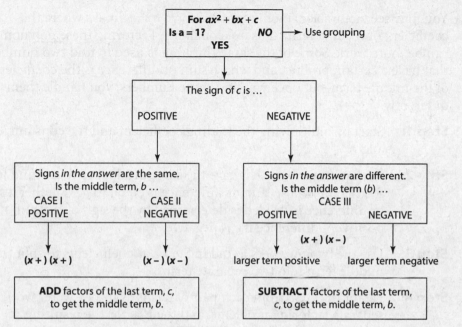

EXERCISE 7

Factoring Trinomials When *c* Is Negative

Directions: Factor each of the following.

1. $x^2 - 11x - 42$ **2.** $x^2 + 11x - 42$ **3.** $x^2 + 3x - 18$

4. $x^2 - 5x - 36$ **5.** $x^2 + 10x - 24$ **6.** $x^2 - 3x - 54$

Answers are on page 551.

Factoring Trinomials When $a \neq 1$

You may see factorable trinomials of the form $ax^2 + bx + c$ where the coefficient of the first term, a, is not equal to 1. Factoring these polynomials can be more work. Some of the same thinking is used to find two numbers that have a certain product and whose sum or difference is the coefficient of the middle term, but once you find those numbers, you handle them differently.

Step 1: Start by multiplying the leading coefficient and the constant, a and c.

Step 2: Find two numbers that have the same product as that found in Step 1, and whose sum or difference is equal to b. Whether a sum or difference is needed is determined by the sign of c: a sum if c is positive, a difference if c is negative.

Step 3: Use the two numbers found in Step 2 as coefficients to split the middle term into two separate terms.

Step 4: Factor the GCF from each pair of terms as if they were two separate factoring problems, and then factor the resulting common binomial factor as a GCF.

EXAMPLE

Factor $2x^2 + 5x + 3$.

Step 1: Multiply the leading coefficient by the constant: $2 \cdot 3 = 6$.

Step 2: The coefficient of the middle term, 5, is the <u>sum</u> of factors of 6 because c is positive. Pairs of factors of 6 are 1 and 6, and 2 and 3. The factors 2 and 3 add up to 5, so you should use them.

Step 3: Use the 2 and 3 to split the middle term into two terms. $2x^2 + 5x + 3 = 2x^2 + 2x + 3x + 3$. Now, factor each pair of terms separately.

Step 4: In the first pair, factor out $2x$, and in the second pair, factor out 3: $2x^2 + 2x + 3x + 3 = 2x(x + 1) + 3(x + 1)$. Notice that there are two large terms now, each of which has a common binomial factor. **The presence of the common binomial factor is very important.** If no such common binomial is present, an error has been made somewhere. Since there is a common binomial factor, treat it as a GCF and factor it out: $2x(x + 1) + 3(x + 1) = (x + 1)(2x + 3)$. Multiplying the binomials together to check verifies that the factored form of $2x^2 + 5x + 3$ is $(x + 1)(2x + 3)$.

When computing the product $(x + 1)(2x + 3)$, the outer term, $3x$, and the inner term, $2x$, are combined. It may not be easy to tell which numbers were added to get the middle term. The idea behind this procedure is to discover the outer and inner terms.

EXAMPLE

Factor $6x^2 - 13x - 8$.

Step 1: Multiply the leading coefficient by the constant: $6 \cdot 8 = 48$.

Step 2: The coefficient of the middle term, 13, is the <u>difference</u> of factors of 48 because c is negative. Pairs of factors of 48 are 1 and 48, 2 and 24, 3 and 16, and others, but the last pair differ by 13 and are the pair you need for the next step.

Step 3: Use the 3 and 16 to split the middle term into two terms. $6x^2 - 13x - 8 = 6x^2 + 3x - 16x - 8$

Step 4: Now, factor each pair of terms separately. In the first pair, you can factor out $3x$, and in the second term you can factor out -8: $6x^2 + 3x - 16x - 8 = 3x(2x + 1) - 8(2x + 1)$. Since there is a common binomial factor, treat it as a GCF and factor it out: $3x(2x + 1) - 8(2x + 1) = (2x + 1)(3x - 8)$. Multiplying the binomials together to check verifies that the factored form of $6x^2 - 13x - 8$ is$(2x + 1)(3x - 8)$.

EXERCISE 8

Factoring Trinomials When $a \neq 1$

Directions: Factor each of the following.

1. $3x^2 + 8x + 5$ 2. $4x^2 + 5x - 6$ 3. $3x^2 - 7x - 6$

4. $8x^2 + 22x - 21$ 5. $6x^2 - 23x + 20$ 6. $12x^2 + 25x + 12$

Answers are on page 551.

Special Cases

There are some trinomials that are so common that you can memorize how they are factored. One of these is known as a **difference of squares.** If a and b are two separate terms, then $(a + b)(a - b) = a^2 - b^2$. An example of this is $4x^2 - 9y^2 = (2x + 3y)(2x - 3y)$.

Another special case is the **perfect square**, where $a^2 + 2ab + b^2 = (a + b)(a + b) = (a + b)^2$. Examples of this pattern include

$$4x^2 + 12x + 9 = (2x + 3)(2x + 3) = (2x + 3)^2$$

$$4x^2 - 12x + 9 = (2x - 3)(2x - 3) = (2x - 3)^2$$

Being able to recognize these patterns can make factoring polynomials much easier.

Rational Expressions

Rational expressions look a lot like fractions but have polynomials for numerators and denominators. An example is $\dfrac{7x^2 + 3x - 7}{13x^2 y^2 + 5xy}$.

Rational expressions follow all the rules of rational numbers but are more complex because numbers are replaced by variables. This requires you to use some very basic rules and techniques.

Adding and Subtracting Rational Expressions

As with adding and subtracting fractions, the main problem is finding a common denominator.

You find the least common denominator (LCD) by including every different factor in the denominators the greatest number of times that it appears. For instance, if one denominator has a factor of x^3 (i.e., x is a factor three times) and another denominator has a factor of x^5 (x is a factor five times), then the LCD will have a factor of x^5. After finding the LCD, convert each fraction to an equivalent fraction by multiplying its numerator and denominator by the factors that are in the LCD but not in that fraction's denominator. For instance, the fraction that has x^3 in the denominator needs to be converted by multiplying by $\dfrac{x^2}{x^2}$ so that the denominator has x^5. Finally, add or subtract numerators and simplify your answer.

EXAMPLE

Add $\dfrac{4}{x + 2} + \dfrac{7}{x - 2}$.

The least common denominator in this case comes from multiplying the denominators. It is $(x + 2)(x - 2)$. You do not multiply these binomials or other factors in denominators because there is no reason to do so. You need to multiply the numerators in order to combine like terms. Each denominator is missing one of the binomials of the LCD. To get equivalent fractions, multiply each term by 1 in the form of the "missing" binomial over itself. You know you can do this because anything multiplied by 1 is itself.

$$\frac{4}{x+2} + \frac{7}{x-2} = \frac{4}{(x+2)} \cdot \frac{(x-2)}{(x-2)} + \frac{7}{(x-2)} \cdot \frac{(x+2)}{(x+2)}$$

$$= \frac{4x-8}{(x-2)(x+2)} + \frac{7x+14}{(x-2)(x+2)}$$

$$= \frac{4x-8+7x+14}{(x+2)(x-2)}$$

$$= \frac{11x+6}{(x+2)(x-2)}$$

Subtraction is similar.

EXAMPLE

Subtract $\dfrac{4}{x-5} - \dfrac{4}{x^2-25}$.

You can save some effort if, instead of using $x^2 - 25$ as a denominator, you factor it first. It is $(x+5)(x-5)$. In this case, that is the common denominator, since the factors $x + 5$ and $x - 5$ are the distinct factors occurring in the denominators. You need only adjust the first term: $\dfrac{4}{(x-5)} \cdot \dfrac{(x+5)}{(x+5)} = \dfrac{4(x+5)}{(x-5)(x+5)}$. So you get

$$\frac{4}{x-5} - \frac{4}{x^2-25} = \frac{4(x+5)}{(x-5)(x+5)} - \frac{4}{(x-5)(x+5)}$$

$$= \frac{4x+20-4}{(x-5)(x+5)}$$

$$= \frac{4x+16}{(x-5)(x+5)}$$

$$= \frac{4(x+4)}{(x-5)(x+5)}$$

When the numerator of the fraction following the subtraction symbol has more than one term, take care to subtract every term.

EXAMPLE

Subtract $\dfrac{3}{x^2+x-2} - \dfrac{1}{x^2+3x+2}$.

The first denominator factors into $(x - 1)(x + 2)$, the second into $(x + 1)(x + 2)$. The distinct factors occurring in the denominator are $x - 1$, $x + 1$, and $x + 2$. Adjusting the fractions and subtracting,

$$\frac{3}{x^2+x-2}-\frac{1}{x^2+3x+2}=\frac{3}{(x-1)(x+2)}-\frac{1}{(x+1)(x+2)}$$

$$=\frac{3}{(x-1)(x+2)}\cdot\frac{x+1}{x+1}-\frac{1}{(x+1)(x+2)}\cdot\frac{x-1}{x-1}$$

$$=\frac{3x+3}{(x-1)(x+2)(x+1)}-\frac{x-1}{(x+1)(x+2)(x-1)}$$

$$=\frac{3x+3-x+1}{(x-1)(x+2)(x+1)}$$

$$=\frac{2x+4}{(x-1)(x+2)(x+1)}$$

$$=\frac{2(x+2)}{(x-1)(x+2)(x+1)}$$

$$=\frac{2}{(x-1)(x+1)}$$

Note how, in the step in which the fractions are combined into a single fraction, the signs of the second numerator change according to the procedure for subtracting polynomials. Also note how the numerator of the difference could be factored and the fraction could be reduced since one of the factors of the numerator was a factor of the denominator.

EXERCISE 9

Adding and Subtracting Rational Expressions

Directions: Add or subtract as indicated.

1. $\frac{y}{6x}-\frac{3x}{8y}$

2. $\frac{x+3}{2x+5}+\frac{3x-5}{3x+5}$

3. $\frac{7x-9}{4x+8}+\frac{5x+11}{3x+6}$

4. $\frac{x+3}{3x^2}-\frac{x+4}{4x}$

5. $\frac{x}{x+3}-\frac{2x^2}{4x-7}$

6. $\frac{x+2}{x^2+6x+9}+\frac{x-1}{x^2-9}$

Answers are on page 551.

Multiplying and Dividing Rational Expressions

The key to success with these problems is this: factor, factor, and factor. Factor all numerators and denominators completely. Cancel common factors from numerators and denominators, and multiply anything left behind.

EXAMPLE

Multiply $\dfrac{5x^2 - 12x - 9}{x^2 + 6x + 9} \cdot \dfrac{4x^2 + 12x}{9 - 25x^2}$.

Begin by factoring numerators and denominators as completely as possible:

$$\frac{(5x + 3)(x - 3)}{(x + 3)(x + 3)} \cdot \frac{4x(x + 3)}{(3 + 5x)(3 - 5x)}$$

Cancel out like factors: $\dfrac{\cancel{(5x + 3)}(x - 3)}{(x + 3)\cancel{(x + 3)}} \cdot \dfrac{4x\cancel{(x + 3)}}{\cancel{(3 + 5x)}(3 - 5x)}$

The answer is $\dfrac{4x(x - 3)}{(x + 3)(3 - 5x)}$.

Dividing and Simplifying Rational Expressions

These problems are like multiplication except that the divisor is inverted before multiplying.

EXAMPLE

Divide $\dfrac{x + 3}{x - 3} \div \left(x^2 + 6x + 9\right)$.

Make a fraction of the second term by putting it over 1.

$$\frac{x + 3}{x - 3} \div \frac{\left(x^2 + 6x + 9\right)}{1}$$

Next, invert the second term and multiply.

$$\frac{x + 3}{x - 3} \div \frac{\left(x^2 + 6x + 9\right)}{1} = \frac{x + 3}{x - 3} \cdot \frac{1}{x^2 + 6x + 9}$$

Factoring and dividing out like terms,

$$\frac{\cancel{(x + 3)}}{(x - 3)} \cdot \frac{1}{(x + 3)\cancel{(x + 3)}} = \frac{1}{(x - 3)(x + 3)}$$

Multiplying and Dividing Rational Expressions

Directions: Multiply or divide as indicated.

1. $\dfrac{6m^2n}{35ab^4} \cdot \dfrac{14a^2b^3}{15m^6}$

2. $\dfrac{45p^4q^6}{28x^2y^7} \div \dfrac{25p^2q^9}{49x^5y^4}$

3. $\dfrac{2x-6}{4x+6} \div \dfrac{4x-12}{6x+9}$

4. $\dfrac{5a+10}{3a-6} \cdot \dfrac{6a-18}{15a+30}$

5. $\dfrac{p^2}{p-5} \cdot \dfrac{p^2+3p-40}{p^2-2p}$

6. $\dfrac{x^2+5x+4}{x^2-16} \div \dfrac{x^2-1}{x^2-5x+4}$

7. $\dfrac{x^2-5x+6}{x^2-9} \cdot \dfrac{x^2-25}{x^2+3x-10}$

8. $\dfrac{x^2-x-6}{9x^2-30x+25} \div \dfrac{x+2}{3x^2+13x-30}$

Answers are on page 551.

CHAPTER 10

Equations and Inequalities

Solving Equations

The ability to solve equations is central to mathematics. An **equation** is a statement that two quantities are identical. Equations typically have variables to represent as-yet-unknown values. A **solution** to an equation is a number or numbers that make the equation a true statement when substituted for the variables in the equation.

EXAMPLES

1. Is -3 a solution of the equation $x^2 = 2x + 11$?

   Replacing the variable with -3 changes the statement into a matter of arithmetic:

   $$(-3)^2 = 2(-3) + 11$$
   $$9 = -6 + 11$$
   $$9 = 5$$

   The statement $9 = 5$ is false, so the answer to the question is *no*.

2. Is 2 a solution of the equation $3x + 7 = 5x + 3$?

   Replacing the variable with 2:

   $$3 \cdot 2 + 7 = 5 \cdot 2 + 3$$
   $$6 + 7 = 10 + 3$$
   $$13 = 13$$

   The last statement is true, so the answer to the question is *yes*.

Solving One-Step Equations

The solutions to an equation are typically not given, as in the example, and must be found by solving the equation. To **solve an equation** means to find all of the solutions to the equation. The general strategy is to replace the given equation with a series of equivalent equations. **Equivalent equations** are equations that have the same solutions. Given an equation, an equivalent equation may be derived by operating on both sides of the equation with the same quantity, or by simplifying one or both sides of an equation. The challenge is deciding what operations to perform, and with what quantities. The goal is to obtain an **obvious equation**, an equation whose solution is obvious. The obvious equation will usually be an equation where the variable is isolated on one side of the equal sign. The means by which operations and quantities are chosen will be uncovered a bit at a time through examples. After Exercise 6, once all of the examples are exposed, the entire process developed will be summarized. For the first few examples, the basic idea is to undo the operations that are being done to the variable.

EXAMPLES

Solve the equation.

1. $x + 5 = 9$

The variable is having 5 added to it. To undo this operation, subtract 5 from both sides of the equal sign. Note that subtraction is often thought of as the opposite of addition.

$$x + 5 = 9$$
$$x + 5 - 5 = 9 - 5$$
$$x + 0 = 4$$
$$x = 4$$

All of the equations are equivalent. In the last equation, the solution is 4, and that is the solution to the original equation.

2. $x - \dfrac{3}{4} = \dfrac{5}{6}$

The variable is having $\dfrac{3}{4}$ subtracted from it. To undo this operation, add $\dfrac{3}{4}$ to both sides of the equation.

$$x - \frac{3}{4} = \frac{5}{6}$$
$$x - \frac{3}{4} + \frac{3}{4} = \frac{5}{6} + \frac{3}{4}$$
$$x + 0 = \frac{5}{6} + \frac{3}{4} = \frac{10}{12} + \frac{9}{12} = \frac{19}{12}$$
$$x = \frac{19}{12}$$

Again, the solution to the last equation is obvious, and it is equivalent to the first equation, so the solution to the first equation is $\dfrac{19}{12}$. With these two examples, the left side turned into $x + 0$, which is the same as x. This is by design, as it serves to isolate the variable, but a constant of 0 will no longer be explicitly written.

3. $-6x = 84$

The variable is being multiplied by −6. To undo this, divide both sides of the equation by −6.

$$-6x = 84$$
$$\frac{-6x}{-6} = \frac{84}{-6}$$
$$1x = -14$$
$$x = -14$$

The division symbol ÷ is not used in equations. Instead, the division is indicated by the fraction bar. If both sides had been divided by 6, without a negative sign, the result would have been $-x = 14$, but the goal is solve for x, not $-x$.

4. $\frac{x}{5} = 3$

The variable is being divided by 5. Multiply both sides by 5. The 5 on the left should be written $\frac{5}{1}$ so as to cancel out the denominator:

$$\frac{x}{5} = 3$$
$$\frac{5}{1} \cdot \frac{x}{5} = 3 \cdot 5$$
$$1x = 15$$
$$x = 15$$

With these last two examples, the left side turned into $1x$, which is the same as x. Again, this is by design, as it serves to isolate the variable, but the coefficient of 1 will no longer be explicitly written.

Solving One-Step Equations

Directions: Solve the equation.

1. $x + 13 = -2$ **2.** $x + 9 = 4$ **3.** $x - 6 = 2$ **4.** $x - 3 = -8$

5. $4x = -24$ **6.** $-7x = -21$ **7.** $\dfrac{x}{8} = -2$ **8.** $-\dfrac{x}{2} = 5$

Answers are on page 552.

Solving One-Step Equations with Fractions

One-step equations involving fractional coefficients can be solved using the following direct approach.

EXAMPLES

Solve the equation.

1. $\dfrac{3}{5}x = 7$

The usual approach to undoing a multiplication is to divide by the same number. Since the coefficient is a fraction, dividing by that fraction will turn into multiplication by its reciprocal. Why not go ahead and invert and multiply to save a step?

$$\frac{3}{5}x = 7$$
$$\frac{5}{3} \cdot \frac{3}{5}x = \frac{5}{3} \cdot \frac{7}{1}$$
$$x = \frac{35}{3}$$

Multiplying the coefficient by its reciprocal cancels out the numerators and the denominators, leaving a 1 (unwritten) behind.

2. $\dfrac{2x}{9} = \dfrac{14}{27}$

Even though the variable is part of the fraction, the same approach as in the previous example will work because $\dfrac{2x}{9}$ is the same as $\dfrac{2}{9}x$:

$$\dfrac{2x}{9} = \dfrac{14}{27}$$

$$\dfrac{9}{2} \cdot \dfrac{2x}{9} = \dfrac{9}{2} \cdot \dfrac{14}{27}$$

$$x = \dfrac{7}{3}$$

EXERCISE 2

Solving One-Step Equations with Fractions

Directions: Solve the equation.

1. $\dfrac{15}{11}x = \dfrac{10}{33}$ 　　　　**2.** $-\dfrac{5}{2}x = 25$

3. $\dfrac{4x}{7} = 6$ 　　　　**4.** $-\dfrac{8x}{15} = -\dfrac{12}{25}$

Answers are on page 552.

Solving Two-Step Equations

When there is more than a single operation to undo in order to isolate the variable, the order in which the operations are undone must be kept in mind. Consider a nonmathematical operation: putting on shoes. The opposite of this operation is taking off shoes. A second operation could be putting on socks. Now, think of the combined operation. Socks are put on first, then shoes. When these are both removed, the shoes have to come off first, then the socks. The point is that to undo the effect of multiple operations, not only must the opposite operations be performed, but they must be carried out in the opposite order. The shoes have to come off before the socks. Such is the case with an equation where the variable has both a multiplication and an addition to be undone. Multiplications usually come before additions, but when solving equations, the additions are usually undone before the multiplications.

EXAMPLES

Solve the equation.

1. $2x + 15 = 39$

If the value of x were known, it would first be multiplied by 2, and the product would be increased by 15 to get 39. To find the value of x that results in 39, the opposite operations must be done in the opposite order: first, subtract 15, and second, divide by 2:

$$2x + 15 = 39$$
$$2x + 15 - 15 = 39 - 15$$
$$2x = 24$$
$$\frac{2x}{2} = \frac{24}{2}$$
$$x = 12$$

2. $\frac{7}{3}x - 26 = 16$

Fractions in equations can be a bother, and coming up is a strategy for solving equations that have more than one fraction. This equation needs to have multiplication by $\frac{7}{3}$ undone and subtraction of 26 undone, so, in this order, add 26 and multiply by $\frac{3}{7}$:

$$\frac{7}{3}x - 26 = 16$$
$$\frac{7}{3}x - 26 + 26 = 16 + 26$$
$$\frac{7}{3}x = 42$$
$$\frac{3}{7} \cdot \frac{7}{3}x = \frac{3}{7} \cdot 42$$
$$x = 3 \cdot 6 = 18$$

3. $\frac{5x}{11} + 6 = -4$

Undo the adding 6 first, then multiply by $\frac{11}{5}$ to take care of the fraction.

$$\frac{5x}{11} + 6 = -4$$
$$\frac{5x}{11} + 6 - 6 = -4 - 6$$
$$\frac{5x}{11} = -10$$
$$\frac{11}{5} \cdot \frac{5x}{11} = \frac{11}{5}(-10)$$
$$x = 11(-2) = -22$$

EXERCISE 3

Solving Two-Step Equations

Directions: Solve the equation.

1. $3x - 5 = 7$
2. $-4x + 6 = 8$
3. $\frac{3}{4}x + 2 = 11$

4. $15 + 6x = -9$
5. $3 - 8x = 15$
6. $\frac{4x}{9} - 3 = -1$

Answers are on page 552.

Clearing Fractions

When the equation has more than a single factor, clearing the equation of the fractions as a first step will leave an equation whose constants and coefficients are integers. This can be done by multiplying both sides of the equal sign by the least common denominator (LCD) of all of the fractions in the equation.

EXAMPLE

Solve the equation.

1. $\frac{2}{3}x + \frac{3}{5} = \frac{1}{2}$

The LCD is 30. Multiply both sides by $\frac{30}{1}$. The Distributive Property must be used on the left because there is more than one term.

$$\frac{2}{3}x + \frac{3}{5} = \frac{1}{2}$$
$$\frac{30}{1} \cdot \frac{2}{3}x + \frac{30}{1} \cdot \frac{3}{5} = \frac{30}{1} \cdot \frac{1}{2}$$
$$10 \cdot 2x + 6 \cdot 3 = 15 \cdot 1$$
$$20x + 18 = 15$$
$$20x + 18 - 18 = 15 - 18$$
$$20x = -3$$
$$\frac{20x}{20} = \frac{-3}{20}$$
$$x = -\frac{3}{20}$$

Work with fractions is minimized by clearing them as soon as possible.

EXERCISE 4

Clearing Fractions

Directions: Solve the equation. Clear the fractions first by multiplying by the LCD.

1. $\dfrac{11}{7}x + \dfrac{3}{2} = \dfrac{5}{14}$

2. $\dfrac{5}{6}x - \dfrac{7}{9} = \dfrac{2}{3}$

3. $-\dfrac{3}{4}x + \dfrac{1}{6} = \dfrac{7}{9}$

4. $-\dfrac{4}{15}x + \dfrac{3}{10} = -\dfrac{7}{6}$

5. $-\dfrac{4}{7}x - \dfrac{1}{3} = \dfrac{2}{5}$

6. $\dfrac{5}{12}x - \dfrac{7}{9} = -\dfrac{3}{8}$

Answers are on page 552.

Variables on Both Sides

An equation can have variable terms on both sides of the equal sign. After any fractions are cleared, variables to the right side of the equal sign can be transposed to the left side by adding them to, or subtracting them from, both sides of the equation.

EXAMPLES

Solve the equation.

1. $7x + 10 = 4x - 5$

There are no fractions to clear. There is a variable term on the right, $4x$, that needs to be transposed to the left. Since the coefficient of the term is positive, subtract the term from both sides of the equal sign. Once the term has been transposed, it can be combined with the other variable term and the solution can continue as before.

$$7x + 10 = 4x - 5$$
$$7x + 10 - 4x = 4x - 5 - 4x$$
$$3x + 10 = -5$$
$$3x + 10 - 10 = -5 - 10$$
$$3x = -15$$
$$\dfrac{3x}{3} = \dfrac{-15}{3}$$
$$x = -5$$

2. $6x + 17 = -3x + 23$

Again, there are no fractions to clear. The variable term on the right has a negative coefficient, so adding its opposite, $3x$, to both sides of the equation will eliminate variables from the right side.

$$6x + 17 = -3x + 23$$
$$6x + 17 + 3x = -3x + 23 + 3x$$
$$9x + 17 = 23$$
$$9x + 17 - 17 = 23 - 17$$
$$9x = 6$$
$$\frac{9x}{9} = \frac{6}{9}$$
$$x = \frac{2}{3}$$

3. $\frac{1}{2}x + \frac{1}{3} = \frac{1}{4}x - \frac{1}{6}$

The LCD is 12. Multiply both sides by $\frac{12}{1}$. This time the Distributive Property needs to be used on both sides of the equation.

$$\frac{1}{2}x + \frac{1}{3} = \frac{1}{4}x - \frac{1}{6}$$
$$\frac{12}{1} \cdot \frac{1}{2}x + \frac{12}{1} \cdot \frac{1}{3} = \frac{12}{1} \cdot \frac{1}{4}x - \frac{12}{1} \cdot \frac{1}{6}$$
$$6x + 4 = 3x - 2$$
$$6x + 4 - 3x = 3x - 2 - 3x$$
$$3x + 4 = -2$$
$$3x + 4 - 4 = -2 - 4$$
$$3x = -6$$
$$\frac{3x}{3} = \frac{-6}{3}$$
$$x = -2$$

Variables on Both Sides

Directions: Solve the equation.

1. $5x - 7 = 2x + 11$

2. $8x + 2 = -2x - 3$

3. $3x - 13 = 7x + 3$

4. $\dfrac{2}{5}x + 1 = 2x - \dfrac{7}{2}$

5. $\dfrac{1}{6}x - \dfrac{2}{3} = \dfrac{3}{4}x + \dfrac{1}{2}$

6. $-\dfrac{3}{2}x + \dfrac{5}{6} = \dfrac{5}{9}x - \dfrac{1}{3}$

Answers are on page 552.

Equations with Grouping Symbols

Some equations will have grouping symbols in them. These can be eliminated from the equation by using the Distributive Property. Even if such an equation contains fractions, it is best to eliminate parentheses before eliminating fractions. It is possible that some denominators are reduced or even eliminated by distributing, making the search for an LCD easier or even unnecessary.

EXAMPLES

Solve the equation.

1. $3(x - 9) = 5 - x$

   Eliminate the grouping symbols by distributing the 3:

$$3(x - 9) = 5 - x$$
$$3x - 27 = 5 - x$$
$$3x - 27 + x = 5 - x + x$$
$$4x - 27 = 5$$
$$4x - 27 + 27 = 5 + 27$$
$$4x = 32$$
$$\frac{4x}{4} = \frac{32}{4}$$
$$x = 8$$

2. $6\left(\dfrac{1}{2}x+\dfrac{1}{3}\right)=8\left(\dfrac{3}{4}x-\dfrac{1}{2}\right)$

There are fractions this time, but since the Distributive Property is used first, some of the factors in the denominators may cancel.

$$6\left(\dfrac{1}{2}x+\dfrac{1}{3}\right)=8\left(\dfrac{3}{4}x-\dfrac{1}{2}\right)$$

$$6\cdot\dfrac{1}{2}x+6\cdot\dfrac{1}{3}=8\cdot\dfrac{3}{4}x-8\cdot\dfrac{1}{2}$$

$$3x+2=6x-4$$

$$3x+2-6x=6x-4-6x$$

$$-3x+2=-4$$

$$-3x+4-2=-4-2$$

$$-3x=-6$$

$$\dfrac{-3x}{-3}=\dfrac{-6}{-3}$$

$$x=2$$

3. $\dfrac{2}{5}\left(\dfrac{3}{4}x+\dfrac{5}{6}\right)=\dfrac{1}{3}\left(\dfrac{3}{5}x-\dfrac{1}{2}\right)$

Use the Distributive Property to eliminate grouping symbols first.

$$\dfrac{2}{5}\left(\dfrac{3}{4}x+\dfrac{5}{6}\right)=\dfrac{1}{3}\left(\dfrac{3}{5}x-\dfrac{1}{2}\right)$$

$$\dfrac{2}{5}\cdot\dfrac{3}{4}x+\dfrac{2}{5}\cdot\dfrac{5}{6}=\dfrac{1}{3}\cdot\dfrac{3}{5}x-\dfrac{1}{3}\cdot\dfrac{1}{2}$$

$$\dfrac{3}{10}x+\dfrac{1}{3}=\dfrac{1}{5}x-\dfrac{1}{6}$$

At this point, the fractions can be eliminated with multiplication of both sides of the equation by the least common denominator of 30. Be sure to distribute the 30 over both terms on each side:

$$\frac{3}{10}x + \frac{1}{3} = \frac{1}{5}x - \frac{1}{6}$$

$$\frac{30}{1} \cdot \frac{3}{10}x + \frac{30}{1} \cdot \frac{1}{3} = \frac{30}{1} \cdot \frac{1}{5}x - \frac{30}{1} \cdot \frac{1}{6}$$

$$9x + 10 = 6x - 5$$

$$9x + 10 - 6x = 6x - 5 - 6x$$

$$3x + 10 = -5$$

$$3x + 10 - 10 = -5 - 10$$

$$3x = -15$$

$$\frac{3x}{3} = \frac{-15}{3}$$

$$x = -5$$

EXERCISE 6

Equations with Grouping Symbols

Directions: Solve the equation.

1. $3(7x - 5) = 11$

2. $5(x + 4) = -2(x - 3)$

3. $6(2x - 1) = 5(3x + 7)$

4. $-\frac{3}{4}(2 + 5x) = \frac{2}{5}(6 - 3x)$

5. $\frac{5}{3}\left(\frac{1}{2}x - \frac{3}{5}\right) = \frac{2}{3}\left(\frac{4}{5}x + \frac{7}{2}\right)$

Answers are on page 553.

Summary of Solving Equations

The process developed for solving equations of the type so far encountered can be summarized in four steps:

1. Eliminate grouping symbols by use of the Distributive Property.

2. If there are fractions, multiply both sides of the equation by the LCD to eliminate denominators.

3. Transpose variable terms to the left side of the equation and constant terms to the right side.

4. Divide both sides by the coefficient.

Special Cases

Before leaving these types of equations behind, mention must be made of two special cases: the contradiction and the identity.

EXAMPLE

Solve the equations.

1. $2x - 5 = 2(x + 1)$

    Using the Distributive Property,

    $$2x - 5 = 2(x + 1)$$
    $$2x - 5 = 2x + 2$$
    $$2x - 5 - 2x = 2x + 2 - 2x$$
    $$-5 = 2$$

    The first equation is equivalent to the last equation, which has no solution, so the first equation also has no solution. An equation with no solution is a **contradiction**.

2. $3(2x + 4) = 2(3x + 6)$

    Using the Distributive Property,

    $$3(2x + 4) = 2(3x + 6)$$
    $$6x + 12 = 6x + 12$$

    There is no need to go any further; it is obvious that the left and right sides are equal for *every* value of x. The same is true for the first equation, which is an **identity**, an equation that is true for any value of its variable or variables.

Equations that are not contradictions or identities are called **conditional** equations. Conditional equations are so called because they are true on the condition that the variable or variables have certain values. The conditional equation $x = 2$ is true on the condition that x is 2. All of the equations in the examples and exercises have been conditional equations.

Solving Inequalities

The equations that have been used for examples and offered as exercises are first-degree equations. A **first-degree equation** is an equation in which the variable occurs to the first power, and not part of any radicand, denominator, exponent, or absolute value symbol. First-degree equations are also called **linear** equations. The process just explored for solving linear equations may also be used to solve linear inequalities. A **strict inequality** is a statement that one quantity is less than (or greater than) another. A **loose inequality** is a statement that one quantity is less than or equal to (or greater than or equal to) another. There are only two differences between linear inequalities and linear equations that need be mentioned. The first of these affects the last step of the solving process. **If both sides of the equation are multiplied or divided by a negative number, the direction of the inequality symbol must be reversed**: a less-than statement turns into a greater-than statement, and a greater-than statement turns into a less-than statement. To see why this is so, take the statement $-5 < 5$. Multiplying both sides of the inequality by 2 changes the statement to $-10 < 10$, but multiplying by -2 changes it to $10 > -10$. Multiplying both sides by any negative number leaves a negative product on the left side and a positive product on the right side, and multiplying by any negative number will leave a positive product on the left and a negative product on the right. The same is true of division: dividing both sides by a negative number requires a reversal of the inequality symbol, but dividing both sides by a positive number leaves the direction of the inequality unchanged. Addition and subtraction have no effect on the inequality symbol.

EXAMPLES

Solve the inequalities.   **1.** $2x < -8$ **2.** $-2x < -8$

These two inequalities serve to illustrate the issue with multiplying and dividing both sides of the inequality symbol by negative numbers, and contrasts the manner in which they are treated.

1. $2x < -8$ **2.** $-2x < -8$

$$\frac{2x}{2} < \frac{-8}{2} \qquad\qquad \frac{-2x}{-2} > \frac{-8}{-2}$$

$$x < -4 \qquad\qquad\qquad x > 4$$

In the solution to both examples, the sign of the number on the right side is not relevant. In Example 1, the coefficient is positive, and dividing both sides by that coefficient doesn't change the inequality symbol. On the other hand, in Example 2 the coefficient is negative, and dividing both sides by it changes the inequality sign from < to >. Notice that whether the inequality is strict or loose doesn't change.

The second difference between linear inequalities and linear equations is that the solution to an inequality is often depicted graphically on the number line. If every point x for which $x > 4$ were plotted on the number line, including all the points between the whole numbers, there would be so many points so close together that the line would look as if it had been continuously shaded. The inequalities $x < -4$ and $x > 4$ are graphed below.

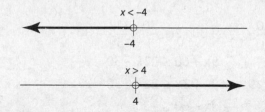

The numbers that appear in the solutions to inequalities appear in the graph as endpoints. The endpoints are the only numbers that are relevant to the inequality, so there is no need to include any other numbers on the number line. The strict inequalities are shown in the graph by using open circles as endpoints. Loose inequalities are shown using solid circles. Arrowheads are used to show that the shading continues in the direction indicated.

EXAMPLES

Solve the inequality and graph the solution on the number line.

1. $-5(x - 3) \geq 3(x + 13)$

   Even though finding the solution to this inequality begins with a multiplication by -5, the inequality symbol doesn't change because the multiplication isn't being done to both sides of the inequality. The part of the solving process where grouping symbols are eliminated doesn't count as an operation being done to both sides of the inequality.

   $$-5(x - 3) \geq 3(x + 13)$$
   $$-5x + 15 \geq 3x + 39$$
   $$-5x + 15 - 3x \geq 3x + 39 - 3x$$
   $$-8x + 15 \geq 39$$
   $$-8x + 15 - 15 \geq 39 - 15$$
   $$-8x \geq 24$$
   $$\frac{-8x}{-8} \leq \frac{24}{-8}$$
   $$x \leq -3$$

   Note that a solid circle is used to indicate the endpoint because of the loose inequality.

2. $\frac{3}{10}x + 2 \leq \frac{11}{15}x - 1$

The LCD is 30. Multiplying both sides by a positive number will not change the direction of the inequality symbol.

$$\frac{3}{10}x + 2 \leq \frac{11}{15}x - 1$$

$$\frac{30}{1} \cdot \frac{3}{10}x + 30 \cdot 2 \leq \frac{30}{1} \cdot \frac{11}{15}x - 30 \cdot 1$$

$$9x + 60 \leq 22x - 30$$

$$9x + 60 - 22x \leq 22x - 30 - 22x$$

$$-11x + 60 \leq -30$$

$$-11x + 60 - 60 \leq -30 - 60$$

$$-11x \leq -90$$

$$\frac{-11x}{-11} \geq \frac{-90}{-11}$$

$$x \geq \frac{90}{11}$$

EXERCISE 7

Solving Inequalities

Directions: Solve the inequality and graph the solution on the number line.

1. $2x + 11 > 7$

2. $4x - 15 \leq 6x + 3$

3. $6(x - 2) \geq 3(4x - 10)$

4. $-\frac{5}{6}x + \frac{1}{2} > \frac{2}{3}$

5. $\frac{3}{4}x + \frac{1}{2} < \frac{2}{5}x - \frac{3}{10}$

6. $\frac{3}{2}\left(\frac{4}{3}x - \frac{1}{6}\right) \geq \frac{2}{3}\left(\frac{1}{2}x + \frac{3}{4}\right)$

Answers are on page 553.

Systems of Equations

Another feature of the equations encountered above is that they are all in a single variable. Equations may also come in more than one variable. The solutions to equations in two variables are not individual numbers, but instead are ordered pairs (x, y).

EXAMPLE

Show that $(7, -2)$ and $(2, 0)$ are solutions to the equation $2x + 5y = 4$.

Substitute the values into the equation:

$$2 \cdot 7 + 5(-2) = 4 \qquad 2 \cdot 2 + 5 \cdot 0 = 4$$
$$14 - 10 = 4 \qquad 4 + 0 = 4$$
$$4 = 4 \qquad 4 = 4$$

Other ordered-pair solutions to the example may easily be found. (Choose any even number for y, substitute, and solve for x.) The example illustrates another difference between first-degree equations in one and two variables: the number of solutions. A single equation in two variables has an infinite number of ordered-pair solutions. However, if another two-variable equation is included, the pair of equations, when taken together, have only one ordered pair for a solution (except for special cases). A set of two or more equations to be solved so that the values found for the variables satisfy all of the equations simultaneously is called a **system of equations**. In Chapter 11, first-degree equations in two variables will be plotted as lines on a coordinate grid; that is why first-degree equations are sometimes called linear equations. When the lines are not parallel, they intersect at a single point. The coordinates of this point of intersection are the ordered pair that is the unique solution to the system of linear equations.

Solving Systems of Equations by Substitution

Systems of linear equations are central to contemporary mathematics, and a great many techniques have been developed to find their solutions. Two such techniques are **substitution** and **addition**. With the substitution method, one of the equations is solved for one of the variables, and the result is substituted into the other equation. The value of one variable is found, and this value is back-substituted to find the value of the remaining variable.

EXAMPLE

Solve the system $\begin{cases} 3x + y = 5 \\ 5x + 2y = 6 \end{cases}$ by substitution.

Solve one of the equations for one of the variables, it doesn't matter which. The easiest choice for this system would be to solve the first equation for y.

$$3x + y = 5$$
$$3x + y - 3x = 5 - 3x$$
$$y = 5 - 3x$$

Now substitute: rewrite the second equation, but instead of writing y, write the expression in x just found for y.

$$5x + 2(5 - 3x) = 6$$
$$5x + 10 - 6x = 6$$
$$-x + 10 = 6$$
$$-x + 10 - 10 = 6 - 10$$
$$-x = -4$$
$$x = 4$$

Lastly, substitute $x = 4$ into the equation $y = 5 - 3x$:

$$y = 5 - 3 \cdot 4 = 5 - 12 = -7.$$

The solution to the system is the ordered pair $(4, -7)$.

EXERCISE 8

Solving Systems of Equations by Substitution

Directions: Solve the system by substitution.

1. $\begin{cases} 6x - 11y = 8 \\ x + 2y = 9 \end{cases}$ 2. $\begin{cases} -3x + 5y = -3 \\ 4x + y = -21 \end{cases}$ 3. $\begin{cases} x - 3y = 7 \\ 7x - 5y = 17 \end{cases}$

Answers are on page 553.

Solving Systems of Equations by Addition

The addition method for solving systems is so called because a key step in the process of solving the system is adding the equations together. Before adding, the system is prepared by multiplying one or both equations by appropriate constants chosen so that once the equations are added, a variable vanishes.

EXAMPLE

Solve the system $\begin{cases} 15x+8y= \ \ 9 \\ 25x+6y=-7 \end{cases}$ by addition.

Finding the constants to multiply the equations by is similar to finding least common denominators. After deciding which variable to eliminate, the coefficients have to be made larger, and of different signs, so that when adding, their sum is 0. Focusing on y, determine the LCD of 8 and 6: 24. Multiply the top equation by 3 and the bottom equation by –4 so that the coefficients of y are 24 and –24, respectively.

$$3(15x + 8y) = \ \ 3 \cdot 9 \ \ \ \rightarrow \ \ \ 45x + 24y = 27$$
$$-4(25x + 6y) = -4 \cdot (-7) \rightarrow -100x - 24y = 28$$

Now add the equations, left side plus left side and right side plus right side, combining like terms:

$$45x + 24y = 27$$
$$\underline{-100x - 24y = 28}$$
$$- 55x \ \ \ \ \ \ = 55$$

Solve for x and back-substitute to find y:

$$\frac{-55x}{-55} = \frac{55}{-55}$$
$$x = -1$$
$$15(-1) + 8y = 9$$
$$-15 + 8y = 9$$
$$8y = 24$$
$$y = 3$$

The solution to the system is $(-1,3)$.

EXERCISE 9

Solving Systems of Equations by Addition

Directions: Solve the system by addition.

1. $\begin{cases} 2x - 3y = 7 \\ 5x + 2y = 8 \end{cases}$

2. $\begin{cases} -4x + 7y = 2 \\ 6x + 5y = 28 \end{cases}$

3. $\begin{cases} 5x + 3y = 13 \\ 8x + 5y = 20 \end{cases}$

Answers are on page 553.

EXERCISE 10

Solving Systems of Equations

Directions: Solve the system by either method.

1. $\begin{cases} 4x + 7y = -1 \\ 3x + 5y = 0 \end{cases}$

2. $\begin{cases} 5x + 2y = 5 \\ x - y = 15 \end{cases}$

3. $\begin{cases} 4x - y = 7 \\ 7x - 2y = 11 \end{cases}$

4. $\begin{cases} 9x + 7y = -4 \\ 4x + 3y = -2 \end{cases}$

5. $\begin{cases} 2x + 5y = 1 \\ 3x - 7y = 16 \end{cases}$

6. $\begin{cases} 9x - 4y = 13 \\ 5x + 6y = -1 \end{cases}$

Answers are on page 553.

Quadratic Equations

The last type of equation to be solved in this chapter is the second-degree, or **quadratic equation**, where the variable occurs to the second power. A quadratic equation may have two, one, or no solution. If this seems strange, consider the equations $x^2 = 1$, $x^2 = 0$, and $x^2 = -1$. The first equation has two solutions, $x = 1$ and $x = -1$, sometimes written $x = \pm 1$. The second has only one solution, $x = 0$, and the last has no solution. There are four techniques for solving quadratic equations.

Solving Quadratic Equations Using the Square Root Property

The first method can be used when there is a second-degree term in the equation but no first-degree term. It relies on a property of square roots: if a is positive and $x^2 = a$, then $x = \pm\sqrt{a}$. This property says

1. A certain form of equation may be solved by taking the square root of both sides of the equal sign.

2. Both square roots, positive and negative, must be accounted for.

3. The number whose square root is being taken must be positive.

EXAMPLE

Solve $4x^2 - 9 = 0$.

The equation is missing x^1, so the square root property can be used. Before using the square root property, solve for x^2:

$$4x^2 - 9 = 0$$

$$4x^2 - 9 + 9 = 0 + 9$$

$$4x^2 = 9$$

$$\frac{4x^2}{4} = \frac{9}{4}$$

$$x^2 = \frac{9}{4}$$

$$\sqrt{x^2} = \pm\sqrt{\frac{9}{4}}$$

$$x = \pm\frac{3}{2}$$

EXERCISE 11

Solving Quadratic Equations Using the Square Root Property

Directions: Solve the equation by using the square root property.

1. $x^2 - 25 = 0$ **2.** $16x^2 = 49$ **3.** $x^2 + 9 = 0$ **4.** $25x^2 - 36 = 0$

5. $x^2 = 20$ **6.** $(x - 1)^2 = 4$ **7.** $(x + 2)^2 = 5$ **8.** $x^2 = 4x$

Answers are on page 554.

Solving Quadratic Equations by Factoring

A second technique for solving quadratic equations relies on a property of multiplication: if $ab = 0$, then $a = 0$ or $b = 0$. If two numbers have a product of zero, then one or both of the numbers is zero. This property can be used with factoring to change a single second-degree equation into two first-degree equations.

EXAMPLE

Solve $6x^2 + 7x - 20 = 0$ by factoring.

Following the procedure from chapter 9, the left side of the equation factors into $(3x + 4)(2x - 5)$. Since there is a zero on the right side, the multiplication property can be applied immediately after factoring:

$$6x^2 - 7x - 20 = 0$$
$$6x^2 + 8x - 15x - 20 = 0$$
$$2x(3x + 4) - 5(3x + 4) = 0$$
$$(3x + 4)(2x - 5) = 0$$
$$3x + 4 = 0 \text{ or } 2x - 5 = 0$$
$$3x = -4 \text{ or } 2x = 5$$
$$x = -\frac{4}{3} \text{ or } x = \frac{5}{2}$$

Before the multiplication property can be used, all terms must be on one side of the equal sign. Expand any products, and transpose and combine terms as necessary before factoring.

EXAMPLE

Solve $(2x + 3)(x - 5) = (x + 4)(x - 1)$ by factoring.

Use FOIL on each side, then transpose the terms from the right to the left. After combining terms, factor and use the multiplication property to solve.

$$(2x + 3)(x - 5) = (x + 4)(x - 1)$$
$$2x^2 - 10x + 3x - 15 = x^2 - x + 4x - 4$$
$$2x^2 - 7x - 15 = x^2 + 3x - 4$$
$$2x^2 - 7x - 15 - x^2 - 3x + 4 = x^2 + 3x - 4 - x^2 - 3x + 4$$
$$x^2 - 10x - 11 = 0$$
$$(x - 11)(x + 1) = 0$$
$$x - 11 = 0 \text{ or } x + 1 = 0$$
$$x = 11 \text{ or } x = -1$$

EXERCISE 12

Solving Quadratic Equations by Factoring

Directions: Solve the equation by factoring.

1. $x^2 + 5x + 6 = 0$ **2.** $2x^2 - 11x + 12 = 0$ **3.** $x^2 + x = 20$

4. $x^2 = 4(x - 1)$ **5.** $2x(x + 4) = 5(x + 7)$ **6.** $3x(x + 1) = 10(1 - x)$

Answers are on page 554.

Solving Quadratic Equations by Completing the Square

The factoring technique won't work on many quadratic equations because many trinomials are not factorable. Another method, called **completing the square**, can be used to solve any quadratic equation. The method finds a number to add to the second- and first-degree terms so that a perfect square trinomial is formed, hence the name. The steps in the process are:

1. Write the equation with variable terms on the left and the constant term on the right.

2. Divide both sides of the equation by the coefficient of x^2.

3. Find half of the coefficient of x and square it.

4. Add the result to both sides of the equation.

5. Factor the left side as a perfect square trinomial.

6. Use the square root property and solve for x.

EXAMPLE

Solve $2x^2 - 8x + 2 = 0$ by completing the square.

This equation cannot be solved by factoring. Following the steps listed above:

$$2x^2 - 8x = -2$$
$$x^2 - 4x = -1$$
$$\frac{1}{2}(-4) = -2; \; -2^2 = 4$$
$$x^2 - 4x + 4 = 3$$
$$(x - 2)^2 = 3$$
$$x - 2 = \pm\sqrt{3}$$
$$x = 2 \pm \sqrt{3}$$

Note that step 2 will involve no extra effort if the number to divide by is 1. When this is so, it will seem that this step is skipped.

The method of completing the square has the advantage that it will find the solutions to any quadratic equation that has solutions, even if they are solutions in radicals. Another advantage is that it can help identify equations that don't have solutions. If you were to try to solve by factoring an equation that had no solution, you wouldn't be able to correctly factor the trinomial. There would be no clue as to whether this was due to a lack of factoring ability on your part or because the equation had no solution. Also, if you tried to factor an equation that had a solution in radicals, you would never be able to factor the trinomial and might incorrectly conclude that the equation had no solution.

EXAMPLE

Solve $x^2 + 3x + 5 = 0$ by completing the square.

This equation has a second-degree term with a coefficient of 1, so step 2 of the process will be trivial.

$$x^2 + 3x = -5$$

$$\frac{1}{2} \cdot 3 = \frac{3}{2}; \left(\frac{3}{2}\right)^2 = \frac{9}{4}$$

$$x^2 + 3x + \frac{9}{4} = -5 + \frac{9}{4}$$

$$\left(x + \frac{3}{2}\right)^2 = -\frac{11}{4}$$

The process should be stopped here. The next step would be to use the square root property, but the equation doesn't meet the conditions of the property. The right side of the equation is negative, and negative numbers don't have square roots. This equation doesn't have a solution.

The factoring of the perfect square in the previous example was a little different from anything else yet encountered, with the fraction involved. This step of the process is easier than it looks because it is known that the left side is a perfect square by design. Keeping this in mind reduces the number of possible forms for the factors to just one: two factors that look exactly the same.

EXAMPLE

Solve $5x^2 - 9x + 3 = 0$ by completing the square.

$$5x^2 - 9x = -3$$

$$x^2 - \frac{9}{5}x = -\frac{3}{5}$$

$$\frac{1}{2}\left(-\frac{9}{5}\right) = -\frac{9}{10}; \left(-\frac{9}{10}\right)^2 = \frac{81}{100}$$

$$x^2 - \frac{9}{5}x + \frac{81}{100} = \frac{21}{100}$$

$$\left(x - \frac{9}{10}\right)^2 = \frac{21}{100}$$

$$x - \frac{9}{10} = \pm\sqrt{\frac{21}{100}}$$

$$x = \frac{9}{10} \pm \frac{\sqrt{21}}{10}$$

$$x = \frac{9 \pm \sqrt{21}}{10}$$

EXERCISE 13

Solving Quadratic Equations by Completing the Square

Directions: Solve the equation by completing the square.

1. $2x^2 + 12x - 8 = 0$ **2.** $x^2 - 8x + 5 = 0$ **3.** $3x^2 - 18x - 7 = 0$

4. $2x^2 - 3x + 4 = 0$ **5.** $4x^2 + 7x - 1 = 0$ **6.** $x^2 + 2x + 4 = 0$

Answers are on page 554.

Solving Quadratic Equations Using the Quadratic Formula

For particular values a, b, and c, with $a \neq 0$, the equation $ax^2 + bx + c = 0$ represents every quadratic equation. If the process of completing the square is carried out on $ax^2 + bx + c = 0$, the result is the **quadratic formula**:

$$x = \frac{-b \pm \sqrt{b^2 - 4ac}}{2a}$$

To use this formula to solve a quadratic equation, write the equation in the form $ax^2 + bx + c = 0$, identify the coefficients a, b, and c, substitute the values of the coefficients into the formula, and simplify.

EXAMPLE

Solve $x^2 = 7x - 3$ by using the quadratic formula.

Transpose terms to get $x^2 - 7x + 3 = 0$. Identify the coefficients: $a = 1$, $b = -7$, and $c = 3$. Substitute these values into the formula and simplify:

$$x = \frac{-(-7) \pm \sqrt{(-7)^2 - 4 \cdot 1 \cdot 3}}{2 \cdot 1}$$

$$x = \frac{7 \pm \sqrt{49 - 12}}{2}$$

$$x = \frac{7 \pm \sqrt{37}}{2}$$

The quadratic formula reduces an algebraic problem to an arithmetic one. It can identify equations with no solutions when the discriminant, $b^2 - 4ac$, is negative.

EXAMPLE

Solve $x^2 + x + 1 = 0$ by using the quadratic formula.

All of the coefficients are equal to 1. Substituting,

$$x = \frac{-1 \pm \sqrt{1^2 - 4 \cdot 1 \cdot 1}}{2 \cdot 1}$$

$$x = \frac{-1 \pm \sqrt{1 - 4}}{2}$$

$$x = \frac{-1 \pm \sqrt{-3}}{2}$$

The discriminant is –3, and the equation has no solution.

The solutions produced by use of the quadratic formula should be simplified when possible. This may involve extraction of perfect square factors from the radical and reducing the fraction to lowest terms. When reducing, don't cancel factors from individual terms in the numerator. Instead, factor a constant from the numerator and use that factor to cancel a common factor with the denominator.

EXAMPLE

Solve $3x^2 + 4x = 2$ by using the quadratic formula.

Writing the equation in the form $ax^2 + bx + c = 0$, the coefficients are found from $3x^2 + 4x - 2 = 0$ to be $a = 3$, $b = 4$, and $c = -2$. Substituting and simplifying,

$$x = \frac{-4 \pm \sqrt{4^2 - 4 \cdot 3 \cdot (-2)}}{2 \cdot 3}$$

$$x = \frac{-4 \pm \sqrt{16 + 24}}{6}$$

$$x = \frac{-4 \pm \sqrt{40}}{6}$$

$$x = \frac{-4 \pm \sqrt{4 \cdot 10}}{6}$$

$$x = \frac{-4 \pm 2\sqrt{10}}{6}$$

$$x = \frac{2\left(-2 \pm \sqrt{10}\right)}{6}$$

$$x = \frac{-2 \pm \sqrt{10}}{3}$$

Solving Quadratic Equations Using the Quadratic Formula

Directions: Solve the equation by using the quadratic formula.

1. $x^2 + 3x - 5 = 0$

2. $2x^2 - 4x + 1 = 0$

3. $x^2 + 2 = x$

4. $x^2 = 5x + 3$

5. $3x^2 = 9x - 4$

6. $x^2 + 6 = 4x$

7. $2x(x + 3) = 5(1 - x)$

Answers are on page 554.

CHAPTER 11

Graphing

One way to make data more understandable and increase its usefulness is to depict it on a graph.

The Graph and Axes

Most graphs are done on a **Cartesian** coordinate system, which is essentially two number lines placed at right angles to each other. Each number line is called an **axis**; the axes cross at the zero value on each line. The crossing point is known as the **origin**. This type of graph is perfect for plotting equations in two variables, such as $3x - 4y = 9$ or $x^2 + y^2 = 16$. You plot the values of x on the horizontal axis and the values of y on the vertical axis. If variables other than x and y are used, say t for time and d for distance, the horizontal axis is used to plot the independent variable and the vertical for the dependent variable. The **independent variable** is the variable whose values do not depend on the other variable. It is the "input" into the equation. The **dependent variable** is one whose value depends on the value of the independent variable. It is the "output." In mathematics, the independent variable is usually x, and the dependent is usually y.

Locating Points on a Graph

A point on a graph represents a pair of numbers, one for x and one for y, and is written (x, y). To find a point, you go to the first value in the coordinate pair on the x-axis. Next, at this point, draw a line perpendicular to the x-axis. Then use the second number in the ordered pair. Locate that number on the y-axis, and at that point draw a line perpendicular to the y-axis. Where the two lines meet is where you plot the point. The x and y values are called the **coordinates**.

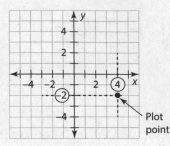

Plotting x = 4, y = –2, or (4, –2).

1. Locate each point on the appropriate axis.

2. Draw perpendicular lines.

3. Plot point where lines meet.

Getting Coordinates from a Graph

To get the coordinates of a point on a graph, reverse the process just explained. Draw a line passing through the point and perpendicular to the *x*-axis. Next, draw a line passing through the point and perpendicular to the *y*-axis. Record the numbers where each line crosses each axis. The location of the point is represented by the *x* and *y* values, listed in that order, separated by a comma, within a pair of parentheses.

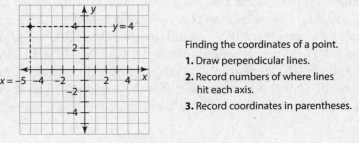

Finding the coordinates of a point.

1. Draw perpendicular lines.

2. Record numbers of where lines hit each axis.

3. Record coordinates in parentheses.

Coordinates of point (–5, 4)

Plotting a Line

The most common type of curve that you will plot is a straight line. The line covers the coordinates of all the possible ordered pairs of *x* and *y* that solve an equation (all pairs for which the equation is true). Equations of the type $3x - 2y = 12$ plot as straight lines. Notice that the two variables *x* and *y* are to the first power. Any equation with two variables, both to the first power, has a line for a graph and is called a **linear equation**.

To graph a line for a given equation, select a series of values for *x*, including negative numbers. Substitute each value of *x* into the equation, and solve for *y*. Using the equation above as an example, substituting *x* = 2 produces *y* = −3 as follows:

$$3(2) - 2y = 12$$
$$6 - 2y = 12$$
$$-6 + 6 - 2y = -6 + 12$$
$$-2y = 6$$
$$\frac{-2y}{-2} = \frac{6}{-2}$$
$$y = -3$$

So the point (2, −3) is a point on the line. Do the same with *x* = −4, 0, 2, 4 in turn and record the results in a table

x (input)	y (output)
−4	−12
−2	−9
0	−6
2	−3
4	0

The two numbers in each row form an ordered pair for a point on a graph. When these points are plotted and connected, you get a straight line.

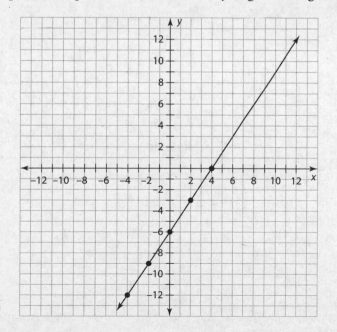

Plotting a Line

Directions: Plot lines on the graphs as instructed.

1. Plot the line represented by the values below.

x coordinate	−6	−4	−2	0	2	4
y coordinate	−13	−7	−1	5	11	17

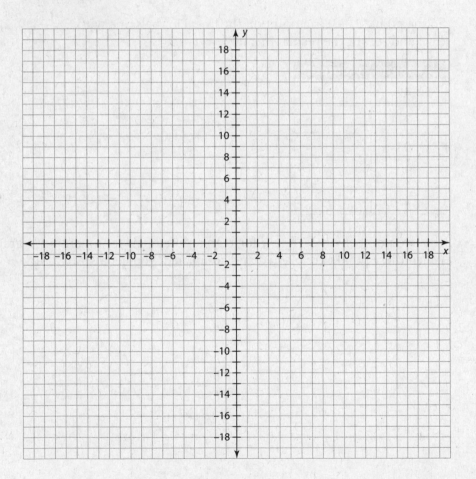

2. Graph the line with equation $2x + y = 5$.

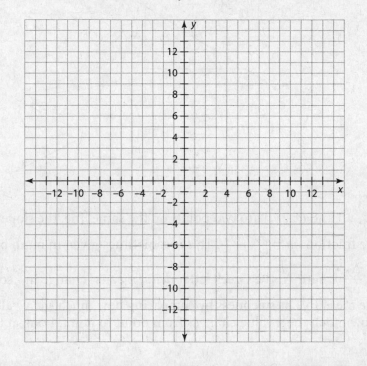

Answers are on page 555.

Linear Equations

The equation for a straight line is often written in what is known as the **standard form** of the equation of a line. It looks like $4x - 3y = 7$, or in general $Ax + By = C$, with the condition that A and B cannot both be 0. Another form is called the **slope-intercept** form of the equation of a line and looks like $y = \frac{4}{3}x - \frac{7}{3}$, or in general $y = mx + b$, where m is the slope of the line and $(0, b)$ is the y-intercept. The **slope** of a line is a measure of how steep it is. The **y-intercept** is the value at which the line crosses the y-axis. Like every point on the y-axis, the y-intercept has an x coordinate of 0.

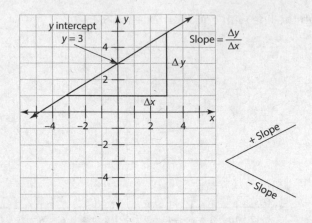

If (x_1, y_1) and (x_2, y_2) are two points on the same line, the slope of the line is the fraction: $m = \dfrac{y_2 - y_1}{x_2 - x_1}$. This is sometimes given in math books as $m = \dfrac{\Delta y}{\Delta x}$ where Δ, the Greek letter *delta*, means "change in," so the slope of a line measures its steepness by comparing how much the y value changes to how much the x value changes from point to point. Look at the following table.

x (input)	y (output)
–4	–4
–2	0
–1	2
0	4
1	6
2	8
4	12

Every time x goes up 1, y goes up 2. When x changes by 2, y changes by 4. The slope here is $\dfrac{2}{1}$, or $\dfrac{4}{2}$, or simply 2. Note that when $x = 0$, $y = 4$. This line has a y-intercept at (0, 4). A quick way to find the y-intercept of the graph of any equation is to solve the equation for y after substituting $x = 0$.

Once you know the slope and y-intercept, you can write down the equation in slope-intercept form, $y = mx + b$, where m is the slope and

(0, *b*) is the *y*-intercept. For the line in the previous table, the equation is $y = 2x + 4$.

Converting from Slope-Intercept Form to Standard Form

Starting with the slope-intercept form, clear fractions from the equation by multiplying both sides of the equal sign by the least common denominator of all fractions in the equation. Transpose the term with *x* by adding its opposite to both sides of the equation. The *x* term is written first, and the coefficient of *x* must also be positive, so when it is not, you may need to multiply both sides by –1.

EXAMPLE

Put the equation $y = \frac{2}{3}x - \frac{4}{5}$ in standard form.

First, clear the fractions by multiplying both sides of the equation by the least common denominator, 15, to get $15y = 10x - 12$. Now transpose the term with *x* by adding –10*x* to both sides of the equation: $15y - 10x = -12$. The *x* term must be placed first, so write the left side as $-10x + 15y = -12$. Finally, the first term should be positive, so multiply both sides of the equation by –1 to get $10x - 15y = 12$.

EXERCISE 2

Converting from Slope-Intercept Form to Standard Form

Directions: Write equations for lines in slope-intercept form and then convert to standard form.

	m	*y*-intercept
1.	2	0
2.	–3	3
3.	$\frac{3}{4}$	4
4.	$-\frac{1}{3}$	6

Answers are on page 556.

Converting from Standard Form to Slope-Intercept Form

Converting an equation from standard form to slope-intercept form makes it easier to find the slope of the line. To accomplish this conversion, add the opposite of the x term to each side. Next, divide both sides of the equation by the coefficient of the y term.

EXAMPLE

Convert $7x - 4y = 1$ to slope-intercept form.

First, subtract the x term from both sides of the equation, yielding $-4y = -7x + 1$. Next, divide both sides of the equation by -4, the coefficient of y: $y = \frac{7}{4}x - \frac{1}{4}$. The slope of the line is now the coefficient of x, $\frac{7}{4}$, and the y-intercept is $\left(0, -\frac{1}{4}\right)$.

EXERCISE 3

Converting from Standard Form to Slope-Intercept Form

1. Convert to slope-intercept form.

   A. $6x + 4y = 8$ **B.** $21x - 15y = -25$

2. Find the slope and y-intercept.

   A. $12x + 4y = -20$ **B.** $10x - 15y = 30$

Answers are on page 556.

Slopes

As you have seen in the exercises, slopes can be positive or negative. Positive-sloped lines slope up from left to right while negative-sloped lines slope down. Horizontal lines have zero slope (they are flat), and vertical lines have an undefined slope.

EXERCISE 4

Slopes

Directions: Match the lines with their slopes.

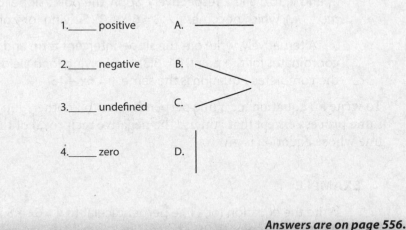

1. _____ positive   A.
2. _____ negative   B.
3. _____ undefined   C.
4. _____ zero   D.

Answers are on page 556.

Parallel and Perpendicular Lines

Two lines with equal slopes and different y-intercepts are parallel. Lines perpendicular to each other have slopes that are opposite in sign and whose absolute values are reciprocals; this latter condition is usually expressed by saying the slopes are negative reciprocals. For example, two lines with slopes of 3 and $-\frac{1}{3}$ are perpendicular to each other, but two lines with slopes $-\frac{1}{3}$ are parallel if they have different y-intercepts.

Often, the equation of a line passing through a point (x_1, y_1) needs to be found. If a value for a slope can be determined, there are two ways to get an equation. You can use the point-slope form, $y - y_1 = m(x - x_1)$, where m is the slope and (x_1, y_1) is the given point, or you can write out the equation as $y = mx + b$, substitute the coordinates of the point for x and y, and solve for b. Both of these techniques can be used to find the equation if one point and a slope is known, or if one point and the equation of a parallel or perpendicular line is known, or if another point is known so that you find the slope using $m = \dfrac{y_2 - y_1}{x_2 - x_1}$.

EXAMPLE

Write the equation of a line parallel to the line $y = 6x + 5$ and passing through the point $(3, 2)$.

In the problem, the slope of the parallel line must be 6. Setting x_1 and y_1 to 3 and 2 respectively, apply the point-slope form $y - y_1 = m(x - x_1)$, which becomes $y - 2 = 6(x - 3)$. Solving for y gives $y = 6x - 16$.

Alternatively, write out the slope-intercept form and substitute the coordinates for the point, $2 = 6(3) + b$. Solving for b yields $b = -16$, and the completed equation is the same: $y = 6x - 16$

To write an equation for a line perpendicular to another, you follow the same process except that you use the negative reciprocal of the slope of the line whose equation is given.

EXAMPLE

Write the equation for a line perpendicular to $y = 6x + 5$ and passing through the point $(3, 2)$.

The negative reciprocal of the slope is $-\frac{1}{6}$. This is the slope of the perpendicular line. Using the point-slope form $y - y_1 = m(x - x_1)$ and substituting, you get $y - 2 = -\frac{1}{6}(x - 3)$. Solving for y produces $y = -\frac{1}{6}x + \frac{5}{2}$. (Try to get this result using the alternative method.)

EXERCISE 5

Parallel and Perpendicular Lines

Directions: Write the slope-intercept forms of the equations of these lines.

Line 1	Parallel to $y = 3x + 2$	Passing through $(4, 1)$
Line 2	Parallel to $4x - 3y = 7$	Passing through $(3, 9)$
Line 3	Perpendicular to $y = 2x - 9$	Passing through $(4, 7)$

Answers are on page 556.

Equations of Lines Between Two Points

When asked for the equation of a line passing between two points, choose one point as *point 1* and the other as *point 2*. It does not matter which you choose as 1 or 2, but make sure you keep them straight. The x and y coordinates of point 1 will be x_1 and y_1, while those for point 2 will be x_2 and y_2. Use the formula $m = \dfrac{y_2 - y_1}{x_2 - x_1}$ to find the slope, and then select either point and use the point-slope form $y - y_1 = m(x - x_1)$ to find the equation.

EXAMPLE

Find the equation of the line running through points (2, 3) and (4, 6).

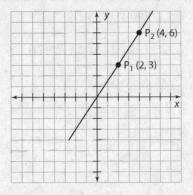

In the diagram, point 1 is (2, 3) and point 2 is (4, 6). Then $y_1 = 3$; $x_1 = 2$; $y_2 = 6$; $x_2 = 4$. Using the slope formula, $m = \dfrac{6 - 3}{4 - 2} = \dfrac{3}{2}$.

Now use the slope in the second formula to get $y - 3 = \dfrac{3}{2}(x - 2)$, which works out to $y = \dfrac{3}{2}x$. But you get a neater and more satisfying equation after multiplying both sides by 2, to get $2y = 3x$.

You can use the coefficients of the other point to check your work. Take the equation $2y = 3x$, and substitute the coefficients of the other point, (4, 6), for x and y in the equation. You get $2(6) = 3(4)$, or $12 = 12$. The equation checks out.

There are two special cases of slope that you need to be aware of. One is the horizontal line. The slope is always zero for a horizontal line. The equation of a horizontal line is $y = k$, where k is a constant. If you think about it, a flat table does not slope in any direction, so a slope of zero for a horizontal line makes sense. The second special case is the vertical line. The equation of a vertical line is $x = k$, where k is a constant. On a vertical line, the x coordinate never changes: it is the same for every point on the line. This presents an issue when finding a slope, for when you calculate $m = \dfrac{\Delta y}{\Delta x}$, you find $\Delta x = 0$, and you cannot divide by zero. Vertical lines are said to have a slope that is undefined because division by zero is undefined.

EXERCISE 6

Equations of Lines Between Two Points

Directions: Write the standard form of the equation of the line passing through the given points.

1. (2, 5) and (7, 4)   **2.** (–3, –7) and (–7, –11)   **3.** (3, 3) and (7, –9)

4. (5, 5) and (5, 9)   **5.** (6, 7) and (11, 7)

Answers are on page 556.

Comparing Data in Various Forms

Coordinate data may be given in three ways: in table form, as an equation, or as a graph. Several key ideas apply to the conversion between forms.

1. All points on the graph of an equation satisfy the equation (make it true).

2. Any anomalous features on a graph must be reflected in the equation or chart at the same values.

3. The specific special points on a graph, such as maximum or minimum values, are also to be found in the equation or chart.

When showing data in graph form, be sure that the axes are labeled and scaled to fit the problem. If you are dealing with time and distance traveled, time is usually expressed on the horizontal axis (whenever it is the independent variable), and distance is usually expressed on the vertical axis (whenever it depends upon the time traveled).

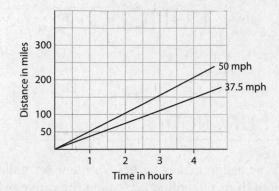

It is also important to remember that if the line passes through the origin, its slope is the **constant of proportionality** between the independent and dependent variables. In the time-distance graph above, the slope is the ratio of the change in distance and the change in time, otherwise known as speed (for instance, miles per hour). Notice that the line representing the slower speed has a smaller slope and is closer to horizontal. You can compute the slopes by picking two points on the line and plugging their coordinates into the formula for slope. Remember that although this chapter focuses on straight lines, graphs of equations can have all sorts of shapes. Circles, ellipses, even spirals can be created using equations and the data they generate. Graphs add to our understanding of all of these mathematical constructs.

CHAPTER 12

Functions

What Is a Function?

A **function** is an assignment of values from one set, called the **domain** of the function, to those of another set, called the **range** of the function. The nature of a function is that **any value from the domain is paired with exactly one value from the range**. The items in a function are **ordered pairs** (d, r), where d is a value from the domain and r is a value from the range. The domain values are often thought of as **inputs**, and the range values as **outputs**. Since ordered pairs are also used in graphing equations in the coordinate plane, the domain and range values are often referred to as x and y values as well. The types of values in the domain and range are not restricted to numbers.

> **EXAMPLE**
>
> If a domain is specified as all of the students in a particular classroom and a range as all of the subjects taught in school, the ordered pairs would look like (Max, art). Suppose the teacher asked each student for his or her single most favorite subject. The ordered pairs (student, favorite subject), assigning to each student their named favorite subject, would be a function.
>
> Most functions in mathematical settings have domains and ranges that are sets of numbers, and we will restrict our attention to such functions for the remainder of this chapter.

Representations of Functions

There are several ways to represent a function, such as verbal descriptions, tables, algebraic expressions, graphs, and lists of ordered pairs. Some of the representations are better than others, depending on how the function is being used. (Using a table and listing the ordered pairs are very nearly the same thing.) Using functions in mathematics and the real world often involves changing the representation of a function from one form to another.

Functions as Tables

One of the most common ways to represent a function is as a table.

EXAMPLE

Here is a function represented by a table:

x (input)	2	6	4	–3	1	–8	–6	3	0
y (output)	5	–4	7	9	0	–1	–5	2	1

Why does this table represent a function? Look at the first input value, 2. It is paired with the output value 5. Is that input ever paired with a different output? Looking at the rest of the table, the answer is clearly *no*. The same is true for every input value. Thus, the entries in the table satisfy the definition of a function.

How else could you represent the function in the example? The values jump around seemingly randomly, even once arranged by increasing input value, so it might be difficult to find an equation that unites the input and output pairs satisfactorily. The entries are ordered pairs, so plotting them in a graph might be fruitful. The **graph** of a function results from plotting the ordered pairs (*x, y*) that are members of the function as points in the *xy*-coordinate system.

EXAMPLE

Treating the table entries as the points (2, 5), (6, –4), and so on, can produce the following graph:

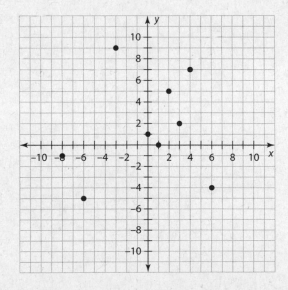

The graph might seem to not convey any extra information, but at least it is even more apparent how haphazard and scattered the points are.

EXAMPLE

Here is another table:

x (input)	5	0	–4	–6	8	2	–4	3	7
y (output)	–6	3	–8	1	1	1	9	2	0

Is this a function? If not, why not? Look at the third input value, –4. There, the value –8 is its corresponding output value, but the same input value occurs four columns to the right, paired with a different output value, 9. Having an input value paired with more than a single output value violates the definition of a function. Therefore, this table does not represent a function.

Some things to note:

- It isn't the repeated input value that prevents the table from being a function; it's that the input can result in more than one output value.

- If the output 9 were replaced with –8, the table would then represent a function. Even though the ordered pair would be included twice, they would be the same ordered pair.

- The repeated output value 1 has nothing to do with whether the table is a representation of a function. In a function, multiple inputs can have the same output.

Although the table in the previous example isn't a function, you can plot the ordered pairs:

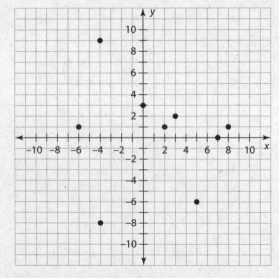

How does the graph show that the table doesn't represent a function? The answer may not be apparent, since both graphs look like randomly scattered points. The issue is with the input value –4 being paired with two different output values, –8 and 9. What can be said about the points (–4, –8) and (–4, 9)

that can't be said about any of the points in the previous graph? They are on a common vertical line. This idea leads to the **Vertical Line Test: If any vertical line has two or more points on a graph, the graph does not represent a function.**

EXERCISE 1

Functions as Tables

Directions: Examine the following tables and, for each one, decide if it represents a function.

1.

x (input)	4	2	1	0	2	7	9	2	8
y (output)	3	7	0	1	7	1	9	6	3

2.

x (input)	1	2	3	4	5	4	3	2	1
y (output)	6	2	8	4	8	4	8	2	6

3.

x (input)	5	8	3	1	2	6	4	7	9
y (output)	3	3	3	3	3	3	3	3	3

Answers are on page 557.

Function Notation

Functions in mathematics are most often represented by algebraic expressions. The letter f is very often used for the name of a function. Then, given an input x, the associated output is $f(x)$. This is read "f of x." This may look like multiplication, but it is just notation borrowed from multiplication. Often, $f(x)$ takes the place of y in ordered pairs, so that (x, y) is the same as $(x, f(x))$. A typical use of the notation follows:

EXAMPLE

The output values of a function are specified by $f(x) = x^2 - 2x + 7$. What is the output associated with the input $x = -3$?

The question is asking for $f(-3)$. To find this output value, replace all occurrences of x in the algebraic expression with -3 and evaluate the resulting arithmetic expression: $f(-3) = (-3)^2 - 2(-3) + 7 = 9 + 6 + 7 = 22$.

This means

- The input row of a table for *f* has a –3; below it is the output 22.
- The ordered pair (–3, 22) is a member of *f*.
- The point (–3, 22) is on the graph of *f*.
- $f(-3) = 22$

The bulleted statements are all equivalent.

EXERCISE 2

Function Notation

Directions: Solve the following problems.

For the function $f(x) = x^2 - 9$, evaluate the following:

1. $f(-5)$　　**2.** $f(-1)$　　**3.** $f(0)$　　**4.** $f(3)$　　**5.** $f(5)$

Find the output associated with the input $x = 4$ for the following functions:

6. $g(x) = 3x - 7$　　**7.** $h(x) = \dfrac{x - 2}{x + 2}$　　**8.** $p(x) = 9$　　**9.** $r(x) = \sqrt{x}$

Answers are on page 557.

Graphing Functions

The graph of a function is the graph of the equation $y = f(x)$. In other words, plot the points obtained by inputting values from the domain of the function and use the output values as the *y*-values of ordered pairs. The input values and the associated output values are often recorded in a table. Which domain values are used depends on the function as well as on an individual's experience with graphing functions. When possible, it is advisable to choose input values on either side of zero—that is, some positive numbers and some negative numbers. Sometimes picking fractions is helpful. Unfortunately, there is no general rule that provides a robust way to choose input values for every type of function.

EXAMPLE

Graph $f(x) = -2x + 5$.

The randomly chosen input values –2, –1, 0, 1, and 2 are substituted for *x* in the function, and the corresponding output values are computed.

For instance, $f(-2) = -2(-2) + 5 = 4 + 5 = 9$. The results are recorded in the table:

x	-2	-1	0	1	2
$f(x)$	9	7	5	3	1

Plotting the entries in each column as an ordered pair produces this graph:

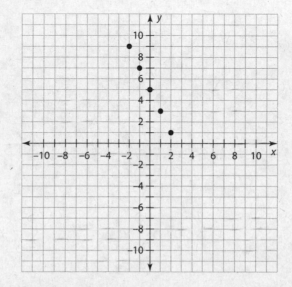

The points appear to lie along a straight line. This is not a surprise; the equation of a line can be written in the form $y = mx + b$, where m is the slope of the line and $(0,b)$ is the y-intercept. Functions of the form $f(x) = mx + b$ are called linear functions. Taking advantage of this insight, draw a straight line through the points.

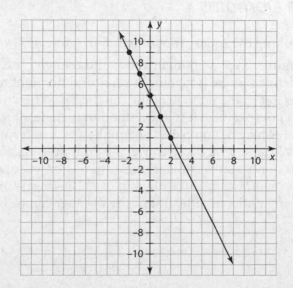

EXERCISE 3

Graphing Functions

Directions: Graph both functions in the supplied coordinate system.

1. $f(x) = \dfrac{1}{2}x - 2$ **2.** $g(x) = \sqrt{x + 4}$

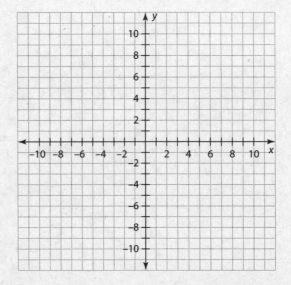

Answers are on page 557.

Finding Domains

When graphing the square root function in Exercise 3, you may have tried using the number –5 as an input and found that you had to find $\sqrt{-1}$. As this is undefined, there is no output value and no point to plot. The reason is that –1 is not in the domain of the function g. When the domain of a function is not specified, it is understood to include all numbers for which computations may be completed and make sense in terms of the use of the function. With the function g above, the domain is restricted so that the radicand is non-negative, or algebraically, $x + 4 \geq 0$. Solving this inequality produces $x \geq -4$, which is the domain of g. The linear function f above has no such computational difficulties. Any number can be halved and then decreased by two, so the domain of *f* is all numbers. Rational expressions lead to rational functions, the domains of which need to exclude numbers that make denominators vanish.

EXAMPLE

If $r(x) = \dfrac{x-1}{x+4}$, then $x + 4 \neq 0$. Solving gives $x \neq -4$, so the domain of this rational function is all numbers except -4.

Other functions may have domains restricted due to the way the function is used.

EXAMPLE

The function $h(t) = 16t^2$ gives the distance *h* an object falls in feet *t* seconds after being dropped. The domain of *h* is given by $t \geq 0$, not because a negative number cannot be squared and the result multiplied by 16, but because negative times don't make sense for the use of this function.

The domain of a function may also be found from its graph. The domain is that part of the *x*-axis that has points of the graph above or below it.

EXAMPLE

The domain of the function graphed below is $-7 \leq x \leq 8$.

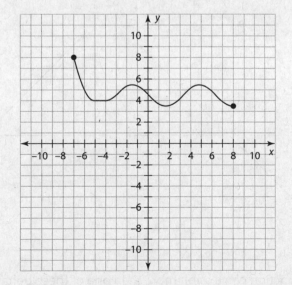

EXERCISE 4

Finding Domains

Directions: Find the domain of the function.

1. $f(x) = 3x - 7$ **2.** $g(x) = \sqrt{x - 2}$ **3.** $h(x) = \dfrac{x + 5}{x - 5}$

Answers are on page 557.

Properties of Functions

We say a function is **increasing** when the y-values of the function get larger as the x-values get larger, and a function is **decreasing** when the y-values get smaller as the x-values get larger. Graphically, think of a point on the graph moving from left to right. If the point also moves upward, the function is increasing. If the point moves downward, the function is decreasing. If the point doesn't move up or down, the function is said to be **constant**.

EXAMPLE

The function on the left is increasing, and the function on the right is decreasing.

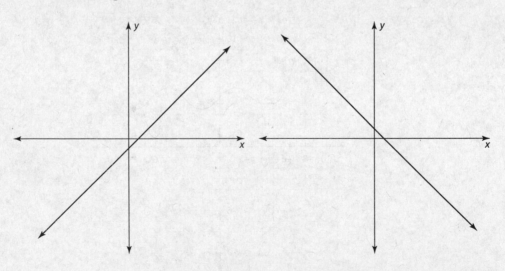

A function can exhibit more than one of these behaviors.

EXAMPLE

The function below is decreasing for $x < -4$, increasing for $x > 4$, and constant for $-4 < x < 4$.

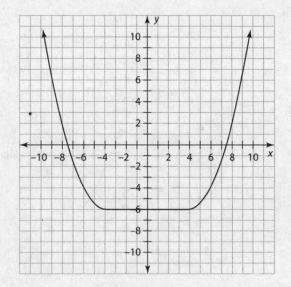

This function also exhibits another feature: **symmetry about the y-axis**. Graphically, this means that the graph can be folded on the y-axis and the left and right halves of the graph will coincide. Other types of symmetry that can be displayed in a graph are **symmetry about the x-axis** and **symmetry about the origin**. If a graph is symmetric about the x-axis, the graph can be folded on the x-axis and the lower and upper halves of the graph will coincide. A graph is symmetric about the origin if rotating the coordinate system 180° around the point (0,0) produces the same graph.

EXAMPLES

Graph (a) is symmetric about the origin, and graph (b) is symmetric about the *x*-axis. Neither is symmetric about the *y*-axis.

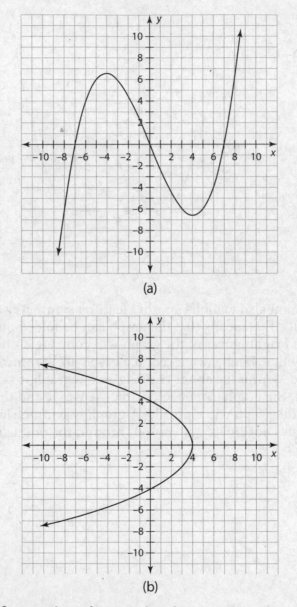

(a)

(b)

   The first graph is a function, but the second graph is not. Why? Remember that the definition of a function doesn't allow an *x*-value to be paired with more than one *y*-value. There are two points on the graph corresponding to *x* = 3. Their *y*-values are 2 and –2. For this graph, every *x* < 4 is paired with two different *y*-values. Notice that this graph doesn't pass the Vertical Line Test mentioned earlier. At least one vertical line crosses the graph more than once. The *y*-axis is one such line.

There are other properties of functions that can be determined from graphs. The **intercepts** are points where the graph crosses the coordinate axes. The **x-intercept** is where the graph crosses the x-axis; it is a point where $y = 0$. The **y-intercept** is where the graph crosses the y-axis; it is a point where $x = 0$.

EXAMPLE

What are the intercepts of the graph?

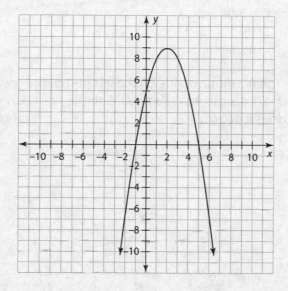

The graph crosses the y-axis at $y = 5$; therefore the y-intercept is (0, 5). The graph crosses the x-axis at $x = -1$ and $x = 5$, so the x-intercepts are (–1, 0) and (5, 0).

The function in the previous example shows another feature: it has a maximum value. The **maximum value** of a function is the largest y-value that the function attains. Graphically, it is the y-value of the highest point on the graph. Similarly, **the minimum value** of a function is the smallest y-value that the function attains. Graphically, it is the y-value of the lowest point on the graph. The maximum value of the function in the previous example is $y = 9$. The maximum occurs when $x = 2$. The function doesn't have a minimum value.

EXERCISE 5

Properties of Functions

Directions: Use the following graph to answer the questions.

1. Where is the function increasing? Decreasing? Constant?

2. What are the intercepts?

3. What is the domain?

4. What is the maximum value on the left part of the graph, and where does it occur? What is the minimum value on the right part of the graph, and where does it occur?

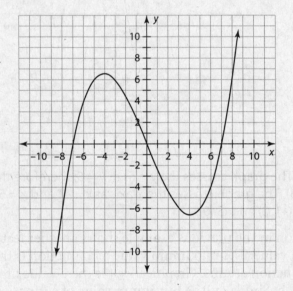

Answers are on page 557.

Science

The Science Test

The Science section of the GED® test measures your knowledge of key science topics and how well you understand basic scientific practices. There are approximately 40 questions on the Science test, and you will have 90 minutes to complete the entire test. About 40 percent of the questions focus on life science, about 40 percent focus on physical science, and the remaining 20 percent focus on Earth and space science.

Questions on the Science test may ask about the information in a short passage, a graph, a table, or some other graphic presentation of scientific data. Sometimes two or three questions will refer to the same passage, graph, or table. These questions measure your ability to interpret scientific data.

Most Science questions are multiple-choice with four answer choices. Others use interactive formats such as drag-and-drop, fill-in-the-blank, drop-down, and short answer. See "Introducing the GED® Test" at the start of this book for an explanation and samples of these formats.

The Science Review

The following section of this book presents a comprehensive review of the knowledge that is tested on the Science test. Each main topic is followed by an exercise to measure how well you have mastered that subject.

Answers for all of the exercises in this section are located in the Exercise Answer Key section at the back of this book.

CHAPTER 1

Life Science

Life science includes those areas of natural science that deal with the structure and behavior of living organisms, such as microorganisms, plants, and animals (including human beings). Its findings are applied in health, agriculture, medicine, the pharmaceutical industry, and the food science industry. While biology is still the main focus of the life sciences, advances in technology have led to many new interdisciplinary fields.

From Molecules to Organisms: Structures and Processes

We all know that cats give birth only to cats, frogs to frogs, and so on for every type of living thing. This is so because of a molecule called deoxyribonucleic acid (DNA). DNA is the hereditary material in humans and most other organisms that contains the instructions that make each species unique. DNA, along with the instructions it contains, is passed from adult organisms to their offspring during reproduction.

DNA

DNA found inside the area of the cell called the nucleus is referred to as **nuclear DNA**. Because the cell is very small and because organisms have many DNA molecules per cell, each DNA molecule must be tightly packaged. A distinct package of DNA is called a chromosome. During DNA replication, the chromosomes unwind so that the DNA can be copied. At other times in the cell cycle, DNA unwinds so that its instructions can be used to make proteins and for other biological processes. But during cell division, DNA is in its compact chromosome form to enable transfer to new cells. An organism's complete set of nuclear DNA is called its **genome**.

DNA is located not only in cell nuclei; small amounts of DNA are also present in cell structures known as mitochondria. **Mitochondria** generate the energy a cell needs to function properly. Mitochondrial DNA contains the instructions for the functioning of the mitochondria. In sexual reproduction, organisms inherit half of their nuclear DNA from the male parent and half from the female parent. On the other hand, organisms inherit their entire mitochondrial DNA from the female parent. This occurs because only egg cells, and not sperm cells, keep their mitochondria during fertilization.

EXERCISE 1

DNA

Directions: Write a short-response answer to each of the following items.

1. Explain when a cell's DNA is packaged in chromosomes and when it is unwound.

2. A typical human cell contains about two meters of DNA, if the DNA strands could be laid end to end. A typical cell nucleus is so small that 10,000 nuclei could fit on the head of a needle. This is equivalent to packing 24 miles of thin thread into a tennis ball. Why is it necessary for DNA to be tightly packaged as chromosomes for cell division?

Answers are on page 558.

Structure of DNA

A DNA molecule is formed from chemical building blocks called **nucleotides**. Nucleotides consist of three parts: a phosphate group, a sugar group, and one of four types of nitrogen bases. To form a strand of DNA, nucleotides are linked in chains of alternating phosphate and sugar groups. Two strands of phosphate and sugar groups are joined by pairs of nitrogen bases. The entire molecule looks like a ladder, with the nitrogen bases forming the rungs of the ladder. The DNA molecule is twisted into a shape known as a double helix. The four types of nitrogen bases found in nucleotides are adenine (A), thymine (T), guanine (G) and cytosine (C). A always pairs with T, and C always pairs with G. The order, or sequence, of these bases determines what biological instructions are contained in the strand of DNA. For example, the sequence ATCGTT might instruct for blue eyes, while ATCGCT might instruct for brown.

DNA's unique structure enables the molecule to copy itself during cell division. When a cell prepares to divide, the DNA double helix splits down the middle and becomes two single strands. These strands serve as templates for building two new, double-stranded DNA molecules—each a replica of the original DNA molecule. In this process, an A base is added wherever there is a T, and C where there is a G. The process continues until all of the bases once again are paired.

Each DNA sequence that contains instructions to make a single protein is known as a **gene**. The size of a gene may vary greatly, ranging from about 1,000 bases to 1 million bases in humans. The human genome contains about 3 billion bases and about 20,000 genes on 23 pairs of chromosomes.

DNA contains the instructions needed for an organism to develop, survive, and reproduce. To carry out these functions, DNA sequences must be converted into messages that can be used to produce proteins, which are the complex molecules that do most of the work in our bodies. DNA's instructions are used to make proteins in a two-step process. When proteins are being made, the double helix unwinds and splits to allow a single strand to serve as another template. This template strand is then transcribed into a molecule called messenger ribonucleic acid, or mRNA. The information contained in the mRNA molecule is translated into the "language" of amino acids, which are the building blocks of proteins. This language tells the cell's protein-making machinery the precise order in which to link the amino acids to produce a specific protein. This is a major task because there are 20 types of amino acids, which can be placed in many different sequences to form a wide variety of proteins.

Although DNA was first observed in the late 1800s, its importance did not become clear until 1953, as a result of the work of scientists James Watson, Francis Crick, Maurice Wilkins, and Rosalind Franklin. By studying X-ray diffraction patterns and building models, the scientists discovered the double helix structure of DNA, which is shown in the following illustration.

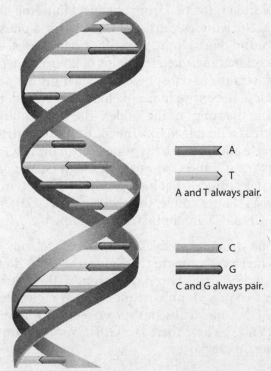

A

T

A and T always pair.

C

G

C and G always pair.

EXERCISE 2

Structure of DNA

Directions: Read the following passage. Then, write a short response to each of the items that follow.

Suppose you are a scientist studying the structure of a DNA molecule. You find that the nitrogen base sequence of one strand of the molecule's double helix is AATGAC.

1. What is the nitrogen base sequence for the opposite strand? Explain how you know this.

2. Compare the functions of DNA and mRNA.

Choose the *best* answer to each of the following items.

3. Most of an organism's DNA is

   A. X chromosome DNA.
   B. mitochondrial DNA.
   C. muscular DNA.
   D. nuclear DNA.

4. The code contained in DNA is encrypted in the

   A. nitrogen bases.
   B. nucleus.
   C. phosphate groups.
   D. sugar groups.

Answers are on page 558.

Interacting Body Systems

Cells are the most basic unit of life in the body. In most multicellular organisms, not all cells are alike. For example, the cells that make up your skin are different from the cells that make up your liver, your blood, or your eyes. Yet all of these specialized organs developed from one fertilized egg cell, which means that all your cells have the same DNA. But your skin, liver, blood, and eyes are very different from each other in form and function. While most of the body's cells are specialized for a specific job, other cells remain unspecialized. These unspecialized cells multiply continuously to replace the millions of different body cells that die and need to be replaced every day.

Cells group together to form tissues that perform specific functions. For example, the inner surface of the stomach is lined with a tissue layer known as the **gastric mucosa**. The gastric mucosa secretes a mucus that coats the inside of the stomach and protects the stomach from being destroyed by its own digestive juices.

An **organ** is a structure made up of two or more tissues that work together for a common purpose. The stomach is an organ composed of four layers of tissues that work together to churn and partially digest the foods we eat. This grouping of cells and tissues is referred to as levels of **organization**. Organs can be as primitive as the brain of a flatworm (a group of nerve cells) or as complex as the human liver. The human body has many different organs, such as the heart, the kidneys, the pancreas, and the skin.

The most complex organisms have organ systems. An organ system is a group of organs that act together to carry out complex, interrelated functions, with each organ focusing on one part of the task. The human organ systems are described in the following table.

Organ System	Function	Organs, Tissues, Structures Involved
Cardiovascular	Transportation of oxygen, nutrients, and other substances to the body cells, and of wastes, carbon dioxide, and other substances away from body cells. It also helps stabilize body temperature and pH.	Heart, blood, blood vessels
Lymphatic	Defense against infection and disease	Lymph, lymph nodes, lymph vessels
Digestive	Processing of food and absorption of nutrients, minerals, vitamins, and water	Salivary glands, esophagus, stomach, liver, gall bladder, pancreas, small intestine, large intestine
Endocrine	Communication within the body via hormones, directing long-term change over other organ systems to maintain homeostasis	Pituitary gland, pineal gland, thyroid, parathyroid, adrenal glands, testes, ovaries, and others

Organ System	Function	Organs, Tissues, Structures Involved
Integumentary	Protection from injury and fluid loss; defense against infection; temperature control	Skin, hair, and nails
Muscular	Movement, support, and heat production	Skeletal, cardiac, and smooth muscle; tendons
Nervous	Collecting, processing, and transmitting information; directing short-term change over other organ systems in order to maintain homeostasis	Brain, spinal cord, nerves, sense organs (eyes, ears, tongue, skin, nose)
Reproductive	Production of sex cells and sex hormones, production of offspring	Fallopian tubes, uterus, vagina, ovaries, mammary glands, testes, vas deferens, seminal vesicles, prostate, penis
Respiratory	Delivery of air to sites where gas exchange can occur	Mouth, nose, pharynx, larynx, trachea, bronchi, lungs, diaphragm
Skeletal	Support and protection of soft tissues, movement at joints, production of blood, mineral storage	Bones, cartilage, ligaments
Urinary	Removal of excess water, salts, and waste products from blood and body; control of pH	Kidneys, ureters, urinary bladder, and urethras

EXERCISE 3

Interacting Body Systems

Directions: Choose the *best* response to each of the following items.

1. Select the correct sequence for human levels of organization.

    A. cell < tissue < organ
    B. organ < cell < organ system
    C. tissue < cell < organ
    D. tissue < organ < cell

2. Muscle cells and nerve cells

    A. develop from different areas of an egg cell.
    B. develop from different egg cells.
    C. have different DNA sequences.
    D. have the same DNA sequences.

Read the following passage and refer to the previous table to respond to the following item.

3. What organ system is described in this passage?

Insects "breathe" through spiracles (small holes) in their abdomens. Air enters the spiracles and travels through a network of tubes, called trachea, to directly reach the cells of the insect's body. In small insects, the distance from the outside atmosphere to the cells is short enough for oxygen to travel by simple diffusion to the cells. In larger insects, there is a need for an additional way of moving air in and out of the insect's body. Larger insects pump their abdomens to move gases in their tracheae to help bring fresh air into the body.

Answers are on page 558.

Homeostasis and Feedback

Homeostasis is the state of balance inside the body, achieved when healthy body systems work together to keep the body functioning normally. It refers to the body's ability to control its internal conditions regardless of changing external conditions. A system of feedback controls and stabilizes the functioning of the body's systems. By releasing chemicals called **hormones** into the blood stream or lymph vessels, the endocrine system helps maintain the necessary internal conditions. The release of these hormones is controlled by negative and positive feedback systems.

A **negative feedback system** is designed to counteract a change in the body's condition in much the same way that a thermostat helps to keep your home's inside temperature within a normal range. When the temperature rises above the normal range, the thermostat turns on the air conditioner. Eventually, the inside temperature is restored to the normal range. This process is illustrated in the following diagram.

Homeostasis and Temperature Control

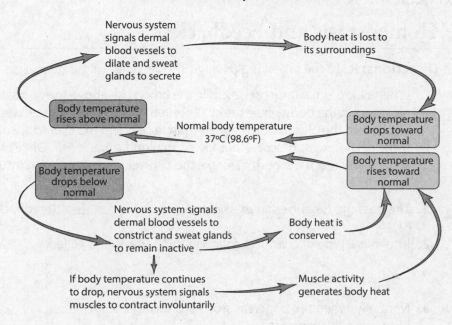

Examples of negative feedback systems that help maintain internal body conditions include these:

- **Body temperature:** If body temperature drops below the normal range, the body shivers to warm up. If the body is too warm, it responds by sweating to cool off.

- **Blood pressure:** As blood pressure increases past the normal range, signals are sent to the brain. The brain uses hormones to communicate with the heart, telling the heart to slow down. Slowing the heart rate helps blood pressure return to the normal range.

- **Production of red blood cells:** If the oxygen level of the blood drops below the normal range, the kidneys release a hormone to stimulate the production of red blood cells.

Unlike negative feedback that counteracts a change in the body's condition, **positive feedback** amplifies a change in the body's condition. An example of positive feedback is of a woman giving birth. As the baby's head pushes against the cervix, signals are sent to the brain, which in turn stimulates contractions. The baby's head is then pushed even more tightly against the cervix. This cycle repeats, causing the contractions to become stronger and stronger until the baby is born. Positive feedback is not always good for the body. If an infection is present in the body, the body may respond with a fever. If the infection spreads, the body may continue to raise its temperature in an attempt to kill the infection. If body temperature rises significantly over the normal range, it can have a deadly effect.

EXERCISE 4

Homeostasis and Feedback

Directions: Read the following passage and respond to the items that follow.

When blood sugar (glucose) levels in the blood rise above the normal range, receptors in the body sense the change. In turn, the pancreas releases insulin into the blood, which signals muscle cells and the liver to absorb some of the excess glucose, thus lowering blood sugar levels. Once blood sugar levels reach the normal range, the pancreas stops secreting insulin.

1. The passage describes an example of _____ feedback.

2. Insulin is a type of chemical, found in the body, that is called a

   _____.

3. Normally, when the pancreas stops producing insulin, _____ has been achieved.

Answers are on page 558.

Mitosis

When an egg cell and a sperm cell combine, a new cell is created that is about as big as the dot over this *i*. From this tiny cell develops an organism as complex as you and me. The mechanism that enables a whole new organism to develop from one small cell is called mitosis. **Mitosis** is a cellular process that replicates chromosomes and produces two identical nuclei in preparation for cell division. Generally, mitosis is immediately followed by the division of the cell nuclei and other cell contents into two equal daughter cells.

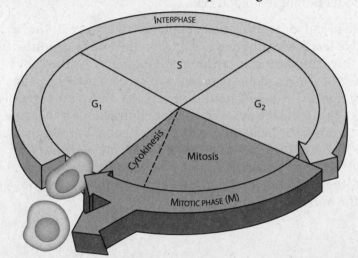

The **cell cycle**, shown in the diagram, describes the life of a cell, which extends from the cell's birth to its division into two cells. The cell cycle can be divided into two major phases: the interphase and the mitotic phase. During **interphase**, the cell performs its normal functions within the organism. It might, for example, produce enzymes or secrete hormones, depending on what kind of cell it is. The cell also grows in size and increases its supply of proteins and cell organelles. Each cell spends 90 percent of its time in interphase. The interphase can be divided into three phases: G_1, S, and G_2. G stands for *gap*. In the G_1 and G_2 phases, the cell grows.

The S phase (synthesis) is most important for cell reproduction. During the S phase, the chromosomes are duplicated. That means that the DNA in the cell nucleus doubles. Thus, in the G_2 phase, the cell contains double the amount of DNA. Now, the cell prepares to divide. A cell that does not enter the S phase but stays in the G_1 phase will not divide anymore.

Cell division occurs in the mitotic phase. This phase can again be divided in two sub-phases—mitosis and cytokinesis. **Mitosis**, which makes up 10 percent of a cell's life cycle, is the division of the nucleus. Mitosis is followed by the division of the entire cell, called **cytokinesis**.

Cell Replacement

Cells divide to replace damaged, dying, or lost cells. Your skin, for example, consists of millions of cells that protect your body against damage and pathogens. The cells on the surface slough off after a while—for example, when you scratch yourself. The lost cells are replaced by new cells.

Growth

You started out as a single cell. Then, the cell divided by mitosis often enough to produce the millions of cells in your body. All the cells of your body work together in tissues and organs in very complex ways so that you can speak, learn, eat, play, and perform all the other activities that are part of your daily life.

Asexual Reproduction

Sometimes, mitosis even functions to produce a whole new organism. Asexual reproduction occurs in single-celled organisms and also in plants and some more complex animals. If you clip part of a plant off, for example, it can develop into a whole new plant. Sea stars can also reproduce asexually. If a sea star loses an arm, for example, the arm can grow into a whole new sea star.

Mitosis

Directions: Choose the *best* response to each of the following items.

1. During interphase, the cell

    A. divides into daughter cells.
    B. performs its normal functions.
    C. spends about half its life.
    D. undergoes mitosis.

2. During the mitotic phase, the cell

    A. grows.
    B. performs its normal functions.
    C. undergoes cytokinesis.
    D. undergoes interphase.

3. Which is NOT a reason for cell division by mitosis?

    A. Asexual reproduction
    B. Growth of organism
    C. Replacement of dead cells
    D. Faster DNA duplication

Answers are on page 558.

Cell Differentiation

Undifferentiated cells of an embryo are known as **embryonic stem cells**. The fertilized egg divides many times to form a ball of undifferentiated cells. At a point, the cells begin to differentiate. Some cells form the brain, others begin to form kidneys, and so on. While some cells have differentiated to form these organs, others are still undifferentiated. Those cells that remain undifferentiated will continue to form new tissues as time goes on.

Even when all tissues are created, some cells within those differentiated tissues remain undifferentiated and are known as adult stem cells. An **adult stem cell** is an undifferentiated cell found among differentiated, specialized cells in a tissue or organ. Adult stem cells can generate some or all of the specialized cells of the tissue or organ in which they are found. The primary roles of adult stem cells in a living organism are to maintain and repair the tissue in which they are found.

Stem Cells and Medical Research

Medical scientists are interested in adult stem cells because of their ability to divide indefinitely and produce all the cell types of the organ from which they came, potentially growing an entire organ from a few cells. Unlike the use of embryonic stem cells, the use of adult stem cells in medicine is not considered controversial, as adult stem cells are extracted from adult tissues rather than from human embryos.

Human embryonic and adult stem cells each have advantages and disadvantages regarding their potential uses in medicine.

- Embryonic stem cells can become all cell types of the body, while adult stem cells are thought to be limited to differentiating into cell types of their tissue of origin.

- Embryonic stem cells can be grown relatively easily in culture. Adult stem cells are rare in mature tissues, so finding and growing these cells from adult tissue is challenging. Large numbers of cells are needed for stem cell replacement therapies such as bone marrow transplants.

- The use of adult stem cells and tissues derived from the patient's own stem cells makes cells less likely to be attacked by the immune system.

EXERCISE 6

Cell Differentiation

Directions: Read the following passage. Then write a short answer to the item that follows.

Scientists are studying ways to treat diabetes. Presently, there is a procedure being tested in which insulin-producing cells are transplanted from deceased tissue donors to diabetic patients. However, there are serious issues to be overcome. For instance, transplant patients will face a lifetime of drug therapy to prevent their immune systems from attacking the transplanted cells. Also, not enough donors are available to fulfill the current need for transplantable cells.

1. Explain how using stem cell therapy could reduce the problems associated with this method of treating diabetes.

Choose the *best* answer to the following item.

2. Adult stem cells

    A. are easily harvested from mature tissues.
    B. are less likely to be rejected by the body.
    C. are capable of developing into any cell of the body.
    D. can be grown relatively easily in culture.

Answers are on page 558.

Amino Acids

Amino acids are molecules made out of hydrogen, oxygen, carbon, and nitrogen atoms (and a little sulfur). There are 20 types of amino acids in living things. While plants are able to make all of the amino acids, animals can make only 10 but need all 20 types to survive. Therefore, animals get all their necessary amino acids by eating plants or by eating animals that eat particular plants.

Amino acid molecules are known as the building blocks of life. They form long chains called **proteins**. Proteins, in various forms, control much of the functioning of an organism. Also, many of an organism's structures are formed from proteins.

As shown in the following diagram, a single amino acid molecule has a central carbon atom, called the **alpha carbon**, bonded to a hydrogen atom, a carboxyl group, an amino group, and an "R" group. The R group differs with each type of amino acid.

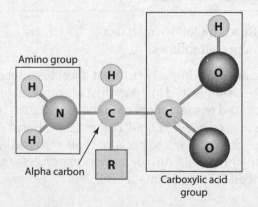

The order of the amino acids in an amino acid chain is determined by the information found in the organism's DNA. DNA's genetic code determines a protein's structure and function.

Amino Acids

Directions: Write a short response to the following item.

1. How are all amino acid molecules alike, and how are they sometimes different?

Choose the best response to the following item.

2. Amino acids

   A. are formed only by animals.
   B. are formed only by plants.
   C. form chains of proteins.
   D. form DNA molecules.

Answers are on page 559.

Photosynthesis

Plants provide the oxygen we need to breathe and the nutrients we need to thrive. Green plants are self-sufficient because they are able to produce their own food, while human beings and lower animals must obtain their food. **Photosynthesis** is the food-making process by which green plants convert light from the sun into useful forms of chemical energy. The process of photosynthesis involves several steps.

Photosynthesis begins within the **chloroplasts**, where chlorophyll molecules absorb light. Chlorophyll is the substance that gives plants their green color. Using the energy that chlorophyll releases from the sunlight, the plant splits water into its two components—oxygen and hydrogen. The oxygen is released to the atmosphere, and the hydrogen recombines with carbon dioxide in the air to produce carbohydrate molecules (a form of starch) in the plant.

Two other chemicals inside the leaves do the same job as chlorophyll. **Xanthophyll** and **carotene** appear as yellow- and orange-colored pigments that are masked during the summer by the chlorophyll. Eventually, the shorter daylight hours of fall cause the plant to stop the production of chlorophyll, allowing us to see the other pigments.

The food that is created by photosynthesis is transported through the plant by the **phloem**. The cellular transport system carries the newly created food down the stem of the plant to the storage center, called the **root**. Water is transported by a similar system called the **xylem**. This cellular system allows the roots to take in water from the soil and transport it up to the leaves through the stem for the process of photosynthesis.

EXERCISE 8

Photosynthesis

Directions: Read the following passage. Then choose the *best* response to the item that follows.

The leaves of certain plants have some areas that lack chlorophyll and some areas containing chlorophyll. A coleus plant, with its brightly colored leaves, is one example. In an experiment in which the pigment (color) of the coleus leaf is removed, an iodine solution will identify areas where starch is present by turning that part of the leaf brown.

1. Which of the following would you predict will happen to a coleus leaf in such an experiment?

   A. The areas that were green originally would turn brown.
   B. The leaf would turn yellow and red.
   C. The entire leaf would turn brown.
   D. Only half the leaf would turn brown.

The answer is on page 559.

Cellular Respiration

All living things require some form of fuel as a source of chemical energy. Both animals and plants release the energy from food by using the process of **cellular respiration**. **Aerobic respiration** is cellular respiration in the presence of an abundance of oxygen. Just as fire needs oxygen to release energy from burned fuel, aerobic respiration requires oxygen to release the energy from food. Without oxygen, cellular respiration does not release all the available energy and is called **anaerobic respiration**.

Aerobic respiration occurs in the cells' mitochondria. Fuel and oxygen are carried to the cells in animals by the circulatory system. The fuel usually used as an energy source in living organisms is glucose. **Glucose** is a sugar produced as carbohydrates are digested. When glucose is burned in the mitochondria, there are two waste products—carbon dioxide and water.

These are the same waste products produced when a fuel such as natural gas is burned. The process of aerobic respiration is represented by the following equations.

fuel (glucose) + oxygen → carbon dioxide + water + energy

$$C_6H_{12}O_6 + 6O_2 \rightarrow 6CO_2 + 6H_2O + energy$$

Most cells can function for a short time even when oxygen levels are low. And some simple microbes are completely anaerobic—they grow and reproduce without any oxygen. Anaerobic respiration, or **fermentation**, occurs in the cell's cytoplasm, and not in the mitochondria. Fermentation is not as efficient at producing energy for cells as aerobic respiration is. There are two types of fermentation—lactic acid fermentation and alcohol fermentation.

In **lactic acid fermentation**, glucose is converted to lactic acid. Skeletal muscle produces lactic acid when the body cannot supply enough oxygen, such as during periods of strenuous exercise. When lactic acid builds up in muscle cells, muscles become fatigued and might feel sore. Lactic acid is also produced by some microorganisms that are often used to produce many foods, including cheese, yogurt, and sour cream. **Alcohol fermentation** occurs in yeast and some bacteria. Alcohol fermentation converts glucose to alcohol.

EXERCISE 9

Cellular Respiration

Directions: Write a short response to the following item.

1. Construct an outline showing how these terms relate to each other: *cellular respiration, fermentation, anaerobic respiration, aerobic respiration, alcohol fermentation,* and *lactic acid fermentation*.

Choose the *best* response to the following item.

2. Which situation might allow your body to use anaerobic respiration?

    A. Eating before exercising
    B. Running a long distance
    C. Sleeping
    D. Breathing deeply

Answers are on page 559.

Ecosystems

An **ecosystem** is a biological community of living organisms and their physical environment. It can include plants, animals (including people), microorganisms, water, and soil. Ecosystems vary widely in size and the elements that make them up. An ecosystem can be as small as a single tree or as large as an entire forest. When an ecosystem is healthy, it is said to be **sustainable**. This means that all the plants and animals in the ecosystem live in balance and can continue to reproduce. Also, there is usually **biodiversity**, meaning that there is a variety of organisms living in that environment.

Carrying Capacity of an Ecosystem

In an ecosystem, **carrying capacity** is defined as the maximum number of individuals of a given species that an environment can support indefinitely. The carrying capacity is the population size at which the population growth rate equals zero. The population size of a species is limited by predators, diseases, competition with other species, and food availability. If the population size is smaller than the carrying capacity, the population will grow. If the population is greater than the carrying capacity, the population will decrease. Populations increase or decrease in size until they reach carrying capacity. The following graph illustrates a population that grows and reaches the ecosystem's carrying capacity for that species. However, notice that the population continues to increase past the carrying capacity.

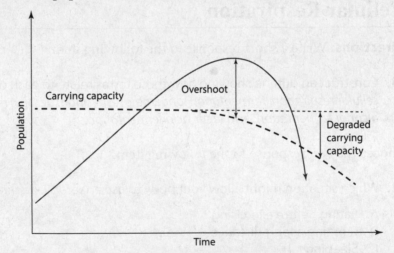

When a population surpasses its carrying capacity, it enters a situation known as **overshoot**. Overshoot must be temporary. How long a species stays in overshoot depends on how much excess resource, such as food, is available to support their greater numbers. A species may enter overshoot when it discovers a vast but exhaustible supply of a resource. A population in overshoot will eventually decline to (or below) the carrying capacity. As the inflated population exhausts the extra supplies of resources, the overpopulated species damages or destroys the original daily supply of resources in its attempt to survive. Eventually, the species begins to starve. Most of the population dies. This collapse of the population is known as a **crash**, or **die-off**.

A frequent result of a crash is that the carrying capacity for the overshot species falls below what it was before the overshoot existed. The species may remain at the lower population level for a short period of time, possibly forever. If the ecosystem does recover and is once again able to produce adequate daily supplies of resources, the species population may recover, too. However, it is possible for a species to undergo a series of overshoots and crashes.

EXERCISE 10

Carrying Capacity of an Ecosystem

Directions: Write a short-response answer to the following item.

   1. Define carrying capacity.

Read the following passage. Then, choose the *best* answer for the item that follows.

> In 1944, 29 reindeer were brought to St. Matthew Island off the coast of Alaska. At first, there were abundant resources and the reindeer population quickly increased. About 20 years later, there was a sudden, massive die-off. Ninety-nine percent of the reindeer died of starvation.

   2. The die-off of the reindeer was probably related to

   A. a disease brought to the island by the original reindeer.
   B. insufficient food for the 29 originally introduced reindeer.
   C. the inability of the reindeer to reproduce in adequate numbers.
   D. the reindeer's exceeding the carrying capacity of the island.

Answers are on page 559.

Biodiversity and Populations

Biodiversity refers to the variety of plants, animals, and other living things in an ecosystem. Everything that lives in an ecosystem is part of a complex system of relationships. Plant, animal, insect, and even microbial species depend on each other for food, shelter, oxygen, and soil enrichment. Maintaining a large diversity of living organisms in all ecosystems is necessary to maintain all the living systems that exist on our planet.

Biodiversity is the life-support system of our planet. We depend on it for the air we breathe, the food we eat, and the water we drink. Wetlands filter pollutants from water; trees and plants reduce global warming by absorbing carbon; and bacteria and fungi break down organic material and fertilize the soil. It has been shown that a large diversity of native species is linked to the health of ecosystems, as is the quality of life for humans.

Biodiversity is vitally connected to our sustainable future. In view of our need to conserve biodiversity, it is important to consider how humans negatively impact the biodiversity of Earth. Human factors that affect biodiversity are explained in the following paragraphs.

Habitat loss and fragmentation

This occurs as humans convert ecosystems to human-dominated systems. Some consider this to be the primary cause of biodiversity loss. Habitats and the organisms in them are destroyed by clearance of native vegetation for agriculture, housing, timber, and industry, as well as draining wetlands and flooding valleys to form reservoirs. In addition, such destruction makes some habitats too small for some organisms to survive. And fragments of formerly whole ecosystems may be too far apart to support migrating animals.

Overexploitation

This occurs as humans use up resource organisms faster than the organisms can reproduce.

Introduction of exotic species

This can also have a devastating effect on biodiversity. Invasive species are the second greatest threat to biodiversity worldwide. Whether introduced deliberately or accidentally, nonnative plants and animals can severely damage the ecosystems they invade. For instance, zebra mussels were introduced from Europe into the Great Lakes during the 1980s. They have voracious appetites and eat much of the plankton that native species depend on. Virtually all ecosystems worldwide have been affected by the invasion of nonnative species. This situation is predicted to worsen in the future because of climate change and more worldwide tourism and trade.

Pollution

This is poisoning many species, both on land and in the water, and is contributing to climate change (see next section). Transportation, industry, construction, mining, electric power plants, and other sources contribute pollutants to the air, land, and water. Dangerous chemicals in an ecosystem can affect biodiversity and ultimately kill individuals, or even entire species and habitats.

Climate change

This is thought to be largely caused by greenhouse gas emissions from the burning of fossil fuels, making the environment too hot for some species and too cold for others. It is changing the distribution of individual species around the globe, affecting the crops we can grow, causing sea levels to rise, and damaging coastal ecosystems.

Elimination of "pest" animals

Elimination of animals viewed as pests. For example, wolves were hunted to extinction in various parts of the country because of their perceived threat to humans and livestock. Without the wolves, populations of such other creatures as coyotes, elk, pronghorn, small prey, and scavengers have gone out of balance, resulting is drastic declines in many species and overgrazing of many areas. Reintroducing wolves has been shown to benefit 20 or more vertebrate species, including bald eagles, grizzly bears, cougars, and songbirds.

EXERCISE 11

Biodiversity and Populations

Directions: Match the human factor that affects biodiversity with a way people can minimize the negative effects.

1. _____ Climate change   a. plant only native flowers

2. _____ Elimination of pest animals   b. use alternative fuel sources

3. _____ Habitat loss and fragmentation   c. drive electric cars

4. _____ Pollution   d. do not wear natural fur coats

5. _____ Overexploitation   e. educate people about predators

6. _____ Nonnative species   f. build fish stairs around water dams

Answers are on page 559.

Socialization Within Populations

Individuals of a single species that share the same geographic location at the same time are a **population**. **Social behavior** refers to the interactions among individuals of a population. A wide range of social behaviors exists among different species. Some animals virtually never interact with each other. Nonsocial animals include mosquitoes and polar bears. Highly socialized animals live in large groups, often cooperating in many ways. Packs of wolves and schools of fish are highly socialized organisms. The most highly socialized animals, such as all ants and termites and some bees and wasps, build homes together and form close colonies.

Many social behaviors are adaptive, meaning that they increase an individual's chances to reproduce. One example of an adaptive social behavior is when individuals of a species congregate in large groups to ward off predators. This applies to schools of fish as well as to flocks of birds. When individuals belong to a group, the likelihood of any given individual being killed by a predator is reduced. However, there are costs to this group behavior. For example, there may not be adequate grazing land for all members of a large herd of bison.

Social behaviors are not only acted out by large groups. Often, individuals play important roles in protecting the interests of the larger group. For example, an act of **altruism** occurs when one member of a population acts in a way that benefits one or more other members of the population but incurs a cost or risk to itself. For example, a ground squirrel may sound a warning when a hawk is nearby. However, this warning draws attention to that individual, thus increasing that individual's risk of attack. Altruistic behavior is perplexing to many biologists. Most social behaviors improve an individual's chances to live long enough to successfully reproduce. Altruism appears to create an opposite situation, in which an individual's chances to reproduce are actually decreased.

Reciprocity is a variant of altruistic behavior. An individual may perform an altruistic act for another individual member of the population when there is a reasonable expectation that the favor will be returned at some later time. Some vampire bats will share a blood meal with another bat, but only with another bat that they will probably see again in the future. The cost of giving up food (when it is plentiful) may be less than the benefit of receiving food in the future (when it is scarce).

EXERCISE 12

Socialization Within Populations

Directions: Choose the *best* response to each of the following items.

1. Adaptive behaviors

   A. are always reciprocal.
   B. increase an individual's chances to reproduce.
   C. increase the resources of an ecosystem.
   D. reduce the numbers of predators in an ecosystem.

2. Dolphins often swim below sick animals for long periods of time, pushing them to the surface so they can breathe. This is an act of altruism because

   A. in nature, the sick animal will probably die despite the help it is receiving.
   B. the dolphin doing the pushing increases its chances to reproduce.
   C. the dolphin doing the pushing is exerting effort with no apparent benefit to itself.
   D. reciprocity is never an issue when help is offered; altruism is its own reward.

Answers are on page 559.

Flow of Energy in an Ecosystem

One way to study the interactions of organisms in an ecosystem is to follow the energy that flows through an ecosystem. Let's begin by looking at how organisms obtain energy. All organisms are classified as either autotrophs or heterotrophs.

Autotrophs

All green plants and other organisms that produce their own food in an ecosystem are primary producers, called autotrophs. An **autotroph** is an organism that collects energy from sunlight or inorganic substances to produce food. Autotrophs are the foundation of all ecosystems because they make energy available for all other organisms in an ecosystem.

Heterotrophs

A **heterotroph** is an organism that meets its energy requirements by consuming other organisms. Heterotrophs are also called consumers. A heterotroph that eats only plants is an **herbivore**, such as a cow, rabbit, or grasshopper. Heterotrophs that prey on other heterotrophs, such as lions and wolves, are called **carnivores**. There are also organisms that eat both plants and animals, called **omnivores**. Humans are omnivores (biologically speaking, though they may choose to limit their diets). **Detritivores** eat fragments of dead matter in an ecosystem, returning nutrients to the soil, air, and water. Detritivores include worms and many aquatic insects. **Decomposers**, similar to detritivores, break down dead organisms by releasing digestive enzymes. Fungi and bacteria are decomposers.

All heterotrophs, including detritivores, perform some decomposition when they consume another organism. However, it is primarily the decomposers that break down organic compounds and make nutrients available to producers to reuse. Without the detritivores and decomposers, the biosphere would be littered with dead organisms. Their bodies would contain nutrients no longer available to other organisms. The detritivores and decomposers are an important part of the cycle of life because they make nutrients available to other organisms.

EXERCISE 13

Flow of Energy in an Ecosystem

Directions: Write a short answer to the following item.

1. Compare and contrast *carnivores* and *detritivores*.

Choose the *best* answer to the following item.

2. If there were a total loss of autotrophs in an ecosystem,
    A. all heterotrophic species would die.
    B. carnivores would survive, but herbivores would not survive.
    C. herbivores would survive, but carnivores would not survive.
    D. only omnivores would survive.

Answers are on page 559.

Models of Energy Flow

Ecologists use food chains and food webs to model the energy flow through an ecosystem. Each step in a food chain or food web is called a **trophic level**. Autotrophs make up the first trophic level in all ecosystems. Heterotrophs make up the remaining levels. With the exception of the first trophic level, organisms at each trophic level get their energy from the trophic level before it.

Food Chains

A food chain is a simple model that shows how energy flows through an ecosystem. The following diagram shows a simplified but typical grassland food chain. Arrows represent the one-way energy flow that typically starts with autotrophs and moves through heterotrophs.

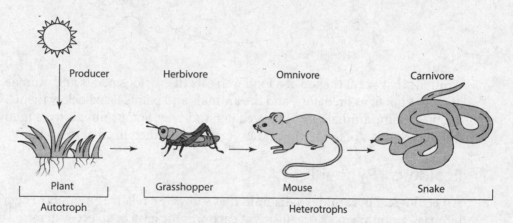

The plant uses energy from the sun to make its own food. The grasshopper gets its energy from eating the plant. The mouse gets its energy from eating the grasshopper. Finally, the snake gets its energy from eating the mouse. Each organism uses a portion of the energy it obtains from the organism it eats for cellular processes to build new cells and tissues.

Food Webs

Feeding relationships usually are more complicated than a single food chain because most organisms feed on more than one species. Some birds, for instance, eat a variety of seeds, fruits, and insects. The model most often used to represent the feeding relationships in an ecosystem is a food web. A **food web** is a diagram that explains the feeding relationships between different plants and animals in an ecosystem. The following diagram shows a food web.

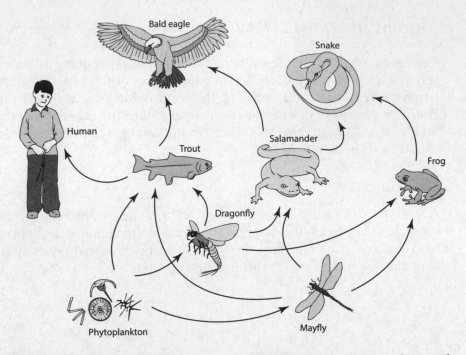

Animals that are at the top of a food web eats the various plants and animals and are known as predators, and the animals and plants listed below them are prey. Some animals are both predator and prey. Some animals have many different sources of food, while others are more limited in what they eat.

Ecological Pyramids

An **ecological pyramid** is a diagram that shows the relative amounts of energy, biomass, or numbers of organisms at each trophic level of an ecosystem.

Pyramid of Energy
In a pyramid of energy, each level represents the amount of energy that is available to that trophic level. With each step up, there is an energy loss of 90 percent.

Pyramid of Biomass
In a pyramid of biomass, each level represents the amount of biomass consumed by the level above it.

Pyramid of Numbers
In a pyramid of numbers, each level represents the number of individual organisms consumed by the level above it.

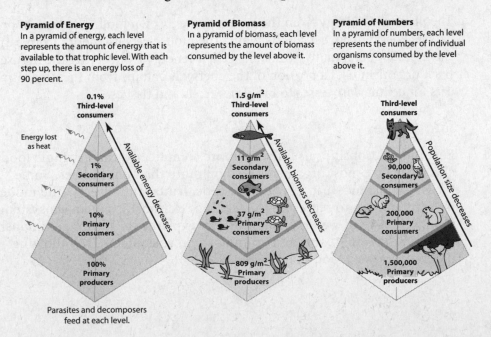

Notice in the preceding diagram that in a pyramid of energy, approximately 90 percent of all energy is not transferred to the level above it. This occurs because most of the energy contained in the organisms at each level is consumed by cellular processes or released to the environment as heat. Usually, the amount of **biomass**—the total mass of living matter at each trophic level—decreases at each trophic level. As shown in the pyramid of numbers, the relative number of organisms at each trophic level also decreases because there is less energy available to support organisms at higher levels of the pyramid.

EXERCISE 14

Models of Energy Flow

Directions: Choose the *best* answer to the following item.

1. A food chain

   A. is a simpler version of a food web.
   B. is a more detailed version of a food web.
   C. is another name for a food web.
   D. shows trophic layers reversed from those in a food web.

Write a short answer to the following item.

2. Can a lion be both a second trophic level consumer and a third trophic level consumer? Explain.

Answers are on page 559.

Cycling of Matter in the Biosphere

Matter is anything that takes up space and has mass. The law of conservation of mass states that matter is neither created nor destroyed. Therefore, natural processes cycle matter through the environment. A **nutrient** is a chemical substance that an organism needs to sustain life and to undergo life processes. The bodies of all organisms are built from water and nutrients such as carbon, oxygen, and nitrogen.

The Water Cycle

Living organisms cannot exist without water. Hydrologists study water found underground, in the atmosphere, and on the surface of Earth in the forms of lakes, streams, rivers, glaciers, ice caps, and oceans. Use the following diagram to trace processes that cycle water through the biosphere.

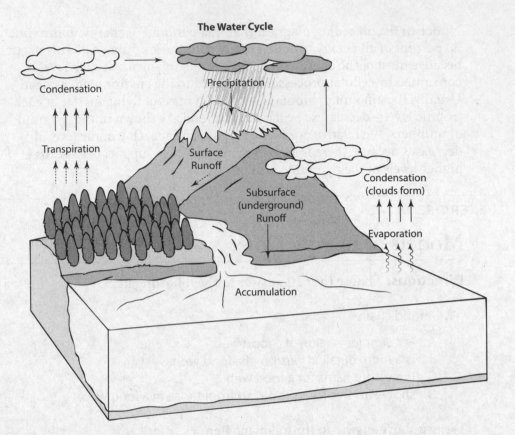

The Water Cycle

Condensation

Precipitation

Transpiration

Surface Runoff

Subsurface (underground) Runoff

Condensation (clouds form)

Evaporation

Accumulation

Water is constantly evaporating into the atmosphere from bodies of water, soil, and organisms; water in the atmosphere is called **water vapor**. As it rises, it begins to cool. Clouds form when the cooling water condenses into water droplets around dust particles in the atmosphere. Water falls from clouds as precipitation in the form of rain, sleet, snow, or hail, transferring water to Earth's surface. As you can see in the figure, groundwater and runoff from land surfaces flow into streams, rivers, lakes, and oceans. Later they will evaporate into the atmosphere to continue the water cycle. Approximately 90 percent of water vapor evaporates from oceans, lakes, and rivers; about 10 percent evaporates from the surface of plants through a process called transpiration.

All living things rely on freshwater. Freshwater constitutes only about 3 percent of all water on Earth. Water available for living organisms is about 31 percent of all freshwater. The other 69 percent of freshwater is found in ice caps and glaciers and is unavailable for use by most living organisms. Even ocean-dwelling organisms rely on freshwater flowing to oceans to prevent high saline content and maintain ocean volume.

The Carbon and Oxygen Cycles

All living things are composed of molecules that contain carbon. Atoms of carbon form the framework for important molecules such as proteins, carbohydrates, and fats. Oxygen is another element that is important to many life processes. Carbon and oxygen often make up molecules essential to life, including carbon dioxide and sugar.

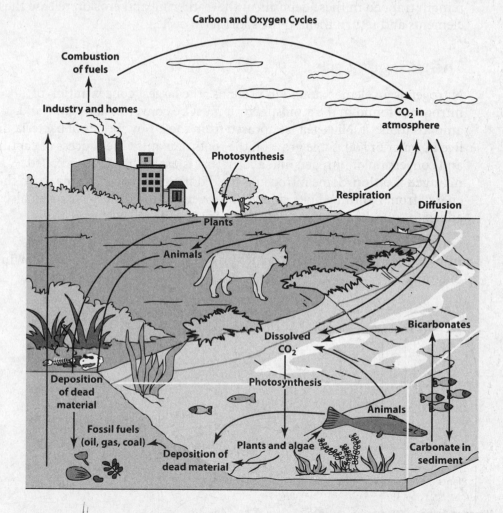

Carbon and Oxygen Cycles

Look at the cycles illustrated in the diagram. During photosynthesis, green plants and algae convert carbon dioxide and water into carbohydrates and release oxygen back into the air. These carbohydrates are used as a source of energy for all organisms in the food web. Carbon dioxide is recycled when autotrophs and heterotrophs release it back into the atmosphere during cellular respiration. Carbon and oxygen generally recycle quickly through living organisms.

Carbon enters a long-term cycle when organic matter is trapped underground and converted to peat, coal, oil, or gas deposits. The carbon might remain trapped as fossil fuel for millions of years. Carbon is released from fossil fuels when they are burned, which adds carbon dioxide to the atmosphere.

In addition to the removal of carbon from the short-term cycle by fossil fuels, carbon and oxygen can enter a long-term cycle in the form of calcium carbonate. Calcium carbonate is found in the shells of plankton and animals such as coral, clams, and oysters. As these organisms die, their shells fall to the sea floor, creating vast deposits of limestone rock. Carbon and oxygen remain trapped in these deposits until weathering and erosion release these elements and return them to the short-term cycle.

The Nitrogen Cycle

Nitrogen is an element found in proteins. The largest concentration of nitrogen is found in the atmosphere; it must be converted for plants and animals to use it. Nitrogen is captured from the air by species of bacteria that live in water or soil; some grow on the roots of plants. The process of capture and conversion of nitrogen into a form that is usable by plants is called **nitrogen fixation**. Some nitrogen is fixed during electrical storms when the energy from lightning bolts changes nitrogen gas to nitrates. Nitrogen also is added to soil when chemical fertilizers are applied to lawns and crops.

Nitrogen enters the food web when plants absorb nitrogen compounds from the soil and convert them into proteins, as illustrated in the following diagram.

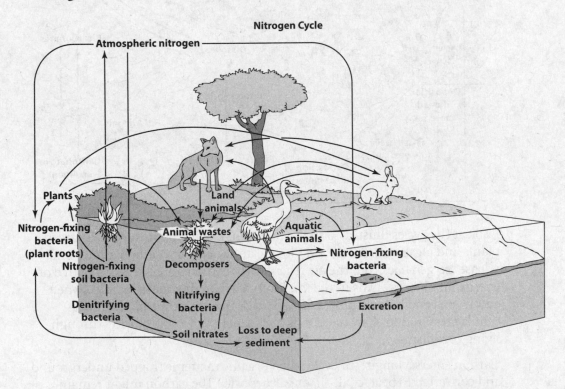

Consumers get nitrogen by eating plants and animals that contain nitrogen. They reuse the nitrogen and make their own proteins. Because the supply of nitrogen in a food web is dependent on the amount of nitrogen that is fixed, nitrogen availability often is a factor that limits the growth of producers.

Nitrogen is returned to the soil in many ways, also shown in the previous diagram. When an animal urinates, nitrogen returns to the water or soil and is reused by plants. When organisms die, decomposers transform the nitrogen in proteins and other compounds into ammonia. Organisms in the soil convert ammonia into nitrogen compounds that can be used by plants. Finally, in a process called **denitrification**, some soil bacteria convert fixed nitrogen compounds back into nitrogen gas, which returns it to the atmosphere.

Cycling of Matter in the Biosphere

Directions: Select the *best* response to each of the following items.

1. Which is NOT a part of the water cycle?

    A. photosynthesis
    B. precipitation
    C. snow melt
    D. transpiration

2. Calcium carbonate (limestone) deposits were formed from the remains of

    A. algae.
    B. animals with shells.
    C. forests.
    D. primitive bacteria.

3. Nitrogen fixation

    A. transfers nitrogen from plants to animals.
    B. converts nitrogen into a form that is usable by plants.
    C. converts nitrogen into a form that is usable only by humans.
    D. recycles by-products of nitrogen from plants.

4. Where is the largest concentration of nitrogen found?

    A. animals
    B. bacteria
    C. atmosphere
    D. plants

Answers are on page 559.

Heredity

Heredity is the passing of genetic traits from parent to offspring. A **gene** is a portion of a chromosome and directs the production of a specific protein, which in turn helps control the structure and/or function of a given trait. Over time, genes of individuals within a population can change. This gene variation plays an important role in the process of natural selection.

Inheritance and Variation of Traits

The selection of favorable traits by a population is the result of interactions between gene variations and the environment. More favorable traits (those that enhance a population's ability to reproduce and survive) are passed on to the population as a whole. Genetic variation occurs mainly through DNA mutation, gene flow (movement of genes from one population to another), and sexual reproduction.

DNA Mutation

A mutation is the changed structure of a gene, resulting in a variant form of a trait that may be transmitted to subsequent generations. A single mutation can have a large effect, but in many cases, evolutionary change is based on the accumulation of many small mutations. Mutations are caused by the alteration, deletion, insertion, or rearrangement of a section of a gene or chromosome. Mutations in DNA sequences generally occur through one of two processes:

1. **Environmental agents:** Ultraviolet light (in sunlight), nuclear radiation, and certain chemicals are some of the agents that can change an organism's DNA by altering the nucleotide bases.

2. **Natural changes:** Recall that a cell copies its DNA as it prepares for cell division. Prior to cell division, each cell must duplicate its entire DNA sequence. This process is called DNA replication. As DNA replication progresses, unintended changes occur in the nucleotide base pairings about once in every 100,000,000 pairings. Repair proteins can help reverse some but not all of these natural changes in DNA sequencing.

Gene Flow

Gene flow—also called migration—occurs as genetic material from one population moves into another. Gene flow involves many types of events, including pollen being blown into a new ecosystem or humans moving to new countries. If genes end up in a population where those genes have not existed at all before, gene flow can be a very important source of genetic variation.

Sexual Reproduction

During fertilization, millions of genetically unique sperm compete to fertilize an egg. The sperm that fertilizes one egg will be genetically different from the sperm that fertilizes the next egg. Also, each egg is genetically unique. Thus, fertilization produces almost limitless opportunities for variation. Except for identical twins, which develop from the same egg and sperm and are genetic copies of each other, every individual is genetically unique.

Because ecosystems are ever-changing, genetically varied populations are better able to adapt and survive in their changing environments than those populations with less variation.

EXERCISE 16

Inheritance and Variation of Traits

Directions: Write a short answer to the following item.

1. Why would you expect natural mutations to very rarely produce a beneficial variation?

Choose the *best* response to the following item.

2. Which is an example of gene flow?
   A. birds migrating to a new destination and breeding with other birds
   B. a bird laying more eggs than usual for that species
   C. learning to eat a more varied diet in response to environmental changes
   D. mutating the DNA sequence through exposure to UV light

Answers are on page 560.

Mendelian Genetics

In 1866, Gregor Mendel, an Austrian monk and plant breeder, published his findings on the method and mathematics of inheritance of garden pea plants. Mendel noticed that certain varieties of pea plants produced specific forms of a trait, generation after generation. For instance, he noticed that some varieties always produced green seeds and others always produced yellow seeds. In order to understand how these traits are inherited, Mendel performed cross pollination by transferring male gametes (pollen) from the flower of a true-breeding green-seed plant to the female organ of a flower of a true-breeding yellow-seed plant. Mendel called the green-seed plant and the yellow-seed plant the parent generation—also known as the P generation.

F_1 and F_2 Generations

When Mendel grew the seeds from the cross between the green-seed and yellow-seed plants, all of the resulting offspring had yellow seeds. The offspring of this P cross are called the first (F_1) generation. The green-seed trait seemed to have disappeared in the F_1 generation. Mendel decided to investigate whether the trait was no longer present, or whether it was hidden, or masked. Mendel planted the F_1 generation seeds, allowed them to self-fertilize, and then examined the seeds from this cross. Of the seeds Mendel collected, 6022 were yellow and 2001 were green, which is almost a perfect 3:1 ratio of yellow to green seeds.

Genes in Pairs

Mendel concluded that there must be two forms of the seed trait in the pea plants—yellow-seed and green-seed—and that each was controlled by a factor, which is now called an allele. An **allele** is an alternative form of a single gene passed from generation to generation. Therefore, the gene for yellow seeds and the gene for green seeds are each different forms of a single gene.

Mendel concluded that the 3:1 ratio observed during his experiment could be explained if the alleles were paired in each of the plants. He called the form of the trait that appeared in the F_1 generation **dominant** and the form of the trait that was masked in the F_1 generation **recessive**.

Dominance

Because the yellow-seed form of the trait is dominant, its allele is represented by a capital Y. The allele for the green-seed form of the trait is represented by a lowercase y because it is recessive. An organism with two of the same alleles for a given trait is **homozygous** for that trait. Homozygous yellow-seed plants are YY and homozygous green-seed plants are yy. An organism with two different alleles for a particular trait is **heterozygous** for that trait, in this case Yy. When alleles are present in the heterozygous state, the dominant trait will be observed.

Genotype and Phenotype

A yellow-seed plant could be homozygous or heterozygous for the trait form. The outward appearance of an organism does not always indicate which pair of alleles is present. The organism's actual allele pairs are called its **genotype**. In the case of the plants with yellow seeds, their genotypes could be either *YY* or *Yy*. The observable characteristics or outward expression of an allele pair is called the **phenotype**. The phenotype of pea plants with the genotype *YY* or *Yy* will be yellow seeds. The phenotype of pea plants with the genotype *yy* will be green seeds.

EXERCISE 17

Mendelian Genetics

Directions: Write a short response to the following items.

1. Distinguish between genotype and phenotype.

Choose the *best* response to each of the following items.

2. Mendel concluded that in pea plants,

    A. all individuals are homozygous.
    B. all phenotypes are dominant.
    C. only one form of a trait could be passed on to the next generation.
    D. there are two factors controlling individual traits.

3. The notation "*RR*" represents a trait that is

    A. heterozygous dominant.
    B. heterozygous recessive.
    C. homozygous dominant.
    D. homozygous recessive.

Answers are on page 560.

Punnett Squares

In the early 1900s, Dr. Reginald Punnett developed what is known as the Punnett square to predict the possible offspring of a cross between two known genotypes. Punnett squares make it easier to keep track of the possible genotypes involved in a cross.

Can you curl your tongue like the person in the following illustration?

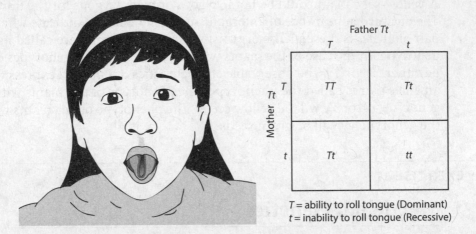

Father *Tt*

	T	*t*
T	*TT*	*Tt*
t	*Tt*	*tt*

Mother *Tt*

T = ability to roll tongue (Dominant)
t = inability to roll tongue (Recessive)

Tongue-rolling ability is a dominant trait that can be represented by *T*. Suppose both parents can roll their tongues and are heterozygous (*Tt*) for the trait. To determine the possible phenotypes in their offspring, examine the Punnett square in the illustration. The number of squares is determined by the number of different types of alleles—in this case, *T* or *t*—produced by each parent. In this case the Punnett square is 2 squares × 2 squares because each parent produces two different types of gametes. Notice that the male gametes are written across the top, horizontal side, and the female gametes are written on the left, vertical side of the Punnett square. The possible combinations of each male and female gamete are written inside each of the corresponding squares.

How many different genotypes are found in the Punnett square? One square has *TT*, two squares have *Tt*, and one square has *tt*. Therefore, the genotypic ratio of the possible offspring is 1:2:1. The phenotypic ratio of tongue curlers to non–tongue curlers is 3:1.

EXERCISE 18

Punnett Squares

Directions: Answer the following question.

1. Fruit flies can have curly wings (*C*) or straight wings (*c*). If a homozygous dominant (*CC*) fruit fly is crossed with a homozygous recessive (*cc*) fruit fly, what will the ratio of phenotypes be? (Draw a Punnett square to help you, if you would like.)

The answer is on page 560.

Biological Evolution

When Charles Darwin boarded the HMS *Beagle* in 1831, many people thought that Earth was about 6,000 years old. The primary mission of the *Beagle* was to survey the coast of South America. Darwin's role on the ship was as naturalist and companion to the captain. Over the course of the ship's five-year voyage, Darwin made extensive collections of rocks, fossils, plants, and animals.

Common Ancestry and Biological Evolution

A few years after Darwin returned to England, he began reconsidering his observations. He realized that species of birds that lived on remote islands off the coast of South America did not live anywhere on the continent. The new species closely resembled species from the mainland, although the islands and mainland had different environments. Island and mainland species should not have resembled one another so closely unless populations from the mainland migrated to the islands and then changed somewhat after reaching the islands.

Darwin hypothesized that new species could appear gradually through small changes in ancestral species, but he could not understand how such a process would work. To understand this better, he studied and bred pigeons. Different breeds of pigeons have distinctive traits. Breeders can promote these traits by selecting and breeding pigeons that have the most pronounced expressions of these traits. Darwin called this **artificial selection**. Darwin hypothesized that this process could produce new species.

Darwin also studied the tendency of populations to increase until they outgrow their food supply. This phenomenon leads to a competitive struggle for existence. He reasoned that some individuals would be better equipped for survival than others. Those less equipped would die sooner and produce fewer offspring. Darwin's theory has four basic principles that explain how traits of a population can change over time:

- Individuals in a population show differences, or variations.
- Variations can be inherited, meaning that they can be passed down from parent to offspring.
- Organisms have more offspring than can survive on available resources.
- Variations that increase reproductive success will have a greater chance of being passed on than those variations that do not increase reproductive success.

Darwin called this theory **natural selection**. He reasoned that given enough time, natural selection could modify a population enough to produce a new species.

If an extreme version of a trait makes an individual more fit, **directional selection** might occur. This form of selection increases the expression of the extreme version of the trait in a population. One example is the evolution of moths in industrial England. The peppered moth has two color forms—those with light-colored wings and those with dark wings. Until the mid-1850s, nearly all peppered moths in England had light-colored wings. Beginning around 1850, dark moths began appearing. By the early 1900s, nearly all the peppered moths were dark. Industrial pollution created an environment that favored the dark-colored moths at the expense of the light-colored moths. The darker the moth, the more closely it matched the sooty background of its habitat's surfaces, and the harder it was for predators to see. Thus, more dark moths survived, adding more genes for dark wings to the population.

EXERCISE 19

Common Ancestry and Biological Evolution

Directions: Select the *best* response to each of the following items.

1. If an average dog weighs about 30 pounds, the development of the Chihuahua, which typically weighs 4–8 pounds, is most likely the result of

   A. a mutation.
   B. artificial selection.
   C. natural selection.
   D. recessive breeding.

2. Which is NOT a principle of natural selection?

   A. Individuals show variation.
   B. Organisms have more offspring than can survive.
   C. Variations can be inherited.
   D. Breeders select and breed for traits they find desirable.

Study the graph. Then, write a short response to each of the items that follow.

> The following graph shows the percentage of melanic (dark-colored) moths in the peppered moth populations in three states between 1959 and 2001.

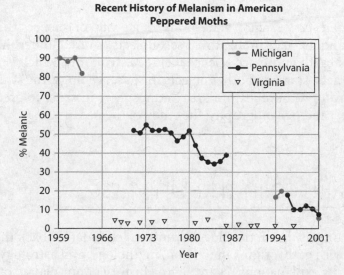

Recent History of Melanism in American Peppered Moths

3. What was the approximate percentage of melanic moths in the peppered moth population in Pennsylvania in 1980?

4. Why might the percentage of melanic moths have remained at a relatively low level in Virginia?

Answers are on page 560.

CHAPTER 2

Earth and Space Science

Earth and space science is the name for a group of sciences that examine Earth and its place in the universe. Subjects covered under the broad topic of earth and space science include **astronomy**, which is the study of the planets, stars, and other objects in space; **geology**, the study of Earth; **meteorology**, the study of Earth's atmosphere in order to predict the weather; and **oceanography**, the study of the ocean.

Earth's Place in the Universe

Astronomy is one of the oldest scientific fields, dating back thousands of years, with early origins in religion, mythology, and astrology. Astronomers search for explanations regarding the history of our planet, our solar system, galaxies of stars, and the beginning of the universe.

The Big Bang Theory

It is virtually impossible to contemplate a time when there was no universe, but everything has a starting point. A leading current theory regarding the beginning of the universe is known as the **big bang theory**. According to this theory, about 13.8 billion years ago a tiny, superdense, superheated kernel, which contained all the matter of the universe, exploded. At that moment, the entire universe began to form. The universe expanded rapidly over the next hundred thousand years. During this expansion, the young universe cooled enough for atoms to form.

The force of gravity pulled atoms, such as hydrogen and helium, which had been suspended in space since the big bang, into dark cloud formations called **nebulae**. Some of these gaseous nebulae became compressed by gravitational force. Collisions of compressed particles produced huge amounts of thermal energy. When the temperature of the compressed particles reached 15 million degrees Celsius, the nuclear reaction called fusion occurred, and a star developed. Over time, more stars developed. Gravity pulled billions of the new stars together into groups called **galaxies**.

Substantial evidence supports the big bang theory. For example, scientists have observed that some stars appear to be redder than others. This is because of a lightwave phenomenon called **redshift**. Light from an object that is moving away shifts to appear slightly more red. If some stars and galaxies appear redder than others, that is because they are moving away from Earth—and from each other. The phenomenon of redshift indicates that the universe is expanding. An expanding universe supports the idea that the universe began with a huge explosion.

In addition, in the 1960s, astronomers discovered faint microwave radiation falling on Earth from every direction. Scientists believe that this radiation, known as **cosmic microwave background (CMB) radiation,** is energy that is left over from the big bang.

EXERCISE 1

The Big Bang Theory

Directions: Choose the *best* response to the following item.

1. Which of the following statements summarizes the big bang theory?
   A. Particles collided to create thermal energy that produced stars.
   B. Two or more atomic nuclei collided at very high speeds, creating fusion.
   C. Electromagnetic radiation from the sun traveled to Earth.
   D. A dense, hot kernel exploded, leading to the formation of the entire universe.

The answer is on page 560.

Stars and Elements

Stars formed after the big bang, when gravity drew hydrogen and helium atoms together. The collision of these atoms resulted in a reaction called nuclear fusion. **Nuclear fusion** is a nuclear reaction in which two or more atomic nuclei collide at a very high speed and join, forming a new atomic nucleus. Most stars, including the sun, are composed of high amounts of hydrogen, along with smaller amounts of helium and oxygen.

As nuclear fusion occurs, it produces successively heavier elements, such as helium, oxygen, and iron, and it releases visible light and other forms of electromagnetic energy.

Stars and Light

As powerful as modern telescopes are, and despite dramatic advances in technology, astronomers can see little of the surface of stars (other than the sun, which will be discussed later). Astronomers study a star by analyzing its **light spectrum**—the range of light it emits—and its brightness.

The light spectrum of a star looks like a rainbow with some colors missing. Scientists can analyze the various light spectra of stars to determine what elements are in the star. Atoms of each element emit and absorb unique combinations of colors of light when they become excited, such as when a large amount of energy passes through the element. The specific colors associated with a given element are known as the element's light spectrum. Even microscopic quantities of an element can be detected by its light spectrum. Common elements found in stars include hydrogen, calcium, iron, and magnesium.

The following illustration shows how these elements present themselves as a light spectrum. The lines of the light spectrum can also indicate whether a star is moving toward or away from Earth. If a star is traveling toward Earth, its spectral lines might shift toward the blue end of the spectrum. The spectral lines of a star moving away from Earth might shift toward the red end of the spectrum. The greater the shift of its spectral lines, the faster the star is moving.

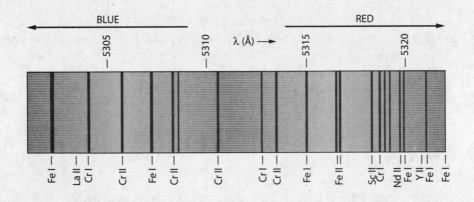

Another important characteristic of a star is its brightness. The brightness of a star is called the star's **magnitude**. There are two types of magnitude: **apparent magnitude** is a star's brightness as it appears from Earth, and **absolute magnitude** is how bright the star would appear from the standard distance of 32.6 light-years. A **light-year** is the distance that light travels during one year. Two stars with the same absolute magnitude might not have the same apparent magnitude. One may be much farther away from Earth than the other. In general, the farther a star is from Earth, the less its apparent magnitude will be.

Death of a Star

Nuclear fusion continues for most of a star's lifetime, which can range from a few hundred thousand years to billions of years. Then the star dies. The death of a star occurs in several stages:

1. The star uses up its supply of hydrogen.

2. The loss of hydrogen ends nuclear fusion, and temperatures drop.

3. Gravity at the center of the star pulls the remaining atoms together. Compression occurs, but without hydrogen, relatively little energy is generated.

4. The compression at the center without the energy source forces the outer layers to swell.

What happens next varies according to the size of the star.

5. The outer layers swell.

   - **Small or medium star (such as the sun):** The outer layers swell until the star is about 100 times its previous size and becomes a **red giant**.

   - **Large star:** The outer layers swell even more significantly, and the star becomes a **supergiant**, red in color.

6. The outer layers are cast off.

   - **Small or medium star:** The outer layers are eventually cast off, and the star becomes a **nova**. The center of the nova becomes a white, hot, dense star called a **white dwarf**.

   - **Large star:** Gravity pulls the outer layers in with such force that an explosion called a **supernova** occurs. During this explosion, the dying star might undergo a process called **nucleosynthesis**, which produces a variety of elements heavier than iron, including plutonium and uranium. The supernova casts gas and dust into space to form a nebula. After the explosion, a very dense and small **neutron star** might remain. Or, if the supernova is very large, the gravity within the collapsing star becomes so powerful that even light cannot escape, turning the star into a **black hole**.

EXERCISE 2

Stars and Elements

Directions: Read the passage, then answer the question.

On January 9, 2008, NASA's Swift Observatory caught a bright X-ray burst from an exploding star. Carnegie-Princeton fellows Alicia Soderberg and Edo Berger were on hand to witness this event. A few days later, SN 2008D appeared in visible light. "We were in the right place, at the right time, with the right telescope on January 9th and witnessed history," remarked Soderberg. "We were looking at another, older supernova in the galaxy, when the one now known as SN 2008D went off. We would have missed it if it weren't for Swift's real-time capabilities, wide field of view, and numerous instruments."

1. What can you infer from this paragraph?

A. Astronomers observed SN 2008D as it was running out of hydrogen.
B. SN 2008D had previously been a red giant.
C. Astronomers observed the formation of SN 2008D.
D. Gravity had pulled in the outer layers of SN 2008D with enormous force.

The answer is on page 560.

The Sun

The sun serves as our planet's primary source of energy. It provides light and heat, which are essential to life on Earth. In addition, the sun completely dominates our solar system, constituting more than 90 percent of its entire mass. But in the vast context of the universe, the sun is rather ordinary. Middle-aged and of average size, it is one of about 100 billion stars that make up the **Milky Way**, the galaxy that contains Earth.

Astronomers estimate that the sun is between four billion and five billion years old and that it is about halfway through its life span. Although scientists are not able to study the interior of the sun directly, they have been able to draw several conclusions based on the energy that it generates.

As is the case with all stars, the sun produces energy through **nuclear fusion**. During nuclear fusion, four hydrogen nuclei fuse to become the nucleus of one new helium atom. This process releases tremendous amounts of energy. The energy released from the sun, called **solar radiation**, travels through space as electromagnetic waves. A small amount of this energy reaches Earth.

Although the sun constantly radiates energy, sometimes the strength and type of that energy vary. Events that can affect the sun's radiation include sunspots and solar flares. **Sunspots** are dark regions on the surface of the sun. They have temperatures of about 3900°C. This is significantly cooler than the temperature of most of the sun's surface, which is estimated to be 5500°C. Studies of sunspots have revealed that the number of sunspots varies throughout an 11-year cycle. Although sunspots are cooler areas of the sun's surface, evidence shows that they are actually a warming force, because they lead to an increase in the sun's radiation.

Solar flares are sudden bursts of energy that appear as a brightening of the region above a group of sunspots. Solar flares, which release an enormous amount of energy, can sometimes result in auroras—also called northern lights and southern lights—on Earth. Auroras look like curtains of light in the atmosphere around one of the poles of the Earth. This spectacular lighting effect can last for several nights.

EXERCISE 3

The Sun

Directions: Choose the *best* response to the following item.

1. A climate phenomenon known as the Little Ice Age occurred for several hundred years during the past millennium. Very few sunspots were observed during this period. This fact suggests that

   A. the Little Ice Age might have occurred despite the lack of sunspots.
   B. the Little Ice Age might have occurred because of the lack of sunspots.
   C. the Little Ice Age had nothing to do with sunspots.
   D. the Little Ice Age might have caused the lack of sunspots.

The answer is on page 560.

The Solar System

More than 2000 years ago, the ancient Greeks theorized that Earth was the center of the universe. They believed the sun and all other objects in the universe orbited Earth. This idea was called the geocentric, or Earth-centered, view, and it was accepted for centuries.

During the Middle Ages, a Polish scientist named Nicolaus Copernicus (1473–1543) stunned fellow scientists with his theory that Earth was one of several planets that orbited the sun. Later, the Italian scientist Galileo Galilei (1564–1642) built a telescope that enabled him to make many discoveries that supported Copernicus's view of the universe. Both scientists concluded that Earth and a host of other planets make up a solar system and that the center of that system—and of the orbits of all the planets—is the sun.

Kepler's Laws of Planetary Motion

Another astronomer, Johannes Kepler (1571–1630), expanded on the work of Copernicus and Galileo with his discovery of three laws of planetary motion.

1. **The law of ellipsis:** Describing the shape of the planets' orbits, this law states that planets move around the sun in an elliptical, or oval-shaped, orbit with the sun at one focus, or fixed point, of the ellipsis.

2. **The law of equal areas:** This law describes the speed of a planet as it orbits around the sun. It states that an imaginary line joining a planet and the sun sweeps over equal areas in equal periods of time. This means that the speed of a planet increases when the planet is nearer to the sun and decreases when the planet is farther from the sun.

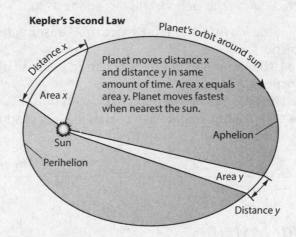

3. **The law of harmonies:** This law describes the relationship between a planet's orbital period (the time it takes to complete one orbit around the sun) and its **radius of orbit** (the average distance between the sun and the orbiting planet). It states that the square of a planet's orbital period is equal to the cube of its radius of orbit. Thus, astronomers can calculate the distance between a given planet and the sun by determining that planet's orbital period. The mathematical formula for the law of harmonies is $P^2 = a^3$, where P is a planet's orbital period and a is its radius of orbit.

EXERCISE 4

The Solar System

Directions: Choose the *best* response to the following item.

1. Which of the following is correct?

   A. Kepler's law of harmonies describes the relationship between the time a planet takes to orbit the sun and that planet's average distance from the sun.
   B. Kepler's law of harmonies describes the relationship between the speed at which a planet moves and that planet's average distance from the sun.
   C. Kepler's law of harmonies describes the relationship between the shape of a planet's orbit and that planet's average distance from the sun.
   D. Kepler's law of harmonies describes the relationship between the size of a planet and that planet's average distance from the sun.

The answer is on page 560.

The Planets

Eight planets, including Earth, orbit, or revolve, around the sun. The four planets closest to the sun, the **terrestrial planets**, are Mercury, Venus, Earth, and Mars. The terrestrial planets are relatively small and dense. They consist mostly of rock and metallic substances and have few satellites. Mercury, the planet closest to the sun, is only slightly bigger than Earth's moon. Though it revolves around the sun quickly, it **rotates**, or turns on its axis, slowly. A planet's day is the time it takes for a planet to complete one entire rotation. A day on Earth lasts 24 hours, split roughly into 12 hours of daylight and 12 hours of night. A night on Mercury, by comparison, lasts about three months, followed by three straight months of sunlight.

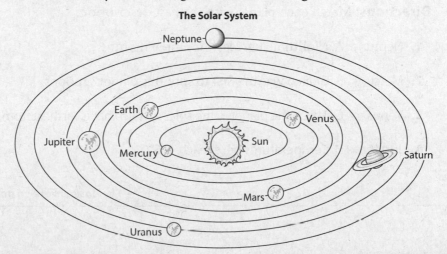

The Solar System

Venus is nearly the size of Earth and takes 255 days to orbit the sun. The surface of Venus is rife with volcanic activity, and its atmosphere is 97 percent carbon dioxide. Temperatures on Venus reach 475°C. Mars is farther from Earth than Venus is, but Mars's reddish color makes its atmosphere highly visible for astronomers. Mars is similar to Earth in that one Martian day lasts approximately 24 hours, and it has seasonal weather patterns, canyons, and volcanoes. For those reasons, it is considered the most hospitable of Earth's fellow planets and the one most likely to undergo further human exploration.

The four planets farthest from the sun, the **Jovian planets**, are Jupiter, Saturn, Uranus, and Neptune. The Jovian planets are giant and gaseous, with many moons and thick atmospheres composed of gases such as hydrogen, helium, methane, and ammonia. Galileo was the first to see Jupiter's four largest moons; through a telescope, they are visible as small points of light near the giant planet they orbit. Jupiter's gaseous surface features include colorful bands that travel in opposite directions. Though all four of the Jovian planets have rings, the rings that surround Saturn are the most readily visible. Several of Saturn's 31 moons are embedded in its rings, forming a complex, highly observable system of objects.

Uranus and Neptune, also large gaseous planets, are the planets in the solar system that are farthest from the sun (and farthest from Earth). Located an average distance of 5.9 billion kilometers from the sun, icy Pluto used to be considered the ninth planet in the solar system, but after the discovery of several other objects Pluto's size or larger, astronomers reclassified Pluto as a dwarf planet in 2006.

EXERCISE 5

The Planets

Directions: Match each planet with the *best* description.

1. Neptune A. Nighttime here lasts for three months.

2. Mercury B. Galileo was the first to spot this planet's moons.

3. Venus C. This is the planet in the solar system that is farthest from the sun.

4. Jupiter D. Temperatures here reach 475°C.

The answers are on page 560.

The History of Planet Earth

Earth has its own history—one that goes back more than 4.5 billion years. Scientists believe that Earth, along with the sun and the other seven planets in the solar system, began as clumps of matter that formed from an enormous rotating cloud called the solar nebula. The solar nebula was composed mostly of helium and hydrogen, with a small amount of some other elements. The sun eventually formed at the center of the nebula. As the remaining nebula cooled, rocky and metallic materials solidified into tiny particles. Those particles collided with each other repeatedly, and eventually formed large asteroids that became the four planets closest to the sun—Mercury, Venus, Earth, and Mars. Those planets did not have sufficient gravitational pull to hold light gases such as helium and hydrogen from the nebula. Those materials combined with each other farther away from the sun and formed the outer, gaseous planets of the solar system.

The particles that had collided to form Earth continued to collide during the planet's early history. This generated a great deal of heat, which melted part of the Earth's interior and allowed denser elements on its surface, including iron and nickel, to sink toward the planet's center. The lighter rocky components of the young planet began moving toward Earth's surface. The constant sinking and floating of elements, which still occur but more slowly, eventually led to the formation of the layers of the Earth.

EXERCISE 6

The History of Planet Earth

Directions: Answer the question.

1. Place the following stages of the formation of Earth into their proper order.

   A. formation of asteroids from metallic particles
   B. formation of the sun
   C. formation of Earth, Mercury, Venus, and Mars
   D. formation of rotating solar nebula

The answer is on page 560.

Earth's Surface

Throughout its history, Earth has undergone dramatic geologic changes that have dramatically altered and sometimes destroyed much of its oldest rock formations. In the early 1900s, geologists began using a technique called radiometrics to estimate the age of Earth. **Radiometrics** is a process that involves measuring the gamma radiation that some decaying elements emit. Scientists used radiometrics to study the elements in some of Earth's rock formations, as well as those of asteroids and meteorites that had crashed into Earth billions of years ago. From these observations geologists ascertained that the planet's continental rocks, some of which are about 4 billion years old, are often much older than rocks found on the ocean floor, which are often about 200 million years old. In the late 1960s, astronauts brought back rocks from the surface of the moon. Analysis of those rocks confirmed geologists' estimates of the age of Earth.

Plate Tectonics

Probably the most significant of all recent findings regarding Earth has been the theory of **plate tectonics**, which explains the development of mountains and ocean trenches and the occurrence of earthquakes and volcanic eruptions.

If you look at a world map, you will notice that Africa and South America look almost like separate pieces of a jigsaw puzzle. A German scientist named Alfred Wegener noticed this in 1912 and formulated the theory of **continental drift,** which says that the land masses that form the seven continents today were originally part of one supercontinent millions of years ago. This supercontinent, which geologists call Pangaea, split into land masses that drifted apart and eventually became the seven continents.

Supercontinent Pangaea

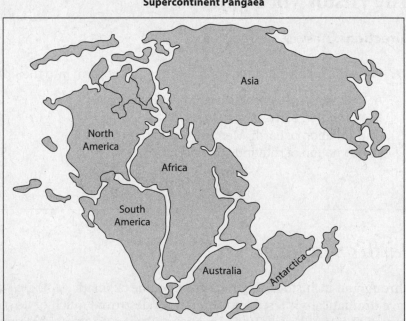

The theory of continental drift explains why the continents look like separated pieces of a jigsaw puzzle. But scientists still did not know what caused the continents to drift apart in the first place. Then in the 1960s, the theory of plate tectonics provided an explanation.

According to this theory, Earth is composed of a crust, mantle, outer core, and inner core. About 20 overlapping tectonic plates make up the upper mantle and crust. Floating on the mantle, these tectonic plates are similar to dishes floating on the surface of water in a large basin. The tectonic plates move very slowly—about one-half inch to four inches a year. Attached to the plates are the continents and the ocean floor.

The movement of the plates is driven by **convection** in Earth's mantle. Convection occurs when hot material from deep in the mantle slowly rises and the cooler plates of Earth's crust descend into the mantle. The movements of the plates create volcanoes, cause earthquakes, and turn large masses of rock into mountains.

EXERCISE 7

Earth's Surface

Directions: Fill in the blanks.

1. The observation that North America and Europe are moving away from each other at a rate of about 2.5 centimeters per year corresponds to the

   theory of _____.

2. The eruption of Mt. Vesuvius, a volcano in Italy, destroyed the city of Pompeii in A.D. 79. This action occurred as the result of

   _____ movement.

3. Scientists used the process of _____ to study elements in a large meteorite that had struck Earth during an era known as the Cretaceous Period.

4. Hot, rising material pushes the surface of the planet upward, as colder sinking material pulls the surface of the planet downward. This process is

   known as _____.

Answers are on page 561.

Earth's Systems

Suppose you take several small rocks and place them in water for 24 hours. Then you place the wet rocks in a freezer for another day or so. When you take the rocks out of the freezer, you might find that one or two of them had broken apart, changing their shape. This can occur because water seeps into spaces within the rocks and then expands as it freezes, a process known as mechanical weathering of rocks.

This "rock popsicle" activity demonstrates one way in which different Earth systems interact. Earth is a dynamic, ever-changing planet made up of four overlapping systems, or spheres, that interact with each other. The four systems of the Earth are the **atmosphere** (the air), the **lithosphere** (land areas), the **hydrosphere** (water areas) and the **biosphere** (areas that contain life). The study of the ways in which Earth's systems work together is called Earth system science.

The Carbon Cycle

The interaction of Earth's systems is closely related to the ways in which certain materials cycle through the different spheres of Earth's systems. A good way to understand how materials and energy move through Earth's systems is to examine the **carbon cycle** (see figure). Pure forms of the element carbon are rare in nature. Most carbon is bonded to other elements to form compounds. A common example of a carbon compound is carbon dioxide, which is one important source of the carbon needed by many living things. The following steps chronicle one possible path of carbon as it enters, leaves, and reenters Earth's atmosphere:

1. Humans and other animals emit carbon dioxide into the atmosphere through respiration, or breathing.

2. Plants and algae, which grow in the lithosphere and hydrosphere, respectively, use the process of **photosynthesis** to convert sunlight, water, and carbon dioxide to energy. Through photosynthesis, these organisms remove carbon from the atmosphere and convert it into carbohydrates.

3. Some animals feed on the plants of the biosphere. Then, through respiration, they return some of the carbon to the atmosphere as carbon dioxide, as explained in step 1.

4. Eventually the plants and animals of the biosphere die. As organisms decompose, their bodies release carbon dioxide into the atmosphere and the soil of the lithosphere. Carbon dioxide also dissolves into the surface waters of the oceans.

Carbon Cycle

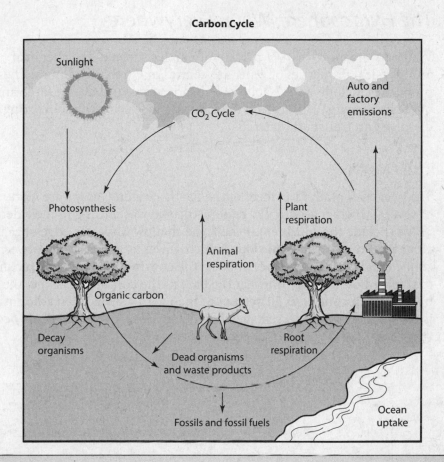

EXERCISE 8

The Carbon Cycle

Directions: Read the passage, then fill in the blanks.

During the photosynthesis stage of the carbon cycle, carbon dioxide is used and oxygen is produced. During the metabolism phase of the carbon cycle, oxygen is used and carbon dioxide is produced. Identify the following steps in the cycle as either photosynthetic or metabolic.

1. Plants convert resources to energy. _____

2. Plants and animals in the biosphere die, and their bodies decompose. _____

3. Animals feed on the plants of the biosphere. _____

4. Humans and other animals respire. _____

Answers are on page 561.

The Hydrosphere: Water Everywhere

Water covers more than 71 percent of Earth's surface. The chemical and physical properties of water are central to Earth's dynamics. These properties include water's ability to absorb, store, and release large amounts of thermal energy; absorb and reflect sunlight; expand upon freezing; and dissolve and transport materials.

The Oceans

The oceans contain 91 percent of the Earth's water. Oceans are made up of several distinct geographic regions that vary according to their depth. These include the **continental shelf**, the shallow undersea edge of each continent; the **continental slope**, which serves as a transition between the continental shelf and the ocean floor; the **continental rise**, which consists of thick amounts of sediment at the base of the continental slope; the **ocean basin**, which comprises 30 percent of the Earth's surface (an amount that is comparable to the percentage of land above sea level); and **deep-ocean trenches**, long creases in the ocean floor.

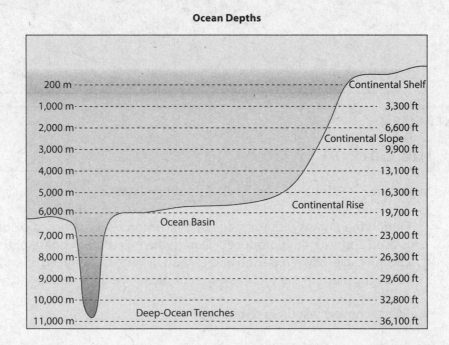

Among the most observable of ocean features are the tides. **Tides,** the rising and falling of the ocean's surface, result from the pull of the sun, the rotation of Earth, and the gravitational pull of the moon. As Earth spins, the area of the ocean directly beneath the moon bulges or rises up, creating a tide. On the opposite side of Earth, a lesser bulge occurs at the same time. Because Earth rotates 180 degrees every 12 hours and the moon revolves 6 degrees around Earth every 12 hours, bodies of water on Earth experience a high tide every 12 hours and 25 minutes. The tides create **currents**, the flowing motion of water. Currents occur not only in oceans but also in bays and coastal estuaries, where saltwater from the ocean mixes with freshwater from lakes and streams.

About 25 percent of Earth's marine life lives in ecosystems known as coral reefs. **Corals** are very small, invertebrate animals, called polyps. Hard corals have skeletons composed of layers of calcium carbonate. Thousands of coral polyps living close together form a coral reef, which provides habitat and food for an enormous variety of living organisms. One such organism, phytoplankton, provides through its photosynthetic process more than half of the oxygen we breathe.

The Water Cycle

Water is constantly in motion. It moves from the hydrosphere to the atmosphere, then to the biosphere and lithosphere, and back again to the hydrosphere. This constant cyclic motion is called the **water cycle**.

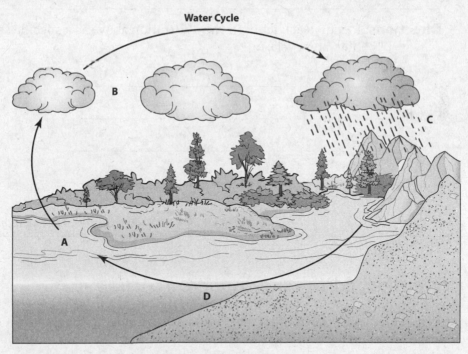

The water cycle includes the following steps:

1. **Radiation:** The sun radiates heat into the atmosphere.

2. **Evaporation:** The sun's heat evaporates water from oceans, lakes, and rivers, as well as some from the land, into the atmosphere.

3. **Condensation:** The moisture-rich air eventually becomes clouds.

4. **Precipitation:** Rain or snow from the clouds falls onto the land and the ocean. Precipitation that falls to the ocean has completed a cycle, but the water in the lithosphere has a few more steps to complete.

5. **Infiltration:** Some of the water on the ground soaks into rocks and soil—a process called infiltration.

6. **Reentry:** The rest of the water moves through the lithosphere and eventually reenters the ocean. Precipitation that falls in very cold places might freeze and become part of glaciers, where it might remain for hundreds or thousands of years.

After step 6 is completed, the cycle begins again, as ocean water evaporates once again into the atmosphere. Plants on the ground that have absorbed water also release it into the air, in a process called **transpiration**.

EXERCISE 9

The Hydrosphere: Water Everywhere

Directions: Identify each letter in the illustration above as a specific step in the water cycle.

A. _____

B. _____

C. _____

D. _____

Answers are on page 561.

Weather: Earth's Atmosphere in Action

When predicting the weather, meteorologists consider the ways in which the atmosphere and hydrosphere interact. These include not only the various steps of the water cycle but also features of the atmosphere, such as humidity and temperature, as well as wind.

Humidity and temperature affect how air masses interact in the atmosphere. Air masses are bodies of air that reflect the climate characteristics of the land or water where they originally formed. For example, an air mass from Canada might be dry and cool, whereas an air mass from Mexico is likely to be warm and humid. Meteorologists track air masses; in the United States air masses tend to travel from west to east.

Warm air masses tend to rise. Cold air masses tend to sink. A **front** occurs when two air masses collide. When warm air enters a region and rises up and over denser, colder air, a **warm front** forms. A **cold front** forms when cold, dry air enters a region, moves under warm, moist air, and then undercuts it. Cold fronts move more quickly than warm fronts; they form a steep slope as they push the warm air upward, an action that often results in heavy rainstorms. When fronts collide, turbulent weather often results. For example, during springtime, warm, moist air from Mexico arrives in the central part of the United States and meets cold, dry air from Canada, spawning thunderstorms and tornadoes.

Tornadoes are violent, funnel-shaped seasonal windstorms. They often begin with the development of a **mesocylone**, a vertical cylinder of spinning air that occurs in the updraft of a thunderstorm. Then, if conditions are favorable, the updraft, which will have a counterclockwise spin owing to the rotation of the Earth, can generate wind speeds approaching 500 km per hour. When conditions change, the funnel will narrow and start to rise toward the cloud. Most tornadoes occur in Oklahoma, Kansas, and Missouri, as well as parts of Texas, Iowa, and Illinois. About 1000 tornadoes of various sizes occur in the United States every year.

Hurricanes are also seasonal storms. They begin as tropical depressions, which are created when a group of thunderstorms come together in the right atmospheric conditions over an ocean. Ocean surface temperatures must be warm enough to provide the atmosphere with large supplies of heat and moisture. As ocean water evaporates, it combines with the hot and moist air to form a powerful atmospheric engine. If winds reach about 64 km per hour, the depression becomes a tropical storm. And when sustained wind speed reaches 120 km per hour, the storm is, by definition, a hurricane. Most hurricanes occur during the late summer. About 10 to 15 storm systems approach hurricane status in water systems adjacent to the United States each year, though the average number varies and might be increasing.

Tornadoes and hurricanes can both wreak enormous damage. Over the short term, they can lead to serious flooding as well as to the destruction of homes and landforms. Possible long-term damage includes the destruction of trees, which take decades to grow back, and also the decimation of local economies. Because more people are now living on islands and in coastal areas, hurricanes can be particularly damaging, over both the short term and the long term. In many coastal areas, efforts are under way to build storm shelters and to build up levees and dikes, which are structures that hold back water.

EXERCISE 10

Weather: Earth's Atmosphere in Action

Directions: Study the illustration, then answer the question.

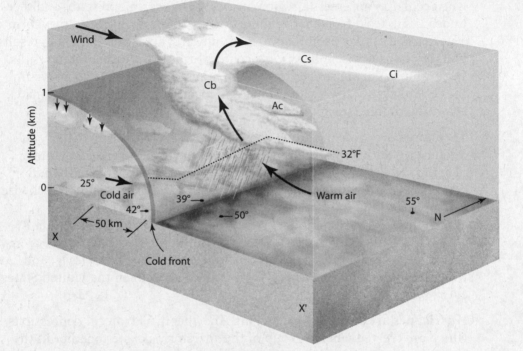

1. In the above illustration, which of the following is occurring?

   A. A hurricane is forming over the ocean.
   B. A tornado is about to hit land.
   C. A warm front is forming.
   D. A cold front is forming.

The answer is on page 561.

The Lithosphere: Layers of Earth

Earth's lithosphere is composed of several layers. Each layer consists of minerals and rocks in various forms. There are three types of rocks, categorized according to their origins: igneous, metamorphic, and sedimentary. **Igneous rocks** form when molten rock, or magma, hardens underground or when lava cools on Earth's surface. **Metamorphic rocks** are those that have been changed within the crust by high pressure and temperature. **Sedimentary rocks** are composed of pieces, or sediments, that have been compacted together.

To probe deep into Earth and study its layers, scientists measure and interpret **seismic waves**, waves produced inside Earth by the movement of tectonic plates. The following illustration shows Earth's layers—the crust, mantle, outer core, and inner core—as well as the thickness of each layer.

Earth's Layers

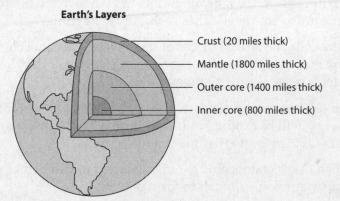

Crust (20 miles thick)

Mantle (1800 miles thick)

Outer core (1400 miles thick)

Inner core (800 miles thick)

Crust: This relatively cool, rocky layer of Earth includes the continental and oceanic crusts, which are composed of a variety of igneous, metamorphic, and sedimentary rocks. Some of the rocks that form the continental crust are more than 4 billion years old. Rock in the oceanic crust is significantly younger—much of it less than 2 million years old.

Mantle: A semisolid layer that contains more than 82 percent of Earth's volume, the mantle consists mostly of igneous rock. The upper regions contain soft, flowing rocks that are at a temperature close to their melting point. The lower mantle, that part of the mantle bordering on the outer core, features both hard and soft rock.

Outer core: The outer core is a layer of hot liquid iron and nickel that lies between the mantle and the inner core (defined below). The iron in this layer is what produces Earth's magnetic field. Temperatures in the outer core range from 4400°C (close to the mantle boundary) to 5500°C (near the inner core).

Inner core: This solid sphere at the center of Earth is composed of iron and nickel. The inner core's temperature is believed to be between 5000°C and 7000°C, which rivals temperatures on the surface of the sun. Despite these high temperatures, the material of the inner core is compressed into a solid state by the immense pressure of the three surrounding layers.

The Rock Cycle

Recall from the beginning of this section that water plays a pivotal role in the way that rocks transform as they move through the various stages of the **rock cycle**. A good way to examine the rock cycle is to trace the movement of an igneous rock as it moves from Earth's inner layers to the crust.

1. Rocks melt deep within Earth's inner layers, forming magma.

2. The magma cools and solidifies. Igneous rock forms.

3. On the surface, the igneous rock is worn down and broken apart by exposure to air, water, other rocks, or living things.

4. Eventually the broken pieces of the rock will become compacted and cemented. Sedimentary rocks form, which might then be moved by water, glacier, wind, or gravity.

5. The sedimentary rock might become buried deep within the Earth, where it will be exposed to intense heat and gravitational pressure, forces that will turn it into new metamorphic rock.

6. When this metamorphic rock is subjected to still higher pressure and temperatures, it will melt to form magma.

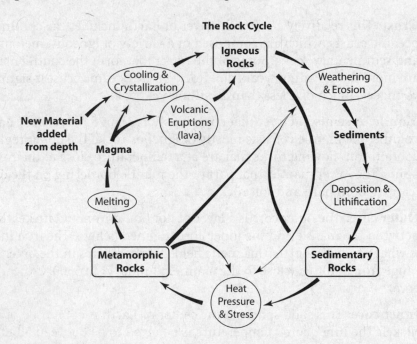

Tectonic Plate Motion

The lithosphere is divided into several **tectonic plates**. The last section described how thermal convection in the mantle sets the tectonic plates in motion. **Thermal convection** occurs when heated molecules move from one place to another. The decay of radioactive elements in Earth's crust and mantle generates the heat that causes thermal convection.

The tectonic plates move incredibly slowly, but because this movement has been occurring for millions of years, it has resulted in tremendous changes. Every stunning plateau, spectacular canyon, and dramatic mountain range has been formed through the movement of tectonic plates.

Constructive and Destructive Forces

Landforms such as mountains, canyons, and plateaus all result from the **constructive forces** that affect Earth's surface. Constructive forces include orogeny, tectonic uplift, and some types of volcanism (volcanic activity). **Orogeny**, the process of mountain building, occurs when tectonic plates move toward each other and collide. **Tectonic uplift** occurs when the movement of tectonic plates raises a geographical area. Tectonic uplift can lead to the formation of seas, lakes, and other inland bodies of water.

Volcanism occurs at tectonic plate boundaries, often when tectonic plates **diverge**, or move away from each other. When an underwater volcano erupts, it discharges lava, or hot, liquid rock that cools and forms islands. Underwater volcanism can also result in several types of sea-floor formations, including seamounts (underwater mountains) and ridges (underwater mountain ranges).

Earth can also be affected by **destructive forces**. These include weathering, coastal erosion, and mass wasting. **Weathering** is the breaking down of rocks on Earth's surface. The two types of weathering are mechanical weathering and chemical weathering. **Mechanical weathering** is the breaking down of rock without any change to its chemical makeup. **Chemical weathering** occurs when rock transforms chemically into another compound. Other types of destructive forces include coastal erosion, which is the wearing away of land by ocean tides, wave currents, or drainage; and mass wasting, which occurs when soil, sand, or rock move downhill. There are several types of mass wasting, including landslides, flows, and rock falls such as avalanches.

Natural Hazards

Other major occurrences that affect the lithosphere are natural hazards. These include earthquakes and volcano eruptions, both of which are caused by tectonic-plate motion, as well as meteorological events such as hurricanes and tornadoes.

Earthquakes occur when tectonic plates grinding past each other cause shifting and breaking of crustal rocks. This plate boundary action is called **translocation** or **transform faulting**. Earthquakes usually occur on **faults**, which are fractures in the Earth caused by tectonic-plate motion. The biggest fault system in the world is the San Andreas Fault in California. Its fault line, which is the portion of the fault seen on Earth's surface, runs for 1300 kilometers.

When volcanoes occur underwater, they can be constructive forces that form islands. Volcanoes that erupt on land have more dire—and destructive—consequences. When Mount St. Helens in Washington state erupted in 1980, it ejected nearly a cubic kilometer of ash, which eventually scattered to 11 states. Lava from the volcano melted glaciers on the side of the mountain, causing tremendous mudslides that extended as far as 65 kilometers. The Mount St. Helens eruption killed 57 people and thousands of animals.

People living in places that are prone to volcanoes and earthquakes often take measures to protect themselves. For example, communities in areas that are close to fault lines might require that houses and other buildings be designed to withstand the force of an earthquake.

EXERCISE 11

The Lithosphere: Layers of Earth

Directions: Match each layer with the choice that *best* describes a characteristic of it.

1. Crust   A. Materials in it are compressed by immense gravitational pressure.

2. Mantle   B. The age of its rocks ranges from 2 million years old to 4 billion years old.

3. Outer Core   C. This layer contains more than 82 percent of Earth's volume.

4. Inner Core   D. The iron in its liquid produces Earth's magnetic field.

Identify the constructive or destructive force that caused each of the following.

5. Formation of the Alps _____

6. Shrinking of the Mississippi Delta _____

7. A sinkhole formed by the decay of rock _____

8. Formation of the Hawaiian Islands _____

Answers are on page 561.

Interactions of Earth's Systems

From studying **fossils**, which are the remains of ancient organisms, paleontologists estimate that life on Earth began about 2 billion years ago. From that time forward, the interaction of solar radiation with Earth's systems and processes has been vital to the evolution of life on the planet. As the biosphere has evolved, it has, in turn, played a vital role in the ways in which Earth's systems have changed. For example, the photosynthetic process plants use to turn sunlight, water, and carbon dioxide into food has produced oxygen. Oxygen has affected the lithosphere by increasing weathering rates during the rock cycle. Oxygen has also increased the biosphere by making animal life possible. Earth's four systems continue to interact today.

Climate Change

One event related to the interaction of Earth's systems is **climate change**. For much of its existence, Earth has experienced various types of climate change. Atmospheric changes to the planet millions of years ago, for example, had profound effects on Earth's climate. Thousands of years ago, changes in the shape of Earth's orbit and the directions in which its **axis of rotation** tilted had major climactic impacts, causing various warming trends as well as several ice ages. You can think of Earth's axis of rotation as an imaginary line that runs between the North and South Poles. Today the tilt of Earth's axis of rotation causes the seasons.

Beginning in the mid-1900s, scientists noted several other causes of climate change, such as volcanic eruptions. Volcanic eruptions disperse large amounts of carbon dioxide into the air, which has a warming effect; but this effect is more than counterbalanced by large-scale cooling created by the volcanic dispersal of particulate matter and sulfur droplets in the atmosphere. Other causes of climate change that have been studied are ocean currents, solar output, and human activity.

Greenhouse Gases

An important event that affects all of Earth's systems is the increase in **greenhouse gases**, which is linked to climate change. Greenhouse gases in Earth's atmosphere, such as carbon dioxide, trap some of the radiation of the sun to help keep the planet warm. This is known as the **greenhouse effect**. Excessive amounts of carbon dioxide in the atmosphere prevent much of the sun's energy from re-radiating, or reflecting, back into space. Instead, the energy remains trapped around Earth. The warmer air temperatures caused by that energy leads to warmer ocean temperatures, which in turn leads to a reduced ability for carbon dioxide to leave the atmosphere. This then leads to a further increase of carbon dioxide in the atmosphere and an increase in the greenhouse effect. This cycle is known as a **feedback effect**.

The increasing greenhouse effect extends beyond Earth's atmosphere. It also affects the hydrosphere, causing major glaciers to melt and the shrinking of polar ice caps. The release of liquid water owing to the melting of the glaciers and polar ice caps is causing a rise in sea level, which is leading to coastal flooding and affecting Earth's lithosphere.

Interactions of Earth's Systems

Directions: Choose the *best* response to the following item.

1. Which of the following is *not* currently linked to climate change?

   A. tectonic plate motion
   B. the increase of greenhouse gases
   C. the eruption of volcanoes
   D. ocean currents

The answer is on page 561.

Earth and Human Activity

Earth's natural resources have played an enormous role in modern culture. Fuels refined from petroleum have powered cars and airplanes. Coal mined from within Earth's crust has provided heat and, along with water, generated electricity. Areas cleared of trees and forests have turned into zones of industry and housing. And natural minerals such as iron, aluminum, copper, and gold have been used in the manufacture of products ranging from steel and industrial wires to dentists' materials and jewelry.

Just as there are benefits to humans from the use of Earth's natural resources, there are costs as well. The greatest of these costs is the impact the use of natural resources has had on our planet. Scientists agree that Earth's climate is becoming increasingly warmer. There is ample evidence that **human activity** plays a significant role in current climate change. There is also evidence that if action is taken immediately, we may be able to control its pace and overall effects.

Climate and Weather

Before we delve farther into the issues of climate change, let's define some terms related to Earth's atmosphere. **Weather** refers to the immediate conditions of the atmosphere. Rain, snow, cold temperatures, and periodic storms are all examples of weather conditions. A weather condition normally lasts for a short period of time. Weather is subject to a variety of variables, which is why it is often difficult to predict. **Climate**, by contrast, is the overall trend of weather in an area and can be predicted with much higher accuracy. When meteorologists and other scientists discuss climate change, they are referring to long trends of weather patterns, lasting for years, centuries, or even millennia.

One way in which climate and weather are related is that an area's climate affects that area's weather. Humid climates, for example, experience more rainfall than dry climates. Climate that is becoming warmer also affects the weather, in ways that might seem surprising. For example, snow may fall in areas that were once too dry to experience snowfalls. Places that once were hit hard by snow might experience rain instead. Rain, snow, thunderstorms, and even hurricanes can become more extreme. And because melting ice caps increase water levels, flooding during or after storms will increase in frequency and severity.

EXERCISE 13

Climate and Weather

Directions: Choose the *best* response to the following item.

1. Hurricane Sandy ravaged parts of the northeastern United States in the fall of 2012. Which of the following statements suggest that Hurricane Sandy might have occurred as a result of climate change?

   A. Hurricane Sandy was the second costliest hurricane in United States history.
   B. In 2012 ocean surface temperatures in the U.S. Northeast were much higher than average.
   C. The Caribbean islands of Haiti and Cuba were heavily damaged, too.
   D. It took Hurricane Sandy 11 days to complete its course.

The answer is on page 561.

Climate Change and Human Activity

Human actions have dramatically increased the amount of carbon dioxide in the atmosphere. They have done so in two major ways: through the burning of fossil fuels and through deforestation.

Burning Fossil Fuels

Fossil fuel is the general term for any naturally occurring hydrocarbon (compound containing hydrogen and carbon) that can be used as fuel. Fossil fuels include coal, petroleum, and natural gas. Fossil fuels are the remains of organisms from the geologic past. The burning of large amounts of fossil fuels is thought to be causing a steady rise in atmospheric temperatures around the globe. The following graph shows how global temperatures have risen since 1880.

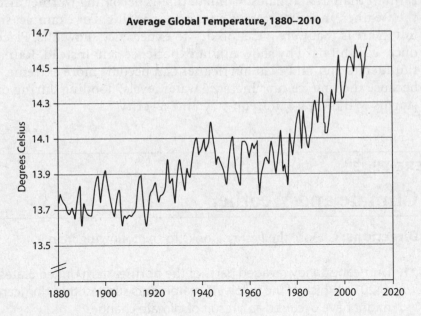

Deforestation

Deforestation is the cutting down and clearing of large areas of trees for various purposes. Reasons for deforestation range from creating new areas for human development to using the wood for buildings or as fuel. When trees are cut down, they are no longer available to remove carbon dioxide from the atmosphere through photosynthesis. And decaying trees release stored carbon into the atmosphere. In addition to the dramatic increase of atmospheric carbon dioxide levels it leads to, deforestation can have a devastating effect on **biodiversity**, which is the variety of life forms in a certain climate, such as a tropical rainforest. The following graph shows the extent of deforestation that has taken place since 1970 in the Amazon Basin in South America, the home of one of Earth's greatest rain forests.

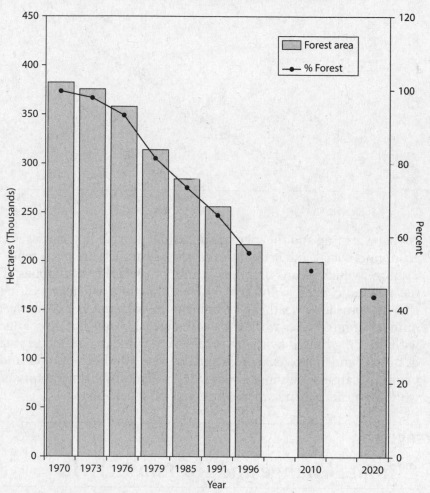

Deforestation in the Amazon Basin, 1970–2020

Dire Predictions

Through computer simulations and other studies, scientists continue to discover ways in which increasing carbon dioxide levels caused by human activity affect the systems of Earth (see next figure). There is evidence that high carbon dioxide levels also cause **ocean acidification**, the increase of acid levels in the ocean. Higher levels of acid in the ocean endanger marine populations. Scientific models predict that if nothing is done to modify human activity, global temperatures will continue to rise.

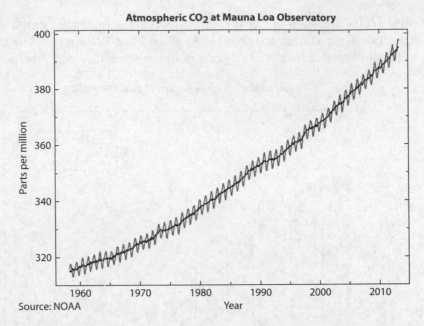

Atmospheric CO$_2$ at Mauna Loa Observatory

Source: NOAA

Global warming and the increase in carbon dioxide that causes it have economic, social, and geopolitical costs. Fossil fuels are not a renewable resource, which means that they cannot be replaced. As supplies of fossil fuels dwindle, oil, gas, and coal will become more expensive. Climate changes can cause weather to become more extreme. For example, the number of hurricanes worldwide will increase. And climate change, along with flooding caused by rising water levels, will damage and ultimately destroy island and coastal areas and displace hundreds of thousands of people. Dealing with those issues will burden future generations as the world becomes warmer, more extreme, and less habitable.

EXERCISE 14

Climate Change and Human Activity

Directions: Match the climate-change event with its consequence.

Event	Consequence
1. Ocean acidification	A. Fuel becomes more expensive.
2. Fossil fuel scarcity	B. The number of hurricanes increases.
3. Melting ice caps	C. Marine populations are endangered.
4. More extreme weather	D. Water levels rise.

Answers are on page 561.

Maintaining a Healthy Planet

Climate change is a crisis, but there are actions we can take every day to help the health of the planet. Two such strategies are recycling and conservation. **Recycling** reusable resources, such as paper and aluminum, is already a regular practice in many communities. **Conserving**, or limiting use of, non-reusable resources has also become widespread.

Other strategies to minimize the impact of human activity on non-reusable resources include using best practices in various industries. **Best practices** in agriculture, for example, might involve contour plowing and strip cropping. **Contour plowing**, or plowing across rather than along hillside slopes, limits soil erosion. **Strip cropping**, or planting crops with different nutrient requirements in adjacent rows, preserves the fertility of the soil. Best practices in coal mining might include identifying engineering controls that control dust levels, which might decrease air pollution.

Sometimes measures that meet some best-practices criteria pose potential hazards as well. For example, some businesses have invested in efforts to extract natural gas and petroleum from sedimentary rock called **oil shale**. Natural gas is a relatively clean-burning fuel, but is non-renewable. The cleaner-burning natural gas emits half as much carbon into the atmosphere as petroleum. Oil shale is located deep within Earth's crust. Extracting the petroleum and natural gas from the oil shale formations involves a process called **hydraulic fracturing**, or **fracking**. During fracking, large amounts of fluid—water mixed with sand and chemicals—are injected at high pressures into the oil shale. The pressure creates small fractures in the rock, which allow natural gas, as well as petroleum, to be removed from the rock. Advocates of fracking say that it not only taps into reserves of cleaner-burning natural gas but also creates jobs and new industry. Opponents of fracking say that the practice endangers natural water supplies. Moreover, some activists claim that without meticulous regulation, fracking could damage the land and seriously threaten wildlife. The illustration that follows shows how fracking works.

Hydraulic Fracturing

Gas reservoir
(sandstone)

Seal

Gas/source rock
(shale, coalbed methane)

Evaluating Strategies

Hydraulic fracturing is a good example of the complex nature of strategies that alter the ways in which we use natural resources. When evaluating such strategies, it is important to consider a range of issues, including cost, safety, and reliability. It is also useful to consider the social and environmental impacts that strategy might have.

Imagine creating a computer simulation that helps you evaluate the costs and benefits of the uses and management of all our natural resources.

Let's begin with the major advantage of managing natural resources responsibly. This benefit involves the relationships among the management of natural resources, sustainability of human populations, and the maintenance of biodiversity. It is a circular relationship, as the diagram below illustrates. You will notice that while biodiversity depends on the responsible management of natural resources, the sustainability of human populations depends on both the management of natural resources and biodiversity.

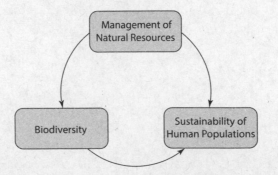

Of course natural-resource management has costs as well. Investing in best-practice methods can be time-consuming. **Waste management**, which is the collecting, transport, and disposal of waste materials, costs money and takes time, as does **urban planning**, which is the design and organization of town and city spaces. Another cost to consider for managing natural resources is the expense of developing new technologies to protect the environment.

Technological Solutions

Scientists and engineers are developing many technologies to help lessen the impact of humans on the environment. These strategies have costs and benefits worth measuring. For example, urban planners have designed sustainable cities that include additional green spaces such as parks. Designing and building sustainable cities benefit us by helping the environment. However, green building can sometimes mean additional costs, such as increases in taxes to pay for construction.

Another type of environmental technology is a range of strategies known as **geoengineering**. The goal of geoengineering techniques is to make changes to the environment in order to counteract the effects of climate change. Geoengineering techniques are still in planning stages and have yet to be implemented. One geoengineering proposal is known as atmospheric seeding. The idea behind atmospheric seeding is to release light-colored sulfur particles into the atmosphere. Those particles would then work to re-radiate the sun's rays into space, which would, in turn, help cool the climate.

Some scientists believe that geoengineering can become a key strategy in the ongoing challenge to control climate change. But some experts warn that geoengineering has its own hazards and that altering Earth's natural atmosphere might lead to issues that could be more challenging than the ones that we currently face.

EXERCISE 15

Maintaining a Healthy Planet

Directions: Read the following passage, then write a short response of one or two paragraphs.

> The United States has large reserves of oil shale. Experts estimate that American energy independence is a real possibility if the hydraulic fracturing ("fracking") industry gains support. Are you in favor of or against fracking? Include at least one cost or benefit of fracking to support your opinion.

A sample answer is on page 561.

CHAPTER 3

Physical Science

Physical science is the study of the composition, structure, and properties of matter as well as the changes matter undergoes.

Matter and Its Interactions

Matter is any substance that occupies space and has mass. Your chair and table are composed of matter. The air you breathe is composed of matter. Matter exists in four states—**solid, liquid, gas,** and **plasma.** You are probably familiar with solids, liquids, and gases. **Plasma** is an ionized gas containing a significant number of electrically charged particles. The sun is made of plasma.

Elements, Atoms, and the Periodic Table

Elements are pure substances composed of atoms. You may be familiar with elements such as hydrogen, carbon, and oxygen. An **atom** is the smallest particle of an element that retains the properties of the element. One hydrogen atom contains the properties of the element hydrogen, just as one atom of copper has all the properties of the element copper and one atom of iron has all the properties of iron.

An atom has two distinct parts, a nucleus and an electron cloud. The **nucleus** is the center of the atom and is composed of positively charged **protons** and electrically neutral **neutrons.** Moving about the nucleus are negatively charged particles called **electrons.** The **electron cloud** is the area where the electrons orbit around the nucleus.

Each element has its own atomic number. The **atomic number** is equal to the number of protons in the nucleus of an atom and determines the identity of the element. For example, all hydrogen atoms have one proton in the nucleus. Therefore, hydrogen's atomic number is 1. The element sodium has 11 protons in its nucleus and the atomic number 11. Sodium also has 11 electrons. An atom in its natural state contains as many electrons as it has protons.

Even though all atoms of a given element contain the same number of protons as electrons, different atoms of the same element can contain different numbers of neutrons. The total number of protons and neutrons determines an atom's mass. Therefore, atoms of the same element having the same number of protons and different number of neutrons can have different masses. Atoms with the same atomic number but with different masses are called **isotopes**. Isotopes are identified by the total number of protons and neutrons in the nucleus. For example, see the following table, which lists the isotopes of the element hydrogen.

Isotopes of Hydrogen			
	H-1	H-2	H-3
Number of protons	1	1	1
Number of neutrons	0	1	2
Number of electrons	1	1	1

A typical hydrogen atom contains one proton and no neutrons. This isotope of hydrogen is identified as H-1. Another isotope of hydrogen contains one proton and one neutron and is known as H-2. And finally, a very rare isotope of hydrogen contains one proton and two neutrons and is called H-3.

In 1869, the Russian chemist Dmitri Mendeleev published a periodic table similar to the one used today. Mendeleev placed the elements in vertical columns (groups) and horizontal rows (periods) which show that certain properties of elements repeat *periodically* when arranged by atomic number. In this way, the periodic table illustrates the periodic law. The **periodic law** states that many of the physical and chemical properties of elements recur systematically with increasing atomic number.

According to the periodic law, as the atomic number increases for elements in a group, similar properties occur regularly and to a greater degree. For example, the elements in the first group, with atomic numbers 3, 11, 19, and 37—lithium, sodium, potassium, and rubidium, respectively—are all chemically active elements. The second member of this group, sodium, is chemically active when placed in water, and the fourth member, rubidium, is so highly active that it bursts into flame simply upon exposure to air.

The periodic table appears on the next page. Each box represents one of the known elements. The number at the top of a box is the element's atomic number, followed by the element's symbol and full name. At the bottom is the atomic mass of the element. **Atomic mass** is the average weight of all the atoms of all the isotopes of the element.

Periodic Table of the Elements

1	2	3	4	5	6	7	8	9	10	11	12	13	14	15	16	17	18
1 H Hydrogen 1.008																	2 He Helium 4.0026
3 Li Lithium 6.94	4 Be Beryllium 9.0122											5 B Boron 10.81	6 C Carbon 12.011	7 N Nitrogen 14.007	8 O Oxygen 15.999	9 F Fluorine 18.988	10 Ne Neon 20.180
11 Na Sodium 22.990	12 Mg Magnesium 24.305											13 Al Aluminum 26.982	14 Si Silicon 28.085	15 P Phosphorus 30.974	16 S Sulfur 32.06	17 Cl Chlorine 35.45	18 Ar Argon 39.948
19 K Potassium 39.098	20 Ca Calcium 40.078	21 Sc Scandium 44.956	22 Ti Titanium 47.867	23 V Vanadium 50.942	24 Cr Chromium 51.996	25 Mn Manganese 54.938	26 Fe Iron 55.845	27 Co Cobalt 58.933	28 Ni Nickel 58.693	29 Cu Copper 63.546	30 Zn Zinc 65.38	31 Ga Gallium 69.723	32 Ge Germanium 72.630	33 As Arsenic 74.922	34 Se Selenium 78.97	35 Br Bromine 79.904	36 Kr Krypton 83.798
37 Rb Rubidium 85.468	38 Sr Strontium 87.62	39 Y Yttrium 88.900	40 Zr Zirconium 91.224	41 Nb Niobium 92.906	42 Mo Molybdenum 95.95	43 Tc Technetium (98)	44 Ru Ruthenium 101.07	45 Rh Rhodium 102.91	46 Pd Palladium 106.42	47 Ag Silver 107.87	48 Cd Cadmium 112.41	49 In Indium 114.723	50 Sn Tin 118.71	51 Sb Antimony 121.76	52 Te Tellurium 127.60	53 I Iodine 126.90	54 Xe Xenon 131.29
55 Cs Cesium 132.91	56 Ba Barium 137.33	57-71	72 Hf Hafnium 178.49	73 Ta Tantalum 180.95	74 W Tungsten 183.84	75 Re Rhenium 186.21	76 Os Osmium 190.23	77 Ir Iridium 192.22	78 Pt Platinum 195.08	79 Au Gold 196.97	80 Hg Mercury 200.59	81 Tl Thallium 204.38	82 Pb Lead 207.2	83 Bi Bismuth 208.98	84 Po Polonium (209)	85 At Astatine (210)	86 Rn Radon (222)
87 Fr Francium (223)	88 Ra Radium (226)	89-103	104 Rf Rutherfordium (265)	105 Db Dubnium (268)	106 Sg Seaborgium (271)	107 Bh Bohrium (270)	108 Hs Hassium (277)	109 Mt Meitnerium (276)	110 Ds Darmstadtium (281)	111 Rg Roentgenium (280)	112 Cn Copernicium (285)	113 Uut Ununtrium (284)	114 Fl Flerovium (289)	115 Uup Ununpentium (288)	116 Lv Livermorium (293)	117 Uus Ununseptium (294)	118 Uuo Ununoctium (294)

Lanthanide Series

57 La Lanthanum 138.91	58 Ce Cerium 140.12	59 Pr Praseodymium 140.91	60 Nd Neodymium 144.24	61 Pm Promethium (145)	62 Sm Samarium 150.36	63 Eu Europium 151.96	64 Gd Gadolinium 157.25	65 Tb Terbium 158.93	66 Dy Dysprosium 162.50	67 Ho Holmium 164.93	68 Er Erbium 167.26	69 Tm Thulium 168.93	70 Yb Ytterbium 173.05	71 Lu Lutetium 174.97

Actinide Series

89 Ac Actinium (227)	90 Th Thorium 232.04	91 Pa Protactinium 231.04	92 U Uranium 238.03	93 Np Neptunium (237)	94 Pu Plutonium (244)	95 Am Americium (243)	96 Cm Curium (247)	97 Bk Berkelium (247)	98 Cf Californium (251)	99 Es Einsteinium (252)	100 Fm Fermium (257)	101 Md Mendelevium (258)	102 No Nobelium (259)	103 Lr Lawrencium (262)

EXERCISE 1

Elements, Atoms, and the Periodic Table

Directions: Match each term on the right with its description on the left.

1. _____ the second lightest element, with two protons in its nucleus
   - A. oxygen

2. _____ a negatively charged particle
   - B. neutron

3. _____ the part of the atom that determines the atom's mass
   - C. proton

4. _____ a particle that has no charge
   - D. helium

5. _____ a positively charged particle
   - E. electron

6. _____ an element containing eight protons in its nucleus
   - F. nucleus

Choose the *best* answer to the following item.

7. Elements listed in the same group of the periodic table have

   _____

   - A. similar properties that intensify as atomic number increases.
   - B. similar properties that lessen as atomic mass decreases.
   - C. the same number of protons in the nucleus.
   - D. the same number of neutrons in the nucleus.

Answers are on page 562.

Compounds and Bonding

Compounds are formed as atoms of two or more elements combine during a chemical reaction. The resulting product usually has properties different from those of the reacting elements. Table salt, or sodium chloride, is a compound composed of sodium atoms and chlorine atoms. The properties of sodium chloride are different from the properties of sodium and from those of chlorine. Sodium chloride is a white solid whereas sodium is a silvery metal and chlorine is a gas.

Sodium atoms and chlorine atoms that combine to make sodium chloride are held together by a bond. A **bond** is a force that that holds together two or more atoms. Bonding may result from either the transfer or the sharing of electrons between atoms.

Both sodium and chlorine atoms are electrically neutral or have no charge. Recall that a neutral element has the same number of protons and electrons. However, when the sodium atom loses one of its negatively charged electrons, it becomes a positively charged ion. The sodium atom then has more protons than electrons. An **ion** is an electrically charged atom. When the chlorine atom receives the electron from the sodium atom, the chlorine atom becomes a negatively charged ion. It then has more electrons than protons. The oppositely charged ions attract each other, forming an ionic bond. The following diagram shows this process.

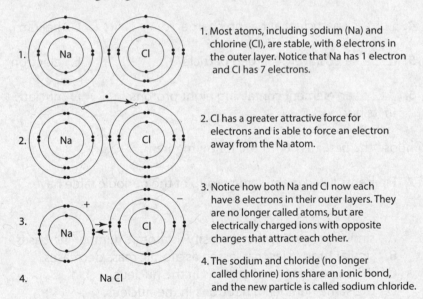

1. Most atoms, including sodium (Na) and chlorine (Cl), are stable, with 8 electrons in the outer layer. Notice that Na has 1 electron and Cl has 7 electrons.

2. Cl has a greater attractive force for electrons and is able to force an electron away from the Na atom.

3. Notice how both Na and Cl now each have 8 electrons in their outer layers. They are no longer called atoms, but are electrically charged ions with opposite charges that attract each other.

4. The sodium and chloride (no longer called chlorine) ions share an ionic bond, and the new particle is called sodium chloride.

An **ionic bond** is formed when electrons are transferred from one atom to another. In the previous example, an ionic bond is formed when an electron from the outermost shell of a sodium atom is transferred to the outermost shell of a chlorine atom. The result is sodium chloride (table salt).

You can use the periodic table to predict how elements will react. Elements in the same groups as sodium and chlorine will react similarly. For example, potassium is in the same group as sodium, and bromine is in the same group as chlorine. Like sodium and chlorine, atoms of potassium and bromine will form an ionic bond, making potassium bromide, used in medicines and photography. Even though sodium chloride and potassium bromide are both ionic compounds, the strength of their bonds differs. You can test the strength of various ionic bonds by observing the solubility (the ability to dissolve) of different ionic substances in water.

When atoms of two or more elements share electrons to form a molecule, a **covalent bond** is formed. As shown in the following illustration, covalent bonds are formed when two hydrogen (H) atoms bond to one oxygen (O) atom to make a molecule of the compound H_2O (water).

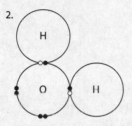

Note: This diagram shows only the outer electron layers. Hydrogen is one of only two elements that are stable with two electrons in a single layer.

1. The hydrogen atoms, each with one electron, need two electrons to be stable. The oxygen atom, with six electrons in its outer layer, needs eight electrons to be stable.

2. The two hydrogen atoms and the oxygen atom can share electrons. Notice that now there are two electrons in the hydrogens' electron layers and eight electrons in oxygen's outer layer. All of the atoms are now stable due to these covalent bonds.

The periodic table allows you to predict how sulfur, which is in the same group as oxygen, will react with hydrogen and what type of bond they will form. Two atoms of hydrogen will share electrons with one atom of sulfur to produce hydrogen sulfide, a gas with a rotten-egg odor.

Covalent bonds can be broken when energy, such as thermal energy or electrical energy, is applied to a covalent compound. An electrical current passed through water will break the covalent bonds between the hydrogen and oxygen atoms of the water molecules. Oxygen atoms easily form new covalent bonds with other oxygen atoms and form oxygen gas. The same is true of the individual hydrogen atoms. Released hydrogen atoms will combine to form hydrogen gas.

One of two things will happen as bonds are broken or created—energy will be released or energy will be absorbed. In the previous example, water molecules release atoms of oxygen and hydrogen, which then combine to form molecules of oxygen gas and hydrogen gas. In this process, energy is absorbed. The release of energy occurs when hydrogen is burned with oxygen. As hydrogen burns and produces water, energy is released as thermal energy, sound, and light.

EXERCISE 2

Compounds and Bonding

Directions: Choose the *best* answer for each question.

1. Before atoms of sodium and chlorine form an ionic bond, the atoms are

   electrically _____.
   A. charged
   B. negative
   C. neutral
   D. positive

2. If two atoms of hydrogen share electrons to form a molecule of hydrogen

   gas, a(n) _____.
   A. covalent bond is broken
   B. covalent bond is formed
   C. ionic bond is formed
   D. ionic bond is broken

Write a short answer to complete the following item.

3. Water molecules exert a force of attraction on the individual ions that
   make up ionic compounds. If the ionic bonds are weak enough, this
   force breaks the ionic bonds, and the compound dissolves in the water.
   Suppose you want to compare the strength of the ionic bonds of two
   ionic compounds—calcium chloride (a road de-icer) and calcium sulfate
   (a food additive). You stir a sample of each compound in test tubes of
   water. You observe that the calcium chloride dissolves in the water, but
   the calcium sulfate does not dissolve. You conclude that

   _____.

Answers are on page 562.

Reaction Rates

Chemical reactions occur as moving particles, such as atoms or molecules,
collide with each other. Upon contact, they either bond or break apart.
Reaction rates generally increase with an increase in the number of
collisions between the particles, as collision theory explains. **Collision**

theory states that not all collisions between particles result in a reaction. Two conditions must be satisfied for atoms or molecules to react with each other. First, the particles must have sufficient energy to break existing bonds and form new ones. Second, reacting particles must be properly oriented with each other to allow a bond to be created. Increasing the number of collisions will increase the probability that conditions will allow a successful reaction to take place.

Several methods exist to increase a reaction rate:

- Increase the temperature of the particles of the reactants. Increasing the temperature will increase the energy and the speed of the particles. The increased speed of the particles creates more collisions and assures that more of the particles will have sufficient energy and orientation to react. As the particles move faster, there will be more collisions between particles, and thus the opportunity for more successful collisions.

- Increase the concentration of the reacting particles. By adding more reacting particles, the distance between the particles decreases. This will result in additional successful collisions. For example, hydrogen peroxide naturally breaks down into water and oxygen gas. To produce the oxygen gas faster, chemists often increase the concentration of the hydrogen peroxide solution.

- Use a **catalyst**. A catalyst is a chemical that is added to the reacting substances, or reactants, to reduce the temperature necessary for the particles to react. A catalyst provides a way for the reacting molecules to collide more frequently. Increasing the number of collisions causes more reactions. For example, catalysts are used in automotive catalytic converters to allow harmful exhaust gases to be burned before they can escape into the atmosphere.

EXERCISE 3

Reaction Rates

Directions: Read the following passage. Then choose the *best* answer for each question.

Enzymes are protein catalysts that control many organics reactions in the body. One reaction is the burning of a sugar, glucose, which releases the energy necessary for the body to function. Without a proper enzyme present, glucose normally burns at a high temperature—hot enough to kill the human body. At body temperature (37°C, 98.6°F), glucose burns too slowly to be practical. Therefore, the body uses enzymatic catalysts that allow the reaction to take place fast enough and at a safe temperature.

1. Catalysts _____.

    A. are used to slow down a reaction to a safe rate
    B. decrease the energy needed by particles to successfully collide
    C. increase a reaction's rate by decreasing successful collisions
    D. raise the concentration of the reacting particles

2. Collision theory suggests that _____.

    A. all particle collisions result in some form of reaction
    B. faster moving particles will collide with other particles more often
    C. increasing the pressure of the reactants slows down a reaction
    D. reactions occur only in the presence of a catalyst

Write a short response to the following item.

3. Explain why increasing the concentration of reactants and increasing the temperature affect the reaction rate.

Answers are on page 562.

Le Châtelier and Equilibrium

Sometimes reactions create more than one product. Often, the products of a chemical reaction react with each other to re-form the original reactants. For instance, examine the following chemical equation for the reaction between methane gas (CH_4) and water vapor (H_2O), which produces carbon monoxide gas (CO) and hydrogen gas (H_2).

$$CH_4(g) + H_2O(g) \longleftrightarrow CO(g) + 3H_2(g)$$

This equation shows that as CO and H_2 are formed (forward reaction going to the right); the CO and H_2 react with each other to produce methane and water (reverse reaction going to the left).

When the rate of the forward reaction equals the rate of the reverse reaction, **chemical equilibrium** occurs. In the late 1800s, French chemist Henri Le Châtelier devised a rule about chemical equilibrium. **Le Châtelier's Principle** states that if you change any of the conditions of a chemical system in equilibrium, the system will respond in a way that minimizes the effects of what you changed. Following are examples of situations that are explained by Le Châtelier's Principle.

• If more of a reactant is added to a system in equilibrium, the equilibrium will shift to use up the added reactants by producing more products.

- In a reaction in which the number of reactant particles is more than the number of product particles, increasing the pressure of the system pushes all the particles closer together. The system relieves the increased pressure by creating more product particles.

- If the temperature of an energy-absorbing system is increased, the equilibrium shifts to use up the thermal energy by producing more products.

EXERCISE 4

Le Châtelier and Equilibrium

Directions: Choose the *best* answer to the following question.

1. A chemical system is most likely to be in equilibrium when the

_____.

A. products on the right side of the chemical equation are decreasing
B. reactants on the left side of the chemical equation are decreasing
C. temperature of the system is constant
D. temperature of the system is increasing

The answer is on page 562.

Conservation of Mass

Water is produced when hydrogen gas reacts with oxygen gas. This process is illustrated by the following equation:

2 atoms of hydrogen + 1 atom of oxygen → 1 molecule of water

In order to make water in large enough quantities for practical use, you need to be able to accurately measure large quantities of hydrogen gas and oxygen gas. Scientists use the mole as a base unit for counting atoms and molecules. Because atoms and molecules are so incredibly small, it takes a large quantity of atoms and molecules to make one mole. A mole is a very large number (approx. 6.02×10^{23}). That is about 602,000,000,000,000,000,000,000!

To understand how to count objects as small as atoms and molecules, start off by counting large eggs. Each egg has a mass of about 60 grams. To measure a dozen (12) eggs, you could do one of two things. You could count 12 eggs one by one. Or you could measure out 720 grams of eggs, which roughly equals a dozen eggs. A mole has too many atoms and molecules to count out individually; atoms and molecules are too small to count. However, looking at the periodic table, you see that the atomic mass of hydrogen is 1.008. If you place a mass of 1.008 grams of hydrogen in a bottle, you will have one mole of hydrogen atoms. Likewise, 15.999 is the atomic mass of oxygen. If you measure out 15.999 grams of oxygen into a bottle, you will have one mole of oxygen atoms in the bottle. Therefore, you can change the above equation to the following:

2 moles of hydrogen atoms + 1 mole of oxygen atoms → 1 mole of water molecules

or

2.016 g H + 15.999 g O → 18.015 g water

Notice that the mass of the produced water equals the combined mass of the reacting hydrogen and oxygen. This may seem like a simple observation. However, it represents a very important concept in science: the **law of conservation of mass**. This law states that in a closed system (a place where nothing can get in or out), no matter what you do to the contents of the system, the total mass of the system always remains the same.

EXERCISE 5

Conservation of Mass

Directions: Read the following passage. Then write a short response to the question. Use the periodic table to help you.

1. Suppose you build a campfire with 100 pounds of wood. When the fire eventually goes out, only 1 pound of ashes remains. Assuming the law of conservation of mass is correct, how can you explain this apparent loss of mass?

The answer is on page 562.

Radioactive Decay, Fission, and Fusion

Recall that elements have various isotopes—atoms of the same element but with differing numbers of neutrons. Some isotopes are stable and do not change; unstable isotopes change and thus are radioactive.

Radioactive decay is the process by which an unstable nucleus becomes stable by emitting different forms of radiation. The three basic types of radioactive decay are alpha decay (α), beta decay (β), and gamma decay (γ). **Alpha decay**

occurs when there are too many protons in a nucleus. In this case the element emits radiation in the form of positively charged particles called alpha particles (helium nuclei). **Beta decay** occurs when there are too many neutrons in a nucleus. In this case the element emits radiation in the form of negatively charged particles called beta particles (electrons). **Gamma decay** occurs when there is excess energy in the nucleus. To achieve a stable energy level, gamma particles, or high-frequency photons of electromagnetic energy, are emitted from the nucleus. The following diagram shows how a large, unstable uranium nucleus spontaneously ejects some of its protons as an alpha particle. This results in a smaller thorium nucleus, which itself is unstable. Further decay occurs as the thorium nucleus ejects a beta particle (electron). A progression of decay steps continues until a stable nucleus is formed.

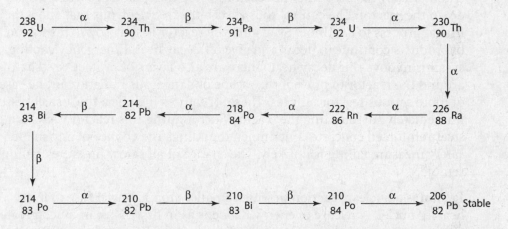

Fission is the splitting of an atomic nucleus into approximately equal parts. Sometimes an unstable nucleus will split spontaneously. Sometimes scientists will fire a subatomic particle, such as a neutron, into a nucleus to cause the nucleus to split. When a nucleus splits, there is usually a release of energy in the form of gamma radiation, thermal energy, and visible light.

In the following illustration, a neutron is shown colliding with a uranium nucleus. The neutron sticks to the nucleus, making the nucleus slightly heavier but unstable. As a result, the nucleus splits into a krypton nucleus and a barium nucleus. Two outcomes occur in this splitting: (1) energy is released, and (2) neutrons are ejected. The ejected neutrons collide with other uranium nuclei. This process continues as a chain reaction that progresses quickly and can ultimately release very large amounts of energy.

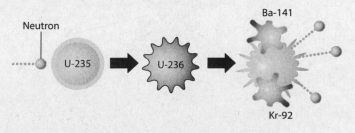

Nuclear fission is used in some power plants to produce electricity. The principal risks associated with nuclear power arise from the biological effects of radiation. Some of the subatomic particles and radiation emitted during fission can penetrate the human body and can damage living cells and possibly cause cancer. If they strike sex cells, they can cause genetic defects in offspring.

Although strict regulations govern the operation of all nuclear power plants, there will always be a possibility for some type of accident to occur. Safety measures are built into nuclear power plants to minimize the risks. For example, excess heat is normally removed from the reactor by the primary coolant system. If cooling water flow cannot be maintained, control rods are automatically inserted into the reactor to stop the fission process and shut down the reactor. The control rods absorb the free neutrons that allow the fission process to continue. Even after the reactor is shut down, the fission byproducts continue to decay and give off decay heat. Emergency cooling systems remove this decay heat. There are also layers of protective structures around the reactor to prevent the escape of dangerous radiation in the case of more serious reactor failures. These structures include a thick steel vessel immediately surrounding the reactor. Surrounding this reactor vessel is a steel-reinforced concrete containment building. The chance of any single safety measure failing is unlikely. The chance of all safety measures failing is remote.

Fusion is a nuclear reaction in which smaller atomic nuclei fuse to form heavier nuclei. A release of energy happens as in fission but in much greater amounts. Fusion is the nuclear reaction occurring within the sun. Presently, there are no containment systems that can hold a reaction that releases so much heat.

During one form of fusion, nuclei of two types of hydrogen atoms (atomic number 1) collide and fuse to form a helium nucleus (atomic number 2). However, this type of helium has three neutrons and is unstable. To become stable, the unstable helium nucleus ejects a neutron with an accompanying burst of energy. This reaction continues until there is no more hydrogen that can be fused into helium.

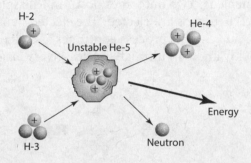

EXERCISE 6

Radioactive Decay, Fission, and Fusion

Directions: Choose the *best* answer to each of the following questions.

1. An unstable nucleus undergoes radioactive decay until _____.

   A. a stable nucleus is formed
   B. no more alpha particles are available
   C. the number of protons in the nucleus equals the number of neutrons
   D. there are no more neutrons in the nucleus

2. Nuclear fission is the _____.

   A. splitting of a nucleus
   B. breaking of a covalent bond
   C. emission of an alpha particle
   D. joining of two nuclei

3. During nuclear fission _____.

   A. only neutrons are released from the nucleus
   B. only protons are released from the nucleus
   C. neutrons and energy are released from the nucleus
   D. protons and energy are released from the nucleus

4. The energy released during nuclear fusion is _____.

   A. approximately equal to the energy given off during nuclear fission
   B. greater than the energy released during fission
   C. less than the energy released during nuclear fission
   D. less than the energy released during radioactive decay

5. Presently, nuclear fusion is not used in nuclear power plants because _____.

   A. fusion produces too little heat to be practical
   B. fission produces too little heat to be practical
   C. fission produces more heat
   D. fusion produces too much heat to contain

Answers are on page 562.

Motion and Stability: Forces and Interactions

Physics is the branch of science that studies the forces that cause matter to behave as it does. Why do objects fall to the ground? Physics uses the concept of force to explain this phenomenon. **Force** is the presence of energy in the environment. **Energy** is the capacity to cause change. The area of physics that deals with forces, energy, and their effects on objects is **mechanics**.

The ancient Greek philosopher Aristotle theorized that heavier objects fall faster than lighter ones. This theory was proved false in the early seventeenth century by the Italian scientist and mathematician Galileo Galilei. However, the force acting upon objects was not fully understood at that time. It was the English scientist and mathematician Sir Isaac Newton who formulated laws of gravity and motion that explained how different forces act on objects. Newton's laws of gravity and motion explain why objects fall to the ground.

Balanced and Unbalanced Forces

To move a grocery cart full of items, you have to exert a force on that cart. A **force** is any push or pull on an object. If you push a full cart yourself, you may have to push hard before the cart starts moving. If a friend pushes with you, you do not need to push as hard. When two or more forces act on an object, the forces combine into what is known as the **net force.**

The motion of an object can change in three ways—it can speed up, slow down, or change direction. Newton's laws of motion can explain how a force on an object can change the object's motion. **Newton's first law of motion** states that an object's motion does not change unless the object is acted upon by an unbalanced **net force.** The net force is the sum of all forces acting on an object. If the net force is zero, the forces are said to be **balanced** and do not cause a change in the object's motion. If you are pushing your cart down the aisle with a given force and a friend is pushing back with an equal force, your cart will stand still. If the net force on an object is not zero, the forces are **unbalanced** and there will be a change in the motion of the object. For example, if you push on your grocery cart and no one pushes back, there will be an unbalanced net force acting on the cart and it will speed up.

EXERCISE 7

Balanced and Unbalanced Forces

Directions: Choose the *best* answer to this question.

1. "Any push or pull on an object" is the definition of _____.

   A. energy
   B. friction
   C. force
   D. work

Write a short answer to this question.

2. What motion would automobile passengers undergo if they failed to use their seat belts and the car was brought to a sudden halt by a collision with a stationary object?

Answers are on page 562.

Force, Mass, and Acceleration

Recall the three ways you can change the motion of an object—speeding up, slowing down, and changing direction. In physics, all of these kinds of changes are called **acceleration**. An **acceleration** is any change in the motion of an object. When you are pushing a grocery cart and turning the corner to go down a different aisle, the cart is accelerating (though in everyday speech, we use the word *acceleration* only to refer to increasing speed). You apply a **force** to a grocery cart when you push or pull on its handle. **Mass** is the amount of matter that makes up an object. When you add items to your grocery cart, the cart's mass increases. The cart has more mass when it is full of groceries than when it is empty.

Isaac Newton's second law of motion sums up the relationships among acceleration, force, and mass. It states that an object's acceleration is proportional to the amount of force applied to it. For example, the greater the force you apply to your grocery cart, the more quickly it will speed up. Once the cart is moving forward, you could pull back on the handle with a small force to make the cart slowly come to a stop.

Newton's second law of motion is expressed using the mathematical equation shown below.

a = F/m

where *a* is the object's acceleration

F is the force applied to the object

m is the mass of the object

EXERCISE 8

Force, Mass, and Acceleration

Directions: Fill in the blanks with the correct terms.

1. An acceleration is any change in the _____ or

   _____ of motion of an object.

2. According to Newton's second law of motion, *a = F/m*. If the force exerted on an object doubles and the mass of the object is constant, the object's

   acceleration will _____.

   A. be cut in half
   B. double
   C. not change
   D. quadruple

Answers are on page 563.

Graphing Motion

Two measurements frequently compared to each other are *distance* and *time*. The relationship between the two can be shown with graphs. Graphs show one measurement compared to another. While pushing your grocery cart, your speed may change many times. However, the following graph describes the motion of an object whose speed does not change. The graph shows the distance it might travel when distance measurements are made every second. Follow the height of the line from the left side of the graph, starting at time 0, to the right side, ending at time 8. You can see how the distance the object moves changes over time. Notice that the change in the distance traveled is the same each second on the graph. The slope of the line at any given time is the speed of the moving object. A greater slope indicates a greater speed. Constant speed is shown as a straight line on a distance-time graph.

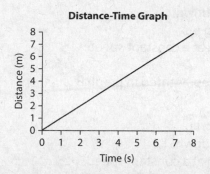

A *speed-time* graph is a convenient way to illustrate acceleration. Notice in the following speed-time graph, section A shows that the speed of the object increases over time. At section B, the object is moving at a constant speed until it reaches section C, where the object's speed begins increasing again. The object's speed is constant once more over section D. Over section E, the object's speed decreases over time until the object comes to a stop at the end of the graph. During sections A, C, and E, the object is shown to be accelerating (changing speed). During sections B and D, the motion of the object is not changing.

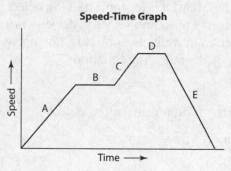

EXERCISE 9

Graphing Motion

Directions: The following graphs describe the motion of two objects. Use the information in the graphs to help you select the *best* answer to each question.

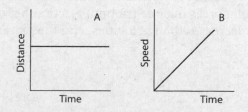

1. The object represented in graph A is

   A. stopped.
   B. slowing down.
   C. speeding up.
   D. traveling at a constant speed.

2. The object represented in graph B is

   A. stopped.
   B. speeding up.
   C. slowing down.
   D. traveling at a constant speed.

Answers are on page 563.

Momentum

If a large truck and a small car move at the same speed, the truck is harder to stop. Because the truck has more mass, it has more momentum. **Momentum** is a measure of how hard it is to stop a moving object. Momentum is the product of an object's mass and velocity. **Velocity** refers to an object's speed as well as the direction in which the object is moving. Momentum is represented mathematically by the following equation:

$p = mv$

where p is the momentum of the object

m is the object's mass

v is the velocity

If two cars of equal mass move at different speeds, the faster car has more momentum and is harder to stop.

In any collision, one object transfers momentum to another object. When a billiards cue ball strikes another ball, it slows down and the other ball speeds up. The momentum of the cue ball decreases as the momentum of the struck ball increases. The total momentum of the system does not change. According to the **law of conservation of momentum**, the total momentum of a group of objects does not change unless an outside force acts on the objects. Outside forces include friction. Friction between the billiard balls and the table decreases their velocities, and they lose momentum.

EXERCISE 10

Momentum

Directions: Read the passage and write a short response to this question.

1. An inelastic collision occurs when one moving object strikes another
    object and the two objects stick together as one. Consider two identical
    lab test carts—one is moving toward the other at a rate of 1 m/s. The
    second cart is standing still. The first cart collides with the second, they
    stick together, and together, they continue to move in the direction of
    the first cart, but at a speed of 0.5 m/s. Explain how momentum was
    conserved in this situation.

The answer is on page 563.

Strength of Noncontact Forces

Lift a pencil and then release it, and it falls toward the floor. A parachutist falls
toward Earth even though nothing is touching her. Objects fall to the ground
because Earth exerts a pulling force, known as **gravity**, on them. A force
that one object applies to another without touching it is a **noncontact force**.
Gravity, which pulls the pencil and parachutist down, is a noncontact force.
Other examples of noncontact forces are magnetic force and electrostatic
force. The **magnetic force** attracts certain metals to magnets. The **electrostatic
force** can also sometimes cause your hair to stand on end after you comb it.

Gravity is a force that exists between any two objects that have mass. Sir
Isaac Newton developed the **law of universal gravitation.** It states that the
amount of the force of gravity between two objects depends on the masses of
the objects and the distance between the objects. When the mass of one or
both of the objects increases, the gravitational force between the objects also
increases. As the distance between the objects increases, the gravitational
force between them decreases. The following proportion represents Newton's
law of universal gravitation.

$$G = \frac{m_1 \times m_2}{r_2}$$

where G is gravitation

m_1 and m_2 are the mass of the two objects

r is the distance between the two centers

For example, if the total mass of the objects doubles, the gravitational force between the objects also doubles. However, if the distance between the centers of the original objects doubles, the gravitational force between the objects drops to one-fourth its original value.

The region surrounding an electrically charged object is called an **electric field.** An electric field applies a noncontact electrostatic force to electrically charged objects. The electrostatic force applied by an object's electric field either attracts or repels other charged objects. Objects with similar electric charges repel each other, while objects with opposite charges attract each other.

The strength of the electrostatic force depends on two variables—the total amount of charge on both objects and the distance between the objects. As the total amount of charge on the objects increases, so does the force of attraction or repulsion. And as the distance between the centers of the charged objects increases, the electrostatic force between the objects decreases. The proportion that describes these electrostatic relationships is the same as the proportion that describes gravitational force. You will learn more about electrostatic charges later in this chapter.

EXERCISE 11

Strength of Noncontact Forces

Directions: Select the *best* answer to the following question.

1. Standing on the surface of Earth, a 200-pound man is about 4000 miles from the center of the planet. What would happen to the man's weight if he could stand on an imaginary tower 4000 miles above Earth's surface?

   A. His weight would decrease to 50 pounds.
   B. His weight would decrease to 100 pounds.
   C. His weight would increase to 400 pounds
   D. His weight would increase to 800 pounds.

The answer is on page 563.

Electricity and Magnetism

A **magnet** is any object that attracts the metal iron. Hair dryers and computers contain magnets. The magnets are used to produce the electric energy that makes these familiar devices work. An invisible magnetic field surrounds all magnets. It is this magnetic field that applies a non-contact force on other magnets as well as on charged particles, such as electrons in a wire. This can be demonstrated by passing a magnetic field over a coil of wire that is part of a closed electric circuit. As the magnetic field moves over the wire coil, an electric current is produced in the circuit. To create an electric current in a wire, the magnetic field near the wire must be moving. Holding a magnet motionless beside a coil will not produce a current.

A magnetic field also surrounds an electric current. This is why a compass needle moves when placed near a current-carrying wire. The needle moves because the magnetic field around the wire applies a force to the compass needle. A magnetic field surrounds all moving, charged particles. An electric current is the flow of an electric charge through a conductor. In a current-carrying wire, the individual magnetic fields of the flowing charges combine to produce a magnetic field around the entire wire. The magnetic field around the wire becomes stronger as the current increases or as more electric charges flow in the wire.

EXERCISE 12

Electricity and Magnetism

Directions: Write a short answer to this question.

1. If a magnet is near but does not touch a coil of wire, what causes a current to flow in the wire?

The answer is on page 563.

Electromagnets

Many electrical devices, including stereo speakers and hair dryers, contain electromagnets. An **electromagnet** is a magnet created by wrapping a current-carrying wire around a core made of iron or similar material. The following diagram illustrates a basic electromagnet.

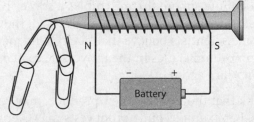

An electromagnet can be made simply by wrapping
a current-carrying wire around an iron core.

The strength of the magnetic field surrounding an electromagnet can be controlled by manipulating the features of the magnet. For instance, increasing the number of loops in the coil or increasing the electric current in the coil will increase the strength of the field. If a device uses electricity and has moving parts, chances are an electromagnet is inside.

EXERCISE 13

Electromagnets

Directions: Fill in the blanks to complete the following sentences.

1. A basic electromagnet can be made by wrapping a current-carrying

   _____ around an iron _____.

2. Summarize the steps in building an electromagnet. Include one way to control the strength of the electromagnet's magnetic field.

Answers are on page 563.

Materials Engineering

Materials engineering is an area of science and engineering that studies the practical uses of different forms of matter. In materials engineering, scientists study the relationship between a substance's atomic or molecular level and its large-scale properties.

Buckyballs

Carbon, one of the most common elements in nature, is present in all living organisms. Coal, diamonds, and space dust are made of carbon. Recently, scientists have discovered a new form of carbon— buckminsterfullerenes, commonly known as buckyballs. Buckyballs are molecules of pure carbon in the shape of a hollow sphere that resembles a soccer ball. The spherical shape makes them extremely stable. When compressed, they become as hard as diamonds. Some scientists believe that buckyballs may be one of the oldest and most common molecules in the universe, created in red giant stars more than 10 billion years ago.

Engineers think that thousands of new products may come out of research on buckyballs. For example, bulletproof vests may eventually be made using buckyballs. Buckyballs might be used someday as rocket fuel. And the round shape of buckyballs could make them excellent lubricants to reduce friction.

The hollow shape of a buckyball allows scientists to place another element inside the carbon sphere. This is called *doping the buckyball* and is shown in the following diagram. Buckyballs doped with potassium, for instance, are excellent electrical superconductors.

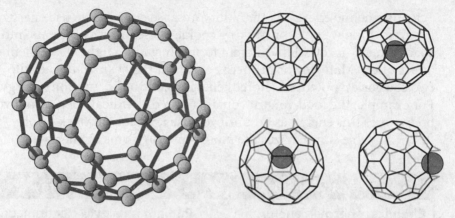

Buckminsterfullerenes, or buckyballs, are hollow spheres of carbon atoms that can be doped with other elements.

Electrical Wires

Even simple electrical wires are engineered based on the properties of metals—ductility, conductivity, flexibility, and non-corrosiveness. A wire's material needs to be **ductile**—that is, have the ability to be drawn out into a thin wire. A wire also needs to be a **good electrical conductor** so that electrons can flow through it. Metals contain electrons that are not bound to any given nucleus. These free electrons are able to move easily through metals, creating an electrical current. Next, a wire needs to be **flexible**, not brittle. In addition, a wire needs to be **non-corrosive** if it is to last. And, for practical uses, a wire needs to be made of a metal that is **economical**.

Most common electrical wire is made of copper. It is ductile, an excellent electrical conductor, very flexible, not easily corroded, and relatively inexpensive.

EXERCISE 14

Materials Engineering

Directions: Write an extended response to this question.

1. Think of a modern engineered structure you are familiar with, such as a long bridge or a tall building. What engineered materials were used to allow the structure to be bigger or better than older structures? Hypothesize about what qualities have been engineered into modern building materials to allow the greater modern structures to be built.

The answer is on page 563.

Energy

Scientists define **energy** as the ability to cause change. We use energy for everything we do, from baking cookies to sending astronauts into space. Energy is found in different forms, including light, heat, chemical, and motion. Many forms of energy exist, but they can all be put into two categories: **potential** (stored) energy and **kinetic** (motion) energy. For example, the food you eat contains stored chemical energy, and your body stores this energy as fat until you use it when you work or play. The following table summarizes the most common forms of energy.

Potential Energy	Kinetic Energy
Chemical energy is energy stored in the bonds of molecules. Batteries, petroleum, natural gas, and coal are examples of chemical potential energy. Example: Chemical energy is transformed into thermal energy when a car's engine burns gasoline.	**Radiant energy** is electromagnetic energy that travels in waves. Radiant energy includes radio waves, visible light, X-rays, and gamma rays.
Mechanical energy is stored in objects by tension. Compressed springs and stretched rubber bands are examples of mechanical potential energy.	**Thermal energy** is the vibration and movement of the atoms and molecules within substances. As an object heats up, its atoms and molecules collide faster. Geothermal energy is the thermal energy within Earth.
Nuclear energy is stored in the nucleus of an atom. Energy can be released when nuclei are combined or split apart.	**Motion energy** is the energy of an object in motion. The faster an object moves, the more energy it contains.
Gravitational potential energy, or GPE, is stored in an object when the object is raised to a given height. The higher the object is raised, the more GPE is stored. Water stored behind a hydroelectric dam is an example of GPE.	**Sound** is the movement of waves of energy through a medium. Sound is produced when a force causes an object or substance to vibrate.
	Electrical energy is delivered by tiny charged particles called electrons. Lightning is an example of electrical energy in nature.

Conservation of Energy

One of the basic scientific concept is the **law of conservation of energy**. It states that the total amount of energy in the universe is constant. In other words, energy cannot be created or destroyed. Only its form can change.

One form of energy is mechanical energy. An object, such as a bowling ball, can contain mechanical energy. There are two types of mechanical energy— mechanical potential energy and mechanical kinetic energy. **Potential energy** is the stored energy of position. Typically, mechanical potential energy is increased in an object, including the bowling ball, as the object is lifted against the force of gravity. Therefore, mechanical potential energy is often referred to as **gravitational potential energy (GPE)**. GPE is due to the vertical position of an object on Earth. When you hold the bowling ball in your hand before you roll it down the lane, the bowling ball has gravitational potential energy.

GPE is calculated using the following equation.

$$GPE = m{\cdot}g{\cdot}h$$

where m is the mass of the object in kilograms

g is the acceleration due to gravity (9.8 m/s/s or 9.8 m/s^2)

h is the height of the object in meters

The unit of energy, including GPE, is the joule (J). For example, if a 7 kg bowling ball is raised to a height of 0.75 m, the ball will have GPE of approximately 51 J.

$$GPE = 7 \text{ kg (mass)} \times 9.8 \text{ m/s}^2 \text{ (acceleration)} \times 0.75 \text{ m (height)} = 51.45 \text{ J}$$

When the bowling ball is rolling down the lane, it has mechanical kinetic energy. **Mechanical kinetic energy (KE)** is the energy of an object due to its motion. Only moving objects have kinetic energy. The KE of an object depends upon the object's mass and velocity. Mechanical kinetic energy is calculated using the following equation:

$$KE = 0.5 \cdot m \cdot v^2$$

where m is the mass of the object in kilograms

v is the velocity of the object, in meters per second

If the same bowling ball with a mass of 7 kg is moving at a velocity of 5 m/s, its kinetic energy is 87.5 J.

$$KE = 0.5 \cdot 7 \text{ kg (mass)} \cdot (5 \text{ m/s})^2 \text{ (velocity)} = 87.5 \text{ J}$$

The total mechanical energy of an object is the sum of its kinetic and gravitational potential energies (GPE). This means that as the bowling ball is being raised, it is gaining GPE. As the ball is held motionless 0.75 m above the ground, its GPE remains unchanged. If the ball is not in motion, it has no kinetic energy. When the ball is released, it falls with continually increasing speed as its height decreases. The increasing speed means the ball is gaining kinetic energy. At the same time, the decreasing height of the ball means the ball is losing potential energy. The instant the ball touches the ground, its height is zero and it is moving at its maximum velocity. Zero height means the ball has no remaining potential energy. But the ball does have maximum kinetic energy. As the ball hits the ground, the ball's kinetic energy equals the ball's potential energy before it was dropped. The change of energy that the ball undergoes as it falls is summarized in the following graphs.

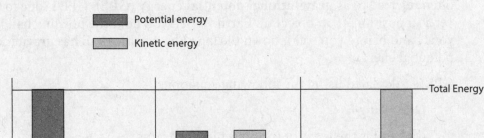

Total mechanical energy of the ball is conserved as the ball falls. The equations for potential energy and kinetic energy can be used to solve for any one of the variables if the other two are known. For instance, you may want to know how fast the ball is traveling when it hits the ground. If the maximum potential energy equals the maximum kinetic energy, you can solve for the ball's velocity using the formula for kinetic energy.

$$KE = 0.5 \times m \times v^2$$
$$50J = 0.5 \times 7\,kg \times v^2$$
$$\frac{50J}{0.5 \times 7\ kg} = v^2$$
$$\sqrt{\frac{50J}{0.5 \times 7\ kg}} = v$$
$$4\,m/s = v$$

EXERCISE 15

Conservation of Energy

Directions: Choose the *best* answer to each question.

1. The law of conservation of energy states that _____.

   A. as the universe expands, the total energy of the universe increases
   B. as the universe expands, the total energy of the universe decreases
   C. energy is constantly being created
   D. the total energy of the universe is constant

2. GPE = _____

   A. $0.5mv^2$
   B. KE
   C. mgh
   D. mv

3. A 7 kg concrete block is lifted 1 meter off the ground. It is then dropped. At the instant the block touches the ground, its GPE is

   _____.

   A. 0 J
   B. 70 J
   C. 700 J
   D. 7000 J

Answers are on page 563.

Thermodynamics

Thermodynamics is the branch of science that deals with the relationships among heat and other forms of energy, such as mechanical, electrical, and chemical energy. Recall that the law of conservation of energy states that energy cannot be created or destroyed. It only can change form or move from one location to another. One aspect of thermodynamics looks at the transfer of heat between two objects of different temperatures. When a hot object is in contact with a cold object, thermal energy flows from the hotter object into the colder object until the temperature of both objects is the same. Think of dropping an ice cube into a cup of hot water. Thermal energy is transferred from the hot water to the ice cube, and the ice cube warms up and finally melts. Eventually the cold water that was once an ice cube continues to warm up until all the water in the cup is at the same temperature. Thermodynamics tells us that the opposite will never happen. On its own, a cup of warm water never will separate into hot and cold areas and form an ice cube.

Another example of this principle is what happens when you drop a glass bottle onto a hard floor. The bottle may break into many pieces. The opposite will never happen. Dropping broken pieces of glass onto the floor will not make the pieces come together to form a bottle.

The melting ice cube and the breaking bottle obey an important law of thermodynamics—matter in a closed system will always tend to move toward a state of greater disorder, unless work is done on the matter to make the matter more orderly. You know that setting out water in a warm room will not create ice. A freezer must be used to do work on the water, changing random water molecules into orderly ice crystals. To make broken glass back into a bottle, work must be done on the glass. The measure of the amount of disorder in a system is known as **entropy**. The entropy of a system will naturally increase until the matter in the system is of uniform consistency. To reverse the trend toward increased entropy, energy must be brought in from outside the system so that work can be done on the system's matter.

EXERCISE 16

Thermodynamics

Directions: Choose the *best* answer for each question.

1. According to the laws of thermodynamics, systems left on their own will

   tend toward _____.

   A. higher entropy
   B. lower entropy
   C. maximum kinetic energy
   D. maximum potential energy

2. A situation that shows the reversal of naturally increasing entropy is a(n)

   _____.

   A. automobile engine burning molecules of gasoline
   B. man carrying a board up a ladder to build a house
   C. paint stirrer mixing different colors
   D. wrecking ball smashing the wall of an old building

3. In a closed system, energy can be _____.

    A. created but not destroyed
    B. created or destroyed
    C. destroyed but not created
    D. neither created nor destroyed

Answers are on page 563.

Electrostatic Forces

If you rub a balloon on a wool sweater, the balloon probably will become electrically charged. The charged balloon will exert a force on other objects. This force is known as an **electrostatic force**. For example, the electrostatic force exerted by the balloon could cause an attraction between the balloon and small bits of paper near the balloon. This attraction might be strong enough to cause the paper to stick to the balloon. The electrostatic force is a noncontact force that acts on the paper and other objects as well, even over great distances. All charged objects exert this force on other objects, both charged and uncharged.

There are two types of electrically charged objects. Objects with more protons than electrons are said to be **positively charged**. Objects with more electrons than protons are **negatively charged**. Objects with opposite charges attract each other, and objects with similar charges repel each other.

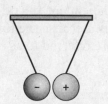   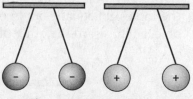

Oppositely charged objects attract   AND   Objects with like charges repel

If a charged object is brought near another charged object, it will experience either a pushing or a pulling force. The objects will therefore have potential energy. When charged objects repel each other, bringing the objects together requires work to be done on the objects. This increases the potential energy of the objects. When charged objects attract each other, increasing the distance between the objects requires work to be done on the objects, and the potential energy of the objects increases.

The electrostatic force between two charged objects, just like such other forces as gravity and friction, obeys **Newton's law of action-reaction,** also known as **Newton's third law.** This law states that a force is simply an interaction between two objects. This interaction results in an equal and opposite push or pull exerted by one object upon the other.

Newton's law of action-reaction explains the interaction of two electrically charged objects, each with the same electric charge. The following illustration shows object A pushing object B to the right, and object B pushing object A to the left. The two forces are equal in strength but opposite in direction. The push on object B by object A is directed away from object A. And the push on object A by object B is directed away from object B. Because these forces push the objects away from each other, the force is referred to as **repulsive.**

Like Charges Repel

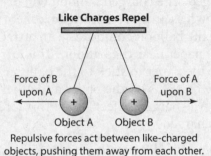

Force of B upon A — Object A (+)   Object B (+) — Force of A upon B

Repulsive forces act between like-charged objects, pushing them away from each other.

Newton's action-reaction law also applies to two oppositely charged objects. The following diagram shows object C exerting a pulling force on object D to the left. And object D is exerting a pulling force on object C to the right. Each object pulls on the other object independently. And as before, the forces act equally but in opposite directions. Because the forces on each object act toward the other object, the forces are referred to as **attractive.**

Opposite Charges Attract

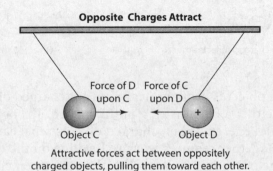

Force of D upon C   Force of C upon D
Object C (-)   Object D (+)

Attractive forces act between oppositely charged objects, pulling them toward each other.

Electrostatic Forces

Directions: Choose the *best* answer to each question.

1. Two plastic foam spheres are hanging straight down near each other.

   Apparently, the spheres are _____.

   A. charged or not charged. It is impossible to speculate
   B. not charged
   C. oppositely charged
   D. similarly charged

2. An electrically charged object _____.

   A. can exert a force on an uncharged object
   B. can exert a force only if the objects are close to each other
   C. can exert only a force of repulsion on an uncharged object
   D. cannot exert a force on an uncharged object

Fill in the correct terms to complete the following sentence.

3. Newton's law of action-reaction tells us that two positively charged

   objects will exert _____ and _____ forces on
   each other.

Answers are on page 563.

Waves

Imagine you are floating on a raft in the middle of a calm pool. Suddenly, your friend does a cannonball dive into the pool. You start bobbing up and down in the water. Your friend created waves by jumping into the pool. A **wave** is a disturbance that transfers energy from one place to another without transferring matter. You moved up and down because the waves transferred energy from your friend to you.

Mechanical Waves

A water wave is an example of a mechanical wave. A wave that can travel only through matter is a **mechanical wave**. Mechanical waves can travel through solids, liquids, and gases. They cannot travel through a vacuum. A material through which a wave travels is called a **medium**. Two types of mechanical waves are transverse waves and longitudinal waves.

Transverse Waves

A transverse wave is a wave in which the disturbance is perpendicular to the direction the wave travels. A transverse wave occurs, for instance, when you shake a rope up and down, as shown in the following figure. The figure shows that the rope moves up and down as the wave travels horizontally. The dotted line in the figure indicates the position of the rope before you started shaking it. This is called the **rest position**. The highest points on the transverse wave are **crests** and the lowest points are **troughs**. The distance from the rest position to the crest is the wave's **amplitude (A)**. And the distance from one crest to the next crest is the wave's **wavelength (λ)**.

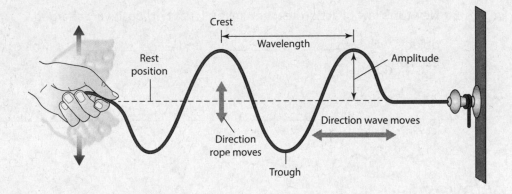

A wave's **frequency (*f*)** is the number of wave crests that pass a given point every second. The unit waves per second is more commonly known as Hertz (Hz). A wave's **speed**, or **velocity (v)**, denotes how far a wave travels every second. The unit for a wave's speed is meters per second (m/s). A wave's **period (T)** is how long it takes a wave to complete one full cycle.

Some of these wave variables have very specific mathematical relationships. For example, the relationship between the frequency (f) of the wave and the period (T) of the wave is represented by the following equation:

frequency = 1/period

or

$f = 1/T$

Knowing a wave's period allows you to calculate the wave's frequency. And, conversely, if you know the wave's frequency, you can calculate the wave's period.

When a wave passes from one medium to another, the frequency of the wave stays constant. In the case of waves of visible light, green light passing from air into glass remains green. However, its velocity decreases. You can see from the following equation that as the wave's velocity changes, its wavelength must change proportionately.

frequency = wave velocity/wavelength,

or

$f = v/\lambda$

In other words, if a wave's velocity is reduced by one-half, its wavelength must also be reduced by one half to maintain a constant frequency.

Longitudinal Waves

Longitudinal waves make the particles in a medium move parallel to the direction that the wave travels. A longitudinal wave traveling along a spring is shown in the following illustration. As the wave passes, the coils of the springs move closer together, then farther apart, and then return to their original positions.

Before a wave moves through the spring, the coils are the same distance apart. This is the resting position of the spring. The illustration shows that the wave produces regions in the spring where the coils are closer together **(compressions)** and regions where the coils are farther apart **(rarefactions)**.

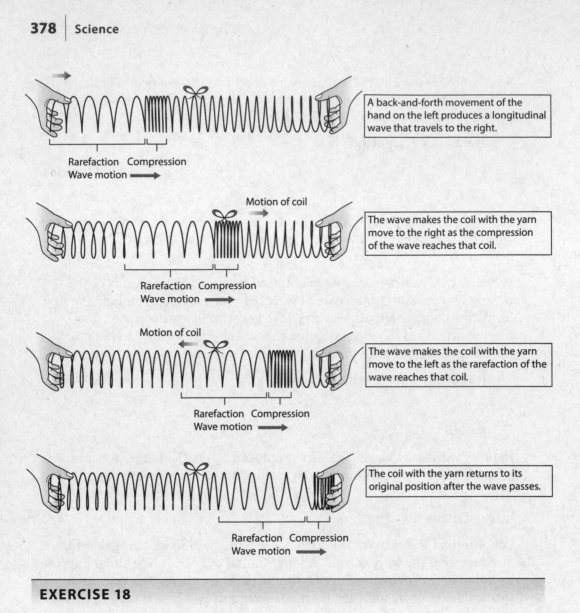

A back-and-forth movement of the hand on the left produces a longitudinal wave that travels to the right.

Rarefaction   Compression
Wave motion ➡

Motion of coil

The wave makes the coil with the yarn move to the right as the compression of the wave reaches that coil.

Rarefaction   Compression
Wave motion ➡

Motion of coil

The wave makes the coil with the yarn move to the left as the rarefaction of the wave reaches that coil.

Rarefaction   Compression
Wave motion ➡

The coil with the yarn returns to its original position after the wave passes.

Rarefaction   Compression
Wave motion ➡

EXERCISE 18

Mechanical Waves

Directions: Fill in the correct terms to complete the following sentences.

1. You tie a rope to a doorknob. Then, you shake the rope, causing a wave to travel from your hand to the door. The rope is the wave's

   _____.

2. The wave in the rope is perpendicular to the direction the wave travels; thus, the wave is a _____ wave.

3. If the rope is 2 meters long and the wave takes 1 second to travel to the door, the wave's speed is _____ m/s.

4. As a light wave traveling through air enters the glass of a window, its

_____ remains constant, but its _____
changes.

Answers are on page 564.

Waves and Digital Information

Computers are **digital** devices. They perform functions using information that has been transformed from a continuous wave to a code that uses only ones and zeroes. Such a code is referred to as a **binary** system, which is the basis of digital technology. Hard drives, CD recorders, and DV camcorders are digital devices. They read and write information digitally in a binary code.

VCRs, tape players, and record players, on the other hand, are **analog** devices. They record and play back data as a continuous wave that matches the source wave from one point to another, such as the sound wave of a singer's voice.

Advantages of Digital Information Systems

A great advantage of storing and transmitting information in digital form is that the information cannot be damaged, or corrupted, as easily as in analog storage systems. Often, information is stored on a magnetic medium, such as a magnetic tape, or on a disk drive. In analog systems, the information is stored as continuous waves of energy on the magnetic material. All portions of the wave are important to an analog device that is reading the information. Any device that reads an analog signal uses every part of the wave, even a corrupted portion, which it misreads as legitimate data. In other words, an analog reader cannot tell the difference between good data and unwanted noise. In addition, as the magnetic material ages, the strength of an analog signal fades, and the original information stored on the medium deteriorates. Even the smallest change can have a great impact on the quality of an analog signal.

Digital data is stored as a series of discrete pulses, not as a continuous wave. These pulses are read as binary data—the signal is either a 1 or a 0, with nothing in between. Therefore, even if there is some corruption of the signal, the high 1 portions and the low 0 portions of the signal can generally still be recognized by the reader.

Being able to make high-quality copies of data, such as from disk to disk, is another advantage of digital systems. Recall that digital reading devices can ignore moderate amounts of signal corruption and still translate information accurately. This also helps in the copying process. Digital copying requires only that the reader and writer recognize the discrete low and high signal pulses. This allows a reader/writer to make copies—and copies of copies—accurately, with no corruption between the generations. Making analog copies usually introduces corruption and signal weakening with each successive generation.

The following factors are also advantages to using digital systems.

- Improved technologies in design and manufacturing have made digital systems less costly than equivalent analog systems.

- Digital systems have very few moving parts. The lack of mechanical hardware reduces wear and delays eventual system failure.

- Digital information is easy to manipulate. For example, cutting and pasting with a word processor is easier than retyping an entire page on a typewriter. And completely reworking the sounds of a vocal recording is easy to do with digital information.

Recall that moderately corrupted digital information can be transferred without error. Corrupt digital signals may be cleaned up at repeater points along a transmission path as well as at the end points.

EXERCISE 19

Advantages of Digital Information Systems

Directions: Choose the *best* response for each question.

1. Much of a corrupted signal can be _____.

    A. ignored by an analog reader
    B. ignored by a digital reader
    C. corrected by an analog reader
    D. translated inaccurately by a digital reader

2. A digital signal is _____.

    A. a code made up of the values 0 and 1
    B. a code made up of the values 1 and 2
    C. transmitted as a continuous wave
    D. virtually impossible to corrupt

3. Copies of a digital CD can be made _____.

    A. using analog read/write systems
    B. repeatedly with minimum corruption
    C. repeatedly, but with increasing corruption with each generation
    D. using continuous digital waves

Write a short answer to the following item.

4. In your own words, summarize and explain three advantages of using digital information systems rather than analog systems.

Answers are on page 564.

Disadvantages of Digital Information Systems

Even with many advantages to digital information, there are some downsides. Digital media, such as hard drives and CDs, have short lives. Keeping and using digital information for long periods of time requires constant management. Corporations and larger organizations can afford special systems to maintain and protect their digital information. However, individuals have a harder problem protecting their digital information. Yet analog waves on a magnetic medium can last up to 30 years.

Another disadvantage of digital information is sampling. Sampling is part of the process of converting an analog signal, such as the sound waves of a musical instrument, into a digital signal of discrete on-off pulses. It is impossible to make a perfect digital copy of an analog signal. Some of the analog signal always will be lost. Even though modern high-quality sampling minimizes this issue, the output fidelity with the original input will never be perfect. This loss of original information is known as **sampling error**.

The translation of digital signals into usable information requires the communications system to be synchronized. This is similar to when you speak to another person. When you transmit a voice signal, the other person needs to understand where one word stops and the next word begins. Dealing with a seemingly continuous stream of on-off pulses, digital transmitters and receivers also need a system of communication where one piece of information stops and the next begins. Generally, this is not an issue with analog systems.

Digital communications require greater bandwidth than analog does to transmit the same information. **Bandwidth** refers to the amount of information that can be transmitted over a given connection per second.

If not backed up, digital information can be instantly lost in the case of a system failure. Analog information, stored on a magnetic tape for instance, is less susceptible to loss.

EXERCISE 20

Disadvantages of Digital Information Systems

Directions: List three disadvantages of using digital information systems.

1. _____

2. _____

3. _____

Answers are on page 564.

Electromagnetic Radiation—Waves or Particles?

The **electromagnetic (EM) spectrum** is the range of all types of EM radiation. Radiation is energy that travels and spreads out as it goes. The visible light that comes from a lamp in your house and the radio waves that come from a radio station are two types of electromagnetic radiation. As shown in the following figure, other types of EM radiation that make up the electromagnetic spectrum are microwaves, infrared light, ultraviolet light, X-rays and gamma rays.

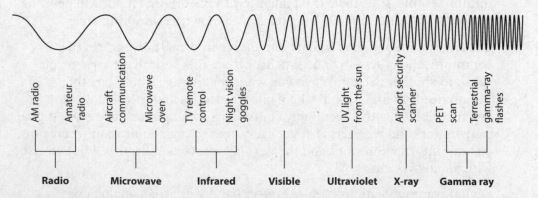

All EM radiation, including visible light, seems to behave as a wave of energy that can travel through a vacuum as well as through various media. It reflects, refracts, and diffracts, just like any other wave, as illustrated in the following diagrams.

Reflection occurs as a wave bounces off a barrier.

Refraction is the bending of a wave as it passes from one medium to another.

Diffraction is the bending of a wave as it passes through an opening or around a barrier.

In 1905, Albert Einstein proposed a new theory of light. He suggested that light is emitted from a source as tiny particles called **photons**. Many experiments have been performed that support the particle theory of light. One phenomenon that supports the particle theory of light is known as the **photoelectric effect**. Scientists have demonstrated that as light shines on a metal surface, electrons are emitted from the metal. When a photon of light with enough energy strikes the surface of the right type of metal and hits an electron in an atom, it knocks the electron away from the atom. This movement of electrons is an electric current. This is the principle behind modern photoelectric cells.

Other experiments on phenomena, such as diffraction, have shown that the wave theory of light apparently is also valid. This seems to present a dilemma. Scientists have conducted some experiments that suggest that light behaves as a wave. Other experiments indicate that light is a stream of particles. These two theories seem to conflict with each other. Scientists have finally decided that this wave-particle duality must be accepted as a perplexing fact. Light, as all forms of EM radiation, is more complex than being a simple wave or a simple stream of particles.

EXERCISE 21

Electromagnetic Radiation—Waves or Particles?

Directions: Choose the *best* answer to each question.

1. A particle of light is called a _____.

2. The photoelectric effect is evidence that light is a _____.

Write a short answer to the following item.

3. Summarize the photoelectric effect.

Answers are on page 564.

Effects of Electromagnetic Radiation

Recall that electromagnetic radiation extends through radio waves, microwaves, infrared light, visible light, ultraviolet light, X-rays, and gamma rays. Each has different properties. For example, radio waves have the longest wavelengths and lowest frequencies and contain the least energy of all EM wave types. Gamma rays have the shortest wavelengths and highest frequencies and are the most energetic of all EM wave types.

Radio waves are used to transmit information. Broadcast television, cell phones, and wireless networking use radio waves.

Microwaves are absorbed by certain molecules in liquids, such as water. Microwave ovens use this property to heat food. Low levels of microwave radiation are used in wi-fi communication but do not cause heating. Radar is another practical application of microwave radiation.

Infrared radiation is subdivided into three frequency ranges—far infrared, with the longest wavelengths; mid infrared; and near infrared, with the shortest wavelengths. The atmosphere blocks virtually all of the far infrared radiation from reaching the surface of Earth. Hot objects emit mid infrared radiation. The human body radiates mid infrared as body heat. Near infrared can be detected by some photographic films and by solid-state sensors for infrared photography.

Visible light is the most familiar form of the electromagnetic radiation. The sun emits vast amounts of energy as visible light. Visible light is the part of the electromagnetic spectrum to which the eye is the most sensitive. White light is perceived by the human brain when all visible wavelengths of light are viewed simultaneously. A prism can be used to split white light into its component visible colors.

The next shortest wavelength of electromagnetic radiation is **ultraviolet (UV)**. UV rays have a shorter wavelength than visible light, but longer than X-rays. The shortest wavelengths of UV are capable of ionizing atoms. This means that photons of high-energy UV can knock electrons off atoms in organisms, including atoms that make up the DNA of the organism. This can cause cells to malfunction or even mutate into cancers. Mid-range UV can break chemical bonds, making the molecules highly reactive. This can result in sunburn and skin cancer. The sun radiates about 10 percent of its energy as UV. The very short wavelengths of UV could destroy most life on Earth. However, the atmosphere, including the ozone layer, absorbs most of this dangerous radiation.

The next shortest wavelength of electromagnetic radiation is **X-rays.** Like short-wavelength UV, X-rays can ionize atoms. X-rays can pass through many substances and can be used to see through some objects. This property is used in medicine to make diagnostic images, a process known as **radiography**.

The shortest wavelength of electromagnetic radiation is **gamma rays.** Like short-wavelength UV and X-rays, gamma rays are highly ionizing. Gamma-ray detection is used in astronomy to study high-energy objects in space. This radiation is also used to sterilize food and seeds and can be used in medicine to do diagnostic imaging such as PET scans.

EXERCISE 22

Effects of Electromagnetic Radiation

Directions: Choose the *best* answer for each question.

1. Which EM waves are in the correct sequence?

    A. gamma rays, radio waves, visible light
    B. gamma rays, visible light, X-rays
    C. radio waves, visible light, microwaves
    D. X-rays, ultraviolet, visible light

2. Gamma rays can _____.

    A. be released by the skin as body heat
    B. be used in radar systems
    C. ionize DNA
    D. transmit digital information

Write a short answer to the following item.

3. Compare the wavelength of an electromagnetic wave and its ionizing ability. Explain your answer with reference to the waves' energy levels.

Answers are on page 564.

Social Studies

The Social Studies Test

The Social Studies section of the GED® test measures your knowledge of key social studies topics and how well you are able to analyze and interpret documents and other social studies information. There are approximately 45 questions on the Social Studies test, and you will have 90 minutes to complete the entire test, including 25 minutes for writing an extended response (essay). Half of the questions focus on U.S. government and civics. The rest cover U.S. history, world history, economics, and geography.

Questions on the Social Studies test may ask about the information in a short passage, a map, a graph, a table, or some other graphic presentation of social studies data. Sometimes two or three questions will refer to the same passage, graph, or table.

Most Social Studies questions are multiple-choice with four answer choices. Others use interactive formats such as drag and drop, fill-in-the-blank, and drop-down. See "Introducing the GED® Test" at the start of this book for an explanation and samples of these formats.

The Social Studies Review

The following section of this book presents a comprehensive review of the knowledge that is tested on the Social Studies test. Each main topic is followed by a short exercise to measure how well you have mastered that subject. Answers for all of the exercises in this section are located in the Exercise Answer Key section at the back of this book.

CHAPTER 1

Civics and Government

Foundations of American Democracy

A government is a set of institutions through which a society makes and enforces public policies. Governments are composed of individuals, usually either elected or appointed, who have various responsibilities, from creating and enforcing laws to setting public policy on issues such as taxation, health care, and defense. In addition, a government establishes and maintains relationships with other nations through diplomacy and sometimes through conflict. The scope of a government's authority can be vast and far-reaching.

Our Political Heritage

The foundations of the government of the United States can be traced to the political ideas of ancient Greece and Rome. The ancient Greeks in classical Athens developed the idea of a **direct democracy**, a government in which all eligible citizens had a say in the government by voting. The ancient Roman republic was a very limited **representative democracy** in which bodies of eligible citizens elected some officials to act on their behalf. Both of these ideas were incorporated into the governing institutions of early colonial America. In New England, town meetings were a form of direct democracy in which every resident had the right to speak. The Virginia colony was a representative democracy in which eligible citizens elected representatives to a legislature called the House of Burgesses.

Early American colonists also drew on their knowledge and experience of English laws and institutions to form their colonial governments. The first English settlers in North America brought knowledge of a political system that had been in place in England for centuries. Some key documents in English legal history are summarized in the following chart.

| Key Documents in English History That Influenced American Government ||
Name of Document	What It Did
Magna Carta (1215)	Guaranteed fundamental rights to individuals, such as trial by jury and due process of law (protection against a government's arbitrarily taking a person's life, liberty, or property)
Petition of Right (Magna Carta 1215)	Limited the power of the king; government could no longer imprison or punish individuals unless they had broken the law; government could not impose martial law in peacetime or force soldiers to be housed by citizens without the citizens' consent
English Bill of Rights (1689)	Prevented potential abuses of power by the monarchy; guaranteed an individual's right to a fair trial, to petition the government, to bear arms, and to not be subject to cruel punishment; established free parliamentary elections

The concept of an **ordered government** provided the early English colonists with the framework for an ordered society, like the one they had left in England. The colonists also eventually wanted to institute a **limited government**, a government that was restricted in what it could do. By limiting a government's power, the colonists emphasized that an individual has certain rights that no government can take away.

One of the earliest colonial governing documents was the **Mayflower Compact**, which the English colonists aboard the ship *Mayflower* created on November 11, 1620. By signing the compact, or agreement, the colonists agreed to establish a government for the newly created Plymouth colony and to obey its laws.

EXERCISE 1

Foundations of American Democracy

Directions: Choose the *best* answer to each of the following questions.

1. Which of the following is an example of a direct democracy?

    A. Congresspersons in the House of Representatives debating a bill
    B. A forum in which people can ask questions of a presidential candidate
    C. School board members voting on whether or not to buy new textbooks
    D. Town residents voting on whether or not to institute a sales tax on food

2. What important concept is represented by the Petition of Right?

    A. People are protected from unjust actions by a government.
    B. A government has the duty to protect all of its citizens.
    C. All people can participate in choosing their government.
    D. The right to petition is the most important right of the people.

Answers are on page 565.

The Influence of the Enlightenment

By the middle of the eighteenth century, tensions began to grow between the American colonists and the English government. The colonists believed their rights as English citizens were being denied, as the king and Parliament imposed increasingly strict laws within the colonies. Colonial leaders recognized that something needed to be done. Eventually, the colonists decided to separate from the British empire, and in 1775, Thomas Jefferson wrote the **Declaration of Independence**.

Jefferson and other American colonists derived many of their political ideas from a seventeenth-century European intellectual movement called the Enlightenment. One major Enlightenment thinker was the English philosopher **John Locke**, who wrote that all men were born with **natural rights** to life, liberty, and property and that no government could take away those rights. Locke also believed that citizens gave governments the power to rule in order to protect these natural rights. Further, Locke believed that citizens could change a government or revolt against it when it failed to protect the rights of its citizens.

Two French Enlightenment thinkers also influenced Jefferson. **Jean-Jacques Rousseau** introduced the idea that a **social contract** exists between a government and its people. According to this idea, the people promise to obey the government as long as the government provides safety and justice in administering the laws. Rousseau believed revolution is justified when a government breaks that contract by failing to serve the needs of the people. **Baron de Montesquieu** wrote that for a government to be truly beneficial for the people, its power needs to be divided among more than one branch. He also believed that a government should be organized in a way that best benefits its citizens.

Finally, the writings of the English judge and politician **William Blackstone** also helped shape Jefferson's ideas. Blackstone's writings on the rights of Englishmen under the British Constitution include the idea of **unalienable rights**, a concept that appears in the Declaration of Independence.

EXERCISE 2

The Influence of the Enlightenment

Directions: Match each passage from the Declaration of Independence to the correct Enlightenment thinker.

_____ **1.** John Locke

A. "whenever any form of government becomes destructive to these ends, it is the right of the people to alter or to abolish it, and to institute new government . . . "

_____ **2.** William Blackstone

B. "to institute new government, laying its foundation on such principles and organizing its powers in such form, as to them shall seem most likely to effect their safety and happiness . . ."

_____ **3.** Jean-Jacques Rousseau

C. "that among these are Life, Liberty and the Pursuit of Happiness."

_____ **4.** Baron de Montesquieu

D. "that all men . . . are endowed by their creator with certain unalienable Rights . . ."

5. Describe the ideas of the social contract and natural rights that helped shape the Declaration of Independence.

_____

_____

_____

Answers are on page 565.

Creating a New Government

After declaring their independence from the British empire, the American colonies adopted the **Articles of Confederation** on November 15, 1777. The articles created a loose confederation of 13 states that were sovereign entities with greater power than that of the weak, central government. This preference for a weak central government reflected the colonists' fear of a strong central authority.

Under the authority of the Articles, the states created a national congress, a **unicameral**, or single-house, legislative body consisting of delegates from each of the states. There was no president or chief executive. Each state had one vote in Congress, and, in most cases, decisions were made based on majority rule. However, Congress was limited in its powers. For example, Congress had no power to levy taxes and could only request that the individual states raise revenue to cover their share of national expenses. The central government had to rely on the states' allocating funds from their treasuries to pay for its needs. In addition, the central government had no control over foreign commerce, and while it could pass laws, it could not force states to comply with those laws. Finally, any amendments to the Articles of Confederation had to be approved unanimously by all the states.

It soon became apparent that the Articles were not an adequate foundation for the new government. After several years, delegates were chosen to meet in Philadelphia to revise the Articles. However, it soon became clear to the delegates that a new governing document was necessary. The new document, now known as the United States Constitution, established the framework for a new government that would be divided into three distinct branches:

- **Executive branch:** Provides leadership and enforces laws
- **Legislative branch:** Makes laws for the nation
- **Judicial branch:** Explains and interprets laws

In addition, the legislative branch would be **bicameral**—that is, it would have two houses, the Senate and the House of Representatives. Each state would have two senators, and the numbers of representatives each state would send to the House was based on that state's population. To ensure protection of individual freedoms, a **Bill of Rights** was added to the Constitution soon after its ratification.

EXERCISE 3

Creating a New Government

Directions: Fill in the following Venn diagram with phrases from the list to show the differences and similarities between the Articles of Confederation and the United States Constitution. (Note: On the real GED test, you will click on the phrases and "drag" them into position on the diagram.)

The Articles of Confederation   vs.   The U.S. Constitution

- Outlines powers and duties of Congress
- No president
- Bicameral legislature
- Bill of Rights
- President
- Only states have power to tax
- Unicameral legislature
- Outlines three-branch federal government

Answers are on page 565.

The Structure and Design of the U.S. Government

The Constitution of the United States is the law of the land. The document sets out the basic principles upon which our government is organized and operates. It also states how our leaders are to be elected and how they are to govern. Most importantly, the Constitution outlines what authority the government does and does not have and describes the basic rights that all Americans are entitled to.

The Constitution

The Constitution is introduced by the Preamble and is then divided into seven numbered sections called articles, as listed here:

Preamble—States the purpose of the Constitution
Article I—Creates the legislative branch
Article II—Creates the executive branch
Article III—Creates the judicial branch
Article IV—Relations among the states
Article V—Amending the Constitution
Article VI—National debt, supremacy of national law, oaths of office
Article VII—Ratifying the Constitution

The Six Basic Principles

The Constitution is built around six basic principles.

Principle	What It Means
1. Popular sovereignty	The people are the legitimate and final source of a government's authority—the government answers to the people.
2. Limited government	Government may do ONLY what the people have directed it to do.
3. Separation of powers	Government power is divided among three equal branches: • Legislative: makes laws • Executive: carries out laws • Judicial: interprets laws
4. Checks and balances	Each branch limits the powers of the other two branches: • Executive: may veto laws passed by Congress; has power to appoint federal judges • Legislative: has power to impeach chief executive (the president) and federal judges • Judicial: may review actions of the executive and legislative branches; decides the constitutionality of actions taken by the executive and legislative branches

Principle	What It Means
5. Judicial review	Courts have the power to determine the constitutionality of governmental actions.
6. Federalism	Governmental power is divided between national and state governments.

EXERCISE 4

The Six Basic Principles

Directions: Answer the following questions.

1. What is judicial review, and why is it important to the U.S. government?

   _____

   _____

2. Explain the principles of popular sovereignty and limited government.

   _____

   _____

3. Explain the meaning of the term "checks and balances."

   _____

   _____

Answers are on page 566.

The Three Branches of the Federal Government

The framers of the Constitution wanted to create a government that did not allow one person or one institution to have too much control. The framers gave each of the three separate branches its own responsibilities while also allowing for the three branches to work together to govern the nation effectively. Each branch may use its powers to check, or restrain, the powers of the other two branches.

The three branches of government are the executive, the legislative, and the judicial. The **executive branch** consists of the president, the vice president, and the president's cabinet. The **legislative branch** consists of the Senate and the House of Representatives. Finally, the **judicial branch** consists of the Supreme Court, which is the highest court in the land, and other federal courts.

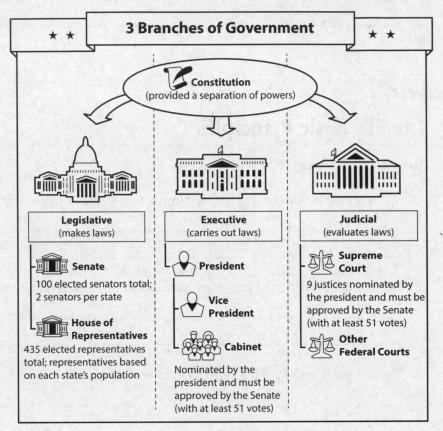

Source: http://kids.usa.gov/three-branches-of-government/index.shtml

EXERCISE 5

The Three Branches of the Federal Government

Directions: Choose the *best* answer to the following questions.

1. Members of the Cabinet are directly responsible to

   A. Congress
   B. the Senate
   C. the Supreme Court
   D. the president

2. Which of these *best* illustrates how the system of checks and balances works?

    A. George Washington sent the army to stop a revolt by Pennsylvania farmers.
    B. South Carolina and other Southern states seceded from the Union.
    C. President Eisenhower ordered federal troops to enforce school integration in Arkansas.
    D. The Senate approved the appointment of Sonia Sotomayor to the Supreme Court.

3. Which of the following is a responsibility of the Senate?

    A. appointing members of the electoral college
    B. approving the president's cabinet nominees
    C. creating a congressional committee system
    D. forwarding nominations for the president's cabinet

Answers are on page 566.

Federalism and the Concurrent Powers

Federalism is one of the most important ideas contained in the Constitution, even though the word never appears in the document. Considered a radical idea at the time of the Constitution's ratification, federalism remains one of the most enduring principles of American government. **Federalism** is the sharing of power between national and state governments. The relationship between national and state governments and the proper role of each in governing the nation are still debated today.

Some powers are exclusive to the federal government. These include the power to establish foreign policy and to declare war, to coin money, and to regulate interstate and foreign trade.

Under the Tenth Amendment, all powers not granted to the federal government or prohibited to the states are left to the states or the people. Such powers include the right to enact laws affecting family relations such as marriages and divorces, the right to regulate commerce that takes place within a state's borders, and the right to provide for the public safety through local law enforcement. State governments are also responsible for establishing local governments and schools as well as conducting elections.

Although both federal and state governments have powers that are designated exclusively for each, they also exercise **concurrent powers**, that is, powers that are shared between the two. Concurrent powers include the power to make and enforce laws, to establish courts, to borrow money, to collect taxes, and to build infrastructure such as roads. Concurrent powers are integral to the success of federalism and make it possible for our federal system of government to function effectively.

EXERCISE 6

Federalism and the Concurrent Powers

Directions: Fill in the Venn diagram with phrases from the list to show the different powers assigned to the federal and state governments and the powers they share. (Note: On the real GED test, you will click on the phrases and "drag" them into position on the diagram.)

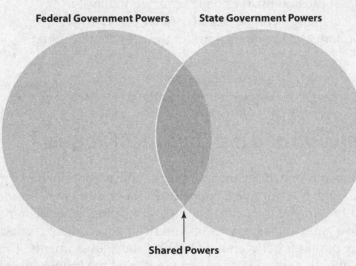

Federal Government Powers   **State Government Powers**

Shared Powers

- Coin money
- Establish courts
- Borrow money
- Establish local government
- Establish schools
- Build roads
- Declare war
- Regulate trade within states
- Collect taxes
- Regulate interstate and foreign trade
- Enact and enforce laws
- Conduct elections
- Maintain local law enforcement
- Establish foreign policy

Answers are on page 566.

The Bill of Rights and Civil Liberties

The first ten amendments to the U.S. Constitution, known collectively as the **Bill of Rights**, define the rights and liberties of the nation's citizens. The Bill of Rights is considered to be one of the landmark achievements in American history.

The Bill of Rights	
Amendment	**What It Does**
First Amendment	establishes freedom of religion, speech, press, assembly, and petition
Second Amendment	establishes the right to keep and bear arms in order to maintain a well-regulated militia
Third Amendment	prohibits quartering of soldiers
Fourth Amendment	establishes freedom from unreasonable searches and seizures
Fifth Amendment	establishes the right to due process of law, freedom from self-incrimination and double jeopardy, protection of private property
Sixth Amendment	enumerates the rights of accused persons—for example, right to a speedy and public trial, right to confront one's accuser, right to legal counsel
Seventh Amendment	establishes the right of trial by jury in civil cases
Eighth Amendment	establishes freedom from excessive bail and from cruel and unusual punishment
Ninth Amendment	tells of other rights of the people
Tenth Amendment	reserves to the states or the people any powers not assigned to the federal government

Over time, as social conditions changed and political ideas evolved, additional amendments have been added to the Constitution to meet these changing needs. These amendments effected such far-reaching changes as ending slavery; creating national guarantees of due process and individual rights; granting the vote to women, African Americans, and citizens age 18 and up; providing for the direct popular election of senators; and limiting the length of presidential terms.

Later Amendments to the Constitution	
Amendment	**What It Does**
Eleventh Amendment	prohibits federal courts from hearing lawsuits brought against states by citizens of another state
Twelth Amendment	specifies the procedure for electing the president and vice president
Thirteenth Amendment	abolishes slavery
Fourteenth Amendment	defines citizenship; requires the states to provide equal protection under the law to all persons (not only to citizens) within their jurisdictions
Fifteenth Amendment	grants voting rights regardless of "race, color, or previous condition of servitude"
Sixteenth Amendment	institutes national income tax
Seventeenth Amendment	provides for the election of senators by popular vote
Eighteenth Amendment	prohibits the production, transport, or sale of liquor (Prohibition)
Nineteenth Amendment	establishes women's suffrage
Twentieth Amendment	changes the dates of terms of office for the president, vice president, and members of Congress
Twenty-first Amendment	repeals Prohibition
Twenty-second Amendment	establishes term limits for the presidency
Twenty-third Amendment	grants suffrage in federal elections to residents of Washington, D.C.
Twenty-fourth Amendment	prohibits poll taxes (requiring citizens to pay a tax in order to vote)
Twenty-fifth Amendment	provides procedures for presidential succession
Twenty-sixth Amendment	grants suffrage to citizens 18 years old and older
Twenty-seventh Amendment	limits congressional pay raises

The Bill of Rights deals with two important areas of freedom: civil rights and civil liberties. **Civil rights** are those freedoms that every citizen has, regardless of sex, race, religion, or national origin. For example, the right to vote and the right to a jury trial are examples of civil rights. **Civil liberties** are the rights of the people to do or say things that are not illegal. In other words, civil liberties are guarantees of the safety of the people, their opinions, and their property from arbitrary actions by the government. Examples of civil liberties include freedom of religion, speech, press, and assembly.

EXERCISE 7

The Bill of Rights and Civil Liberties

Directions: Choose the *best* answer to the following questions.

1. Which of the following *best* describes why amendments have been added to the Constitution over time?

   A. to check the power of the Supreme Court and its rulings
   B. to preserve the federal system of government and its power
   C. to allow government to meet the changing needs of society
   D. to allow for the expansion of the states' powers

2. Which of the following is an example of a civil liberty that is explicitly protected by the Constitution?

   A. the freedom to practice any religion
   B. the freedom of women to serve in the military
   C. the right of children of undocumented immigrants to attend public schools
   D. the right to drive a car

3. Read the following excerpt from the Fourth Amendment to the U.S. Constitution:

   "no warrants shall issue, but upon probable cause . . . and particularly describing the place to be searched, and the persons or things to be seized."

   This excerpt is addressing what issue?

   A. powers granted to the states
   B. separation of powers
   C. concurrent powers
   D. limits on governmental power

Answers are on page 567.

The Expansion of Rights

Under Chief Justice Earl Warren (1953–1969), the Supreme Court rendered a number of important decisions that expanded the rights of individuals as well as the power of the federal government to enforce civil rights legislation. The Supreme Court has rarely exercised as much power to shape American culture, and Earl Warren is remembered as one of the most influential Supreme Court justices in American history. His court is sometimes described as an "activist" court because of the changes brought about by its decisions.

Here is a brief summary of some landmark decisions made by the Supreme Court in the area of civil rights under Chief Justice Warren and in later years.

An Activist Court: Landmark Supreme Court Cases for Civil Rights	
Supreme Court Case	**Significance**
Brown v. Board of Education (1954)	Strikes down "separate but equal" doctrine adopted in an earlier case called *Plessy v. Ferguson*, which had been used to justify racial segregation, especially in the area of education
Gideon v. Wainwright (1963)	Requires state courts, under the Fourteenth Amendment, to provide counsel in criminal cases to represent defendants who cannot afford attorneys
Reynolds v. Sims (1964)	Requires electoral districts to be of as equal population as mathematically possible, so as to ensure equal protection
Miranda v. Arizona (1966)	Requires police to advise criminal suspects of their Constitutional rights to remain silent, to consult a lawyer, and to have a lawyer appointed if the suspect is indigent
Roe v. Wade (1973)	Strikes down laws prohibiting abortion
Frontiero v. Richardson (1973)	Prohibits the U.S. military from discriminating on the basis of gender in the granting of benefits to military families
Romer v. Evans (1996)	Declares that a Colorado state constitutional amendment disqualifying homosexuals from obtaining protections under the law is a violation of the Fourteenth Amendment

EXERCISE 8

The Expansion of Rights

Directions: Choose the *best* answer to each of the following questions.

1. The Fourteenth Amendment provides that any state shall not "deprive any person of life, liberty, or property, without due process of law; nor deny to any person within its jurisdiction the equal protections of the laws." Which of the following best expresses the effect of this amendment on the U.S. justice system?

   A. The process of amending the Constitution became slower and more complex.
   B. States were required to ensure that all persons within their jurisdiction receive equal treatment under the law.
   C. Every citizen gained an absolute right to freedom of speech and assembly.
   D. The power of the federal government was sharply reduced.

2. Why was the Warren Court considered an "activist" court?

   A. because of its reluctance to overturn state laws
   B. because of its insistence on restricting freedom of speech
   C. because of its expansion of individual rights
   D. because of its refusal to reconsider the *Plessy v. Ferguson* case

3. Which of the following statements best summarizes the chart of Landmark Supreme Court Cases?

   A. Many of the Supreme Court's rulings have expanded civil rights and liberties to apply to groups not previously protected.
   B. The Supreme Court has issued many conservative rulings that have helped maintain the civil liberties of select groups.
   C. The Supreme Court has taken a more active role in upholding the constitutionality of the existing laws of the land.
   D. The Supreme Court does not make rulings that challenge the constitutionality of current laws.

Answers are on page 567.

Politics in Action

Political Parties and the Two-Party System

A **political party** is a group of persons who share common views and ideology and who seek to control government. They do so by winning elections and holding political offices. Political parties greatly influence American politics by defining political issues and national priorities and by working to resolve disputes. Today the United States has a mostly **two-party system**, consisting of **Republicans** and **Democrats**. Most of our political leaders come from one of these parties. Nevertheless, American political history has seen the rise and fall of **third parties** that have often influenced the local and national political landscape even though they may not have won major elections. For example, third-party candidates sometimes change an election's outcome by attracting votes that otherwise would have gone to one of the dominant parties or by introducing new concerns and platforms into election discourse.

One reason that a two-party system continues to dominate American politics today is that the organizations of the Republican and Democratic parties are very large and frequently outspend and overshadow any third-party contenders in an election. At times, both parties have worked to ensure that third parties remain weak. For instance, in some states, election laws support the two-party system by making it very difficult to register a third-party candidate on a ballot.

EXERCISE 9

Political Parties and the Two-Party System

Directions: Choose the *best* answer to the following questions.

1. What is the major role of political parties in the United States?

    A. to protect the American public from corrupt public officials
    B. to ensure that free and honest elections are held
    C. to nominate candidates for public office and conduct campaigns
    D. to meet constitutional requirements for choosing the president

2. Which of the following *best* summarizes the state of the two-party system in the United States?

    A. The growing weakness of both parties has opened the way for stronger third parties to emerge.
    B. Both parties have a great deal of control over the American political process.
    C. Most Americans are tired of the two-party system and are looking for alternatives to the election process.
    D. Today one of the two parties has finally triumphed over the other.

Answers are on page 567.

The Election Process

An election is a formal decision-making process by which a population chooses an individual to hold public office. In the United States, elections have been the usual mechanism by which modern representative democracy has operated since the colonial era. Elections fill offices in the legislature, sometimes in the executive and judiciary, and in regional and local government.

According to the Constitution, **presidential elections** are held once every four years. However, the process of picking a presidential candidate gets under way long before election day in November. Politicians from both major and minor political parties and independent politicians begin to raise money and campaign many months or years before the general presidential election. Within each political party, politicians compete against each other during a **primary** process to determine who will be nominated as that party's candidate in the election. This process is a contest that often produces or reinforces factions within political parties. These divisions affect the policy stances and agendas of the politicians running for nomination as they attempt to garner the support of party leaders and activists.

As part of this process, states hold primaries and caucuses between late January and early June during an election year. **Primaries** are elections in which party members vote to determine who will be the party's candidate. **Caucuses** consist of small groups of party members who gather together to decide whom they want to support as the party's candidate. A few states hold caucuses, while most states hold primary elections. These events are the voters' first chance to participate in selecting the next president.

In both primaries and caucuses, party members choose **delegates** committed to support particular candidates. These delegates attend national party conventions held later in the summer. Each state gets a certain number of delegates, depending on its population. At the conventions, the candidate with the most delegate votes becomes the party's candidate for the general election.

On election day, people go to the polls to vote. However, when voting for president, each voter is really casting a ballot for an elector who is committed to support a particular candidate. The electors, who are chosen by each state, make up the **Electoral College**. They are the group of people who officially elect the president and vice president. Each state has as many votes in the Electoral College as it has senators and members of the House of Representatives. The Electoral College meets in December to record its members' votes and send the results to the Senate. When Congress meets in January, the current vice president of the United States announces the results to the Senate. This announcement is the official moment at which the president and vice president are elected.

EXERCISE 10

The Election Process

Directions: For each blank, fill in a definition.

1. caucus _____

2. primary _____

3. Electoral College _____

4. candidate _____

5. delegate _____

Answers are on page 567.

Making Public Policy

It is Congress's duty to make laws for the nation. However, making laws and setting policy is not a simple process. When preparing legislation, members of both the House of Representatives and the Senate meet and debate the issue under consideration. For a bill to become law, it must be passed by both the House and the Senate. Often the House and the Senate will pass different versions of a bill. The differences must then by reconciled by a committee of senators and representatives.

Legislative proposals take various forms, which are summarized in the following table:

Forms of Legislation	
Type	**What It Is/Does**
Bill	Can be public or private: public bills affect the general public or classes of citizens, while a private bill affects an individual or specific group.
Joint resolution	Can originate in the House or Senate; like a bill, it requires the president's approval before it can become law.
Concurrent resolution	Must be voted on by both bodies but does not need the president's approval and does not carry the force of law; it is typically used to regulate Congress's internal affairs.
Simple resolution	Addresses a matter affecting either the House or the Senate and needs to pass only in the body it affects; it is not presented to the president and does not carry the force of law.

After a bill is debated and agreed upon, it goes to the president for approval. The president has a few options when deciding whether or not to sign a bill into law. The president can **pass** the bill, which means he or she signs it. If the president chooses not to sign the bill while Congress remains in session, the bill still becomes a law, as if it had been signed. The president can **veto** a bill, in which case the bill dies or goes back to Congress. Congress can revise a vetoed bill and send it back for the president's signature, or they can vote by a two-thirds majority to override the president's veto and enact the bill into law without his or her signature. The president can also use a **pocket veto**. A pocket veto results when, after receiving a bill, the president neither signs it nor returns it to Congress within 10 days. If Congress has recessed within the 10-day signing period, the bill dies.

When Congress and the president are from different political parties, coming to an agreement on legislation can be difficult. **Gridlock** may result if neither party is willing to compromise and no legislation is enacted.

Government Agencies

In addition to the three branches of government, there are a number of federal agencies that oversee everything from the national parks to the space program to education and health policy. These agencies are sometimes called the "headless fourth branch" of the government, because the Constitution does not explicitly establish them. Most of these agencies are considered part of the executive branch. Although the president usually appoints the head of each agency, each agency has a certain degree of autonomy from the executive branch.

In carrying out their duties, government agencies have the power to legislate by issuing regulations, resolving disputes, and enforcing laws that are subject to that agency's authority. Examples of some government agencies include the Federal Trade Commission (FTC), the Federal Communications Commission (FCC), and the National Labor Relations Board (NLRB). Other agencies at work in the federal government include cabinet-level departments such as the Department of Energy (DOE) or the Internal Revenue Service (IRS).

EXERCISE 11

Government Agencies

Directions: Answer the following questions.

1. The job of most federal agencies is to carry out the laws. This makes them part of which branch of the government?

   A. legislative
   B. executive
   C. judicial
   D. state

2. Which of the following *best* describes the legislative power of a government agency?

   A. The Department of Energy appoints a new department head.
   B. The Internal Revenue Service passes a new tax law.
   C. The Federal Trade Commission enforces a consumer protection law.
   D. The Federal Communications Commission issues a court decision.

Answers are on page 568.

Interest Groups

Interest groups are some of the busiest groups working within the political process. Also known as advocacy groups, **lobbies**, **pressure groups**, or **special interests**, these organizations work to change or promote public policy. The number of interest groups in the United States has increased rapidly over the last several decades. One of the reasons for the increase in the number of groups has been the development of sophisticated technology that makes it easier for groups to make their voices heard in Washington.

There are a number of ways in which an interest group can influence public policy:

- **Lobbying:** Lobbyists are people who represent organized groups; they can be paid lobbyists or volunteers. The primary purpose of a lobbyist is to influence members of Congress. However, lobbyists can also help Congress by providing information, by helping with and creating political strategy for members of Congress, and by being a source of ideas. Lobbying can persuade legislators to support a certain policy. Sometimes the policy promoted by lobbyists benefits a broad section of the public. But other times, lobbyists may promote a policy that benefits only a few and may even harm the interests of other people. Lobbyists have been known to sway a member of Congress's position, but they are often most effective in working with members who already support that lobbyist's group.

- **Electioneering:** For interest groups, electioneering consists mainly of aiding candidates financially. Political action committees (**PACs**) are significant forces in electioneering. These groups solicit funds from their members to support particular candidates or political campaigns. The number of PACs has grown rapidly in recent years.

- **Litigation:** If interest groups fail to change policy in Congress, they sometimes go to court to try to get specific rulings. Environmental groups and civil rights groups have been particularly successful in litigation. In litigation, interest groups often file an *amicus curiae* **brief**, or "friend of the court" brief, that supports a particular side of a case. Another alternative is to file a **class-action suit** in which groups or individuals with similar complaints combine their individual suits into a single lawsuit. Class-action suits have been filed against tobacco companies, large retailers, communications companies, and oil companies.

- **Going public:** Many interest groups work to influence legislators by shaping public opinion in their favor. Some groups spend large sums of money on public-relations campaigns in order to gain exposure and the support of the American public.

Interest Groups

Directions: Answer the following questions.

1. What are *amicus curiae* briefs?

   A. written explanations by a judge for a court decision
   B. lawsuits undertaken by interest groups in an effort to influence policy
   C. written arguments to a court in support of one side in a legal case
   D. lawsuits brought by several plaintiffs on a specific issue

2. What is the value of public opinion to interest groups?

3. Explain briefly why lobbying is both a positive and a negative force in American politics.

Answers are on page 568.

CHAPTER 2

United States History

This chapter highlights some of the most important events in United States history, from European exploration to the present.

The Making of a New World

The Italian explorer **Christopher Columbus**, sailing on behalf of Spain, is often considered to have been the first European to reach the Americas. However, many historians note that Vikings from Scandinavia, led by **Leif Ericson**, landed on the shores of North America more than 400 years before Columbus reached the New World. Their arrival at what is now Newfoundland, Canada, makes them the very first European explorers of North America.

When Columbus set sail in 1492 from Spain, he was searching for a shorter route to the spices and riches of the East Indies. Unlike other explorers who had sailed to the east and around the coast of Africa to reach their destination, Columbus believed that by sailing west, he could reach his destination more directly. Sailing on the uncharted waters of the Atlantic Ocean, he eventually landed on a small island in what is now the Bahamas. Columbus died believing he had found the route to the East Indies; instead, he opened the way for new explorations in the Americas.

Over the course of the early sixteenth century, the European nations of Britain, France, the Netherlands, and Spain all sent ships and men to North America. With each new voyage and exploration, parts of the North American continent, though already inhabited by native peoples, were claimed by different nations. Under the Spanish flag, **Hernando de Soto** explored the Mississippi River, and **Francisco Vasquez de Coronado** claimed for Spain what is now the southwestern region of the United States. For France, **Jacques Cartier** explored the eastern region of Canada and the St. Lawrence River. **Henry Hudson's** voyages for the Netherlands took him to the far north of Canada. Finally, Englishman **John Cabot** sailed to the areas now known as Nova Scotia and Newfoundland. Over time, the Spanish would establish a vast empire encompassing parts of what is now the southeastern and southwestern United States as well as Mexico and Latin America. The French concentrated their explorations and settlements in what is now Canada. The British claimed areas along the Atlantic coast between the Spanish and French.

EXERCISE 1

The Making of a New World

Directions: Using the map, choose the *best* answer for each of the following questions.

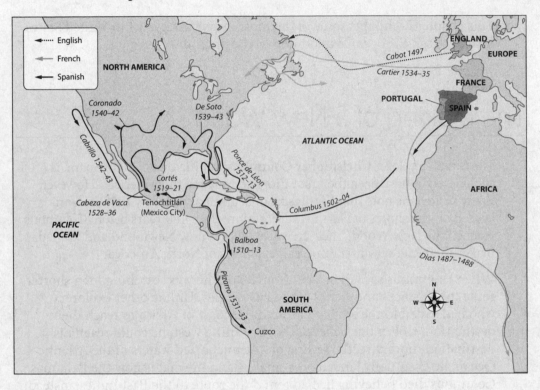

1. Which of the following statements *best* describes what is shown on the map?

   A. The Spanish traveled the furthest into North America.
   B. The French were the only Europeans to explore the area around Newfoundland.
   C. The British started their explorations in Canada but soon moved to the West Indies.
   D. The majority of explorers voyaging to the New World were from France and Britain.

2. Which of the following would be the *best* title for this map?

   A. The British Arrive: The Early Voyages of John Cabot
   B. Voyages of Discovery: European Exploration of the Americas
   C. Building an Empire: Spanish Discovery in North America
   D. The Beginnings of New France: The French in North America

Answers are on page 568.

The 13 Colonies

The British were one of the most important colonizers of North America; for Britain, the English colonies were important economic resources.

British colonization of North America began in earnest in 1607 with the establishment of **Jamestown** in the colony of Virginia. In 1619, that settlement received the first slaves brought from Africa; they were to be used for labor in the colony. By 1733, when they established the colony of Georgia, the British had secured control of most of the Atlantic seaboard; in the process, they also established a number of growing commercial centers.

The British established three types of colonies in North America.

- **Charter colonies**, such as Virginia and Connecticut, were created through joint-stock companies that in turn established their own governments. These governments were independent of the Crown.

- **Proprietary colonies** were created through land grants given to individuals by the Crown in return for political or financial favors. These colonies, such as Maryland and Pennsylvania, had governments headed by a royal governor who reported to the king.

- **Royal colonies** were owned directly by the Crown. Virginia, Massachusetts, and New York would all eventually become royal colonies.

The settling of North America by the British was not without consequences. Relations with Native Americans were often tense, in part because of the vast cultural differences between the Europeans and Native Americans and also because the colonists brought with them diseases to which Native Americans had no resistance. Some of these diseases decimated entire Native American tribes. Overall, the British were more interested in promoting settlement and development in North America than in trading with Native Americans, as the French did.

The rich natural resources found in North America allowed the colonies to prosper. More land for farming meant more food. Farmers in the Southern colonies also produced cash crops such as tobacco, rice, and cotton. Exports of these products, as well as transshipment of molasses (sugar) from the West Indies to Europe, brought wealth to merchants in the coastal towns. The abundance of trees made possible the production of lumber and pine tar, used to build boats. In addition, fur trading and fishing played important roles in the New England colonies.

By the early 1750s, Britain had successfully established 13 colonies along the eastern seaboard of North America. (See map.) With the population in these colonies increasing, many colonists looked to the west, beyond the Appalachian Mountains, for new areas to settle. However, the French laid claim to this land and refused to allow any British settlement. In 1754, hostilities broke out between the British and the French in what became known as the **French and Indian War** in the colonies and the **Seven Years'**

War in Europe. The British would go on to defeat the French in 1763. The subsequent peace treaty, known as the **Treaty of Paris**, gave the British control of the region from the Atlantic coast to the Mississippi River. But British colonists who hoped to settle in those new lands soon learned that the Crown had something else in mind. Under the terms of the **Proclamation of 1763**, Britain prohibited any settlement beyond the Appalachian Mountains.

EXERCISE 2

The 13 Colonies

Directions: Using the map and the passage, choose the *best* answer for each of the following questions.

Eastern North America in 1763

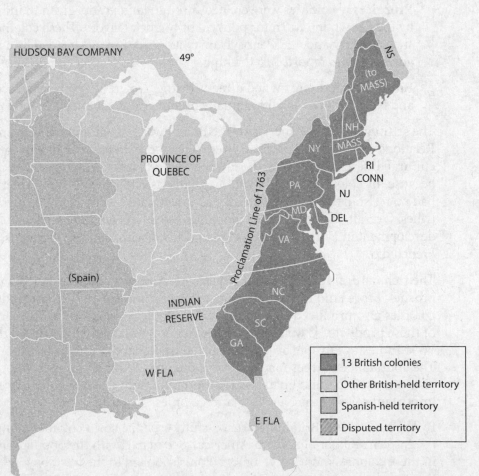

1. Based on details on the map, which of the following statements is true about eastern North America in 1763?

    A. The French still held considerable territory in North America.
    B. The 13 British colonies bordered directly on Spanish-held territory.
    C. The Hudson Bay Company was owned and run by the French.
    D. Britain held the area surrounding the Great Lakes.

2. Who benefited most from the Proclamation of 1763?

    A. Native Americans
    B. British colonists
    C. Dutch fur traders
    D. Spanish soldiers

Answers are on page 568.

Increasing Tensions Between Crown and Colonies

The victory over the French during the French and Indian War came at a high cost for Britain. Faced with mounting debts as a result of the war, **King George III** and the British Parliament decided that the colonists must help pay for the debt, as they benefited from the British victory. To help generate revenue, Parliament passed the **Stamp Act** in 1765; this law placed a tax on all official documents in the colonies, such as deeds, wills, and newspapers. Parliament also passed measures such as the **Townsend Acts**, which forced the colonists to pay additional taxes on imports such as glass, lead, and tea. The colonists, outraged at what they considered interference by the British government, protested, but to little avail. But the actions of the colonists at the **Boston Tea Party** pushed Parliament to even more drastic measures. After the destruction of tea that belonged to the British East India Tea Company, Parliament passed a series of laws that the colonists called the **Intolerable Acts**. These laws placed the Massachusetts colony under the direct authority of the Crown and severely heightened tensions between Parliament and the American colonists.

The colonists responded quickly. In September 1774, delegates met at the **First Continental Congress** in Philadelphia and demanded that the Intolerable Acts be repealed. In addition, the colonists requested that Parliament treat them more fairly and recognize their rights as British subjects. The king and Parliament refused.

EXERCISE 3

Increasing Tensions Between Crown and Colonies

Directions: Choose the *best* answer to each of the following questions.

Question 1 is based on the following passage.

Excerpt from the *Petition to King George III, 1774*

In the magnanimity and justice of your majesty and Parliament, we confide for a redress of our other grievances, trusting that when the causes of our apprehensions are removed, our future conduct will prove us not unworthy of the regard we have been accustomed in our happier days to enjoy. For appealing to that Being who thoroughly searches the hearts of his creatures, we solemnly profess that our councils have been influenced by no other motive than a dread of impending destruction. . . .

1. What is a valid conclusion that can be drawn from the Petition to King George III?

    A. The colonists demanded independence from the king.
    B. The king was right to punish the colonists for their actions.
    C. The colonists claimed that if their grievances were addressed, they would stop their protests.
    D. The colonists believed the Parliament would be more forgiving than the king.

2. Why did the British Parliament pass the Intolerable Acts?

    A. To prevent acts of violence by the colonists against British soldiers
    B. To stop the colonists from demanding independence from Britain
    C. To punish the colonists for resisting acts of Parliament
    D. To stop the colonists from stealing tea and other British products

Answers are on page 569.

The Declaration of Independence and the Revolutionary War

By May 1775, the British and the colonists were at war. During this period, the **Second Continental Congress** met, again in Philadelphia. Inspired by *Common Sense*, a pamphlet in which **Thomas Paine** argued that the colonies should break from Britain, the delegates debated what to do. Many agreed that it was time for the colonies to declare their independence. **Thomas Jefferson** was given the task of drafting what would become known as the **Declaration of Independence**. This important document explains the colonies' grievances and their reasons for revolution. On July 4, 1776, the Continental Congress approved the document.

American troops were woefully unprepared to fight the British army, one of the finest fighting forces in the world. But aid in the form of troops and money from France helped the colonists sustain the long war. In 1781, the British finally surrendered after George Washington defeated General Charles Cornwallis at Yorktown, Virginia. In 1783, the **Treaty of Paris** officially ended hostilities. Although the war proved to be costly for both the Americans and the British, the new American nation had won not only its freedom, but also all British lands that stretched west to the Mississippi River, south to Florida, and north to the Great Lakes.

EXERCISE 4

The Declaration of Independence and the Revolutionary War

Directions: Choose the *best* answer to each of the following questions.

Question 1 is based on the following passage.

Excerpt from the *Declaration of Independence*

We, therefore, the Representatives of the United States of America, in General Congress, Assembled, appealing to the Supreme Judge of the world for the rectitude of our intentions, do, in the Name, and by Authority of the good People of these Colonies, solemnly publish and declare, That these united Colonies are, and of Right ought to be Free and Independent States, that they are Absolved from all Allegiance to the British Crown, and that all political connection between them and the State of Great Britain, is and ought to be totally dissolved; and that as Free and Independent States, they have full Power to levy War, conclude Peace, contract Alliances, establish Commerce, and to do all other Acts and Things which Independent States may of right do. — And for the support of this Declaration, with a firm reliance on the protection of Divine Providence, we mutually pledge to each other our Lives, our Fortunes, and our sacred Honor.

1. Which of the following *best* describes one of the main ideas of this excerpt?

    A. The king of Great Britain must recognize the new nation.
    B. The colonies are pledging to go to war with Britain.
    C. The colonies will no longer obey the authority of the British king.
    D. The colonial government has the right to establish commercial interests.

2. For the Americans, which of the following was one consequence of winning the Revolutionary War?

    A. Recognition of the United States as a world power
    B. Opening lands west of the Appalachian Mountains to new settlement
    C. More peaceful relations with Native Americans
    D. The emergence of the western territories as a new political power

Answers are on page 569.

The Beginnings of a New American Nation

The first new government of the American nation was a loose grouping of the former 13 colonies. Determined to avoid the abuses of power that they had suffered under the English king, Americans organized their new government under the **Articles of Confederation**. This framework guaranteed the sovereignty of each state; however, it also gave the central government very limited powers, hampering its ability to function. A weak central government might not interfere in state affairs, but it also could do little for the nation when it came to national or international issues.

Realizing that the confederation was not working as effectively as hoped, government leaders called for delegates to a new convention to amend the Articles of Confederation. Coming together in Philadelphia in May 1787, the delegates soon realized that the articles needed to be replaced. After many discussions, debates, and compromises, the delegates created a new framework for the governing of the nation—the **United States Constitution**. This document has now governed the nation for more than two centuries.

The Beginnings of a New American Nation

Directions: Choose the *best* answer to each of the following questions.

1. Which of the following *best* describes the purpose of the Articles of Confederation?

   A. To assign representation in the legislature according to each state's population
   B. To fix the division of power between the states and the federal government
   C. To provide a strong central government for the United States
   D. To establish a loose association of the individual states

2. Which of the following statements *best* describes how the Articles of Confederation embodied a major aim of the Revolutionary War?

   A. The Articles created a weak central government in order to prevent the possible rise of tyranny.
   B. The Articles placed power in the hands of the states in order to establish political stability.
   C. The Articles allowed only the states to tax in order to promote a strong economy.
   D. The Articles established permanent peace and harmony among the states.

Answers are on page 569.

The U.S. Constitution

One of the greatest challenges facing the delegates at the Constitutional Convention was the question of how much power to give to the federal government while allowing the states to maintain their sovereignty. To accomplish this, delegates decided that a new federal system of government would be created. This idea of a union formed by the states is known as **federalism**. The delegates also decided that the federal government would have specifically defined powers, such as the ability to regulate trade or to declare war. All others powers would be reserved to the states.

Still, the convention was not without controversy. The Federalists, or those who favored a strong central government with clearly defined control over the states, clashed with the Anti-Federalists, those who feared and distrusted the idea of a strong central government that could take away the powers of the states. The Federalists included Alexander Hamilton and James Madison and were generally members of the merchant class, which supported commercial and industrial expansion of the nation. The Anti-Federalists, among them Thomas Jefferson and Patrick Henry, were often wealthy farmers who favored individual liberties and were not in favor of territorial expansion.

The Constitution has often been called a bundle of compromises. This chart shows some of those compromises.

Debate	Compromise
What will the legislature look like?	**The Great Compromise:** Bicameral legislature Senate: Upper House with all states represented equally The House of Representatives: Lower House with representation based on state population
How will slaves be counted? (The North wanted slaves counted for taxes, the South for representation.)	**The 3/5 Compromise:** Three-fifths of the total slave population would help determine representation for presidential electors and help determine taxes.
Who elects the president?	Creation of the Electoral College, which would vote for the president; each state is given the same number of electors as it has representatives
Does slavery continue?	Yes, although importation of slaves will be banned as of 1808
How are individual rights protected?	**The Bill of Rights** is created.
What will stop one branch of government from assuming too much power?	The system of **checks and balances** in which certain powers of one branch will limit the powers of the other branches

The U.S. Constitution

Directions: Use information from the chart to answer each of the following
questions.

1. Why did Southerners want to have slaves counted for congressional
representation?

   A. Doing so would lead to a more equitable balance between North and
   South in the Senate.
   B. Doing so would reduce tax collections in the Southern states.
   C. Doing so would increase the power of Southern state
   governments.
   D. Doing so would give Southern states more representatives in the lower
   house of Congress.

2. Which of the following would most likely have been considered a victory
for the Anti-Federalists?

   A. the 3/5 Compromise
   B. the Bill of Rights
   C. the creation of the Electoral College
   D. the ban on the importation of slaves

Answers are on page 570.

Domestic and Foreign Affairs, 1791–1853

Between 1791 and 1853, the United States saw its borders increase
dramatically. During the period 1791 to 1796, under the administration
of President **George Washington**, the states of Vermont, Kentucky,
and Tennessee were admitted to the Union. Under **Thomas Jefferson**'s
presidency, the state of Ohio was admitted. But one of the most important
events during Jefferson's presidency was the **Louisiana Purchase**. Jefferson
understood that Americans needed access to the port of New Orleans and
the right to navigate the **Mississippi River**, which was of vital importance
to American commerce. These areas were now owned by France, which had
taken them over from Spain. By paying France $15 million for the territory,

Jefferson not only secured access to the port and the river but also doubled the size of the nation. But the purchase also tested the constitutionality of the president's powers. Although Jefferson believed in strictly adhering to the powers of the presidency as spelled out in the Constitution, he exceeded those powers in making the purchase. However, his concern for the security of the nation was greater. Jefferson later appointed **Meriwether Lewis** and **William Clark** to explore the new territory.

The United States and Adjacent Territories in 1810

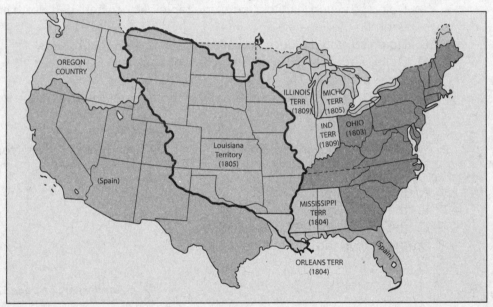

The Monroe Doctrine

After the War of 1812, in which America again fought against the British, the United States entered a period of strong nationalism. This nationalistic spirit was expressed through a continued emphasis on westward expansion and reduced concerns over European interference in American affairs. This **"Era of Good Feelings"** reached its peak in 1820 with the election of **James Monroe** to the presidency.

In an effort to further discourage European intervention in the Western Hemisphere, Monroe proclaimed one of the first significant pieces of American foreign policy—the **Monroe Doctrine**. According to this policy, the United States would remain neutral in European affairs, but if European nations interfered with or attempted to colonize nations in the Western Hemisphere, the United States would view those actions as a threat to its own security. With this policy the United States entered the arena of world affairs.

The Age of Jackson and the Mexican War

By the end of Monroe's presidency in 1825, the nation was troubled by growing sectionalism between the North and the South. **Sectionalism** refers to the economic, political, and/or social differences that may be present between regions within a country. In this case, the agricultural South and West increasingly took issue with the largely industrial Northeast. Nowhere was this conflict more evident than in the halls of Congress, as each section put forth more and more demands. The result was growing political turmoil.

These sectional differences played a large role in the presidential election of 1828. **Andrew Jackson**, a Southerner and a hero of the War of 1812, emerged as the leading candidate. Jackson was considered a **populist**, that is, a candidate who the common people believed represented their best interests. Jackson supported the idea that *the people* should have a stronger voice in their government, and not just a select few. With the passage of universal male suffrage in 1820, more people than ever before could vote. Jackson's popularity among ordinary people secured the presidency for him. His presidency inaugurated a period of so-called Jacksonian Democracy, in which farmers, tradespeople, and other everyday folk gained a greater voice in politics.

A leading controversy during Jackson's time in office involved the National Bank. Created to handle the nation's finances and to help give the country a more solid financial footing, the bank was viewed by Jackson as a tool of wealthy industrialists and merchants of the North to control the nation's money. Jackson eventually shut the bank down. He also engaged in a program that forced Native American peoples living in the Southeast to relocate to the Western territories. However, despite pressure to annex Texas from Mexico, Jackson refused, fearing this would lead to war.

Jackson's successor, **James Polk**, did not share Jackson's apprehension over the annexation of Texas. So in 1845, with the aid of Congress, Polk annexed the Texas Republic. The annexation coincided with an increasing belief in so-called **Manifest Destiny**, the idea that the United States was destined to expand its borders to the Pacific Ocean. But Polk was unable to purchase from Mexico the territory that included New Mexico and California, so in 1846 the United States declared war. Two years later, in 1848, with America victorious, the two nations signed the **Treaty of Guadalupe Hidalgo**, in which the United States gained the territory that would eventually become the states of California, Utah, and Nevada, as well as portions of the states of Colorado, New Mexico, Arizona, and Wyoming. The nation had finally expanded its boundaries from coast to coast, as shown in the following map.

Territorial Expansion of the United States to 1853

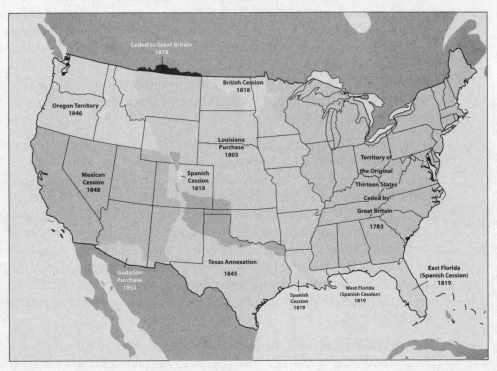

EXERCISE 7

The Age of Jackson and the Mexican War

Directions: Choose the *best* answer to each of the following questions.

1. How did the granting of universal male suffrage change American politics during the early nineteenth century?

    A. Political candidates had to appeal to a more diverse group of people.
    B. Political parties formed for the first time in U.S. history.
    C. Sectionalism emerged as a major political issue.
    D. More populists now ran for political office.

2. Which statement *best* summarizes the intent of the Monroe Doctrine?

    A. It proclaims that the United States would stop European nations from establishing colonies anywhere in the world.
    B. It promises that the United States would help colonies in the Americas achieve democracy.
    C. It states that European interference in the Americas would be viewed as a threat to the national interest of the United States.
    D. It declares that the United States would prevent other nations from trading with South American countries.

Answers are on page 569.

Disunion and Civil War

The end of the Mexican War was followed by increasing political conflict between the Northern and Southern states, particularly over the issue of whether slavery should be permitted in the new territories. Eventually the strife led to secession by a group of Southern states, followed by a devastating civil war.

Sectional Tension and Secession

By the 1850s, sectionalism had become a dominant factor in America's political life. One issue that spawned deep discontent was **tariffs**, taxes placed on goods imported into the country. People living in the South and the West viewed tariffs unfavorably; they believed that because of the lack of manufacturing and industrial centers in those areas, people living in those regions had to pay more for goods than those who lived in the North.

However, the main issue dividing the nation was slavery. As each new territory was added to the nation, the question arose as to whether slavery would be allowed in that new area. One proposed solution was **popular sovereignty**, the idea that the people of a territory should decide for themselves whether to be a free state or a slave state. Others believed that slavery should be banned in all new territories and states, though they were willing to allow slavery to continue in areas where it already existed. Another group, known as **abolitionists**, wanted to completely abolish, or do away with, slavery throughout the nation.

The increasingly strained relations between the North and South were intensified by the Supreme Court's 1857 decision in the **Dred Scott** case. This case centered on a slave, Dred Scott, whose master had moved and taken Scott to a free territory. Scott then sued for his freedom. However, the court ruled that as a slave, Scott was property and so could not sue for his freedom in federal court. Although the South applauded the court's decision, many in the North found it a miscarriage of justice. The case deepened the bitter sectionalism that threatened to tear the nation apart.

With the election of Abraham Lincoln to the presidency in 1860, the question of whether slavery would be allowed to expand appeared to be answered. Although not an abolitionist, Lincoln supported restricting slavery to the states where it already existed. Southern states objected to limitations on the expansion of slavery. They also felt threatened by the North's growing dominance of political and economic affairs. Some states, such as South Carolina, threatened to leave the Union if Lincoln was elected.

In December 1860 a special state convention convened in South Carolina, and the delegates voted to secede from the United States. By the time of Lincoln's inauguration in March 1861, seven Southern states had seceded from the Union and created their own government, the Confederate States of America. The president of the new government was Jefferson Davis, from Mississippi.

Lincoln and his government believed that the secession was illegal. They feared that if the South was allowed to secede, other states that might disagree with federal laws or policies would choose the same route. The Union would thus be perpetually threatened and would descend into political and economic instability. Despite efforts to find a compromise, no agreement could be reached, and when Confederate forces fired on the federal garrison at Fort Sumter, South Carolina, in April 1861, the Civil War began.

EXERCISE 8

Sectional Tension and Secession

Directions: Choose the *best* answer to each of the following questions.

1. Which of the following *best* summarizes the effect of the Dred Scott decision?

   A. African Americans had no legal rights as U.S. citizens.
   B. Slavery could expand into the territories.
   C. Slaves could sue their masters for their freedom.
   D. In the eyes of the federal courts, all people were considered equal.

2. Which of the following *best* describes the immediate effect of Lincoln's election to the presidency?

    A. Confederate forces fired on Fort Sumter.
    B. South Carolina seceded from the Union.
    C. Southern states supported Lincoln's view on slavery.
    D. Southern states formed their own government.

Answers are on page 570.

The Civil War

The Civil War, which was fought mostly in the South, lasted four years. Both sides had certain advantages. The North had the larger army because of its greater population. In addition, its industries helped ensure that the army had everything it needed for the war effort. Its vast abundance of natural resources and a strong transportation system also helped the North. The South had the advantage of fighting on its own territory, as well as the leadership of some of the nation's greatest military leaders.

In 1862, Lincoln issued the **Emancipation Proclamation**, which ordered the freeing of all slaves living in the slave states that were part of the Confederacy. This action prompted 180,000 former slaves to escape to Union-controlled areas; many soon enlisted in the Union army. In the end, the superior military skills of the South's generals could not offset the overwhelming numbers of the Northern armies. The war ended on April 9, 1865, with the surrender of Confederate General **Robert E. Lee** to Union General **Ulysses S. Grant**. With the surrender, Lincoln was faced with new challenges—how best to mend the great divide between North and South and how to rebuild a war-torn region.

Reconstruction

Lincoln never saw the implementation of his plan for the South, known as **Reconstruction**. The president hoped to slowly bring the Southern states back into the Union, but when he was assassinated by a Southern sympathizer, the task fell to Lincoln's successor, **Andrew Johnson**, of Tennessee.

Though Johnson supported the Union, he faced difficulties because he was thought to be sympathetic to the South. Distrust by Congress eventually led to Johnson becoming the first president ever to be **impeached**, or charged with official misconduct. However, the Senate failed in its attempt to convict Johnson.

During Johnson's administration, three important amendments to the Constitution were passed. The **Thirteenth Amendment**, passed in 1865, abolished slavery throughout the nation. The **Fourteenth Amendment**, ratified in 1870, guaranteed citizenship to all people born or naturalized in the United States (including former slaves) and promised all citizens "equal protection of the laws." The **Fifteenth Amendment**, also ratified in 1870, gave voting rights to African American men. Despite these great advances however, African Americans, particularly in the South, continued to struggle to gain equality.

EXERCISE 9

Reconstruction

Directions: Match each term with the choice that *best* describes its significance.

1. _____ Thirteenth Amendment
2. _____ Impeachment
3. _____ Fifteenth Amendment
4. _____ Reconstruction

A. brought the Southern states back into the Union
B. gave African American men the right to vote
C. abolished slavery throughout the United States
D. allows for removing public officials from office on account of unlawful conduct

Answers are on page 570.

America in the Late Nineteenth Century

The late nineteenth century in the United States was a time of tremendous economic growth. New industries developed, railroads pushed westward, and the population expanded rapidly, fueled by immigration from Europe.

The Growth of Big Business and Urbanization

After the Civil War, the rapid spread of **industrialization**, that is, the production of goods by mechanized means, spurred the growth of big business in the United States. Large corporations began emerging as growing companies bought out competitors; soon these large corporations began controlling the marketplace, most notably in the steel, oil, and railroad industries. As businesses thrived, many workers did not; many labored under unsafe conditions and for poor wages. Power became concentrated in the hands of a few industrialists. The economic doctrine called *laissez-faire*, that is, little or no government intervention in business practices, characterized the relationship between big business and government.

With the rise of industry came **urbanization**, the shift in population from rural to urban areas. This shift was created by the need for workers in the growing urban-based manufacturing businesses. By 1890, nearly one-third of the U.S. population lived in urban areas. Cities such as New York, Chicago, and Philadelphia had populations of more than one million. In addition to supplying an abundant labor force for factories and businesses, these cities also developed into major transportation centers for people, goods, and supplies.

Adding to the large number of people coming to the cities from rural areas were growing numbers of immigrants who came to the United States in search of jobs and a better life. Many of these immigrants were fleeing poverty, famine, and persecution in countries such as Ireland, Germany, Scandinavia, Russia, and Italy. Not everyone welcomed the new arrivals. Their willingness to work long hours for very little money caused resentment among other workers, who were often forced to do the same. And immigrants often had to live in less desirable areas of the cities, in cramped and unhealthy conditions. However, over time, communities of immigrants took root, bringing institutions, customs, and culture from their homelands.

EXERCISE 10

The Growth of Big Business and Urbanization

Directions: Use the following chart to answer the question.

Main Sources of European Immigration to the United States, 1841–1860		
	1841–1850	**1851–1860**
	5,074	4,738
	539	3,749
Belgium	77,262	76,358
Denmark	434,626	951,667
France		
Germany		
	32,092	247,125
Great Britain	3,712	38,331
England	229,979	132,199
Scotland		
Not Specified	780,719	914,119
	8,251	10,789
Ireland		
Netherlands	13,903	20,931
Norway ⎫		
Sweden ⎬	4,644	25,011
Switzerland		

1. Which of the following statements *best* summarizes the chart?

   A. In the 1840s and 1850s, Great Britain, Germany, and Ireland were the main sources of European immigrants.
   B. Immigration from France dropped sharply in the 1850s.
   C. In the 1850s, more immigrants came from Ireland than from any other country.
   D. Norwegian and Swedish immigrants arrived in huge numbers in the 1840s and 1850s.

The answer is on page 570.

The Settling of the West

To promote settlement of the West, Congress passed the **Homestead Act** in 1862, which offered 160 acres to anyone who was willing to live on and farm the land. Unfortunately, much of the Great Plains and the West was not suitable for farming; however, ranchers made use of the wide spaces to raise cattle. To further encourage settlement, Congress extended the railroad: the 1862 Pacific Railway Act chartered the Union Pacific Railroad Company and authorized the building of the **transcontinental railroad**. While the Union Pacific built tracks going west, the Central Pacific Railroad Company built tracks going east. The railroads met on May 10, 1869, in Promontory, Utah, marking the completion of the nation's first transcontinental railroad. Only a few years earlier, settlers had had to spend grueling months crossing the nation by wagon or on horseback; rail travelers could now go from coast to coast in a week's time.

The policy of forced resettlement of Native Americans also continued. By the 1860s, the federal government had set aside two large tracts of land for Native Americans. The threat of force convinced many tribes to comply with resettlement. But some tribes, the Sioux in particular, fiercely resisted the government's attempt to move them. In 1874, at the Battle of the Little Bighorn, the Sioux wiped out troops under the leadership of General George A. Custer. In retaliation, the United States Army began a systematic war against the Sioux; by 1890, the Sioux were defeated.

EXERCISE 11

The Settling of the West

Directions: Choose the *best* answer to each of the following questions.

1. Which of the following statements describes the 1862 Pacific Railway Act?

   A. It gave land to people who wanted to settle in the West.
   B. It authorized the building of the first transcontinental railroad.
   C. It established a policy of forced resettlement of Native Americans.
   D. It prevented people from buying farmland.

2. Why did the Homestead Act attract farmers to the frontier?

   A. It guaranteed farmers access to the railroad.
   B. It provided farmers with subsidies for growing certain crops.
   C. It offered tax deductions to people who agreed to settle in the West.
   D. It offered free land to people who would live on and farm the land.

The answer is on page 570.

America as a World Power

Well after winning its independence, the United States made a point of staying out of world affairs; this practice is called **isolationism**. But by the late nineteenth century, the United States was pursuing dreams of building an empire like that of Great Britain more than a century earlier. Americans, seeing the potential for new markets and new sources of raw materials, as well as the possibility of extending the ideals of American democracy, began looking beyond their borders. A powerful U.S. navy—known as the Great White Fleet—was developed, and after a war with Spain in 1898, the United States took control of the Philippines, Puerto Rico, and other former Spanish possessions. Americans believed they were engaged not in **imperialism** (that is, the taking over of other nations to acquire resources or for military purposes), but rather in a kind of "informal colonialism" that promoted not only financial and business interests in other lands but also democracy and other American institutions, too. Rather than politics, the emphasis was on economics, specifically markets and raw materials.

In the early twentieth century, the complex alliances among European nations and the growing militarism and nationalist stances of certain nations set the stage for World War I. The war began in Europe in the summer of 1914. Although the conflict eventually involved many nations, it was primarily a battle between two sides. The **Central Powers** included Germany, Austria-Hungary, Bulgaria, and Turkey. The **Allied Powers** were made up of Great Britain, France, Russia, Belgium, and Italy.

When war first broke out, the United States tried to maintain its neutral status, even though it was loaning money to both the Allies and Germany. However, in 1917, following increased German attacks on ships carrying American citizens, the United States entered the war and sent an army to fight in Europe. American factories shifted production to the manufacture of war materials and weapons. As American men entered the military, women and older children took their places in the factories. To ensure that American soldiers would have enough meat and bread, the government asked Americans to restrict their consumption. With the help of the American forces, the Allied Powers drove the Central Powers forces back to their own borders. When Allied forces approached the German border, the war ended with an armistice.

The **Treaty of Versailles** officially ended the war in 1919. One condition of the treaty was the creation of the **League of Nations**, an international organization that would work to maintain peace throughout the world. Although the idea for the organization came from President **Woodrow Wilson**, leaders in Congress did not want to become entangled again in world affairs and rejected U.S. membership, dooming the league to an early failure. The United States once again retreated to its earlier policy of isolationism and focused instead on domestic issues.

EXERCISE 12

America as a World Power

Directions: Choose the *best* answer to each of the following questions.

Questions 1 and 2 are based on the following passages.

Passage 1

The United States have always protested against the doctrine of international law which permits the subjugation of the weak by the strong. A self governing state cannot accept sovereignty over an unwilling people. The United States cannot act upon the ancient heresy that might makes right . . .

We propose to contribute to the defeat of any person or party that stands for the forcible subjugation of any people. We shall oppose for reelection all who in the White House or in Congress betray American liberty in pursuit of un-American gains. We still hope that both of our great political parties will support and defend the Declaration of Independence in the closing campaign of the century. . . .

Passage 2

And the burning question of this campaign is, whether the American people will accept the gifts of events; whether they will rise as lifts their soaring destiny; whether they will proceed upon the lines of national development surveyed by the statesmen of our past; or whether for the first time American people doubt their mission, question fate, prove apostate to the spirit of their race, and halt the ceaseless march of free institutions.

The Opposition tells us that we ought not to govern a people without their consent. I answer, the rule of liberty that all just government derives its authority from the consent of the governed, applies only to those who are capable of self-government. We govern the Indians without their consent, we govern our territories without their consent, we govern our children without their consent.

1. What issue does passage 1 address?

   A. Why the United States must bring democracy to other nations
   B. Why imperialism goes against American ideals
   C. Why the United States must protect weaker countries
   D. Why it is important to use force in dealing with other nations

2. Which of the following *best* describes passage 2?

 A. The United States should govern nations that cannot govern themselves.
 B. The United States is the one true democracy in the world.
 C. Other nations look to the United States to learn how to be democracies.
 D. People need only to see how the United States has dealt with Native Americans to understand democracy.

Answers are on page 570.

The New Deal and Trouble in Europe

There was no single defining event that served as the catalyst for World War II. Long-simmering tensions left over from World War I set the stage for a new ordeal in Europe. Germans in particular resented the harsh Treaty of Versailles, which had stripped Germany of its overseas colonies and imposed huge war reparations payments. Social and political problems were worsened by the worldwide economic Great Depression that began with bank failures in Europe and the collapse of the U.S. stock market in 1929. Many Europeans saw the depression as a failure of democracy and capitalism. In response, groups in many European countries turned to extremist political parties of the left and right. Some joined **communist** parties, which promised a revolution to overthrow capitalism and replace it with a worker-led state. Communists pointed to the example of the Soviet Union, where a communist party had taken power following a revolution in 1917. Other Europeans turned to **fascism**, a political philosophy based on extreme nationalism and aggression. In Germany an extreme fascist group called the National Socialists ("**Nazis**"), whose beliefs included racism and anti-Semitism, took power in 1933. The hostility among all of these groups, their aim to expand their power, and their hatred for democracy set the stage for a new world conflict.

In the United States, the administration of President Herbert Hoover proved unable to halt the Great Depression or to reverse its effects. In 1932 **Franklin Roosevelt** was elected president and initiated a set of policies called the **New Deal**. These measures were intended not only to end the Depression but also to restore Americans' faith in the nation.

Roosevelt's programs radically changed government functions. Many New Deal agencies created to help Americans, such as the Social Security Administration and the Federal Housing Administration, are still in operation today. To help farmers, Roosevelt proposed the Agricultural Adjustment Act, which paid farmers a subsidy to cut back on growing certain crops so that food prices would remain stable. A number of New Deal programs, such as the Works Progress Administration (WPA), were expressly designed to create jobs and reduce unemployment.

World War II

For the United States, what finally ended the Great Depression was the start of World War II. When Germany launched the war in Europe in 1939, initially most Americans did not want to become involved. Some, however, including President Roosevelt, believed that German military aggression would eventually threaten the United States. Roosevelt's government initiated programs to help Great Britain combat Germany. For example, under the Lend-Lease program, war supplies were made available to Britain and its allies. As the demand for war supplies increased, the U.S. economy at last recovered from the Depression and began to expand.

Meanwhile, Japanese military forces launched campaigns of aggression in Asia. In response, Roosevelt's government imposed economic sanctions against Japan. When the Japanese bombed the U.S. naval base at **Pearl Harbor** in Hawaii in 1941, the United States joined the worldwide conflict and became involved in two theaters of war: in the Pacific against the Japanese and in Europe against the Germans.

After a difficult period during 1942, the Allies—Great Britain, France, the Soviet Union, and the United States—began to gain momentum. Soviet armies achieved crucial victories against the Germans in Eastern Europe and approached Germany from the east. U.S., British, and Canadian forces landed on the Normandy coast of France on June 6, 1944, and approached Germany from the west. The Germans finally surrendered in May 1945.

In the months before the German surrender, the Allies deliberated over how to shape the postwar world. At a meeting at Yalta, in the Soviet Union, a decision was made to divide Germany into four zones, each of which would be headed by one of the Allied powers. Soon after the Yalta conference, President Roosevelt died and was replaced as president by Harry Truman.

Meanwhile in the Pacific, by 1942 the United States had stopped the Japanese advance and began a slow and difficult island-hopping campaign toward Japan. Realizing that an invasion of Japan would result in massive American casualties, President Truman made the momentous decision to use atomic weapons at **Hiroshima** and **Nagasaki** in August 1945, forcing the Japanese to surrender.

Certainly one of the most horrific aspects of World War II in Europe was the **Holocaust**, the systematic extermination of six million European Jews by the Nazis. In the United States, the detention of thousands of Japanese Americans in internment camps during the war remains one of the more shameful episodes in American history.

EXERCISE 13

The New Deal and Trouble in Europe

Directions: Choose the *best* answer to each of the following questions.

Question 1 is based on the following chart.

New Political Ideologies of the Twentieth Century	
Communism	Centralized control of a nation/state by a single group; the state controls production; classless society; equality for all
Fascism	Centralized control of a nation/state by a single group; the nation/state is celebrated above all else; emphasis on an aggressive nationalism and racism
Totalitarianism	A term applied to political and social organization as practiced by both communists and fascists; denotes centralized control of a nation/state by a single individual or group in accordance with a central ideology; state control over all aspects of public and private life; no individual freedoms

1. Which of the following describes the beliefs or practices of both communists and fascists?

    A. Both wanted to create a classless society.
    B. Both thought that the state should control production.
    C. When in power, both did not permit individual freedoms
    D. Both promoted extreme nationalism and racism.

2. Which of the following was a primary goal of the New Deal?

    A. to provide war supplies to Britain and its allies
    B. to help European countries recover from the Great Depression
    C. to help the United States recover from the Great Depression
    D. to promote the spread of democracy in Europe

Answers are on page 571.

The Cold War Era

At the end of World War II, conflict arose among the victorious Allies. The Western powers—the United States, Britain, and France—distrusted the communist-led Soviet Union. By the time of the German surrender, Soviet troops occupied much of Eastern and Central Europe and were setting up "satellite" states in the region. Those states were nominally independent but actually under Soviet domination. The Western powers feared further Soviet attempts to expand communist power and take control of more countries. The result was the emergence of a new kind of war—the Cold War, a decades-long conflict marked by sustained tensions between the world's free and communist nations. Two superpowers had emerged out of the ashes of World War II—the United States and the Soviet Union—and for the next 40 years these two nations would be locked in an ideological battle of wills.

As the Soviets tightened their grip on Eastern Europe, the United States embarked on the first of many efforts to counter Soviet influence. Under the policy of **containment**, steps were taken to prevent the spread of communism in Western Europe. Under the **Truman Doctrine**, announced in 1947, the United States pledged to aid nations threatened by communism. That same year saw the implementation of the **Marshall Plan**, which provided billions of dollars in U.S. economic aid to help rebuild nations devastated by World War II, as well as to shore up unstable governments that could be targets for communist takeover. In 1949 the United States stepped up its military support of Europe by joining the **North Atlantic Treaty Organization (NATO)**, the first security and military alliance that the country had ever entered into in peacetime. The Soviet Union countered with its own multistate alliance, formed in 1955, called the **Warsaw Pact**.

Soon the Cold War conflict spread beyond the borders of Western Europe to Asia, Africa, and Latin America. Asian and African countries seeking to end European colonial rule were especially vulnerable to Cold War tensions, as both the United States and the Soviet Union attempted to influence events in those areas. Although war between the two superpowers was never formally declared, they did engage in a series of **proxy wars** in which each superpower supported a third-party nation as a substitute to fight the other. This was most evident in the conflicts in Korea and Vietnam; in both cases the United States sent troops to help fight against communist forces.

The United States and the Soviet Union also engaged in an arms race in which each nation stockpiled huge amounts of weaponry, especially nuclear missiles and bombs. Both nations also increased the size of their military. Under President John F. Kennedy, the United States added five new army divisions and increased its air power and the number of military reservist units. Nuclear testing by both superpowers also resumed.

The End of the Cold War

By the late 1980s, the Cold War was winding down. The economies of the Soviet Union and its allies were depressed. Communist economic policies failed to promote prosperity, and the cost of maintaining huge armies and weapons stockpiles was an enormous burden. A new Soviet leader named Mikhail Gorbachev attempted to jump-start the Soviet economy by introducing two reformist policies called *glasnost* and *perestroika*. Glasnost, or openness, involved allowing Western ideas and goods into the Soviet Union. Perestroika was permission for Soviet citizens to develop a limited market economy.

In 1989 Gorbachev announced that the Soviet Union would no longer defend communist governments in Eastern Europe with Soviet troops. As a result, communist regimes soon collapsed in Poland, Hungary, and Czechoslovakia. In Germany, crowds tore down the Berlin Wall, a barrier between the Western- and Soviet-controlled sectors of the city and a potent symbol of the Cold War. Finally, in 1991 the Soviet government itself collapsed, to be succeeded by elected governments in Russia and other parts of the former Soviet Union. The Cold War was over, but it had lasting consequences. Both superpowers had spent trillions of dollars arming themselves for a confrontation that never came. And the proxy wars, such as those in Korea and Vietnam, had cost thousands of American lives and the lives of many thousands of others.

EXERCISE 14

The Cold War Era

Directions: Choose the *best* answer to each of the following questions.

1. A *satellite* is a small body that circles around a planet. In regard to the allies of the Soviet Union, why is the term "satellite states" appropriate?

   A. Those nations were formally independent but were under Soviet control.
   B. Those countries needed military protection from the Soviet Union.
   C. Historically, those nations had all been part of the Soviet Union.
   D. The Soviet Union depended on those nations for economic aid.

2. Which of the following could be considered a contributing factor in the collapse of the Soviet economy during the 1980s?

A. A growing religious opposition to communism throughout Eastern Europe

B. The enormous cost of maintaining large stockpiles of weapons

C. The development of peaceful uses of modern technology

D. The adoption of more peaceful approaches to world diplomacy

Answers are on page 571.

America in the Twenty-First Century

Timeline of Significant Events in American History in the Twenty-First Century

- 2000—In a highly contested presidential election, Republican George W. Bush defeats Democrat Al Gore, making Bush the 43rd president of the United States.

- 2001—On September 11, 19 terrorists hijack four airplanes and crash them into the World Trade Center, the Pentagon, and a field in Pennsylvania; an estimated 3000 people die and more than 6000 are injured.

- 2001—The United States launches an invasion of Afghanistan, a country suspected of harboring terrorist leaders.

- 2001—The U.S. Congress passes the Patriot Act, which expands law enforcement powers in cases of suspected terrorist activities.

- 2002—The Department of Homeland Security is created.

- 2003—The United States, Great Britain, and several allies launch an invasion of Iraq.

- 2008—The collapse of the U.S. stock market plunges the world economy into a recession.

- 2008—Democrat Barack Obama is elected president of the United States and becomes the first African American president.

- 2009—U.S. conservatives form "Tea Party" groups to demand fiscal conservatism, lower taxes, and cuts to government programs.

- 2011—Osama bin Laden, leader of al-Qaeda and originator of the September 11 terrorist attacks, is killed in Pakistan by American forces.

- 2012—Barack Obama is reelected to a second term as president.

EXERCISE 15

America in the Twenty-First Century

Directions: Choose the *best* answer to the following question.

1. Based on the timeline, which of the following statements *best* describes the state of American foreign affairs in the first decades of the twenty-first century?

   A. With the end of the Cold War, the United States faced new threats to its interests and security.
   B. After the Cold War, Americans abandoned global responsibilities and retreated into isolationism.
   C. The U.S. role as world peacekeeper diminished as other nations assumed more responsibility for international security.
   D. The United States broke relations with its Cold War allies and sought new partners in Asia and the Middle East.

The answer is on page 571.

CHAPTER 3

Economics

Economics is the study of how people, countries, and institutions make choices to satisfy their unlimited wants using their limited resources. Economists analyze how and why different goods and services are produced, distributed, and consumed.

Factors of Production

The **factors of production** are those things necessary to produce goods and services when attempting to generate an economic profit. These factors are natural resources, capital, labor, and entrepreneurship.

- **Natural resources**, such as land, oil, or iron, encompass all the raw materials that are utilized to produce a good or a service.

- **Labor** represents all of the workers in an organization and the work they perform when generating a good or a service. The type of labor necessary depends on the kind of good or service being generated. For example, a welder might be necessary to build a car and a receptionist might be necessary to greet people in a doctor's office.

- **Capital** is all of the tools and machines that are used to generate a good or perform a service. It also includes the money necessary to purchase those tools, purchase natural resources, and hire workers. An example of capital would be the hammer a carpenter uses as well as the money the carpenter uses to buy the hammer.

- **Entrepreneurship** is the process of identifying what good or service needs to be produced or improved upon and organizing the natural resources, labor, and capital to produce it for an economic benefit. Entrepreneurship can be undertaken by an organization, such as a government or company, or by an individual.

EXERCISE 1

Factors of Production

Directions: Write the factor of production that *best* describes each item.

1. Water

_____

2. Business owner

_____

3. Bank loan

_____

4. Truck driver (contract, not owner-operator)

_____

5. Soil

_____

6. Sales person (employee)

_____

7. Trees

_____

8. Computer

_____

9. Inventor

_____

10. Forklift

_____

Answers are on page 571.

Markets: Supply, Demand, and Prices

The basic foundation of the American capitalist system is the market. The **market** is the environment in which the producers and the buyers of a particular good or service interact. Markets are generally created when the buying public expresses a desire for a good or service—this is called **demand**. Producers, either established organizations or individual entrepreneurs, then evaluate whether to create a **supply** of the desired good or service to meet this demand and calculate the opportunity cost of doing so. A producer's **opportunity cost** is determined by comparing the amount of profit that can be made when meeting the demand for one good or service versus the profit that can be made by meeting the demand for some other good or service. A producer who can make the most profit meeting the demand for a certain good or service will do so and create supply.

The interaction between the producer and the buyer within the market determines the **price** of a good or service. A producer is in business to make a profit by providing a good or service at a price. He or she must charge a price that is high enough to both cover the cost of the natural resources, labor, and capital that are necessary to create the good or service and also generate a profit. In most cases, a producer seeks to charge as high a price as possible in order to generate the highest possible profit. Consumers who are willing to buy a good or service, however, seek to acquire the good or service at the lowest price possible in order to hold on to as much of their own money as they can. If the price of a good or service is high, consumers often will either buy few of it or will not buy it at all.

If consumers will not pay enough to cover the cost to produce a good or service and generate a profit for the producer, the producer generally will not make the good or service.

For a good example of the relationship between supply and demand, consider an electronics company that creates and sells a new and very useful kind of computer. When the new computer is first offered to the public, there is a high demand for it because no other company sells anything quite like it, and the supply of the new computer is limited. The electronics company has a near monopoly on the market for this new kind of computer; that is, there are very few competitors working to meet consumers' demand. The electronics company is therefore able to charge a high price and generate a large profit. However, other companies see how much profit the electronics company is making, so they decide to enter the market and create their own versions of the new kind of computer. As more and more companies enter the market, there is increased competition for the dollars of consumers who want the new computers.

With so many companies entering the market, eventually the supply of new computers offered for sale becomes very large. There may even be a surplus of the new computers in the marketplace. At that point, the companies offering computers for sale may start to cut their prices in order to persuade consumers to buy their computers instead of those of their competitors. As prices fall, the companies make smaller profits. In order to stay in business and keep profits high, they have two choices. They can reduce the costs associated with producing the computers, such as by using cheaper parts or paying their workers less, or they can innovate by adding new features to convince consumers to buy the computers from them at sustained or higher prices.

In general:

- **When prices are high**, demand will be low because consumers will either not buy the product or will buy it from some other producer whose price is lower.

- **When supply is high**, prices will be low because producers will compete among themselves for consumer dollars.

- **When prices are low**, demand will be high because consumers will want to take advantage of the low prices.

- **When supply is low,** demand will be high because consumers will be willing to pay more for goods that are relatively scarce.

When producers generate the exact amount of a product that consumers want to buy at the price they are willing to pay, the market for that product is said to be at **equilibrium**.

EXERCISE 2

Markets: Supply, Demand, and Prices

Directions: Choose the *best* answer to each of the following questions.

1. How are markets initially created?

   A. Producers provide a good or service.
   B. Consumers demand a good or service.
   C. Producers make a profit.
   D. New companies compete with existing companies.

2. If the price of baseballs decreases, why does the quantity of baseballs sold increase?

   A. Consumers are willing to buy more baseballs at a lower price.
   B. Consumers cannot afford to buy as many baseballs.
   C. Consumers' incomes increase as the price of baseballs decreases.
   D. Consumers will choose to play other sports.

Answers are on page 571.

Gross Domestic Product (GDP)

The sum of all the economic activity of a country's markets is called its **gross domestic product (GDP).** A country's GDP is calculated by adding together all of the consumption, government spending, investment, and net exports that happen within a given period of time.

GDP is one of the main ways that economists estimate the health of a country's economy. When GDP in the present year or quarter is greater than in the previous quarter or year, the economy is thought to be growing and healthy. There will typically be more goods and services consumed; therefore, businesses will increase wages, hiring, and investment to meet growing demand. Many new businesses may be created. When GDP is less than in previous periods, the economy is thought to be in trouble. There will typically be less consumption; therefore, businesses will try to maintain profits by reducing wages, laying off workers, and spending less on production. Some businesses will struggle or close. GDP figures help people determine where to invest, where to seek employment, and how to spend money.

EXERCISE 3

Gross Domestic Product (GDP)

Directions: Using the graph, answer the following questions.

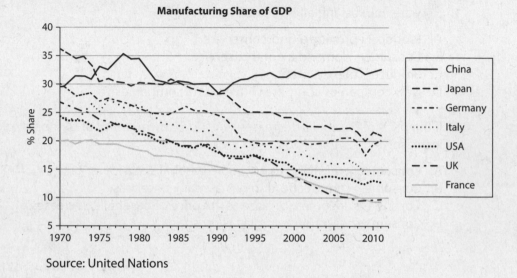

Source: United Nations

1. In which country has manufacturing grown as a percentage of GDP since 1970?

   A. France
   B. Germany
   C. China
   D. Italy

2. What does the graph indicate about manufacturing as a share of overall economic activity in these countries since 1970?

   _____

   _____

   _____

   _____

Answers are on page 572.

Fiscal and Monetary Policy

There are two primary ways that the government influences economic growth in the United States. One way the government influences economic growth is through fiscal policy. **Fiscal policy** largely represents the decisions that the president and Congress make about how much money the government spends, where it spends money, and what the level of tax rates is. For example, if economic growth is slow or contracting, the government can choose to lower taxes and increase employment and the supply of money by spending more on programs like education and infrastructure improvements.

Another way the government influences economic growth is through monetary policy set by the Federal Reserve Bank ("the Fed"). **The Federal Reserve Bank** is the central bank of the United States. It was created by Congress in 1913 to provide the country with a stable and flexible financial system. The Fed oversees 12 regional Federal Reserve Banks, each of which oversees a different part of the country by supervising and regulating banks there.

The primary purpose of the Fed is to promote stable and predictable growth; that is, to prevent the economy from either growing too quickly or from contracting. When the economy is growing too quickly, there is an oversupply of money and credit available to satisfy consumers' demand for goods and services. This causes the value of the dollar to go down, which then causes the cost of goods and services to go up. This condition is known as **inflation.** To slow down economic activity, the Fed can raise interest rates so that it is more expensive for businesses and consumers to borrow money to buy goods and services.

When the economy is growing too slowly or is contracting, there are more goods and services than consumers are willing to buy and there is a shortage of credit and money. This causes the value of the dollar to go up, which then causes the cost of goods and services to go down. This condition is known as **deflation.** When deflation occurs, the Fed tries to increase consumer demand and prices by reducing interest rates and the supply of money.

EXERCISE 4

Fiscal and Monetary Policy

Directions: Answer the following question on the lines provided.

1. What are some ways that the government can help increase economic growth in the United States?

_____

_____

_____

_____

Choose the *best* answer to the following question.

2. How does an increase in the supply of credit and money generally affect the nation's economy?

   A. Prices for goods and services increase.
   B. The supply of goods and services decreases.
   C. Economic growth slows down.
   D. Economic growth increases.

Answers are on page 572.

Consumer Economics

Consumers have seemingly unlimited demands, but they have limited resources with which to satisfy those demands. As a result, consumers must make choices about how to spend their resources to best satisfy their wants and needs. For example, if you decide to buy a car, you may have to forgo buying a new washing machine until a later time. Consumers, therefore, may create budgets. To make a **budget,** a person lists all of his or her demands and decides which ones are necessities—those things that he or she must have, such as food and medicine—and which ones are wants—those things that are not necessary but that he or she wants anyway, such as a vacation or a dinner at a restaurant. After consumers satisfy all of their needs, they must decide which wants they will spend their remaining resources on and which wants they will do without.

Consumers primarily have two options when attempting to satisfy demands that exceed their budget. They can either save money by setting aside extra money over time so that they can buy the things they want at a later time, or they can buy those things on credit. **Credit** is a loan that allows a consumer to purchase a good or service now and pay for it, often a little at a time each month, in the future.

A consumer who buys on credit is referred to as the **lendee.** The person or organization that lends the money is referred to as the **lender.** A lendee repays his or her lender the original purchase price of the product—called the **principle**—plus a little extra for the risk that the lender undertakes by lending the money—called **interest.**

Consumers most often get loans from banks, credit unions, and credit card companies. These lending institutions keep records of how much each consumer borrows and how reliably each makes his or her monthly loan payments. In turn, lenders report this information to credit reporting firms. These firms give each consumer a lending score based on the information that lending institutions report to them. This lending score helps lenders determine what interest rate to charge for a loan. For example, if you borrow a very high percentage of your monthly income and do not make your payments on time, you will earn a low lending score. People with low credit scores have a difficult time finding someone to lend them money, and when they do get a loan, it carries a high interest rate. However, if you borrow a low percentage of your income and consistently make your loan payments on time, lenders will compete to lend to you and give you a lower interest rate.

EXERCISE 5

Consumer Economics

Directions: Choose the *best* answer for each of the following questions.

1. A lendee is considered a good risk by lenders if the lendee

    A. carries a higher percentage of his or her income as a balance on a credit card.
    B. has missed a few credit payments.
    C. has borrowed a small amount of money at a low interest rate.
    D. has a low credit score.

2. A lender uses a consumer's credit score to

    A. set prices for goods and services.
    B. determine the interest rate on a loan to that consumer.
    C. determine what products that consumer should buy.
    D. recommend how much money that consumer should spend.

Answers are on page 572.

Political and Economic Freedom

Markets occurs in civil society and are composed of ordinary people with wants and needs that businesses strive to satisfy. Therefore, it is very important that consumers' political freedoms are protected and that everyone is held accountable to the same rules. This reduces uncertainty so people are confident to create markets and express their demands to producers.

Many economists consider private property rights to be essential political rights that promote stability. The right to control how your own property is used and to benefit from it without coercion reduces uncertainty by increasing confidence in the laws. Economists have shown that countries featuring strong property protections enjoy much greater economic growth rates than countries that do not.

Economists have also shown compelling evidence suggesting that countries with competitive market economies have more democratic governments with greater freedom of expression. Consumers must be free to express themselves so that producers know what goods and services to provide. And because such markets largely operate according to the impersonal forces of supply and demand, people in them are protected from discrimination that is unrelated to their productivity.

EXERCISE 6

Political and Economic Freedom

Directions: Choose the *best* answer to the following question.

1. Strong property rights promote stability in an economy because

    A. property rights slow economic growth.
    B. property rights primarily benefit producers.
    C. property rights reduce uncertainty and increase confidence in the laws.
    D. property rights limit consumers' freedom to express their wants to producers.

Answer the following question on the lines provided.

2. Explain how market economies with strong political rights protect individuals from discrimination.

_____

_____

_____

_____

Answers are on page 572.

CHAPTER 4

Geography and the World

Places and Regions

Geography is the study of Earth's physical features and of human activity as it affects these features. The word *geography* comes from the Greek language and means "Earth description." In addition to studying Earth and the activities of the people who live on it, geographers also study the interactions between people and environments in order to explain the nature of these interactions, why they happen, and how they affect our lives. Geographic study covers a broad range of topics and requires diverse skills. A geographer may be involved in anything from mapmaking to urban planning to environmental management.

The Tools and Skills of Geography

There are two major branches of geography: physical geography and human geography. **Physical geography** is the study of Earth's physical features, including climate, land, water, and plant and animal life. **Human geography**, also known as cultural geography, studies human activities and their relationship to the physical environment. It involves the analysis of the economic, cultural, social, and political impact of these activities.

Geographers rely on many different types of tools to help them in their studies. One of the most basic activities of a geographer is **mapping.** A geographer who designs and makes maps is known as a **cartographer**, and the design and study of maps is **cartography**. Maps are important tools and often illustrate information that is not always easily explained in words alone. Maps allow geographers the opportunity to compare data derived from different locations, such as population density or income distribution.

This chart summarizes the various types of maps a geographer may use.

Type of Map	What It Does
Climate	Presents general information about the climate and precipitation of a region; different colors can show zones
Economic	Features natural resources or different economic activities of an area
Physical	Illustrates the physical features of an area, such as mountains, rivers, and other bodies of water; colors show differences in land elevations
Political	Illustrates government and political boundaries, such as states, nations, and cities
Road	Shows major and minor roads, as well as airports, railroads, cities, and points of interest
Thematic	Illustrates themes or special topics of interest in an area; may show physical features but these may be secondary
Topography	Features contour lines that show the shape and elevation of a region

Most maps contain certain elements that allow a reader to interpret them. For instance, the **title** of the map tells the reader what the map is about. **Distance,** or **scale**, helps a reader understand the relationship between the distance measured on the map and the actual distance measured on the earth. Distance can be measured by verbal, numeric, or graphic form:

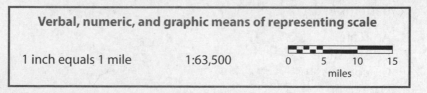

Verbal, numeric, and graphic means of representing scale

1 inch equals 1 mile   1:63,500   0   5   10   15
                                                           miles

A map also usually includes a **compass rose** marking all four directions or a directional finder indicating **true north**. Maps also usually contain a **legend** that includes the various symbols depicted on the map such as towns or cities, water resources, railroads, and highways. The legend will vary depending on what type of map is being used. Finally, **inset maps** can provide detailed information and are often drawn at a larger scale.

In addition to maps, geographers rely on the use of **statistics**, or numerical information, to organize their data and findings in a clear way. Statistics can also identify trends or patterns. For example, census data can be used to understand patterns of living and income distribution, as well as the ethnic or religious composition of an area. Statistics provide geographers with the opportunity to test theories to determine if ideas being studied are valid.

Like other fields of research, geography has also benefited from modern advances in technology. Tools such as satellites and computers have proved invaluable to geographers in collecting, sorting, and analyzing data of all kinds. **Geographic information systems** (GIS) are computer tools that help geographers understand the location of natural resources as well as plan their efficient use. Computer technology has also influenced how cartographers make maps. Digital maps can contain layers, each of which includes a specific type of data, such as roads, houses, or water resources. These layers help cartographers make many different kinds of maps more quickly and efficiently.

EXERCISE 1

The Tools and Skills of Geography

Directions: Choose the *best* answer to each of the following questions.

1. Which of the following statements *best* describes the study of human geography?

   A. a survey of natural vegetation in an area of land
   B. a study to determine economic activities in an area of land
   C. a project to map the location of water bodies in an area of land
   D. a comparison of mountain elevations in an area of land

2. Which of the following do geographers use to help them identify trends or patterns in data?

   A. scale
   B. statistics
   C. compass rose
   D. legend

Answers are on page 572.

Place and Region

The surface of Earth is composed of water and land, with various **bodies of water** occupying almost 70 percent of Earth's surface. The main body of water that circles Earth is conventionally considered to be roughly divided into four oceans: the Pacific, the Atlantic, the Indian, and the Arctic. Approximately 97 percent of the world's water is saltwater; the remaining water consists of freshwater bodies that include lakes, rivers, ponds, and streams.

The remaining surface of Earth is composed of **landforms**, or dry land physical features. Landforms include hills, plateaus, mountains, plains, valleys, canyons, and basins. By far the largest landforms on Earth are the seven land masses known as **continents**. Of the seven, two—Australia and Antarctica—stand alone, while each of the others is joined to at least one other continent. North and South America are connected by the Isthmus of Panama; Asia and Europe are part of one very large landform called Eurasia. Africa is connected to Asia by the Sinai Peninsula.

A **region** is an area of land that has common features that may be natural or artificial. For example, natural features of a region may include forests, deserts, and mountains. Certain climates and even wildlife can help define a region. In the United States, there are five regions, named according to their position on the North American continent: the Northeast, Southwest, West, Southeast, and Midwest. Languages, governments, and religions are among the artificial features that can define a region. In addition, a population's cultural differences or similarities can also distinguish one region from another.

EXERCISE 2

Place and Region

Directions: Label each of the following items to indicate what kind of geographical element it is.

1. Africa _____

2. Rocky Mountains _____

3. Mississippi River _____

4. The West in the United States _____

Answers are on page 572.

Climate

Climate is another important geographical concept. Unlike **weather**, which is an atmospheric condition that is occurring in one area at a particular time, climate describes long-term weather patterns in an area. For example, people who live in the Midwest make sure to have snow tires on their cars during the winter because the climate there is cold enough to produce ice and snow frequently in the winter. In the dry desert of New Mexico, people must take care to protect themselves from the sun and heat common in desert climates.

Many factors determine the climate of a particular region. One such factor is Earth's position relative to the sun at certain times of the year. For example, winter in the United States usually occurs from approximately November to February, while in Australia these months are considered to be summer. This is because Earth tilts on its rotational axis. As Earth revolves around the sun, from November through February the Northern Hemisphere, where the United States is located, is tilted away from the sun and receives less heat. Meanwhile, during those same months, the Southern Hemisphere, where Australia is located, is tilted toward the sun and enjoys a warm summer.

Climate is determined by five other factors:

Factor	How It Affects Climate
Latitude (distance from the equator)	The closer a place is to the equator, the warmer it is.
Elevation	The higher a place is above sea level, the cooler the temperature.
Ocean temperature and wind currents	The temperature of ocean waters determines the directions of the wind currents that move heat.
Closeness to water	Areas closer to water may have more precipitation and have cooler or warmer temperatures than regions further inland.
Terrain	Mountains can block or redirect moist air and cause an area on one side to receive less rain.

People and Environment

An environment is the complex of physical features that determines the form of a given region. The environment includes both human-made and naturally occurring features. **Naturally occurring features** include landforms, the atmosphere, vegetation, and wildlife. **Human-made,** or

artificial, features include housing, transportation infrastructure, and industrial infrastructure. Geographers study the impact of human actions on the environment. Human interventions in the natural environment can cause problems such as soil erosion, global climate change, and pollution.

Geographers look at the relationship between people and the environment in a variety of ways. For instance, some geographers will look at how people use and alter their environment. For example, tobacco farming in some U.S. eastern coastal areas in the early seventeenth and eighteenth centuries exhausted the soil, which caused it to erode and made it unusable for long periods of time. Overgrazing in some U.S. western states also caused soil erosion, which turned some grasslands into desert. Cultural geographers study how the natural environment influences the development of human culture. For example, the climate in a particular area largely determines what kinds of crops are grown and, by extension, the social organizations employed to utilize those crops most effectively. Political geographers can study the impact political events and situations have on the environment, such as conflicts over water rights, grazing areas, and other environmental concerns.

Movement of People

In addition to studying Earth, its landforms, climate, and cultural regions, geographers also study people. Specifically, geographers study the characteristics of populations, including life expectancy, population density, age distribution, and growth rate. This data can help a geographer map settlements and analyze where people live, why they move, and the impact of cultural diversity on a given area. Scientists who study populations are known as **demographers**.

Population Trends and Issues

The world's population is currently more than 7 billion people. Approximately 60 percent of all people live in Asia, making parts of that continent some of the most densely populated regions in the world. By the year 2050, there may be more than 9.7 billion people living on Earth, with the most growth occurring in Asian and African countries. Among the factors that geographers study are the number of live births in a population and the number of deaths. **Birthrates** are calculated as the number of births per year for every 1000 people. **Death rates** are calculated as the number of deaths per year for every 1000 people.

tion density**—that is, the average number of people living within a

ile or kilometer of land. To determine an area's population density,

population of a country is divided by its total land area. The final

angladesh, on the other hand, has one of the highest population

EXERCISE 3

Population Trends and Issues

Directions: Define the following terms.

1. birthrate

2. death rate

3. population density

4. zero population growth

Answers are on page 572.

Human Settlement

A **human settlement** is a place where people live. Settlements come in all sizes, shapes, and locations. A settlement can be as small as a single house or as large as a city with millions of residents. A settlement can be temporary, such as a refugee camp, or permanent, such as a city or town. Sometimes, temporary settlements become permanent settlements.

A settlement is usually established for a particular reason or function. The function of a settlement can often be determined by analyzing its size, its location, and its situation. For example, in the United States, Boston was originally settled because it had a protected harbor with easy access to the Atlantic Ocean. In time the settlement became a center of commerce and a port city.

Some of the largest settlements in the world are cities. The process of **urbanization** occurs when a settlement undergoes major population growth and develops an **infrastructure** (buildings, streets, transportation, etc.) to accommodate the influx of people. People move to cities for a wide variety of reasons, but the most common and compelling reasons are better job opportunities and a higher standard of living. Although people do move to rural areas, it is less common. Almost half of the world's population lives in cities, with more people moving to urban areas every day.

EXERCISE 4

Human Settlement

Directions: Answer the following questions.

1. What is a human settlement?

   _____

   _____

2. Explain the meaning of the term *urbanization*.

   _____

   _____

3. What is one reason that people move to cities?

_____

_____

Answers are on page 573.

Population Movement

Migration is the movement of people from place to place. This can take several different forms. **Immigration** is the movement of people into a country or region where they are not native in order to permanently resettle there; the new arrivals are called **immigrants**. For example, many Italians who left Italy during the nineteenth and twentieth centuries were immigrants *to* the United States. **Emigration** is the movement of people away from their native country or region to live elsewhere. For example, the Pilgrims who settled in North America in the seventeenth century were emigrants *from* England. **Internal migration** is the movement of people to new homes within the boundaries of a given state or country, while **external migration** is the movement of people to new homes across state or national boundaries.

The migration of people can also take other forms. **Seasonal migration** is the movement of people in response to labor or climate conditions, such as farm workers who move as crops ripen and need harvesting or people from the northern U.S. states who travel to the South to escape cold weather months. **Imposed migration** occurs when a government forces people to leave a country. This most often occurs during times of war or political unrest or when a group is facing some kind of persecution. A **diaspora** is the scattering of a group of people in areas away from their native homeland. One of the largest diasporas began in the seventeenth century, when approximately 9 million to 12 million Africans were sold as slaves and transported to places throughout the Western Hemisphere.

People migrate for a variety of reasons. Geographers call those reasons push and pull factors. A **push factor** is a reason to leave a place, usually because some hardship makes staying difficult. Common push factors are wars, famines, political unrest, economic problems, and natural disasters. A **pull factor** is a reason to move to another place, typically because that other place offers better opportunities. Pull factors include better climate, better housing, more food, more jobs, better schools, or more freedom. Push and pull factors often work together—that is, people may leave an area because of a push factor and are drawn to another area because of a pull factor.

Population Movement

Directions: Choose the *best* answer to the following questions.

1. During the late nineteenth century, thousands of Europeans came to the United States to settle and make new lives. This is an example of:

   A. seasonal migration
   B. internal migration
   C. imposed migration
   D. immigration

2. Which *best* illustrates a pull factor?

   A. a country offering free health care to all residents, including recent immigrants
   B. Africans transported from the Ivory Coast to work as slaves in Virginia
   C. a war forcing civilian city dwellers to seek refuge in a neighboring country
   D. seventeenth-century Europeans sending trading expeditions to China

3. Which *best* illustrates a push factor?

   A. millions of acres of new farmland being cleared for settlement
   B. a new industry creating thousands of jobs in a region with few current residents
   C. a famine making it difficult for people to survive in their homeland
   D. a country with mild weather year-round

Answers are on page 573.

Cultural Geography

In addition to studying the physical conditions on Earth and the movement of people, geographers also study **culture**, or the way a group of people who share similar beliefs and customs live. A culture is made up of many different facets, each of which helps a geographer understand a particular group. Geographers who study cultures are called **cultural geographers**.

Elements of Culture

Every culture includes many different elements. One of these is **language**, which is one of the most important parts of a culture. Language allows people to communicate their ideas and experiences as well as pass on cultural traditions. **Religion** can help a group establish a common identity and give meaning and purpose to everyday life. A **social group**, such as a family, is a group of people who interact with one another based on similar characteristics and a sense of unity. Many cultures also have social classes that further distinguish people within a group, based on birth, wealth, or education. **Ethnic groups** are groups that share a common language, history, place of origin, or a combination of these elements. **Cultural diversity** emerges when a variety of distinct cultural groups come together and form one common population.

Two additional features that are important in defining a culture are government and economics. **Government** is the body of laws and institutions that a society uses to establish social order and provide public services and security. There are many different types of government. An **autocracy** is a system in which governmental power is held by a single individual. The traditional monarchies of past ages, headed by a king or queen with unlimited power, were autocracies; so were the totalitarian dictatorships of mid-twentieth-century Europe, in which a single leader exerted influence over almost every aspect of society. An **oligarchy** is a system in which a small group of people, often from a particular social class or ethnic group, holds governmental power. A **democracy** is a system in which power is vested in the people, who elect representatives to make laws and carry out other functions of government.

Economic systems can be just as diverse as any other cultural element. Economic systems have three purposes: to determine what goods and services will be produced, to determine how these goods and services will be produced, and to decide who will get those goods and services. There are three major types of economic systems, and each approaches those three basic purposes differently. A **traditional economy** is one in which long-established customs, habits, and beliefs determine the goods and services a society produces and who will get them. A traditional economy is often found in rural or underdeveloped areas. A **market economy** is one in which supply and demand determine what goods and services a society produces. Consumers choose the products and services they want and businesses produce them in response to that demand. In a **command economy**, or planned economy, goods and services are produced and distributed according to a plan implemented by a central authority, such as a government. Also, the means of production are publicly owned in a command economy.

Elements of Culture

Directions: Define the following terms.

1. language

2. cultural diversity

3. command economy

4. autocracy

5. traditional economy

6. social groups

Answers are on page 573.

CHAPTER 5

Writing the Extended Response

Extended Response Questions

The GED Assessment asks you to demonstrate your ability to generate a text-based argument citing evidence from primary and secondary sources, develop your ideas and write clearly, and use the conventions of standard written English correctly. To test these skills, the Social Studies section includes one 25-minute **Extended Response (ER)** item. The ER requires you to analyze one or more source texts, each 650 words or less. Then you will create a writing sample in response to a prompt. The writing prompt will generally ask you to interpret or explain some important issue or theme in the text(s). To answer the prompt, you will need to develop an argument. An **argument** is a set of reasons for or against a particular idea. You will need to analyze the text(s) and draw conclusions about the topic. You will then need to develop your own point of view about the issue or theme. You will also need to support your argument with evidence from the source text(s). Your argument must be persuasive enough to convince readers that your ideas are correct.

The Extended Response in the Social Studies portion of the GED test is somewhat similar to the Extended Response in the RLA portion. However, the time limit is shorter than for the RLA response: 25 minutes as opposed to 45 minutes. The Social Studies ER is, in turn, scored on a 4-point rubric due to the shorter time limit.

Extended Response Format

You will read the ER source text or texts and respond to the writing prompt online. The item format will be a split screen. The source text(s) will appear on the left side of the screen. Longer texts are tabbed by page, so you can easily page through them. On the right side of the screen are the directions, the prompt, and the area in which you write your response.

Response Guidelines

Please use the guidelines below as you answer the Extended Response question on the Social Studies test.

You will be given guidelines to follow in preparing your response. Here is a simplified version.

1. **You will have 25 minutes to complete this task.** Start by reading the source text(s) and the prompt. Then think carefully about what you want to write. Make sure to plan your response before you begin writing

2. As you write, be sure to

   ☐ **construct an argument** that explains the author's ideas as expressed in the source text(s)
   ☐ **use evidence from the source text(s)** to support your argument
   ☐ **use your own background knowledge** to put your argument into historical context
   ☐ **keep your focus on the source text(s)** and make sure you respond to the directions in the prompt
   ☐ **structure your argument** by arranging your main points in a logical sequence and by elaborating on each point using supporting details from the source text(s)
   ☐ **keep your audience in mind** as you write; choose your words accordingly to make sure your message is clear
   ☐ **express your ideas clearly** by choosing appropriate vocabulary; connect your ideas with appropriate transition words, and vary your sentence structure to enhance the flow of your writing
   ☐ **review your essay and revise it** to correct any errors in grammar, usage, or punctuation

Scoring

Your Extended Response writing sample will be scored across three traits. You will receive a score of 1, 2, or 3 (or 0 for an unscorable response) on each trait.

Trait 1   Creation of Arguments and Use of Evidence

This score measures how well you create a persuasive argument that uses points included in the source text(s) provided to you.

Trait 2   Development of Ideas and Organizational Structure

This score measures how well you develop and organize your writing.

Trait 3   Clarity and Command of Standard English Conventions

This score measures how well you demonstrate fluency with conventions of standard American English.

Materials

Your testing center will provide you with an 8.5 × 14–inch erasable noteboard. This board can be used with an erasable marker. For test security, scratch paper is not allowed.

Understand the Source Text

Your writing sample is scored in part on how well you understand the Extended Response source text or texts. To start, make sure you understand the main idea of each text. The **main idea,** also called the **thesis,** is the central focus of the passage. Think of it as the text's most important idea.

An ER source text may focus on one **position,** or side, of a controversial issue. In that case, the main idea will be subjective, expressing the writer's opinion on the issue. For example, the text might say, "The Electoral College provides the best way of electing the U.S. president." A second text arguing a different position might say, "The Electoral College does not allow for a fair election and should be abandoned."

Another type of Extended Response source text provides an overview of an issue, presenting both positions. In these cases, the main idea is objective, not favoring one side or the other. For example, the main idea might be "there are convincing arguments both for and against the Electoral College."

Making Inferences

Sometimes writers do not state their ideas directly. In these cases, you need to make an **inference,** a conclusion based on information in the text and your own prior knowledge and experience.

EXAMPLE

Statement: Because of the way the Electoral College works, many people don't bother to vote in our presidential elections.

Inference: Under the Electoral College system, a candidate may be elected president without winning the majority of the popular vote. As a result, many people are not motivated to make the effort to vote.

Arguments and Evidence

Once you identify the main idea of the text(s), you can begin to analyze the arguments made by the writer(s). As previously defined, an **argument** is a reason or set of reasons for or against something. For example, a writer who supports the Electoral College system in presidential voting might argue that the system ensures that winning candidates have broad support from diverse areas of the country. A writer who is against the system might argue that the system does not accurately reflect the national will as expressed in the popular vote.

Look for **evidence** the writer uses to support his or her arguments. In most cases, writers state a **claim,** an assertion that some particular idea is true. Then they give evidence to support that claim. Another way to think about this relationship is by using the following formula:

> Claims + Evidence = Argument

Evidence comes in many forms:

- **facts**—statements that can be proven true

    example: The Electoral College is established in the U.S. Constitution.

- **statistics**—numerical facts and data

    example: Arizona had 11 electoral votes in 2012.

- **expert opinions**—quotes from authorities on the topic

    example: Harvard historian Alexander Keyssar observes that no other country has an electoral college.

- **anecdotes**—personal experiences

    example: My father refuses to vote in presidential elections because the president is not elected by popular vote.

As you might guess, anecdotes are not the strongest type of evidence. However, they do provide real-world examples that create a personal connection for readers, a way for them to relate to the topic. Look for all types of evidence in an ER source text, but be wary of any claims that are supported only by anecdotes.

Evaluating Evidence

Part of analyzing an argument is evaluating its evidence. Does the evidence provide good support for the claims made? Check the evidence given in the source text(s) for these factors:

- **specific**—Is the evidence exact, precise information?

    example: Saying that "voting in the Electoral College does not reflect the national will" is not specific; saying that "a candidate who fails to win the popular vote may nevertheless become president by winning the Electoral College" is specific.

* **relevant**—Is the evidence connected to the issue?

    example: Facts about Electoral votes versus popular votes are relevant to a discussion of the Electoral College; facts about votes in primary elections are not.

* **reliable**—Is the evidence trustworthy? Is the source of the evidence an expert? Can the facts be confirmed?

    example: The expert opinion of someone who thoroughly understands the issue, such as a political scientist, can be considered reliable; opinions from a random college student are not as reliable.

* **reasonable**—Is the evidence in line with widely accepted norms? For example, is data derived from credible sources or is it slanted to support one's bias?

    example: An anecdote taken from some random website about a candidate who won the Electoral College vote only through a secret conspiracy is out of line with widely accepted norms and is most likely not credible.

Not all evidence has to meet all four of these factors, but if it meets only one or two, then you might be justified in being unconvinced.

Highlighting as You Read

As you read the source text or texts, be sure to use the on-screen highlighter. The highlighter tool has a variety of different colors you can use to mark up the source text(s). One good use of the tool is to mark a writer's claims in one color and evidence in another color. Or you may want to assign each type of evidence a different color.

Sample Source Text

Here is a sample Social Studies Extended Response source text.

Excerpt

The Electoral College is a process, not a place. The founding fathers established it in the Constitution as a compromise between election of the President by a vote in Congress and election of the President by popular vote of qualified citizens.

The Electoral College process consists of the selection of the electors, the meeting of the electors where they vote for President and Vice President, and the counting of the electoral votes by Congress.

The Electoral College consists of 538 electors. A majority of 270 electoral votes is required to elect the President. Your state's entitled allotment of electors equals the number of members in its Congressional delegation: one for each member in the House of Representatives plus two for your Senate. . . .

The presidential election is held every four years on the Tuesday after the first Monday in November. You help choose your state's electors when you vote for President because when you vote for your candidate you are actually voting for your candidate's electors.

Most states have a "winner-take-all" system that awards all electors to the winning presidential candidate. However, Maine and Nebraska each have a variation of "proportional representation." . . .

—*Excerpted from* What Is the Electoral College? *by the Office of the Federal Registrar, U.S. National Archives and Records Administration*

Excerpt

There have, in its 200 year history, been a number of critics and proposed reforms to the Electoral College system—most of them trying to eliminate it. But there are also staunch defenders of the Electoral College who, though perhaps less vocal than its critics, offer very powerful arguments in its favor.

Opponents of the Electoral College are disturbed by *the possibility of electing a minority president* (one without the absolute majority of popular votes). Nor is this concern entirely unfounded. . . .

One way in which a minority president could be elected is if the country were so deeply divided politically that three or more presidential candidates split the electoral votes among them such that no one obtained the necessary majority. . . . Should that happen today, there are two possible resolutions: either one candidate could throw his electoral votes to the support of another (before the meeting of the Electors) or else, absent an absolute majority in the Electoral College, the U.S. House of Representatives would select the president in accordance with the 12th Amendment. Either way, though, the person taking office would not have obtained the absolute majority of the popular vote. . . .

Opponents of the Electoral College system also point to *the risk of so-called "faithless" Electors*. A "faithless Elector" is one who is pledged to vote for his party's candidate for president but nevertheless votes of another candidate. . . . Faithless Electors have never changed the outcome of an election, though, simply because most often their purpose is to make a statement rather than make a difference. That is to say, when the electoral vote outcome is so obviously going to be for one candidate or the other, an occasional Elector casts a vote for some personal favorite knowing full well that it will not make a difference in the result. . . .

Finally, some opponents of the Electoral College point out, quite correctly, *its failure to accurately reflect the national popular will* . . . primarily from the winner-take-all mechanism whereby the presidential candidate who wins the most popular votes in the State wins all the Electoral votes of that State. One effect of this mechanism is to make it extremely difficult for third-party or independent candidates ever to make much of a showing in the Electoral College. If, for example, a third-party or independent candidate were to win the support of even as many as 25% of the voters nationwide, he might still end up with no Electoral College votes at all unless he won a plurality of votes in at least one State. . . .

Recognizing the strong regional interests and loyalties which have played so great a role in American history, proponents argue that the Electoral College system *contributes to the cohesiveness of the country be requiring a distribution of popular support to be elected president,* without such a mechanism, they point out, presidents would be selected either through the domination of one populous region over the others or through the domination of large metropolitan areas over the rural ones. Indeed, it is principally because of the Electoral College that presidential nominees are inclined to select vice presidential running mates from a region other than their own. . . .

Proponents also point out that, far from diminishing minority interests by depressing voter participation, the Electoral College actually *enhances the status of minority groups.* This is so because the voters of even small minorities in a State may make the difference between winning all of that State's electoral votes or none of that State's electoral votes. And since ethnic minority groups in the United States happen to concentrate in those States with the most electoral votes, they assume an importance to presidential candidates well out of proportion to their number. The same principle applies to other special interest groups such as labor unions, farmers, environmentalists, and so forth. . . .

Proponents further argue that the Electoral College *contributes to the political stability of the nation by encouraging a two-party system.* There can be no doubt that the Electoral College has encouraged and helps to maintain a two-party system in the United States. This is true simply because it is extremely difficult for a new or minor party to win enough popular votes in enough States to have a chance of winning the presidency. Even if they won enough electoral votes to force the decision into the U.S. House of Representatives, they would still have to have a majority of over half the State delegations in order to elect their candidate—and in that case, they would hardly be considered a minor party. . . .

—*Excerpted from* The Electoral College *by William C. Kimberling, Deputy Director FEC National Clearinghouse on Election Administration, revised May 1992*

PROMPT

In your response, develop an argument about the value of the Electoral College from the information presented in both sources and your personal knowledge.

Organize Your Response

After reading the source text(s) but before you begin writing, take time to plan your response. You may feel the need to hurry, but your response will be better if you plan and organize before writing. A plan will help you stay on track in terms of your presentation and also allow you to write your response within the allotted 25 minutes.

A suggested outline is as follows:

I.   Introduction (1 paragraph)

Identify issue.

State the position you support.

II. Body (2–3 paragraphs)

Analyze strongest/weakest arguments.

Evaluate evidence from text(s).

III. Conclusion (1 paragraph)

Summary

Note: If you do write an outline, erase it before submitting your final essay.

Write Your Response

Support Your Ideas

Remember, your writing sample is scored in part on how well you develop your ideas and organize your response. Follow your plan or outline. Defend your ideas with evidence from the source text(s). Try not to merely cut and paste text directly from the source text(s). Put the ideas into your own words, using direct quotations only when the source text writer has expressed an idea in an especially effective way.

Your primary evidence will come from the source text(s); however, you may sparingly include additional evidence from your own prior knowledge or experience to support or attack claims made in the source text(s). For example, if an argument against the Electoral College is that the Electoral College depresses voter turnout, you might point out, if the text does not already, that there are also many other factors that affect voter turnout.

Consider Audience and Purpose

Keep your audience and purpose in mind as you write.

Your **audience** is the readers of your writing sample. You can't know who exactly will read your response. Assume that your audience will know something—but not everything—about the issue. Remember, though, that a reader may already hold an opinion on the issue and may not agree with you. So be sure to respectfully address the position with which you disagree.

Your **purpose** is the primary reason you are writing your sample. Of course, everyone knows you are writing because the GED Assessment requires it. Think beyond that, though, and consider *why* the GED requires it. The Extended Response portion tests you to see how well you can

- analyze arguments
- develop and organize your ideas
- use Standard English

Your purpose, then, is to show through your writing how well you can do these three tasks. Keep them in mind as you write.

Maintain Coherence

To ensure that your response is **coherent,** or logical and well-organized, use transition words and phrases to show how your ideas are connected. Here is a list of common transitions.

- **to add:** also, and, besides, in addition, likewise, next, similarly, too
- **to contrast ideas:** although, but, however, in contrast, instead, nevertheless, on the other hand, or, still, yet
- **to show importance:** first, last, mainly, then, most/least importantly
- **to clarify:** in other words, to put it another way, that is
- **to emphasize:** above all, especially, in fact, more importantly, naturally, obviously
- **to summarize or conclude:** at last, consequently, eventually, finally, in conclusion/summary, lastly, so, summing up, therefore, thus, to conclude

Sample Response

Here is a sample response to the source texts that present the pros and cons of the Electoral College system, including a sample outline. As you read, keep in mind that this is a first unedited draft.

SAMPLE OUTLINE

I. Introduction

Enduring Issue: The most equitable way to elect a U.S. president

The "con" position is better supported.

II. Body

Strongest arguments against: The presidential election does not always reflect the will of the majority of the people.

Claim: It is possible to elect a president who does not win the popular vote.

Evidence: Each state gets a number of electoral votes, equal to the number of its members of Congress.

Evaluate: There are only 538 Electors who vote in the Electoral College; there are millions of Americans who vote for President.

Claim: The Electoral College does not promote unity.

Evidence: The Electoral College gives some states advantage over others because some states have far greater number of representatives in Congress.

Evaluate: Those states with the most votes have an undue influence over the election of the President.

III. Conclusion

Summary

Final thought: The Electoral College should be abolished.

SAMPLE RESPONSE

The excerpts clearly present both sides of the issue of whether the Electoral College is a good way to elect a U.S. President. While the writers present a case for both arguments, I believe that the position stated in opposition to the Electoral College is best supported when you consider how the process of the Electoral College works.

The Electoral College does not reflect the will of the majority of the people. Each state only gets a certain number of votes; in fact, the states get the number of Electoral votes equal to the number of representatives and senators. Although voters can directly vote for members of Congress, they cannot directly vote for President. The "winner takes all" approach that is true for 48 states, including my own, is troubling because it is possible that a large numbers of voters will not see their choice of candidate voted for in the Electoral College because they were not the majority voice of that state.

Although one of the arguments in favor of the Electoral College is that it promotes unity, I do not agree. It seems that large states or states with an abundance of electoral votes have the advantage. I know from media coverage that presidential candidates spend more time and money on those states with the most electoral votes. That means that those areas of the country have more say in our highest elected official. If I were running for president, and I knew that I would need certain states' votes to win then I would be sure to tailor my message to those states. I believe that it is one more way for states with large populations to have more leverage in policy and lawmaking.

In conclusion, the position opposing the Electoral College has better supported convincing claims and stronger evidence that the Electoral College promotes unity and supports minority interests. Only 538 votes really count toward our election of the U.S. President, and these are not equally divided among the states. I can't find the evidence that the Electoral College brings us together and helps minorities have a vote. In my opinion, the number of Electoral votes and the winner-takes-all approach makes it very difficult for the Electoral College to be a true mirror of democracy where we elect our officials to speak for us.

Edit Your Response

Leave time to edit your response. First, make sure the essay is well organized and coherent. Do you need to reorder any paragraphs or ideas? Drag-and-drop or cut-and-paste paragraphs, sentences, or words to create the best flow of ideas. Be sure to reread the edited parts to ensure that they make sense. You may need to add transitional words or phrases to create the best fit. Check your sentences for variety. Avoid overuse of the basic subject + verb sentence pattern, which can make your writing seem repetitive and dull. Try beginning some sentences with introductory words, phrases, or clauses.

How Your Response Will Be Graded

Remember, your writing sample will be scored across three traits.

Trait 1   Creation of Arguments and Use of Evidence

Trait 2   Development of Ideas and Organizational Structure

Trait 3   Clarity and Command of Standard English Conventions

Your response is scored one trait at a time. Here is a simplified version of the scoring rubrics that will be used to score your response.

Score	Description
Trait 1: Creation of Arguments and Use of Evidence	
2	• Creates an argument based on the source text(s). Shows a clear understanding of the relationships among the ideas, events, and persons mentioned in the source text(s) and their historical context. • Supports the argument with evidence from primary and secondary sources. • Connects the argument clearly to both the prompt and the source texts.
1	• Shows some understanding of the relationships among the ideas, events, and persons mentioned in the source text(s). • Supports the argument with some evidence from primary and secondary sources. • Connects the argument to both the prompt and the source text(s).
0	• Shows little or no understanding of the relationships among the ideas, events, and persons mentioned in the source text(s) or their historical context • May or may not create an argument; presents little or no evidence to support the argument. • Does not connect an argument to either the prompt or the source text(s).
Trait 2: Development of Ideas and Organizational Structure	
1	• Organizes ideas in a sensible sequence and clearly shows links between main ideas and details. • Develops ideas in a generally logical manner; elaborates on several ideas. • Shows awareness of the audience and the purpose of the writing task.
0	• Organization of ideas is unclear or lacking. • Develops ideas poorly or illogically; elaborates on just a single idea. • Shows no awareness of the purpose of the writing task.

(continued)

Score	Description
Trait 3: Clarity and Command of Standard English Conventions	
1	• Uses largely correct sentence structure in regard to the following: ○ Frequently confused words and homonyms ○ Subject-verb agreement ○ Pronoun usage, including agreement with antecedent, unclear references, and pronoun case ○ Placement of modifiers and correct word order for logic and clarity ○ Capitalization ○ Use of apostrophes with possessive nouns ○ Punctuation • Uses largely correct sentence structure and varies structure from sentence to sentence; is generally fluent and clear with regard to the following: ○ Correct subordination, coordination, and parallelism ○ Avoidance of wordiness and awkwardness ○ Use of transitional words, conjunctive adverbs, and other words that aid organizational clarity ○ Avoidance of run-on sentences or sentence fragments ○ Standard usage at a level appropriate to on-demand, draft writing • May make some errors in usage and mechanics, but these do not interfere with understanding.
0	• Has minimal control of basic conventions regarding frequently confused words, subject-verb agreement, pronoun usage, word order, and capitalization. • Sentence structure is consistently flawed with little or no variation; has minimal control over conventions regarding correct and fluent sentence structure and standard usage at a level appropriate to on-demand, draft writing. • Makes severe and frequent errors in usage and mechanics that interfere with meaning. OR • Response is insufficient to demonstrate level of mastery over usage and mechanics.

Posttests

How to Use the Posttests

Each of the following Posttests is designed to match the real exam as closely as possible in format and degree of difficulty. When you take these Posttests, your results will help you to determine whether you are ready to take the real GED test, and if not, which topics you still need to review.

To make the best use of these Posttests, follow these four steps:

1. **Take the Posttests one at a time.** Do not try to work through all four Posttests in one session.

2. **Take each Posttest under test conditions.** Find a quiet place where you will not be disturbed. Take the Posttest as if it were the actual GED test. Work through the Posttest from beginning to end in one sitting. Mark your answers directly on the test pages. Observe the time limit given at the start of the test. If you have not finished the Posttest when time runs out, mark the last question you answered, then note how much longer it takes you to complete the test. This information will tell you if you need to speed up your pace, and if so, by how much.

3. **Answer every question.** On the real GED test, there is no penalty for wrong answers, so it makes sense to answer every question, even if you have to guess. If you don't know an answer, see if you can eliminate one or more of the answer choices. The more choices you can eliminate, the better your chance of guessing correctly!

4. **Check your answers in the Posttest Answer Key section at the back of this book.** Pay particular attention to the explanations for questions you missed.

The number of questions and time limit for each Posttest are shown in the following chart.

Posttest	Number of Questions	Time Limit
Reasoning Through Language Arts		
Part 1: Various Formats	23	35 minutes
Part 2: Essay	1 essay question	45 minutes
Mathematical Reasoning	50	90 minutes
Science	10	30 minutes
Social Studies		
Part 1: Various Formats	15	30 minutes
Part 2: Essay	1 essay question	25 minutes

Reasoning Through Language Arts (RLA)

This Reasoning Through Language Arts (RLA) Posttest is designed to help you determine how well you have mastered this GED® test subject area and whether you are ready to take the real GED RLA test.

This test has 23 items in multiple-choice or other formats and one essay question. The question formats are the same as the ones on the real exam and are designed to measure the same skills. Most of the questions are based on reading passages that are selections from either fiction selections or nonfiction sources. Most of the questions are in multiple-choice format, but you will also see questions in other formats, such as fill-in-the-blank items and simulated drag-and-drop and drop-down items. On the real GED test, you will indicate your answers by clicking on the computer screen. For this paper-and-pencil practice test, mark your answers directly on the page. Write your essay in the space provided.

To get a good idea of how you will do on the real exam, take this test under actual exam conditions. Complete the test in one session and follow the given time limit. If you do not complete the test in the time allowed, you will know that you need to work on improving your pacing.

Try to answer as many questions as you can. There is no penalty for wrong answers, so guess if you have to. In multiple-choice questions, if you can eliminate one or more answer choices, you can increase your chances of guessing correctly.

After you have finished the test, check your answers in the Posttest Answer Key section that begins on page 525.

Now begin the Reasoning Through Language Arts (RLA) Posttest.

Reasoning Through Language Arts (RLA)

Part 1: Multiple Choice

23 Questions (various formats) | **35 Minutes**

Use the excerpt for items 1–5:

"The Coming of the Martians"

from The War of the Worlds, *by H. G. Wells*

1   No one would have believed in the last years of the nineteenth century that this world was being watched keenly and closely by intelligences greater than man's and yet as mortal as his own; that as men busied themselves about their various concerns they were scrutinized and studied, perhaps almost as narrowly as a man with a microscope might scrutinize the transient creatures that swarm and multiply in a drop of water. With infinite complacency men went to and fro over this globe about their little affairs, serene in their assurance of their empire over matter. It is possible that the *infusoria* under the microscope do the same. No one gave a thought to the older worlds of space as sources of human danger, or thought of them only to dismiss the idea of life upon them as impossible or improbable. It is curious to recall some of the mental habits of those departed days. At most terrestrial men fancied there might be other men upon Mars, perhaps inferior to themselves and ready to welcome a missionary enterprise. Yet across the gulf of space, minds that are to our minds as ours are to those of the beasts that perish, intellects vast and cool and unsympathetic, regarded this earth with envious eyes, and slowly and surely drew their plans against us. And early in the twentieth century came the great disillusionment.

2   The planet Mars, I scarcely need remind the reader, revolves about the sun at a mean distance of 140,000,000 miles, and the light and heat it receives from the sun is barely half of that received by this world. It must be, if the nebular hypothesis has any truth, older than our world; and

long before this earth ceased to be molten, life upon its surface must have begun its course. The fact that it is scarcely one seventh of the volume of the earth must have accelerated its cooling to the temperature at which life could begin. It has air and water and all that is necessary for the support of animated existence.

3   Yet so vain is man, and so blinded by his vanity, that no writer, up to the very end of the nineteenth century, expressed any idea that intelligent life might have developed there far, or indeed at all, beyond its earthly level. Nor was it generally understood that since Mars is older than our earth, with scarcely a quarter of the superficial area and remoter from the sun, it necessarily follows that it is not only more distant from time's beginning but nearer its end.

4   The secular cooling that must someday overtake our planet has already gone far indeed with our neighbor. Its physical condition is still largely a mystery, but we know now that even in its equatorial region the midday temperature barely approaches that of our coldest winter. Its air is much more attenuated than ours, its oceans have shrunk until they cover but a third of its surface, and as its slow seasons change, huge snowcaps gather and melt about either pole and periodically inundate its temperate zones. That last stage of exhaustion, which to us is still incredibly remote, has become a present-day problem for the inhabitants of Mars. The immediate pressure of necessity has brightened their intellects, enlarged their powers, and hardened their hearts. And looking across space with instruments, and intelligences such as we have scarcely dreamed of, they see, at its nearest distance only 35,000,000 of miles sunward of them, a morning star of hope, our own warmer planet, green with vegetation and grey with water, with a cloudy atmosphere eloquent of fertility, with glimpses through its drifting cloud wisps of broad stretches of populous country and narrow, navy-crowded seas.

5   And we men, the creatures who inhabit this earth, must be to them at least as alien and lowly as are the monkeys and lemurs to us. The intellectual side of man already admits that life is an incessant struggle for existence, and it would seem that this too is the belief of the minds upon Mars. Their world is far gone in its cooling and this world is still crowded with life, but crowded only with what they regard as inferior animals. To carry warfare sunward is, indeed, their only escape from the destruction that, generation after generation, creeps upon them.

POSTTEST

1. Paragraph 1 makes an analogy comparing Martians to

    _____ and the inhabitants of Earth to _____?

    A. microscopic creatures, monkeys and lemurs
    B. beasts, scientists
    C. a missionary, colonized peoples
    D. a scientist, microscopic creatures

2. In paragraph 1, context clues indicate that the word *infusoria* most likely means

    A. minute aquatic creatures.
    B. transient matters.
    C. terrestrial humans.
    D. unsympathetic Martians.

3. Paragraphs 2–4 have the *primary* purpose of

    A. giving details to explain and elaborate the analogy used in paragraph 1.
    B. providing exposition to explain what is about to happen in the story.
    C. acquainting readers with scientific theories about the solar system.
    D. introducing the main characters of the story.

4. The following sentence from the passage includes what rhetorical or figurative device?

    The immediate pressure of necessity has brightened their intellects, enlarged their powers, and hardened their hearts.

    A. chronological order
    B. parallelism
    C. simile
    D. personification

5. The final paragraph indicates that the Martians will "carry warfare sunward." What does this mean?

    A. They will try to colonize the sun.
    B. They will attack Earth during daylight hours.
    C. They will attack Earth, which is closer to the sun than Mars is.
    D. They will teach Earthlings advanced military technologies.

Use the two excerpts for items 6–18:

Excerpt from *Clocks and Culture 1300–1700*

by Carlo M. Cipolla

1   In Europe, where the clock soon became an essential object of everyday life, the modes of thinking of the people, as well as their ways of expression, were deeply influenced by it. Froissart [. . .] wrote a poem of 1174 verses in which he developed an analogy between the mechanical movements of a clock and the sensations and movements of a loving heart. One century later, another poet, Gaspare Visconti, wrote a shorter and more delicate poem in which again feelings of love are compared to the movements of a clock. These might be judged extravaganzas of mechanically inclined poets, but in the course of the sixteenth and seventeenth centuries the clock as a machine exerted deep influence on the speculations of philosophers and scientists. Kepler asserted that "The universe is not similar to a divine living being, but is similar to a clock." Robert Boyle wrote that the universe is "a great piece of clock work," and Sir Kenelm Digby wrote again that the universe was nothing but an immense clock. In the framework of this prevailing mechanistic *Weltanschauung*[1] God was described as an outstanding clockmaker.

2   Per se, these facts may seem to be of interest only to the erudite collector of historical oddities. Their meaning, however, acquires a new dimension when one notices that similar facts are quite common in the history of technology and machines. Each new machine that appears creates new needs, besides satisfying existing ones, and breeds newer machines. The new contrivances modify and shape our lives and our thoughts; they affect the arts and philosophy, and they intrude even into our spare time, influencing our way of using it.

3   The machine is a tool. But it is not a "neutral" tool. We are deeply influenced by the machine while using it. De Saint Exupèry optimistically believes that "little by little the machine will become part of humanity" and that "every machine will gradually take on (man's) patina and lose its identity in its function." However, in a world of machines we too are

---

[1] *Weltanschauung*: particular worldview or view of life.

gradually taking on a patina and are little by little infected by a mechanistic outlook that is not always useful nor beneficial in handling human affairs. As Oscar Wilde reportedly said, "the evil that machinery is doing is that it makes men themselves machines also."

4   Only a fool would undiscriminately condemn the machine as such. We desperately need more and better machines because we desperately need economic and technological development. But we desperately need also a development of our philosophy and of our capacity for handling human affairs so that we can put our machines to good and reputable uses.

6. Which sentence would the author of the passage *most* likely agree with?

   A. The use of machines changes the user.
   B. Machines create more problems than they solve.
   C. Poets and philosophers often exaggerate the effects of machines.
   D. God is like a powerful clockmaker.

7. What kinds of evidence does Cipolla use to support his claims?

   A. numerical statistics
   B. complex metaphors
   C. relevant quotations
   D. personal anecdotes

8. The word *patina* usually describes a greenish film that often appears on the surface of old bronze. In paragraph 3, the word *patina* is used

   as a _____.

   A. scientific term describing the physiological effects of handling machines
   B. term used to personify machines, to liken them to robots
   C. modifier showing De Saint Exupèry's negative view of machines
   D. metaphor creating a striking comparison between (non-metal) humans and metal machines

Use the excerpt for items 9–11:

From "The Coming Robot Army"

by Steve Featherstone

1   Robots have always been associated with dehumanization and, more explicitly, humanity's extinction. The word "robot" is derived from the Czech word for forced labor, *vobota*, and first appeared in Karel Capek's 1920 play, *R.U.R.* (*Rossum's Universal Robots*), which ends with the destruction of mankind.

2   This view of robots, popularized in such movies as the Terminator series, troubles Cliff Hudson, who at the time coordinated robotics efforts for the Department of Defense. I ran into Cliff on the second day of the show [the Association for Unmanned Vehicle Systems International conference], outside Carnegie Mellon's National Robotics Engineering Center's booth. Like the scientists in *R.U.R.*, Cliff saw robots as a benign class of mechanized serfs.[2] Military robots will handle most of "the three D's: dull, dangerous, dirty-type tasks," he said, such as transporting supplies, guarding checkpoints, and sniffing for bombs. The more delicate task of killing would remain in human hands.

3   "I liken it to the military dog," Cliff said, and brought up a briefing given the previous day by an explosive ordinance disposal (EOD) officer who had just returned from Iraq. The highlight of the briefing was an MTV-style video montage of robots disarming IEDs [improvised explosive devices]. It ended with a soldier walking away from the camera, silhouetted against golden evening sunlight, his loyal robot bumping along the road at his heels. Cliff pressed his hands together. "It's that partnership, it's that team approach," he said. "It's not going to replace the soldier. It's going to be an added capability and enhancer."

9. In paragraph 2, the word *benign* means

    A. being.
    B. harmless.
    C. dangerous.
    D. lowly.

---

[2] **serf:** a person in condition of servitude, required to render services to a lord; a servant or slave

10. In paragraph 2, the author compares Cliff Hudson to the scientists in *R.U.R.*, who "saw robots as a benign class of mechanized serfs." The comparison *primarily*

    A. implies that Hudson may be naïve, since the robots in *R.U.R.* destroy humanity.
    B. indicates that Hudson admires Karel Capek's 1920 play *R.U.R.*
    C. implies that Hudson may be involved in classified military work.
    D. indicates that Hudson is well educated, since he is like a scientist.

11. Choose the answer with terms that correctly fill in the blanks in this sentence:

    The main **topic** of the excerpt from "The Coming Robot Army" is

    _____. A key concern of the passage is _____.

    A. robots in literature; whether robots will bring about the destruction of humanity
    B. robots in literature; whether or not robots are benign
    C. robots in the military; whether robots in the military are a positive development
    D. robots in the military; whether robots can replace military dogs

Directions: Statements 12–18 are listed after the following table. Write each number, 12–18, in the correct column to show which passage or passages it applies to.

ONLY the excerpt from *Clocks and Culture*	ONLY the excerpt from "The Coming Robot Army"	BOTH the excerpt from *Clocks and Culture* and the excerpt from "The Coming Robot Army"	NEITHER the excerpt from *Clocks and Culture* nor the excerpt from "The Coming Robot Army"

12. express(es) some ambivalence about a technology

13. wholeheartedly celebrate(s) technological advancement

14. include(s) both third-person and first-person perspectives

15. refer(s) to entertainments from pop culture of the last 50 years

16. use(s) quotations to add specificity and/or provide evidence for claims

17. discuss(es) a technology that has shaped culture for several hundred years

18. compare(s) a technological device with one or more living or natural beings

The following letter contains several numbered blanks, each marked "Select..." Beneath each one is a set of choices. Indicate the choice from each set that is correct and belongs in the blank. (**Note:** On the real GED test, the choices will appear as a "drop-down" menu. When you click on a choice, it will appear in the blank.)

Dear Mr. Jackson:

Thank you very much for writing a letter of recommendation
19. Select... ▼ extremely grateful for your support.

19. Select... ▼
A. on my behalf, I am
B. on my behalf. I am
C. on my behalf I am

I also have some good news to report. I have received a letter from
20. Select... ▼ , dean of admissions at Springdale College, and it says

20. Select... ▼
A. Professor Rothenberg
B. professor Rothenberg
C. professor rothenberg

POSTTEST

that I have been accepted into this [21. Select . . . ▼] entering first-year

21. Select . . . ▼
A. falls'
B. fall's
C. falls

class!

I really appreciate the time and effort you put into mentoring me this [22. Select . . . ▼] especially want to let you know that all of

22. Select . . . ▼
A. year, and I
B. year and, I
C. year and I

[23. Select . . . ▼] help with my college applications has paid off. It is so

23. Select . . . ▼
A. your
B. you're
C. your'

exciting to think about starting college next year!

I will be sure to email you to say how I am doing next year. Thank you again.

Sincerely,

Taylor Wallace

Part 2: Essay

1 Question | **45 Minutes**

Use the following passage for item 24:

Should Middle and High School Students Be Taught to Use Print Reference Books?

1   My sister called me the other day to complain that her son's middle school librarian had—gasp—"wasted" an hour teaching the students to use print reference sources, such as atlases and encyclopedias. "Why would she do that?" she yelped. "The kids can look up everything they need to know on the Internet."

2   I wondered if that were true. I grew up knowing how to use print resources, and I do still use them, from time to time. But it sure is easier, most of the time, to use Google to find information quickly. I decided to investigate whether, given the wealth of online resources available today, there are good reasons to learn to use print reference materials.

3   First, I considered the positive aspects of focusing on the use of online resources rather than print materials. If you go to a library to use print references, chances are that there are a limited number of volumes and that many of them are out of date. Atlases are a good example. With all the strife in the world, borders of countries are changing all the time. Names of regions and countries change. Wetlands erode, and rivers change course. The day an atlas is printed, it is probably full of outdated information. As my sister pointed out, "Remember the atlas in our seventh-grade textbook, which still showed the U.S.S.R. in place of Russia and other countries, even though the U.S.S.R. had dissolved in 1991?"

4   And then there's the accessibility of the Internet: you can look up what you want to from the comfort of your home or car—anywhere with Internet access—without having to have proximity to libraries or the money to own print reference works. As of November 2013, Google Books had scanned 20 million books to make available online. How many libraries do you have access to that have that many volumes? Last, students need very little specialized knowledge to use the Internet: Search engines allow students to

type in a few keywords, without having to understand print indexes, tables of contents, or other features of print texts.

5   Then I spoke to my friend Molly, who is a research librarian. I asked her opinion. She made several compelling points. First, the ability to understand how print texts work is an important skill. Print texts are the foundation of modern culture: without Johannes Gutenberg and his fifteenth-century printing press, we'd still be in the Dark Ages. When students type in a few keywords, they aren't getting a particularly sophisticated idea of the architecture of information that is available. Exposure to information architecture, in turn, will help students learn to structure data and ideas to convey it to others.

6   And then there's the digital divide. Not every student has a computer, a tablet, or a smart phone. Access to these things costs money, too. Students without online resources still need libraries and the resources within them—and they need to know how to use them. And not every location has cell coverage, cable Internet, or wireless availability. Next time you're stuck in a rural area with no cell signal and no Internet, you'll be glad to know how to find a map in a road atlas or how to read a phone book!

7   Plus, most people overestimate the comprehensiveness of Internet information. Molly says that the Internet is a "mile wide and an inch deep." That is, it is great if you need up-to-the-minute information about your favorite pop star's latest scandal. But what if you need old information, obscure information, or access to text that is still under copyright? She gives as an example topographical maps, trail maps, and contour maps. Most really good, detailed maps are not available online (what would the copyright holder's motivation be to provide them for free?). And even for maps that are available, screen resolution is nowhere near as good as the resolution of a printed page.

8   I have learned a lot about information and online access, and it seems to me that there are strong points on both sides. Perhaps time will bear out one position or the other. Reader, what do you think?

24. The passage presents two positions on a specific issue. Write a response in which you compare and contrast the two positions and explain which position you find more persuasive. Use relevant and specific evidence from the passage to support your response.

Write your response in the box. You should plan to spend up to 45 minutes planning, drafting, and editing your response.

Mathematical Reasoning

Now that you have reviewed the topics tested on the GED® Mathematical Reasoning test, take this Mathematical Reasoning Posttest to get a good idea of your readiness to take the actual exam.

This test has 50 items. The questions are in the same formats as the ones on the real exam and are designed to measure the same skills. Some of the questions simply ask you to make calculations. Others describe real-life situations that you must decide how to solve using mathematics. Many of the questions on this test are based on graphs or diagrams. Most of the questions are in multiple-choice format, but you will also see questions that ask you to indicate a point on a graph, write your answer in a box, select an answer from a drop-down menu, or "drag" an answer into the correct position in a math expression or equation. On the real GED test, you will indicate your answers by clicking on the computer screen. For this paper-and-pencil practice test, mark your answers directly on the page.

To get a good idea of how you will do on the real exam, take this test under actual exam conditions. Complete the test in one session and follow the given time limit. If you do not complete the test in the time allowed, you will know that you need to work on improving your pacing.

Try to answer as many questions as you can. There is no penalty for wrong answers, so guess if you have to. In multiple-choice questions, if you can eliminate one or more answer choices, you can increase your chances of guessing correctly.

After you have finished the test, check your answers in the Posttest Answer Key section that begins on page 526.

Now turn the page and begin the Mathematical Reasoning Posttest.

Mathematics Formula Sheet

Area of a:

parallelogram $\quad A = bh$

trapezoid $\quad A = \left(\dfrac{1}{2}\right)h(b_1 + b_2)$

Surface Area and Volume of a:

rectangular/right prism $\quad SA = \pi ph + 2B \qquad V = Bh$

cylinder $\quad SA = 2\pi rh + 2\pi r^2 \qquad V = r^2h$

pyramid $\quad SA = \left(\dfrac{1}{2}\right)ps + B \qquad V = \left(\dfrac{1}{3}\right)Bh$

cone $\quad SA = \pi rs + \pi r^2 \qquad V = \left(\dfrac{1}{3}\right)\pi r^2h$

sphere $\quad SA = 4\pi r^2 \qquad V = \left(\dfrac{4}{3}\right)\pi r^3$

(p = perimeter of base B; $\pi \approx 3.14$)

Algebra

slope of a line $\quad m = \dfrac{(y_2 - y_1)}{(x_2 - x_1)}$

slope-intercept form of the equation of a line $\quad y = mx + b$

point-slope form of the equation of a line $\quad y - y_1 = m(x - x_1)$

standard form of a quadratic equation $\quad ax^2 + bx + c = y$

quadratic formula $\quad x = \dfrac{-b \pm \sqrt{b^2 - 4ac}}{2a}$

Pythagorean theorem $\quad a^2 + b^2 = c^2$

simple interest $\quad I = prt$

(*I* = interest, *p* = principal,
r = rate, *t* = time)

Mathematical Reasoning

50 Questions | **90 Minutes**

Directions: Choose the best answer for each of the following questions.

1. Circle one number in each shaded cell that would make the chart that of a function. (*Note:* On the real GED test, the choices will appear in a drop-down menu, and you will click on your choice.)

x	–2	–1	0	1	2	1	5	–2 ▼
y	1	3	0	2	6	–1	7	5
	3					2		
	4					7		
	5					10		

2. Circle the two points that prove this is not the graph of a function. (*Note:* On the real GED test, you will click on your choices.)

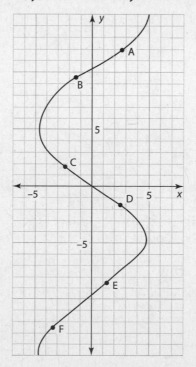

POSTTEST

3. Write the comparison "175 people compared to 70 people" as a proportion. Use a fraction in lowest terms. Write your answer in the box.

4. Choose the correct answer. (*Note:* On the real GED test, the choices will appear in a drop-down menu, and you will click on your choice.)

   The distance on the number line from 4 to –9 is ____ the distance from –5 to 9.

Select... ▼
less than
equal to
greater than

5. Multiply

   A. x

   B. 1

   C. $x^{\frac{13}{6}}$

   D. $\frac{1}{x}$

6. Factor $5x^2 - 17x - 12$

   A. $(5x + 3)(x - 4)$
   B. $(5x - 3)(x + 4)$
   C. $(x + 1)(5x - 15)$
   D. The expression is prime.

7. Divide $\dfrac{x^3 - 9x^2 + 20x}{x - 4}$

   A. $(x^2 - 5x)(x - 4)$
   B. $x(x + 5)$
   C. $x(x - 5)(x - 4)$
   D. $x(x - 5)$

8. Solve for x: $4x - 5 < 3x + 9$.

   A. $x > 7$
   B. $x < 7$
   C. $x > 14$
   D. $x < 14$

9. Divide $\dfrac{x^{-2}y^5}{x^3 y^2}$

   A. 1

   B. $\dfrac{y^3}{x^3}$

   C. $\dfrac{y^3}{x}$

   D. $x^5 y^3$

10. Solve for x: $6x^2 + 7x = 20$.

   A. $x = \dfrac{5}{2}, -\dfrac{4}{3}$

   B. $x = -\dfrac{5}{2}, -\dfrac{4}{3}$

   C. $x = -\dfrac{5}{2}, \dfrac{4}{3}$

   D. $x = \dfrac{5}{2}, \dfrac{4}{3}$

11. What values of x cannot be used in the expression: $y = \sqrt{5x}$?

   A. $x > 0$
   B. $x \neq 0$
   C. $x < 0$
   D. $x \leq 0$

12. At a banquet, 470 people were served at a cost to the organizers of $5640. What was the unit cost per person?

    A. $12.00
    B. $8.33
    C. $11.62
    D. $13.86

13. Solve for x: $5x - 1 = 8x - 7$.

    A. 2

    B. $\frac{1}{2}$

    C. $\frac{8}{3}$

    D. $\frac{3}{8}$

14. Write the correct mathematical symbol in each mathematical relationship: <, >, or =. (*Note*: On the real GED test, you will click on each symbol and "drag" it into the correct position.)

    −3 _____ 2   −1 _____ −5   14 _____ 14

15. Which of the following is equivalent to $\frac{128}{17}$ as a mixed number in lowest terms?

    A. $10\frac{12}{17}$

    B. 7.53

    C. $7\frac{1}{9}$

    D. $7\frac{9}{17}$

16. Solve for x: $25 - 4x = 5$.

    A. 5

    B. -5

    C. $\dfrac{1}{5}$

    D. $7\dfrac{1}{2}$

17. Add $9\dfrac{2}{7} + 3\dfrac{7}{9}$

    A. $13\dfrac{2}{31}$

    B. $27\dfrac{4}{63}$

    C. $13\dfrac{4}{63}$

    D. $6\dfrac{4}{63}$

18. Subtract $\dfrac{4y - 3x}{x} - \dfrac{2x + 3y}{y}$

    A. $\dfrac{2(2x^2 - 3xy - y^2)}{xy}$

    B. $\dfrac{2(2y^2 - 3xy - x^2)}{x - y}$

    C. $\dfrac{2(2y^2 - 3xy - x^2)}{x + y}$

    D. $\dfrac{2(2y^2 - 3xy - x^2)}{xy}$

19. Provide the missing number: 6:11::78: _____

   A. 200

   B. 143

   C. 66

   D. $\dfrac{1}{13}$

20. Choose the correct answer. (*Note*: On the real GED test, the choices will appear in a drop-down menu, and you will click on your choice.)

   The area of a circle of radius 6 is _____ the area of a square 10 units on a side.

Select ... ▼
less than
equal to
greater than

21. Add 12.7 + 22.006 + 9.0101

   A. 42.7161
   B. 43.7161
   C. 43.72
   D. 43.7116

22. What is the equation of a straight line that has slope 2 and that passes through the point (3, 3)?

   A. $y = 2x + 3$
   B. $y = 2x - 3$
   C. $y = x - 3$
   D. $y = 2x - 6$

23. Multiply $7.35 \times 10^{12} \cdot 5.0 \times 10^{2}$

   A. 3.675×10^{15}
   B. 36.75×10^{14}
   C. 3.675×10^{14}
   D. 36.75×10^{15}

24. What fraction equals 0.555?

    A. $\dfrac{111}{200}$

    B. $1\dfrac{89}{111}$

    C. $\dfrac{555}{999}$

    D. $\dfrac{555}{1000}$

25. 22 coffee drinkers use 5 pounds of ground coffee in a month. At the same rate, how many coffee drinkers would use 32 pounds of ground coffee?

    A. 40
    B. 44
    C. 141
    D. 704

26. Add $3 \times 10^9 + 7 \times 10^{10}$

    A. 7.3×10^9
    B. 7.3×10^{10}
    C. 1.0×10^{10}
    D. 1.0×10^{20}

27. Arrange the following decimals in order from greatest to least. Write them in the spaces provided. (*Note*: On the real GED test, you will click on each decimal and "drag" it into the correct position.)

    0.022, 0.077, 0.0203, 0.00105, 0.0905

    _____ > _____ > _____ > _____ > _____

28. What is the circumference of a circle with a diameter of 30 feet?

    A. 2827 feet
    B. 706.85 feet
    C. 94.2 feet
    D. 47.12 feet

29. What is the area of this triangle?

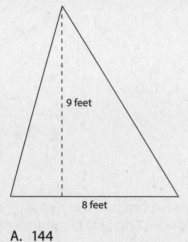

9 feet

8 feet

    A. 144
    B. 108
    C. 72
    D. 36

30. A rectangular crate has a volume of 42 cubic feet. The top of the crate measures 7 feet by 2 feet. How tall is the crate?

    A. 6 feet
    B. 3 feet
    C. 2 feet
    D. 1 foot

31. If $f(x) = x^2 - 2x + 5$, what is $f(6) + f(4)$?

    A 13
    B. 29
    C. 42
    D. 377

32. Tom's makes candies that are 55% sugar. If he has 120 pounds of a mixture of the other ingredients, how much sugar should Tom mix in?

    A. 54 lbs.
    B. 66 lbs.
    C. 146.67 lbs.
    D. 218.2 lbs.

33. Evaluate $(2 + 2 \cdot 7)^2 - 3(2(7 + 14 \div 7))$

    A. 766
    B. 730
    C. 238
    D. 202

34. Evaluate $8^{\frac{-5}{3}}$

    A. $\dfrac{1}{32}$

    B. $8^{\frac{1}{8}}$

    C. 32

    D. $\dfrac{1}{1024}$

35. Divide $\dfrac{2}{3} \div \dfrac{9}{4}$

    A. $1\dfrac{1}{2}$

    B. $\dfrac{8}{27}$

    C. $3\dfrac{3}{8}$

    D. $\dfrac{2}{3}$

36. You are tossing a special 10-sided gamer's die that has a different number between 0 and 9 on each side. How many 6's would you expect to throw in 40 tries?

    A. 0
    B. 4
    C. 5
    D. 13

37. If 2300 students at a college represent 26% of the student body, how many students are at the college?

    A. 598
    B. 1702
    C. 3108
    D. 8846

38. The population of a county is 114,300, which represents a decrease of 10% from last year. What was the population of the county last year?

    A. 102,870
    B. 125,730
    C. 127,000
    D. None of the above

39. Choose the correct answer. (*Note*: On the real GED test, the choices will appear in a drop-down menu, and you will click on your choice.)

    Peter received the following grades: 98, 76, 85, 88, and 79.

    His mean grade is | Select ... ▼ | his median grade.
    | less than |
    | equal to |
    | greater than |

40. Expand: $(5x - 6)^2$

    A. $25x^2 - 36$
    B. $25x^2 + 36$
    C. $25x^2 - 60x + 36$
    D. $25x^2 + 60x + 36$

41. What is the smallest integer that makes $x + 7 > -14$ true?

    A. -20
    B. -21
    C. 21
    D. 20

POSTTEST

42. Arrange the following numbers in order from greatest to least. Write them in the spaces provided. (*Note:* On the real GED test, you will click on each number and "drag" it into the correct position.)

    0.87, 92%, 0.96, $\frac{5}{9}$, $\frac{7}{8}$, $\frac{8}{11}$, 8.3%

    _____ > _____ > _____ > _____ > _____ > _____ > _____

43. If a line has an equation of $4x + 3y = 15$, what is its slope?

    A. $\frac{4}{3}$

    B. $-\frac{4}{3}$

    C. $-\frac{3}{4}$

    D. $\frac{3}{4}$

44. What is the sum of $7x^2 + 9x$ and $13 + 8x - 5x^2$?

    A. $2x^2 + 17x + 17$
    B. $12x^2 + 17x + 13$
    C. $2x^2 + x + 13$
    D. $2x^2 + 17x + 13$

45. Choose the correct answer. (*Note:* On the real GED test, the choices will appear in a drop-down menu, and you will click on your choice.)

    Throwing 4 heads in a row with a fair coin has a probability that is

    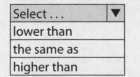

    | Select... ▼ |
    | lower than |
    | the same as |
    | higher than |

    the probability of throwing heads, tails, heads, tails in that order.

46. Graph $y = 2x^2 - 12x + 14$

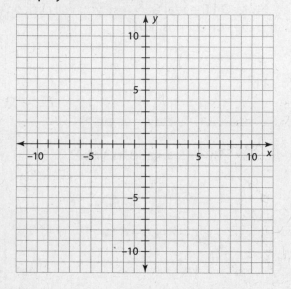

47. What is the probability of getting a 3 or 4 on one throw of a normal, six-sided die?

    A. $\dfrac{1}{6}$

    B. $\dfrac{1}{3}$

    C. $\dfrac{7}{36}$

    D. $\dfrac{2}{3}$

48. If the enrollment at a school was 1500 last year and is 1425 this year, what is the percent decrease in enrollment from last year?

    A. 95%
    B. 94.7%
    C. 5.26%
    D. 5.0%

49. Write the equation of a line passing between the points (5, 9) and (–2, 4).

    A. $y = \dfrac{5}{7}x + \dfrac{38}{7}$

    B. $y = \dfrac{7}{5}x + \dfrac{38}{7}$

    C. $y = -\dfrac{5}{7}x + \dfrac{38}{7}$

    D. $y = 5x + 38$

50. Circle the point where the graph of $y = 6x^3 + 5x^2 + 4$ intersects the y-axis. (*Note*: On the real GED test, you will click on your choice.)

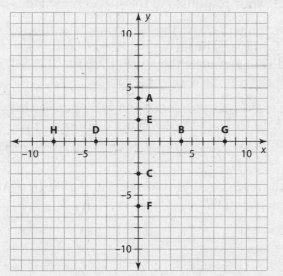

Science

This Science Posttest is designed to help you determine how well you have mastered this GED® test subject area and whether you are ready to take the real GED Science test.

This test has 10 items in various formats. The question formats are the same as the ones on the real exam and are designed to measure the same skills. Some of the questions are based on passages or diagrams.

Most of the questions are in multiple-choice format, but you will also see questions in other formats, such as short-response or fill-in-the-blank items. On the real GED test, you will indicate your answers by clicking on the computer screen. For this paper-and-pencil practice test, mark your answers directly on the page. Write your responses in the spaces provided.

To get a good idea of how you will do on the real exam, take this test under actual exam conditions. Complete the test in one session and follow the given time limit. If you do not complete the test in the time allowed, you will know that you need to work on improving your pacing.

Try to answer as many questions as you can. There is no penalty for wrong answers, so guess if you have to. In multiple-choice questions, if you can eliminate one or more answer choices, you can increase your chances of guessing correctly.

After you have finished the test, check your answers in the Posttest Answer Key section that begins on page 529.

Now begin the Science Posttest.

Science

10 Questions | 30 Minutes

Directions: Choose the best answer for each of the following questions.

Use the passage for item 1:

1 Electric energy is derived from converting other sources of energy, mostly nonrenewable resources such as coal, natural gas, oil, and nuclear power. Half of the electricity used in the United States is produced by burning coal. Coal-burning power plants are a key source of carbon dioxide emission, the primary cause of global warming. Coal-burning plants are also a leading source of other harmful air pollutants. These include sulfur dioxide, which contributes to acidic particles that penetrate human lungs and enter the bloodstream as well as cause acid rain. Acid rain acidifies bodies of water and the soil and also damages plants. Nitrogen oxides cause ozone-based smog and harms lungs and the bronchiolar system.

2 The electricity produced in power plants is transformed in light bulbs. A portion of the electricity is transformed into light and the rest is transformed into heat. The amount of electric energy that a bulb uses to produce light is measured in Watts, with 1 Watt (W) equaling the consumption rate of 1 Joule of energy per second. By law, the United States and other countries are phasing out incandescent bulbs by banning the production or importation of these bulbs. In the table below, information about three different types of lights is arranged according to the amount of light produced, measured in lumens. The lifetime of the bulbs follows the trend of their energy efficiencies

Light Output	Incandescent Light Bulbs	Compact Fluorescent Lights (CFLs)	Light Emitting Diodes (LEDs)
Lumens	Watts	Watts	Watts
450	40	9–13	4–5
800	60	13–15	6–8
1,100	75	18–25	9–13
1,600	100	23–30	16–20
2,600	150	30–55	25–28

POSTTEST

1. Based on the passage and the table, compare the relative energy efficiency of standard metal-filament incandescent bulbs, compact fluorescent lights (CFLs), and light-emitting diodes (LEDs) in transforming electric energy (in Watts) into light energy (in lumens). Describe the likely consequences for the environment and for human health of phasing out the use of incandescent light bulbs.

   Write your response in the box. This task may require approximately 10 minutes to complete.

Use the passage for items 2–3:

Earth and the seven other planets in our solar system revolve around a star that we call the sun. Earth is about 93 million miles from the sun. Earth rotates, or turns completely around, in one day and simultaneously revolves at a slightly tilted angle in an elliptical orbit around the sun in the course of one year. Orbiting around Earth at the relatively close distance of approximately 240,000 miles is its single moon. The moon revolves around Earth in approximately one month in an orbit that is slightly tilted from Earth's orbit around the sun. The sun is about 400 times larger than the moon and about 400 times farther away from Earth, so the sun and the moon appear to be approximately the same size to people on Earth.

Based on the passage, fill in the blanks of the following sentences.

2. The revolution of the _____ around _____ is responsible for the phases of the moon.

3. The seasons, which are most obvious between the poles and the equator on Earth, are due to the _____ revolving around the _____.

Use the passage for item 4:

Plants, phytoplankton, algae, and some bacteria can carry out a light-dependent form of respiration called photosynthesis. In photosynthesis, light energy from the sun is used to synthesize a cellular fuel, glucose. Compare the chemical equations for aerobic respiration and photosynthesis:

Aerobic respiration:

$C_6H_{12}O_6 + 6O_2 \rightarrow 6CO_2 + 6H_2O$ + chemical energy

[1 glucose molecule + 6 oxygen molecules {*the reactants*} $\rightarrow$ 6 carbon dioxide molecules + 6 water molecules + energy {*the products*}]

Photosynthesis:

$6H_2O + 6CO_2$ + light energy $\rightarrow C_6H_{12}O_6 + 6O_2$

[6 water molecules + 6 carbon dioxide molecules + light energy {*the reactants*} $\rightarrow$ 1 glucose molecule + 6 oxygen molecules {*the products*}]

POSTTEST

4. Based on the chemical equations, what is the relationship between photosynthesis and aerobic respiration in terms of their reactants and products, as well as between photosynthetic organisms and humans, who depend largely on aerobic respiration?

Write your response in the space provided. This task may take approximately 10 minutes to complete.

✂ **Cut** 📋 **Copy** 📋 **Paste** ↰ Undo ↱ Redo

Use the energy pyramid below to answer item 5.

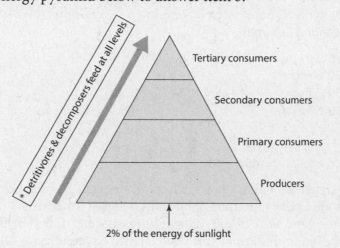

5. Which statement correctly describes the flow of energy through this pyramid?

   A. All of the energy of the producers is eventually transferred to the tertiary consumers.
   B. The largest amount of the energy is transferred from the secondary to the tertiary consumers.
   C. The energy of the producers is directly supplied to the primary consumers.
   D. All of the energy at each level is transferred to the next higher level.

Use the passage for item 6:

Suppose you need to pry up bricks from a walkway so that you can plant grass. You might use a crowbar, which is a simple lever. A lever is an arm that pivots (turns) against a pivot point (fulcrum). First you shove a short portion of the crowbar under the brick. Then you apply force downward at the long end of the crowbar. The crowbar pivots at the point where it meets the edge of the brick (the fulcrum). As a result, the brick is lifted out of the ground.

Physicists define work as what occurs when a force acts upon an object to move it. Work is calculated using the equation $F \times D = W$, in which F is the force applied downward on the crowbar, D is the length of the crowbar, and W is the resulting upward movement of the brick.

6. You need to use a force of 5N to move a brick. How much more work can you do with the same force using a 3-foot-long crowbar instead of a 2-foot-long crowbar?

    A. 25% more
    B. 30% more
    C. 50% more
    D. 100% more

Use the passage for items 7–8:

    Genes are the primary basis of heredity. A gene is a region of DNA on a chromosome. Very few traits of humans or other animals are determined by only one gene. One of the traits of humans determined by one gene is the blood type agglutination factor. There are three versions, or alleles, of this gene, A, B, and O, on chromosome 9. Alleles A and B encode agglutination proteins that are found on the surface of red blood cells. Allele O encodes a non-functional protein. The genes for the A and type B agglutination proteins are co-dominant.

7. The table shows the possible contributions of each parent's chromosomes 9 (Chr. 9), the child's genotype (the two alleles, one from each parent), and the child's blood type trait (phenotype). Fill in the blanks in the table.

Allele Inherited from One of the Chr. 9 of One Parent	Allele Inherited from One of the Chr. 9 of the Other Parent	Child's Genotype (the genetic alleles on the two Chr. 9)	Child's Blood Type
A	A	AA	A
B	B		
B	A	AB	AB
A	B		
A	O	AO	A
B	O		
O	O		

8. A person with the AB blood type has inherited the A allele from one of the first parent's pair of chromosome 9 and the B allele from one of the other parent's pair of chromosome 9. Fill in the Punnett square to show the genotypes of the possible children of two parents with blood type AB.

	Parent 2: A	Parent 2: B
Parent 1: A	Possible child:	Possible child:
Parent 1: B	Possible child:	Possible child:

Use the passage for items 9–10:

In physics, conservation of momentum is demonstrated through collisions. The total momentum of a system before a collision is equal to the total momentum of the system after the collision:

$$P_{before} = P_{after}$$

where p is momentum.

The momentum of an object is equal to its mass multiplied by its velocity:

$$p = mv$$

where p is momentum, m is mass and v is velocity.

Velocity is a vector quantity, meaning that it has both magnitude and direction. To express velocity, the speed and the direction of movement must be stated. For example, when you walk across a room, your velocity might be 10 feet/second east.

Consider the following collision: A 5000 kilogram (kg) car traveling south at 4 meters/second (m/s) collides with an 8000 kg truck traveling north at 2 m/s. After the collision, the car and truck form a system with a certain speed and direction.

9. How much momentum, in kg-m/s, does the car have before the collision?

   A. 10,000 kg-m/s north
   B. 10,000 kg-m/s south
   C. 20,000 kg-m/s north
   D. 20,000 kg-m/s south

10. How much momentum, in kg-m/s, does the truck have before the collision?

A. 16,000 kg-m/s north
B. 16,000 kg-m/s south
C. 32,000 kg-m/s north
D. 32,000 kg-m/s south

Social Studies

This Social Studies Posttest is designed to help you determine how well you have mastered this GED® test subject area and whether you are ready to take the real GED Social Studies test.

This test has 15 items in various formats and one essay question. The question formats are the same as the ones on the real exam and are designed to measure the same skills. Many of the questions are based on historical documents or on short reading passages on social studies topics. Some are based on graphics such as a map, a diagram, or an illustration. You will also see questions based on paired passages.

Most of the questions are in multiple-choice format, but you will also see questions in other formats, such as fill-in-the-blank items and simulated click-and-drag and drop-down items. On the real GED test, you will indicate your answers by clicking on the computer screen. For this paper-and-pencil practice test, mark your answers directly on the page. Write your essay in the space provided.

To get a good idea of how you will do on the real exam, take this test under actual exam conditions. Complete the test in one session and follow the given time limit. If you do not complete the test in the time allowed, you will know that you need to work on improving your pacing.

Try to answer as many questions as you can. There is no penalty for wrong answers, so guess if you have to. In multiple-choice questions, if you can eliminate one or more answer choices, you can increase your chances of guessing correctly.

After you have finished the test, check your answers in the Posttest Answer Key section that begins on page 531.

Now turn the page and begin the Social Studies Posttest.

POSTTEST

Social Studies

Part 1: Multiple Choice

15 Questions (various formats) | **30 Minutes**

1. Which was a form of direct democracy in early colonial America?

   A. the House of Burgesses
   B. Magna Carta
   C. ordered government
   D. town meetings

Use the excerpt for items 2 and 3:

In the name of God, Amen. We whose names are under-written, the loyal subjects of our dread sovereign Lord, King James, by the grace of God, of Great Britain, France, and Ireland King, Defender of the Faith, etc. Having undertaken . . . a voyage to plant the first colony in the northern parts of Virginia, do . . . enact, constitute, and frame such just and equal laws, ordinances, acts, constitutions and offices, from time to time, as shall be thought most meet and convenient for the general good of the Colony, unto which we promise all due submission and obedience.

—*Excerpted from the* Mayflower Compact, *1620*

2. Where were the English colonists when they signed the Mayflower Compact?

   A. They were still in England.
   B. They were on a ship on their way to New England.
   C. They were settled in the Plymouth colony.
   D. They were in the presence of the English king.

POSTTEST

3. Why did the colonists sign the Mayflower Compact?

   A. to get permission to start a new colony
   B. to protest a government order to relocate
   C. to form a government for their new colony
   D. to promise to plant crops in their new colony

Use the excerpt for item 4:

"to institute new Government, laying its foundation on such principles and organizing its powers in such form, as to them shall seem most likely to effect their Safety and Happiness . . .

"We hold these truths to be self-evident, that all men are created equal, that they are endowed by their Creator with certain unalienable Rights, that among these are Life, Liberty and the pursuit of Happiness. —That to secure these rights, Governments are instituted among Men, deriving their just powers from the consent of the governed, —That whenever any Form of Government becomes destructive of these ends, it is the Right of the People to alter or to abolish it, and to institute new Government, laying its foundation on such principles and organizing its powers in such form, as to them shall seem most likely to effect their Safety and Happiness.

—*Excerpted from the* Declaration of Independence *by Thomas Jefferson*

4. Which Enlightenment thinker influenced Jefferson when he wrote "whenever any Form of Government becomes destructive of these ends, it is the Right of the People to alter or to abolish it, and to institute new Government"?

   A. Baron de Montesquieu
   B. John Locke
   C. Jean-Jacques Rousseau
   D. William Blackstone

5. Fill in the blank.

   Under the United States Constitution, the legislative branch is

   _____, meaning that it has two houses, the Senate and the House of Representatives.

6. The United States Constitution is built around six basic principles. Which principle establishes the people as the legitimate and final source of the government's authority?

    A. limited government
    B. popular sovereignty
    C. separation of powers
    D. federalism

7. The first 10 amendments to the U.S. Constitution are known as the Bill of Rights. Which of the following was covered by an amendment added later?

    A. the right to due process of law
    B. freedom from unreasonable searches
    C. the abolition of slavery
    D. protection of private property

Use the chart for item 8:

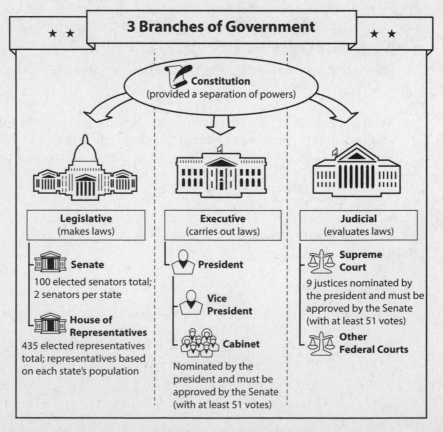

Source: http://kids.usa.gov/three-branches-of-government/index.shtml

POSTTEST

8. Which of the following is an example of the system of checks and balances?

    A. The Senate votes on the president's nominee for Supreme Court.
    B. Each state has a certain number of representatives based on population.
    C. The president nominates candidates to serve in the Cabinet.
    D. All three branches of government deal with laws.

    Indicate the choice that is correct and belongs in the blank. (**Note:** On the real GED test, the choices will appear as a "drop-down" menu. When you click on a choice, it will appear in the blank.)

9. The belief that the United States would inevitably expand its borders to

    the Pacific Ocean was called

Select... ▼
laissez-faire
manifest destiny
federalism
popular sovereignty

10. Which of the following was an advantage the North had over the South in the Civil War?

    A. Most battles were fought in the South.
    B. Industry was concentrated in the North.
    C. Northern generals were more experienced.
    D. The North was more determined than the South.

11. Fill in the blank.

    During the Cold War, the United States adopted a policy of

    _____ to prevent the spread of communism in Western Europe.

POSTTEST

Use the passage for item 12:

An electronics company creates and sells a new and very useful kind of computer. When the new computer is first offered to the public, there is a high demand for it because no other company sells anything quite like it, and the supply of the new computer is limited. The electronics company is therefore able to charge a high price and generate a large profit. However, other companies see how much profit the electronics company is making, so they decide to enter the market and create their own versions of the new kind of computer.

12. Based on the model of supply and demand, what is likely to happen to the market for this new kind of computer?

    A. Profit made from sales of the new computer will rise as supply goes up.
    B. Supply of the new computers will rise and profit will decline.
    C. Demand for the new computer will rise along with supply.
    D. Profit will increase demand for the new computer.

13. A loan that allows a consumer to purchase a good or service now and pay for it in the future is called

    A. principle.
    B. interest.
    C. inflation.
    D. credit.

Use the chart for item 14:

Factor	How It Affects Climate
Latitude (distance from the equator)	The closer a place is to the equator, the warmer it is.
Elevation	The higher a place is above sea level, the cooler the temperature.
Ocean temperature and wind currents	The temperature of ocean waters determines the directions of the wind currents that move heat.
Closeness to water	Areas closer to water may have more precipitation and have cooler or warmer temperatures than regions further inland.
Terrain	Mountains often determine how much rain or sun an area receives.

14. According to the chart, which factor would *best* explain why northern states in the United States are cooler than southern states?

    A. ocean temperature
    B. elevation
    C. terrain
    D. latitude

    Indicate the choice that is correct and belongs in the blank. (*Note:* On the real GED test, the choices will appear as a "drop-down" menu. When you click on a choice, it will appear in the blank.)

15. The growth of population in cities is the process of | Select... ▼ |.

    | urbanization |
    | immigration |
    | emigration |
    | diaspora |

POSTTEST

Part 2: Essay

1 Question | **25 Minutes**

Use the following excerpt for item 16:

1   Fifteen years ago, delegates from 189 countries met in Beijing for the Fourth World Conference on Women. It was a call to action—a call to the global community to work for the laws, reforms, and social changes necessary to ensure that women and girls everywhere finally have the opportunities they deserve to fulfill their own God-given potentials and contribute fully to the progress and prosperity of their societies. . . .

2   So as we meet here in New York, women worldwide are working hard to do their part to improve the status of women and girls. And in so doing, they are also improving the status of families, communities, and countries. They are running domestic violence shelters and fighting human trafficking. They are rescuing girls from brothels in Cambodia and campaigning for public office in Kuwait. They are healing women injured in childbirth in Ethiopia, providing legal aid to women in China, and running schools for refugees from Burma. They are rebuilding homes and re-stitching communities in the aftermath of the earthquakes in Haiti and Chile. And they are literally leaving their marks on the world. For example, thanks to the environmental movement started by Nobel Laureate Wangari Maathai, 45 million trees are now standing tall across Kenya, most of them planted by women.

3   And even young girls have been empowered to stand up for their rights in ways that were once unthinkable. In Yemen, a 10-year-old girl forced to marry a much older man made headlines around the world by marching into court and demanding that she be granted a divorce, which she received. And her courage helped to shine a spotlight on the continuing practice of child marriage in that country and elsewhere.

4   Now, these are just a few of the stories, and everyone here could stand up and tell even more. These are the stories of what women around the world do every day to confront injustice, to solve crises, propel economies, improve living conditions, and promote peace. Women have shown time and again that they will seize opportunities to improve their own and their families' lives. And even when it seems that no opportunity exists, they still find a way. And thanks to the hard work and persistence of women and men, we have made real gains toward meeting the goals set in Beijing. . . .

5   But the progress we have made in the past 15 years is by no means the end of the story. It is, maybe, if we're really lucky, the end of the beginning. There is still so much more to be done. We have to write the next chapter to fully realize the dreams and potential that we set forth in Beijing. Because for too many millions and millions of girls and women, opportunity remains out of reach. Women are still the majority of the world's poor, the uneducated, the unhealthy, the unfed. In too many places, women are treated not as full and equal human beings with their own rights and aspirations, but as lesser creatures undeserving of the treatment and respect accorded to their husbands, their fathers, and their sons. . . .

6   In 1995, in one voice, the world declared human rights are women's rights and women's rights are human rights. And for many, those words have translated into concrete actions. But for others they remain a distant aspiration. Change on a global scale cannot and does not happen overnight. It takes time, patience, and persistence. And as hard as we have worked these past 15 years, we have more work to do. . . .

7   This isn't window dressing, and it's not just good politics. President Obama and I believe that the subjugation of women is a threat to the national security of the United States. It is also a threat to the common security of our world, because the suffering and denial of the rights of women and the instability of nations go hand in hand. . . .

—*Excerpted from* Address to the United Nations Commission on the Status of Women *by Secretary of State Hillary Rodham Clinton, March 12, 2010, United Nations, New York*

POSTTEST

16. Determine and evaluate the purpose of this excerpt. Why does Secretary of State Clinton argue that the "subjugation of women is a threat to the national security of the United States"? What examples does she give to support this claim? Are they effective? Why, or why not?

    Write your response in the box. This task may take 25 minutes to complete.

Reasoning Through Language Arts (RLA)

1. **D**
2. **A**
3. **B**
4. **B**
5. **C**
6. **A**
7. **C**
8. **D**
9. **B**
10. **A**
11. **C**

12–18. See chart below.

ONLY the excerpt from *Clocks and Culture*	ONLY the excerpt from "The Coming Robot Army"	BOTH the excerpt from *Clocks and Culture* and the excerpt from "The Coming Robot Army"	NEITHER the excerpt from *Clocks and Culture* nor the excerpt from "The Coming Robot Army"
17	15	12, 14, 16, 18	13

19. **B**
20. **A**
21. **B**
22. **A**
23. **A**
24. Extended response. In response to this prompt, your essay should compare and contrast the arguments presented for and against teaching middle and high school students to use print reference books. You should choose which side you find more persuasive, and then develop an argument of your own explaining why you support that viewpoint, and why your readers should support it too. Make sure that your essay is structured sensibly and logically. Cite evidence from the passage to support your claim, and explain why you find that evidence more persuasive than the evidence for the opposing argument.

POSTTEST ANSWER KEY

If possible, ask an instructor to evaluate your essay. Your instructor's opinions and comments will help you determine what skills you need to practice in order to improve your essay writing.

You may also want to evaluate your essay yourself using the checklist that follows. Be fair in your evaluation. The more items you can check, the more confident you can be about your writing skills. Items that are not checked will show you the essay-writing skills that you need to work on.

My essay:

_____ Creates a sound, logical argument based on the passage.

_____ Cites evidence from the passage to support the argument.

_____ Analyzes the issue and/or evaluates the validity of the arguments in the passage.

_____ Organizes ideas in a sensible sequence.

_____ Shows clear connections between main points and details.

_____ Uses largely correct sentence structure.

_____ Follows standard English conventions in regard to grammar, spelling, and punctuation.

Mathematical Reasoning

1. **5 and 2** Both are repeats of y values already given for that x.

x	−2	−1	0	1	2	1	5	−2
y	5	3	0	2	6	2	7	5

2. Points A and D show the same x value with two y values.

3. $\dfrac{5}{2}$ $\dfrac{175 \text{ people}}{70 \text{ people}} = \dfrac{175}{70} = \dfrac{5 \cdot 5 \cdot 7}{2 \cdot 5 \cdot 7} = \dfrac{5}{2}$

4. **less than** 4 to −9 is 13 units. −5 to 9 is 14 units.

5. **C** Adding exponents,

$$-\frac{2}{3} + \left(-\frac{3}{2}\right) = -\frac{4}{6} + \left(-\frac{9}{6}\right) = -\frac{13}{6},$$

so $x^{-\frac{13}{6}} = \dfrac{1}{x^{\frac{13}{6}}}$.

POSTTEST ANSWER KEY

6. **A** $(5x+3)(x-4)=5x^2-20x+3x$

7. **D** Factor and cancel:

$$\frac{x^3-9x^2+20x}{x-4}$$

$$=\frac{x\,(x-4)(x-5)}{x-4}=x(x-5)$$

8. **D** $4x-5<3x+9 \rightarrow 4x-3x<9+5$
$\rightarrow x<14$

9. **B** Rearrange before dividing:
$$\frac{x^{-2}y^5}{x^3y^2}=\frac{y^5}{x^5y^2}=\frac{y^3}{x^5}.$$

10. **C** $6x^2+7x-20=20-20 \rightarrow 6x^2$
$+7x-20=0 \rightarrow$
$(2x+5)(3x-4)=0 \rightarrow 2x+5$
$=0$ or $3x-4=0 \rightarrow 2x+5-5$
$=0-5$ or $3x-4+4=0+4 \rightarrow$
$2x=-5$ or $3x=4 \rightarrow \dfrac{2x}{2}=\dfrac{-5}{2}$
or $\dfrac{3x}{3}=\dfrac{4}{3} \rightarrow x=-\dfrac{5}{2}$ or $x=\dfrac{4}{3}$

11. **C** To avoid a negative number under the radical, $5x \geq 0$. Solving, $x \geq 0$. The opposite of this statement is $x<0$.

12. **A** $\dfrac{\$5640}{470 \text{ people}}=\$12$ per person

13. **A** $6=3x \rightarrow 2=x$

14. $<, >, =$

15. **D** $17\overline{)128}$ remainder 9

16. **A** $25-4x=5 \rightarrow 25-5=4x \rightarrow 20$
$=4x \rightarrow 5=x$

17. **C** $9+3=12$ and $\dfrac{2}{7}+\dfrac{7}{9}=\dfrac{9}{9}\cdot\dfrac{2}{7}$

$+\dfrac{7}{7}\cdot\dfrac{7}{9}=\dfrac{18}{63}+\dfrac{49}{63}=\dfrac{67}{63}=1\dfrac{4}{63}$

18. **D** The least common denominator is xy.

$$\frac{4y-3x}{x}-\frac{2x+3y}{y}=\frac{y}{y}\cdot\frac{4y-3x}{x}$$

$$-\frac{x}{x}\cdot\frac{2x+3y}{y}=\frac{4y^2-3xy}{xy}$$

$$-\frac{2x^2+3xy}{xy}=$$

$$\frac{4y^2-3xy-2x^2-3xy}{xy}=$$

$$\frac{4y^2-6xy-2x^2}{xy}=$$

$$\frac{2(2y^2-3xy-x^2)}{xy}$$

19. **B** $\dfrac{n}{78}=\dfrac{11}{6} \rightarrow 78\cdot\dfrac{n}{78}=78\cdot\dfrac{11}{6} \rightarrow n$
$=13\cdot11 \rightarrow n=143$

20. **greater than**

Area of the circle: $A=\pi r^2=3.14(36)$
$=113.04$

Area of the square: $A=s^2=10^2$
$=100$

21. **B**

22. **B** Using $y=mx+b$ with $m=2$, $y=2x+b$. Substituting $x=3$ and $y=3$, $3=2(3)+b \rightarrow 3=$
$6+b \rightarrow -3.$

23. **A** Multiplication gives $36.75\times10^{14}=3.675\times10^{15}$.

24. **A** $0.555 = \dfrac{555}{1000} = \dfrac{5 \cdot 111}{5 \cdot 200} = \dfrac{111}{200}$

25. **C** $\dfrac{22}{5} = \dfrac{n}{32} \to 32 \cdot \dfrac{22}{5} = 32 \cdot \dfrac{n}{32} \to$
$\dfrac{704}{5} = n \to 140.8 = n$

26. **B** $3 \times 10^9 = 0.3 \times 10^{10}$, and
$7 \times 10^{10} + 0.3 \times 10^{10} =$
$(7 + 0.3) \times 10^{10} = 7.3 \times 10^{10}$

27. 0.0905, 0.077, 0.022, 0.0203, 0.00105

28. **C** $C = \pi d \approx 3.14(30) = 94.2$

29. **D** $A = \dfrac{1}{2}bh = \dfrac{1}{2} \cdot 8(9) = \dfrac{1}{2} \cdot 72 = 36$

30. **B** $V = lwh \to 42 = 7 \cdot 2 \cdot h \to 42$
$= 14h \to \dfrac{42}{14} = \dfrac{14h}{14} \to 3 = h$

31. **C** $f(6) = 29$ and $f(4) = 13$

32. **C** 120 pounds – 0.45 of the total
(100% – 55% sugar).
$\dfrac{120}{0.45} = 266.67$, which is the
total weight of the batch. To
find the amount of sugar,
multiply 0.55 · 266.67.

33. **D** $(2 + 2 \cdot 7)^2 - 3(2(7 + 14 \div 7))$
$= 16^2 - 3(2(9)) = 256 - 54 = 202$

34. **A** $8^{-\frac{5}{3}} = \dfrac{1}{8^{\frac{5}{3}}} = \dfrac{1}{\sqrt[3]{8}^5} = \dfrac{1}{2^5} = \dfrac{1}{32}$

35. **B** Invert the second fraction and
multiply: $\dfrac{2}{3} \times \dfrac{4}{9} = \dfrac{8}{27}$

36. **B** $\dfrac{1}{10}$ of 40 throws is 4.

37. **D** $\dfrac{2300}{0.26} = 8,846$

38. **C** Today's population is 90% of
last year's. $\dfrac{114,300}{0.9} = 127,000$

39. **greater than**

His median is 85, and the mean is 85.2.

40. **C** $(5x - 6)^2 = (5x - 6)(5x - 6)$
$= 25x^2 - 30x - 30x + 36 =$
$25x^2 - 60x + 36$

41. **A** Because the inequality sign is
"greater than" and an integer
is asked for, –21 does not
qualify.

42. $0.96 > 92\% > \dfrac{7}{8} > 0.87 > \dfrac{8}{11} > \dfrac{5}{9} > 8.3\%$

43. **B** Solve for y to put the equation
in the slope-intercept form.
$4x + 3y = 15 \to 3y =$
$-4x + 15 \to y =$
$-\dfrac{4}{3}x + 5$, so $m = -\dfrac{4}{3}$

44. **D** $(7x^2 + 9x + 13) + (8x - 5x^2)$
$= (7x^2 - 5x^2) + (9x + 8x) + 13$
$= 2x^2 + 17x + 13$

45. **the same as**

The probability of throwing H, H,
H, H is $\dfrac{1}{2} \cdot \dfrac{1}{2} \cdot \dfrac{1}{2} \cdot \dfrac{1}{2} = \dfrac{1}{16}$.

The probability for H, T, H, T, is also
$\dfrac{1}{2} \cdot \dfrac{1}{2} \cdot \dfrac{1}{2} \cdot \dfrac{1}{2} = \dfrac{1}{16}$.

46.

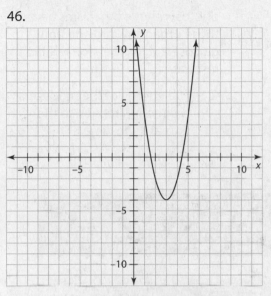

47. **B** The probability is the number of "good" outcomes, 2, divided by the number of all possible outcomes, 6. $\frac{2}{6} = \frac{1}{3}$

48. **B** actual decrease = 1500 – 1425 = 75;

percent decrease = $\frac{75}{1500} = 0.05 = 5\%$

49. **A** The slope is $m = \frac{9-4}{5-(-2)} = \frac{5}{7}$.

Using $y = \frac{5}{7}x + b$ and the coordinates of the point (5, 9),

$9 = \frac{5}{7} \cdot 5 + b \rightarrow 9 = \frac{25}{7} + b \rightarrow \frac{63}{7}$.

$-\frac{25}{7} = b \rightarrow b = \frac{38}{7}$ $y = \frac{5}{7}x + \frac{38}{7}$.

50. **A** Set $x = 0$. $y = 6 \cdot 0^3 + 5 \cdot 0^2$. The point is (0,4).

Science

1. *Sample response:* The lights have different levels of efficiency in transforming electric energy into light energy because to produce the same amount of lumens, they use different amounts of electric energy. Incandescent bulbs are the most inefficient and LEDs are the most efficient. Phasing out incandescent light bulbs and replacing them with CFLs and LEDs should reduce the need for electricity to power lights, which should reduce the production of carbon dioxide, sulfur dioxide, nitrogen oxides, and soot particles. These reductions will slow global warming and reduce acid rain and the amount of smog in the air. That will benefit human respiratory health and the health of plants and of organisms that live in water.

2. The revolution of the <u>moon</u> around <u>Earth</u> is responsible for the phases of the moon.

3. The seasons, which are most obvious between the poles and the equator on Earth, are due to the <u>Earth</u> revolving around the <u>sun</u>.

4. *Sample response*: Aerobic respiration and photosynthesis are opposite processes because in aerobic respiration, glucose is broken down into water and carbon dioxide and yields energy, and in photosynthesis, water and carbon dioxide plus light energy are used to produce glucose and oxygen. Humans consume photosynthetic organisms because those organisms provide both glucose and oxygen for aerobic respiration.

5. **C** The energy of the producers is directly supplied to the primary consumers.

6. **C** 50% more

7.

Allele Inherited from One of the Chr. 9 of One Parent	Allele Inherited from One of the Chr. 9 of the Other Parent	Child's Genotype (the genetic alleles on the two Chr. 9)	Child's Blood Type
A	A	AA	A
B	B	BB	B
B	A	AB	AB
A	B	AB	AB
A	O	AO	A
B	O	BO	B
O	O	OO	O

8.

	Parent 2: A	Parent 2: B
Parent 1: A	Possible child: AA	Possible child: AB
Parent 1: B	Possible child: AB	Possible child: BB

9. **D** 20,000 kg-m/s south

10. **A** 16,000 kg-m/s north

Social Studies

1. Choice **D** is correct. In New England, town meetings were a form of direct democracy in which every resident had the right to speak.

2. Choice **B** is correct. The colonists were aboard the *Mayflower* when they created and signed the document.

3. Choice **C** is correct. The purpose of the Mayflower Compact was to establish a government for Plymouth colony.

4. Choice **C** is the correct answer. Rousseau believed revolution was justified when a government breaks that contract by failing to serve the needs of the people.

5. Blank should be filled in with "bicameral."

6. Choice **B** is correct. Under the principle of popular sovereignty, the people are the final source of a government's power—the government derives its legitimacy from the people and answers to the people.

7. Choice **C** is correct. The abolition of slavery was established in the Thirteenth Amendment to the Constitution. It was not included in the original 10 amendments that form the Bill of Rights.

8. Choice **A** is correct. The Senate can check the powers of the executive branch by voting to approve or reject a nominee for Supreme Court. The president in turn can check the power of the Supreme Court by nominating candidates.

9. "Manifest destiny" should be chosen from the drop-down box.

10. Choice **B** is correct. Industry in the North enabled the Union to manufacture arms and other materials necessary to sustaining the war effort. By contrast, the South was often forced to look abroad for resources.

11. Blank should be filled in with "containment."

12. Choice **B** is correct. As more companies enter the market and produce more of the new computers, the supply will increase until eventually there is a surplus. At that point, to remain competitive, the producing companies will lower prices.

13. Choice **D** is correct. When people buy things on credit, they purchase the good or service now but pay for it in the future, often a little at a time each month.

14. Choice **D** is correct. Although elevation and ocean temperature also affect temperature, the best response is latitude, which explains climate on the basis of proximity to the equator.

15. "Urbanization" should be chosen from the drop-down box.

16. Extended response. In response to this prompt, your essay should describe the many problems associated with the subjugation of women, including health concerns, poverty, and domestic abuse. You may also cite Clinton's examples of the ways in which women and girls contribute to global stability and security, ranging from environmental initiatives to health care reform. By citing examples from around the world, Clinton connects the concerns of women and girls to the national security interests of the United States.

If possible, ask an instructor to evaluate your essay. Your instructor's opinions and comments will help you determine what skills you need to practice in order to improve your essay writing.

You may also want to evaluate your essay yourself using the checklist that follows. Be fair in your evaluation. The more items you can check, the more confident you can be about your writing skills. Items that are not checked will show you the essay-writing skills that you need to work on.

My essay:

_____ Creates a sound, logical argument based on the passage.

_____ Cites evidence from the passage to support the argument.

_____ Analyzes the issue and/or evaluates the validity of the arguments in the passage.

_____ Organizes ideas in a sensible sequence.

_____ Shows clear connections between main points and details.

_____ Uses largely correct sentence structure.

_____ Follows standard English conventions in regard to grammar, spelling, and punctuation.

Reasoning Through Language Arts (RLA)

Chapter 1: Reading and Analyzing Texts

Exercise 1: Main Idea and Supporting Details

1. **B**
2. **D**
3. **A**
4. **D**

Exercise 2: Relationships in Texts

1. **D**
2. **B**
3. **C**

Exercise 3: Vocabulary: The Meaning of Words and Phrases

1. **B**
2. **B**

Exercise 4: Word Choice, and Diction, Connotative and Figurative Meanings

1. **B**
2. **C**
3. **C**

Exercise 5: Author's Purpose or Point of View

1. **D**
2. **C**

Exercise 6: Rhetorical Techniques

1. **A**
2. **C** (or **D**)
3. **D** (or **C**)
4. **B**

Exercise 7: Analyzing Arguments

1. **A**
2. **A**
3. **D**
4. **B**

Exercise 8: Analyzing Data

1. **B**
2. **A**
3. **D**
4. **C**
5. **D**
6. **B**

Chapter 2: Comparing Texts

Exercise 1: Comparing Literature

1. **B**
2. **C**
3. **D**
4. **A**
5. **B**

Exercise 2: Comparing Argumentative Passages

1. **A**
2. **C**
3. **C**
4. **D**

Exercise 3: Comparing Across Genres and Forms

1. **B**
2. **D**
3. **B**
4. **A**
5. **C**

Chapter 3: Writing Extended Responses

Exercise 1: Finding the Main Idea of the Source Text

1. **D**
2. **C**

Exercise 2: Making Inferences

1. **D**
2. **A**

Exercise 3: Identifying Arguments and Evidence

1. **B**
2. **B**
3. **C**
4. **C**

Exercise 4: Evaluating Evidence

1. **C**
2. **A**
3. **B**
4. **D**

Exercise 5: Writing an Extended Response

Answers will vary. Essays should meet all the requirements of the rubric provided in the chapter.

EXERCISE ANSWER KEY

Chapter 4: Editing for Conventions of Standard English: Grammar and Usage

Exercise 1: Parts of Speech

1. river
2. that, he
3. preposition
4. adverb

Exercise 2: Parts of a Paragraph

1. phrase
2. clause
3. phrase
4. clause

Exercise 3: Coordination

1. **A**
2. **B**
3. **B**

Exercise 4: Subordination

1. **A**
2. **A**
3. **B**

Exercise 5: Parallelism

1. **B**
2. Answers may vary. Sample answer: The gems were prized for their value, rarity, and beauty.

3. Answers may vary. Sample answer:
   * Drafting
   * Revising
   * Editing
   * Proofreading
   * Publishing

Exercise 6: Writing Clearly and Concisely

1. **A**
2. **C**

Exercise 7: Using Transitions

1. **D**
2. **C**
3. **A**
4. **A**

Exercise 8: Subject-Verb Agreement and Pronoun-Antecedent Agreement

1. **B**
2. **A**
3. **A**
4. **A**
5. **B**
6. **A**

EXERCISE ANSWER KEY

Exercise 9: Pronoun Case

1. **B**
2. **A**
3. **B**

Exercise 10: Pronoun Reference

1. **B**
2. **B**

Exercise 11: Using Modifiers Correctly

1. **A**
2. **B**
3. **A**
4. **A**

Exercise 12: Nonstandard and Informal Usage: Frequently Confused Words

Revisions are in boldface.

A. That is **a lot** of mulch.

B. **Try to** turn the knob.

E. **You're** going to win the race!

F. Please **accept** my apology.

H. How will that **affect** you?

I. Divide the dessert **among** the four of you.

K. It **doesn't** matter to Connor.

L. He did **well** on that assessment.

N. I **infer** from the results that I misunderstood the directions.

O. Marti saw **their** lost cat hiding in the bushes.

P. Answers may vary. Sample answer: She was, **figuratively speaking,** catapulted to fame.

R. I like swimming more **than** hiking.

EXERCISE ANSWER KEY

Chapter 5: Editing for Conventions of Standard English: Capitalization and Punctuation

Exercise 1: Capitalization

1. **M**y, **B**anjo, **C**himmy
2. **L**incoln **M**emorial, **W**ashington, **D**.**C**.
3. **R**anjan, **A**bby, **W**ebberville **R**oad
4. **A**unt **R**etha, **A**cme **B**ookstore
5. **I**, *Greek Mythology: Classic Myths*
6. **B**uddhism, **H**induism

Exercise 2: Writing Correct Sentences

Corrected sentences may vary.

1. Correct
2. Fragment. I am upset because we will be late.
3. Run-on. I saw that movie. It was good.
4. Run-on. The light turned green, and we turned left.
5. Correct
6. Fragment. Whenever you decide to get your plane ticket, email me.

Exercise 3: End Marks

1. Are you really getting up at 4:00 A.M.?

2. The vegetable garden needs to be watered.
3. Ms. Carter asked all the students to line up in the front hall.
4. The artifact is from 12 B.C. or perhaps A.D. 34.
5. Watch out for that falling anvil!

Exercise 4: Commas in Series and Sentences

1. The recipe calls for peas, carrots, and potatoes.
2. Paint was everywhere: on the sofa, in the carpet, and even under the bookshelves.
3. Kirk wrote the script last winter, and Madge directed the play this season.
4. That is a kind, thoughtful gesture, and I really appreciate it.
5. Well, Annie illustrated the book but did not write it.

Exercise 5: Commas with Nonessential Elements

1. Andy's son, Sly, is an only child.
2. The movie *The Fall*, which I recommended the other night, is available at the library.

EXERCISE ANSWER KEY

3. **C**

4. Leaving in a hurry, Miranda forgot to put the dog in its crate and bring in the mail.

Exercise 6: Commas with Introductory Elements

1. Yes, I'd love to share a salad with you.

2. If you are online, will you please check tonight's weather forecast?

3. Hurrying toward the finish line, the runner experienced a burst of energy.

4. Startled, the chihuahua began barking madly.

Exercise 7: Semicolons

1. The itinerary includes three cities: Houston, Texas; Washington, D.C.; and Gainesville, Florida.

2. The weather on the island will be cold; the team should pack very warm clothes.

3. Robyn volunteers weekly at the homeless shelter; also, she is raising money to help a local family who lost their home in a fire.

4. I like studying insects; however, I still don't like live cockroaches.

Exercise 8: Apostrophes

1. Sarah's new bike lock, which she can't find, is green.

2. All four teams' medals are in that box, but the ribbons in the other box have to be returned.

3. The ribbons have extra *o*'s in the city name.

4. It's unclear to me whether the *'60s* was an unusually turbulent decade or whether its hype is overblown. [*'60's* is also acceptable, though not preferable.]

5. They're coming over to look for something of theirs that they left behind on Monday.

Exercise 9: Review of Capitalization and Punctuation

1. **W**here's the charger for your new phone**?**

2. Well, **I** don't know if they're ready to go; however, **A**na definitely is.

3. Shivering in the icy drizzle, we looked forward to building a cozy, warm fire at our new home at 1230 **H**earthstone **S**treet.

4. The bees, butterflies, and birds all seem to enjoy those two beautiful trumpet vines, which **C**edric planted last year**.**

5. **I**f you could go anywhere, would you go see the **G**rand **C**anyon, the **B**rooklyn **B**ridge, or **H**oover **D**am today**?**

Mathematical Reasoning

Chapter 1: Integers

Exercise 1: The Number Line

Exercise 2: Signed Numbers

1.

2. A. −20

   B. −8

3. A. −5

   B. 10

3. −27

4. 6

5. 4

6. −39

Exercise 3: Order and Absolute Value

1. A. <

   B. >

   C. <

   D. >

2. A. 44

   B. 12

   C. −11

   D. −72

Exercise 4: Adding Signed Numbers

1. −6

2. −7

Exercise 5: Subtracting Signed Numbers

1. 55

2. −32

3. −22

4. −54

5. −67

6. 8

7. 50

8. 9

9. 15

10. 5

Exercise 6: Multiplying and Dividing Signed Numbers

1. 12

2. –15

3. –40

4. 21

5. 5

6. –4

7. –3

8. 4

Exercise 7: The Coordinate Plane

1. (2, –6)

2. (–6, 2)

3. (–5, –5)

Exercise 8: Quadrants and Coordinates

1. A and E are reflections of each other in the x-axis, and B and D are reflections of each other in the y-axis.

2. A. QIV

   B. QIII

   C. QI

   D. QII

Exercise 9: Multiples

1. 9, 18, 27, 36, 45, 54, 63, 72, 81, 90, …

2. 30, 60, 90, 120, …

3. 120, 240, 360, 480, …

4. 60

5. 72

Exercise 10: Factors

1. 1, 2, 4, 8, 16, 32

2. 1, 2, 5, 10

3. 1, 2, 4

4. 12

5. 10

Chapter 2: Exponents and Properties of Numbers

Exercise 1: Exponents

1. *24* is the base; *73* is the exponent.

2. A. $2 \cdot 2 \cdot 2 \cdot 2 \cdot 2 \cdot 2 = 2^6$

   B. $5 \cdot 5 \cdot 5 \cdot 5 \cdot 5 \cdot 5 \cdot 5 \cdot 5 = 5^8$

3. A. $6^4 = 6 \cdot 6 \cdot 6 \cdot 6$

   B. $7^{10} = 7 \cdot 7 \cdot 7 \cdot 7 \cdot 7 \cdot 7 \cdot 7 \cdot 7 \cdot 7 \cdot 7$

4. A. $4^5 = 4 \cdot 4 \cdot 4 \cdot 4 \cdot 4 = 16 \cdot 16 \cdot 4$
   $= 256 \cdot 4 = 1024$

   B. $7^3 = 7 \cdot 7 \cdot 7 = 49 \cdot 7 = 343$

Exercise 2: Exponents—Special Cases

1. $1^{17} = 1$
2. $0^{10} = 0$
3. 0^0 is undefined
4. $3^1 = 3$
5. $7^0 = 1$
6. $10^{11} = 100{,}000{,}000{,}000$
7. $10^9 = 1{,}000{,}000{,}000$
8. $1{,}000{,}000 = 10^6$
9. $10{,}000{,}000{,}000{,}000 = 10^{14}$

Exercise 3: Negative Bases

1. -216
2. 1
3. 25
4. -64
5. -128

Exercise 4: Roots and Radicals

1. 8
2. 15
3. undefined
4. 5
5. -3
6. $2\sqrt{6}$
7. $3\sqrt{5}$
8. $9\sqrt{2}$

9. $3\sqrt[3]{3}$
10. $6\sqrt[3]{2}$

Exercise 5: Properties of Numbers

1. Associative Property of Multiplication
2. Commutative Property of Addition
3. $35 - 14$
4. $18 + 54$
5. $24 + 3 + 15$
6. $x = a$
7. $6 \leq x$
8. $2 = y$
9. $p > a$

Exercise 6: The Product Rule and the Factor Rule

1. 2^{11}
2. 10^{x+3}
3. can't be rewritten
4. x^5
5. 4^{14}
6. $2^3 \cdot 7^3$
7. $5^4 \cdot x^4$
8. $2^8 \cdot 5^8$
9. $3^5 \cdot 7^5 \, a^5$
10. $11^9 \, x^9 \, y^9$
11. $2^6 \cdot 3^4 \cdot 5^{10}$

12. $2^{x+y} \cdot 3^x \cdot 5^y$

13. $2^6 \cdot 5^3 \, x^9$

14. $3^7 \cdot 5^5 \cdot 7^8$

Exercise 7: The Quotient Rule

1. 5^6

2. $\dfrac{1}{8^2}$

3. x^4

4. $\dfrac{3^4}{a^2}$

5. $\dfrac{x^3}{n^2}$

Exercise 8: The Power Rule

1. 2^{12}

2. x^6

3. 3^{4r}

4. 7^{5a}

5. x^{3n}

Exercise 9: Exponent Rules

1. x^{23}

2. $\dfrac{3^{20}}{5^{12}}$

3. $3^2 \, x^{14}$

4. $\dfrac{2^3 \, x^3}{7^3 \, y^3}$

5. $2^7 \, x^{23}$

6. $p^{15} \, q^6$

7. $\dfrac{1}{r^{13}}$

8. $\dfrac{a^9 x^{15}}{b^4 y^{12}}$

Exercise 10: Negative Exponents

1. $\dfrac{1}{7^4}$

2. 3^5

3. $\dfrac{3^2}{5^2}$

4. b^4

5. $\dfrac{5b^5}{6a^6}$

6. $\dfrac{p^4}{8^4}$

7. $\dfrac{m^4 q^7}{n^2 p^3}$

8. $\dfrac{7^4}{t^3}$

9. $\dfrac{v^7}{u^7}$

10. $\dfrac{p^3}{q^5}$

Exercise 11: Fractional Exponents

1. $\sqrt{7}$

2. $\sqrt[3]{5}$

3. $\dfrac{1}{\sqrt{2}}$

4. $\dfrac{1}{\sqrt[3]{9}}$

EXERCISE ANSWER KEY

5. $\dfrac{1}{\sqrt[3]{x}^2}$ or $\dfrac{1}{\sqrt[3]{x^2}}$

6. $10^{\frac{1}{3}}$

7. $3^{-\frac{1}{2}}$

8. $4^{-\frac{1}{3}}$

9. $6^{\frac{1}{2}}$

10. $x^{-\frac{1}{2}}$

11. 7

12. $\dfrac{1}{11}$

13. 3

14. $\dfrac{1}{2}$

15. 4

Chapter 3: Fractions

Exercise 1: Fractions and Mixed Numbers

A. Proper fraction (not reduced)

$\dfrac{7}{21}$ __A__

$1\dfrac{3}{4}$ __C__

B. Improper fraction

$6\dfrac{1}{4}$ __C__

$\dfrac{62}{10}$ __B__

C. Mixed number

$\dfrac{5}{5}$ __B__

$\dfrac{3}{4}$ __D__

D. Proper fraction (reduced)

$\dfrac{3}{8}$ __D__

$\dfrac{6}{32}$ __A__

Exercise 2: Reducing Fractions and Converting Between Fractions and Mixed Numbers

1. $\dfrac{1}{2}$

2. $\dfrac{1}{3}$

3. $\dfrac{1}{2} \times \dfrac{12}{12} = \dfrac{12}{24}$

4. $\dfrac{3}{16} \times \dfrac{3}{3} = \dfrac{9}{48}$

EXERCISE ANSWER KEY

5. $\dfrac{11}{8}$

6. $\dfrac{14}{5}$

7. 5

8. $3\dfrac{3}{5}$

Exercise 3: Adding and Subtracting Fractions and Mixed Numbers

1. Add $3\dfrac{3}{4} + 6\dfrac{3}{4} = 9\dfrac{6}{4} = 10\dfrac{2}{4} = 10\dfrac{1}{2}$

2. Add $7\dfrac{5}{8} + 4\dfrac{3}{5} = 7\dfrac{25}{40} + 4\dfrac{24}{40}$

   $= 11\dfrac{49}{40} = 12\dfrac{9}{40}$

3. Subtract $7\dfrac{1}{6} - 4\dfrac{5}{6} = 6\dfrac{7}{6} - 4\dfrac{5}{6}$

   $= 2\dfrac{2}{6} = 2\dfrac{1}{3}$

4. Subtract $8\dfrac{1}{3} - 3\dfrac{4}{5} = 8\dfrac{5}{15} - 3\dfrac{12}{15}$

   $= 7\dfrac{20}{15} - 3\dfrac{12}{15} = 4\dfrac{8}{15}$

Exercise 4: Multiplying and Dividing Fractions and Mixed Numbers

1. $\dfrac{1}{8} \times \dfrac{3}{32} = \dfrac{3}{256}$

2. $1\dfrac{3}{5} \div 2\dfrac{2}{3} = \dfrac{8}{5} \div \dfrac{8}{3} = \dfrac{8}{5} \times \dfrac{3}{8} = \dfrac{3}{5}$

3. $1\dfrac{3}{4} \div \dfrac{3}{5} = \dfrac{7}{4} \times \dfrac{5}{3} = \dfrac{35}{12} = 2\dfrac{11}{12}$

Exercise 5: Working Problems with Fractions

1. $56 \times \dfrac{1}{4} = \dfrac{56}{1} \times \dfrac{1}{4} = \dfrac{56}{4}$
   = 14 questions
   56 – 14 = 42 left to do.

2. $125 \times 1\dfrac{3}{5} = \dfrac{125}{1} \times \dfrac{8}{5} = 200$

3. $2\dfrac{3}{4}$ = original number $\times \dfrac{1}{2}$

   original number $= 2\dfrac{3}{4} \div \dfrac{1}{2} =$

   $\dfrac{11}{4} \times \dfrac{2}{1} = \dfrac{22}{4} = 5\dfrac{2}{4} = 5\dfrac{1}{2}$

Chapter 4: Decimals

Exercise 1: Place Values in Decimals

1. 8 hundredths

2. 7 tenths

3. 3 thousandths

Exercise 2: Rounding

1. 167.93

2. 0.003

3. 6.7893

4. 123

EXERCISE ANSWER KEY

Exercise 3: Adding and Subtracting Decimal Numbers

1. 262.4765
2. 0.0458
3. 121.063
4. 0.00322

Exercise 4: Multiplying Decimal Numbers

1. 5
2. 6
3. 7
4. 8

Exercise 5: Dividing Decimal Numbers

1. 78,000
2. 0.005
3. 2.27
4. 4.3
5. 1.173
6. 8430

Exercise 6: Converting Between Fractions and Decimals

	Decimal	Fraction
1.	0.002	$\frac{2}{1000} = \frac{1}{500}$
2.	0.1875	$\frac{3}{16}$
3.	0.26667	$\frac{4}{15}$
4.	2.375	$\frac{2375}{1000} = \frac{19}{8}$

Exercise 7: Scientific Notation

	Scientific Notation	Number
1.	6.02×10^5	602,000
2.	1.14525×10^3	1145.25
3.	5×10^{-4}	0.0005
4.	1.7×10^1	17

Exercise 8: Operations in Scientific Notation

1. 7.55×10^6
2. 9.13×10^7
3. 1.87625×10^{17}
4. 6.67×10^{-7}

Chapter 5: Ratios, Rates, and Proportions

Exercise 1: Ratios

1. $\frac{5}{4}$; 5:4

2. $\frac{4}{1}$; 4:1

3. 4:5:2

4. 2:10:1:5

Exercise 2: Rates

1. $\frac{80 \text{ cashews}}{7 \text{ people}}$; 80 cashews:7 people

EXERCISE ANSWER KEY

2. $\dfrac{\$36}{5 \text{ minutes}}$; \$36:5 minutes

Exercise 3: Unit Rates

1. $40 \dfrac{\text{houses}}{\text{block}}$

2. $3\dfrac{1}{2}$ mice per cage

3. $35.5 \dfrac{\text{rooms}}{\text{floor}}$

Exercise 4: Using Unit Rates

1. 660 students
2. \$19.95
3. 42 tons of sand
4. 280 miles
5. 1280 nails
6. \$205.50
7. 640 square feet
8. 168 hours

Exercise 5: Proportions

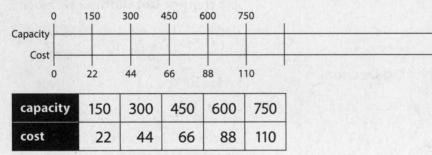

capacity	150	300	450	600	750
cost	22	44	66	88	110

Exercise 6: Solving Problems with Proportions

1. 1.42 miles
2. 99 square feet
3. \$6.35

Chapter 6: Percents

Exercise 1: Converting Between Percents and Decimals

1. 0.45
2. 1.27
3. 0.0025
4. 17%
5. 245%
6. 8.5%

EXERCISE ANSWER KEY

Exercise 2: Converting Between Percents and Fractions

1. 80%

2. 28.8%

3. 9944%

4. $\dfrac{18}{25}$

5. $8\dfrac{27}{100}$

6. $\dfrac{11}{20,000}$

Exercise 3: Basic Percentage Questions

1. 20%

2. 60.35

3. 33.33

4. $11,625

Exercise 4: Percent Increase and Decrease

1. 3120 visitors

2. 25.6% decrease

3. $19.98

4. 90 people

5. 6% increase

6. 30 hours

7. 13 in.

8. $55,027

Chapter 7: Probability and Statistics

Exercise 1: Probability

A. There are 12 face cards in a deck, so the probability is $\dfrac{12}{52} = \dfrac{3}{13}$ $= 0.23 = 23\%$

B. There are 4 aces, so the probability is $\dfrac{4}{52} = \dfrac{1}{13} = 0.077 = 7.7\%$

C. There is only one ace of hearts. The probability is $\dfrac{1}{52} = 0.019 \cong 2\%$

Exercise 2: Probabilities of Repeated Events

The probability of rolling a 3 on a single roll of a die is $\dfrac{1}{6}$. This does not change with the second and third rolls. All rolls are independent, so we have a probability of $\dfrac{1}{6} \times \dfrac{1}{6} \times \dfrac{1}{6} = \dfrac{1}{216}$ $\cong 0.0046$, or just under one-half percent.

Exercise 3: Probability Trees

Br = brown eyes; Bl = blue eyes

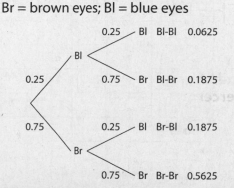

1. The probability of having children with eyes of different colors is $0.1875 + 0.1875 = 0.375$.

2. The probability of having children with the same colored eyes is $0.5625 + 0.0625 = 0.625$, which could also be computed by subtracting $1 - 0.375$.

Exercise 4: Factorials

1. $3! = 3 \times 2 \times 1 = 6$

2. $6! = 6 \times 5 \times 4 \times 3 \times 2 \times 1 = 720$

3. $10! = 10 \times 9 \times 8 \times 7 \times 6 \times 5 \times 4 \times 3 \times 2 \times 1 = 3,628,800$

Exercise 5: Problems Using Permutations and Combinations

1. Order of selection is not important, so this is a combination of 5 items selected from 7 possibilities.

$$_7C_5 = \frac{7!}{(7-5)!5!} = \frac{7!}{2!5!} = \frac{7 \times 6 \times 5!}{2 \times 5!}$$

$$= \frac{42}{2} = 21 \text{ different groups}$$

2. What pattern is used where makes a difference. Any three patterns selected can be used in three different ways. We use a permutation.

$$_5P_3 = \frac{5!}{(5-3)!} = \frac{5!}{2!}$$

$$= \frac{5 \times 4 \times 3 \times 2 \times 1}{2 \times 1} = 60 \text{ different arrangements}$$

Exercise 6: Statistics: Mean, Median, and Mode

1. MEAN: The sum of the data is 202, and $\frac{202}{7} = 28.86$.

   MEDIAN: Listing data in numerical order:

   25.0, 26, 27.5, **27.5**, 30.0, 32.0, 34.0

   Counting from either end, the median is **27.5**, highlighted above.

   MODE: The value 27.5 appears twice and is the mode.

2.

Date	Number of Filters	Price per Filter	Total Cost	
1 Jan	25	$2.50	$62.50	
15 Jan	15	$2.75	$41.25	
21 Jan	10	$3.00	$30.00	
5 Feb	15	$2.50	$37.50	
12 Feb	15	$2.00	$30.00	
Totals	80		$201.25	$2.52

$$\frac{\$201.25}{80} = \$2.52$$

EXERCISE ANSWER KEY

Chapter 8: Geometry

Exercise 1: Circles and Spheres

1. For a circle, $A = \pi r^2$, so $1810 = \pi r^2$. Dividing both sides by π gives $r^2 = 576.14$. Taking the square root gives $r = 24.00$ feet. The restaurant will be 24 feet in radius, or 48 feet across.

2. The surface area of a sphere of radius r is $4\pi r^2$, but you have only half a sphere as a domed roof. The area to be painted will be $2\pi r^2$ $= 2\pi(24)^2 = 3619$ square feet.

Exercise 2: Cubes

1. The volume is $V = s^3 = 15^3 = 3375$ cubic centimeters.

2. The surface area of a cube of edge s is $SA = 6s^2$, but you are leaving off the top, so you need only $5s^2$. Substituting for s, you get $5(15)^2$ $= 1125$ square centimeters.

Exercise 3: Triangles

1. The area of each triangle is $A = \frac{1}{2}bh$ $= \frac{1}{2}(12)(12) = 72$ square feet. For three signs the total is 216 square feet.

Exercise 4: Pyramids

1. Since the volume of a pyramid is $V = \frac{1}{3}Bh$ where h is the height of the pyramid and the slant height is 480 feet, you need to find the true height. To do this you use the Pythagorean theorem. The section of the pyramid looks like this:

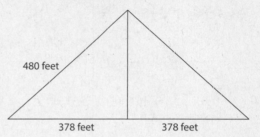

Using the Pythagorean theorem, $(480)^2 = (378)^2 + h^2$, or $h = \sqrt{230{,}400 - 142{,}884} = \sqrt{87516}$ $= 295.8$ feet. The area of the base is $B = 756^2$. The volume is $V = \frac{1}{3}Bh$ $= \frac{1}{3}(756)^2(295.8) = 56{,}353{,}450$ cubic feet.

Exercise 5: Cones

1. The surface area is $A = \pi rl + \pi r^2$ where l is the slant height and r the radius. Substituting, $A = \pi(5.5)(17) + \pi(5.5)^2$ $= 293.74 + 95.03 = 388.77$ square centimeters. To calculate the volume, find the true height. Use the Pythagorean theorem with a side of 5.5 cm and a hypotenuse of 17 cm.

$$17^2 = 5.5^2 + h^2$$
$$289 = 30.25 + h^2$$
$$258.75 = h^2$$
$$16.1 = h$$

For the cone, $V = \frac{1}{3}Bh$ or

$V = \frac{1}{3}\pi r^2 h$.

Substituting, $V = \frac{1}{3}\pi r^2 h = \frac{1}{3}\pi (5.5)^2$

$(16.1) = 510$ cubic centimeters.

Exercise 6: Cylinders

1. $SA = 2\pi r^2 + 2\pi rh = 2\pi r(r + h)$
    $= 2\pi(1.75)(1.75 + 1.25) = 10.5\pi$
    $= 33$ square inches.

2. $V = \pi r^2 h = \pi(1.75)^2(1.25) = 12$
    cubic inches.

Exercise 7: Hexagons

1. The area of the circle is
    $A = \pi r^2 = \pi(6)^2 = 113.1$ square
    units. The side of the hexagon is
    also 6 units. Its area is
    $A = \frac{3\sqrt{3}s^2}{2} = \frac{3\sqrt{3}(6)^2}{2} =$

93.53 square units. The circle has
$113.1 - 93.53 = 19.57$ square units
more area.

Exercise 8: Complex Bodies

1. The pill is a cylinder with a
    hemisphere at each end. The
    volume of a cylinder is $V = \pi r^2 h$.
    The pill has a radius of
    $\frac{0.75}{2} = 0.375$ cm. Substituting,
    $V = 2\pi(0.375)^2(1.25) = 1.104$
    cubic centimeters. The ends form a
    sphere with radius 0.375 cm. The
    volume of a sphere is $V = \frac{4}{3}\pi r^3$.
    Substituting, $\frac{4}{3}\pi(0.375)^3 = 0.221$
    cubic centimeters. Adding, you
    get 1.325 cubic centimeters.

Chapter 9: Polynomials and Rational Expressions

Exercise 1: Writing Polynomials

1. $x^3 - 6$

2. $2x + 4$

3. $(x - 3)^2$

4. $x^3 + 2$

5. $2(x + 1)^3$

Exercise 2: Evaluating Polynomials

1. after 5 seconds: 252.5 meters

2. after 15 seconds: 22.5 meters

Exercise 3: Adding and Subtracting Polynomials

1. $5x^2 + 4x + 1$

2. $-x^3 + 4x^2 + 5x + 4$

3. $2x^3 - x^2 + 6$

4. $4x^4 + 6x^3 - 10x + 11$

Exercise 4: Multiplying Polynomials

1. $-15x^7$

2. $4x^2 - 20x + 12$

EXERCISE ANSWER KEY

3. $6x^3 - 21x^2$

4. $-6x^6 + 4x^5 - 14x^4$

5. $x^2 - 4x - 21$

6. $6x^2 - 11x - 10$

7. $2x^3 - 3x^2 + x + 15$

8. $6x^4 - 52x^3 + 22x^2 + 36x + 4$

Exercise 5: Factoring and Dividing Polynomials

1. $5ab(3a + b - 4)$

2. $-7x^3(2x^3 + 3x - 1)$

3. $\dfrac{3a + b}{2}$ 4. $\dfrac{2xy^3}{3y + 4}$ 5. $\dfrac{7p}{3q}$

Exercise 6: Factoring Trinomials

1. $(x + 1)(x + 4)$

2. $(x - 1)(x - 4)$

3. $(x - 1)(x - 2)$

4. $(x + 2)(x + 1)$

5. $(x - 2)(x - 4)$

6. $(x + 10)(x + 2)$

Exercise 7: Factoring Trinomials When c Is Negative

1. $(x - 14)(x + 3)$

2. $(x + 14)(x - 3)$

3. $(x + 6)(x - 3)$

4. $(x - 9)(x + 4)$

5. $(x + 12)(x - 2)$

6. $(x - 9)(x + 6)$

Exercise 8: Factoring Trinomials When a ≠ 1

1. $(3x + 5)(x + 1)$

2. $(4x - 3)(x + 2)$

3. $(3x + 2)(x - 3)$

4. $(2x + 7)(4x - 3)$

5. $(2x - 5)(3x - 4)$

6. $(3x + 4)(4x + 3)$

Exercise 9: Adding and Subtracting Rational Expressions

1. $\dfrac{(2y - 3x)(2y + 3x)}{24xy}$

2. $\dfrac{9x^2 + 19x - 10}{(2x + 5)(3x + 5)}$

3. $\dfrac{41x + 17}{12(x + 2)}$

4. $-\dfrac{3x^2 + 8x - 12}{12x^2}$

5. $-\dfrac{x(2x^2 + 2x + 7)}{(x + 3)(4x - 7)}$

6. $\dfrac{2x^2 + x - 9}{(x + 3)^2(x - 3)}$

Exercise 10: Multiplying and Dividing Rational Expressions

1. $\dfrac{4an}{25bm^4}$

2. $\dfrac{63p^2x^3}{20q^3y^3}$

3. $\dfrac{3}{4}$

4. $\dfrac{2(a-3)}{3(a-2)}$

5. $\dfrac{p(p+8)}{p-2}$

6. 1

7. $\dfrac{x-5}{x+3}$

8. $\dfrac{(x-3)(x+6)}{3x-5}$

Chapter 10: Equations and Inequalities

Exercise 1: Solving One-Step Equations

1. −15
2. −5
3. 8
4. −5
5. −6
6. 3
7. −16
8. −10

Exercise 2: Solving One-Step Equations with Fractions

1. $\dfrac{2}{9}$
2. −10
3. $\dfrac{21}{2}$
4. $\dfrac{9}{10}$

Exercise 3: Solving Two-Step Equations

1. 4
2. $-\dfrac{1}{2}$

3. 12
4. −4
5. $-\dfrac{3}{2}$
6. $\dfrac{9}{2}$

Exercise 4: Clearing Fractions

1. $-\dfrac{8}{11}$
2. $\dfrac{26}{15}$
3. $-\dfrac{22}{27}$
4. $\dfrac{59}{8}$
5. $-\dfrac{77}{60}$
6. $\dfrac{29}{30}$

Exercise 5: Variables on Both Sides

1. 6
2. $-\dfrac{1}{2}$

EXERCISE ANSWER KEY

3. −4

4. $\frac{45}{16}$

5. −2

6. $\frac{21}{37}$

Exercise 6: Equations with Grouping Symbols

1. $\frac{26}{21}$

2. −2

3. $-\frac{41}{3}$

4. $-\frac{26}{17}$

5. $\frac{100}{9}$

Exercise 7: Solving Inequalities

1. $x > -2$

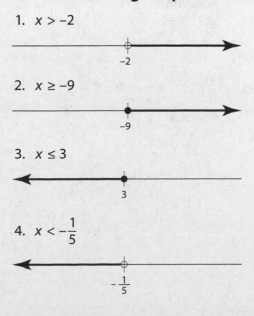

2. $x \geq -9$

3. $x \leq 3$

4. $x < -\frac{1}{5}$

5. $x < -\frac{16}{7}$

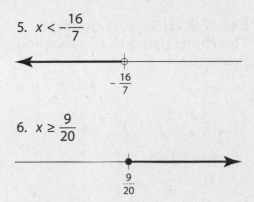

6. $x \geq \frac{9}{20}$

Exercise 8: Solving Systems of Equations by Substitution

1. (5,2)

2. (−6,3)

3. (1,−2)

Exercise 9: Solving Systems of Equations by Addition

1. (2,−1)

2. (3,2)

3. (5,−4)

Exercise 10: Solving Systems of Equations

1. (5,−3)

2. (5,−10)

3. (3,5)

4. (−2,2)

5. (3,−1)

6. (1,−1)

Exercise 11: Solving Quadratic Equations Using the Square Root Property

1. ±5
2. $\pm\dfrac{7}{4}$
3. no solution
4. $\pm\dfrac{6}{5}$
5. $\pm2\sqrt{5}$
6. $-1, 3$
7. $-2\pm\sqrt{5}$
8. not solvable with the square root property

Exercise 12: Solving Quadratic Equations by Factoring

1. $-3, -2$
2. $\dfrac{3}{2}, 4$
3. $-5, 4$
4. 2
5. $-5, \dfrac{7}{2}$
6. $-5, \dfrac{2}{3}$

Exercise 13: Solving Quadratic Equations by Completing the Square

1. $-3\pm\sqrt{13}$
2. $4\pm\sqrt{11}$
3. $\dfrac{9\pm\sqrt{102}}{3}$
4. no solution
5. $\dfrac{-7\pm\sqrt{65}}{8}$
6. no solution

Exercise 14: Solving Quadratic Equations Using the Quadratic Formula

1. $\dfrac{-3\pm\sqrt{29}}{2}$
2. $\dfrac{2\pm\sqrt{2}}{2}$
3. no solution
4. $\dfrac{5\pm\sqrt{13}}{2}$
5. $\dfrac{9\pm\sqrt{33}}{6}$
6. no solution
7. $\dfrac{-11\pm\sqrt{161}}{4}$

EXERCISE ANSWER KEY

Chapter 11: Graphing

Exercise 1: Plotting a Line

1.

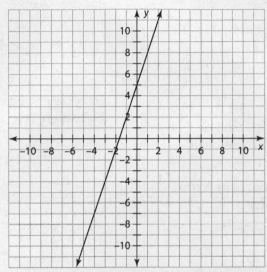

2.

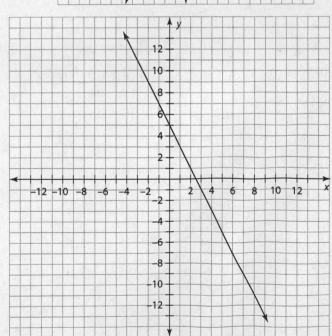

Exercise 2: Converting from Slope-Intercept Form to Standard Form

1. slope-intercept form $y = 2x$;
   standard form $2x - y = 0$

2. slope-intercept form $y = -3x + 3$;
   standard form $3x + y = 3$

3. slope-intercept form $y = \frac{3}{4}x + 4$;
   standard form $3x - 4y = -16$

4. slope-intercept form $y = -\frac{1}{3}x + 6$;
   standard form $x + 3y = 18$

Exercise 3: Converting from Standard Form to Slope-Intercept Form

1. A. $y = -\frac{3}{2}x + 2$

   B. $y = \frac{7}{5}x + \frac{5}{3}$

2. A. $m = -3, (0,b) = (0,-5)$

   B. $m = \frac{2}{3}, (0,b) = (0,-2)$

Exercise 4: Slopes

1. **C**

2. **B**

3. **D**

4. **A**

Exercise 5: Parallel and Perpendicular Lines

1. $y = 3x - 11$

2. $y = \frac{4}{3}x + 5$

3. $y = -\frac{1}{2}x + 9$

Exercise 6: Equations of Lines Between Two Points

1. $x + 5y = 27$

2. $x - y = 4$

3. $3x + y = 12$

4. $m = \frac{9 - 5}{5 - 5} = \frac{4}{0}$. Slope is undefined. This is the vertical line $x = 5$.

5. $m = \frac{7 - 7}{11 - 6} = \frac{0}{5} = 0$. This is the horizontal line $y = 7$.

Chapter 12: Functions

Exercise 1: Functions as Tables

1. not a function

2. function

3. function

Exercise 2: Function Notation

1. 16

2. −8

3. −9

4. 0

5. 16

6. 5

7. $\dfrac{1}{3}$

8. 9

9. 2

Exercise 3: Graphing Functions

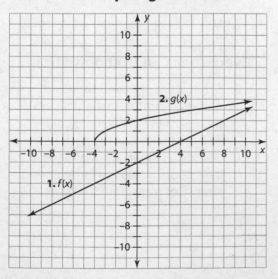

Exercise 4: Finding Domains

1. all numbers

2. $x \geq 2$

3. all numbers except 5

Exercise 5: Properties of Functions

1. increasing: $x < -4$ or $x > 4$; decreasing: $-4 < x < 4$; constant: nowhere

2. x-intercepts: $(-7,0),(0,0),(7,0)$; y-intercept: $(0,0)$

3. all numbers

4. maximum value $y = 6.5$ when $x = -4$

   minimum value $y = -6.5$ when $x = 4$

Science

Chapter 1: Life Science

Exercise 1: DNA

1. During cell division, DNA is packaged as chromosomes. During DNA replication and protein synthesis, DNA is unwound.

2. *Answers will vary somewhat.* Responses may focus on the need for a highly organized form of DNA to accommodate the very small volume of the nucleus.

Exercise 2: Structure of DNA

1. TTACTG. T and A always pair, as do C and G.

2. DNA stores the genetic code; mRNA copies that code and carries it to the protein-synthesizing machinery of the cell.

3. D

4. A

Exercise 3: Interacting Body Systems

1. A

2. D

3. The passage refers to the respiratory system of insects. (Note: Insects and humans have trachea that carry air into the body, but none of the other organs found in the human respiratory system occur in insects.)

Exercise 4: Homeostasis and Feedback

1. negative

2. hormone

3. homeostasis

Exercise 5: Mitosis

1. B

2. C

3. D

Exercise 6: Cell Differentiation

1. Adult stem cells and tissues derived from the patient's own tissues make the cells less likely to be attacked by the patient's immune system. Growing stem cells could provide a large enough supply of transplantable cells.

2. B

Exercise 7: Amino Acids

1. All amino acid molecules have a central alpha carbon, bonded to a hydrogen atom, carboxyl group, amino group, and an "R" group. The R group differs with each type of amino acid.

2. **C**

Exercise 8: Photosynthesis

1. **C**

Exercise 9: Cellular Respiration

1. *Answers may vary somewhat.* Types of Cellular Respiration

   I.   Aerobic respiration

   II. Anaerobic respiration (fermentation)

       A. Lactic acid fermentation

       B. Alcohol fermentation

2. **B**

Exercise 10: Carrying Capacity of an Ecosystem

1. *Carrying capacity* is the maximum number of individuals of a given species that an environment can support indefinitely.

2. **D**

Exercise 11: Biodiversity and Populations

1. **B** or **C**

2. **E**

3. **F**

4. **B** or **C**

5. **D**

6. **A**

Exercise 12: Socialization Within Populations

1. **B**

2. **C**

Exercise 13: Flow of Energy in an Ecosystem

1. *Answers may vary somewhat.* Both are heterotrophs. Carnivores eat flesh, while detritivores eat plant and animal material.

2. **A**

Exercise 14: Models of Energy Flow

1. **A**

2. A lion cannot be a second-level consumer. Second-level consumers must eat plants. Lions are carnivores.

Exercise 15: Cycling of Matter in the Biosphere

1. **A**

2. **B**

3. **B**

4. **C**

EXERCISE ANSWER KEY

Exercise 16: Inheritance and Variation of Traits

1. *Answers will vary.* Mutations are rare and are often corrected during DNA replication. Effects of individual mutations are often very slight.

2. **A**

Exercise 17: Mendelian Genetics

1. *Answers may vary somewhat.* "Genotype" is an organism's full hereditary information. "Phenotype" is an organism's actual observable attributes.

2. **D**
3. **C**

Exercise 18: Punnett Squares

1. 100% heterozygous, *Cc*. (All offspring will have curly wings.)

Exercise 19: Common Ancestry and Biological Evolution

1. **B**
2. **D**
3. Approx. 50%
4. *Answers will vary somewhat.* Virginia is not a heavily industrialized state and does not have much sooty pollution. Light-colored moths have been able to survive.

Chapter 2: Earth and Space Science

Exercise 1: The Big Bang Theory

1. **D**

Exercise 2: Stars and Elements

1. **D**

Exercise 3: The Sun

1. **B**

Exercise 4: The Solar System

1. **A**

Exercise 5: The Planets

1. **C**
2. **A**
3. **D**
4. **B**

Exercise 6: The History of Planet Earth

Answer: D, B, A, C

EXERCISE ANSWER KEY

Exercise 7: Earth's Surface

1. continental drift
2. tectonic
3. radiometrics
4. convection

Exercise 8: The Carbon Cycle

1. photosynthetic
2. metabolic
3. metabolic
4. metabolic

Exercise 9: The Hydrosphere: Water Everywhere

Wording of answers may vary slightly.

A. Evaporation (water evaporates)

B. Condensation (moisture in the air becomes clouds)

C. Precipitation (rain, snow, or ice falls)

D. Reentry (the water on the ground reenters a body of water)

Exercise 10: Weather: Earth's Atmosphere in Action

1. **D**

Exercise 11: The Lithosphere: Layers of Earth

1. **B**
2. **C**

3. **D**
4. **A**
5. orogeny
6. erosion
7. weathering
8. volcanism

Exercise 12: Interactions of Earth's Systems

1. **A**

Exercise 13: Climate and Weather

1. **B**

Exercise 14: Climate Change and Human Activity

1. **C**
2. **A**
3. **D**
4. **B**

Exercise 15: Maintaining a Healthy Planet

Answers will vary.

Benefits students might mention: creates jobs, cleaner-burning than petroleum, makes energy independence more feasible

Costs students might mention: uses water, endangers lands, threatens wildlife

Chapter 3: Physical Science

Exercise 1: Elements, Atoms, and the Periodic Table

1. D
2. E
3. F
4. B
5. C
6. A
7. A

Exercise 2: Compounds and Bonding

1. C
2. B
3. *Answers may vary somewhat.* The ionic bonds of calcium nitrate are weaker than the bonds of calcium sulfate.

Exercise 3: Reaction Rates

1. B
2. B
3. *Answers may vary somewhat.* Increasing the concentration of reactants decreases the distance between particles. Increasing the temperature increases the speed of the particles. Both conditions create more collisions between reactants. The more collisions, the more reactions.

Exercise 4: Le Châtelier and Equilibrium

1. C

Exercise 5: Conservation of Mass

1. Something had to escape the system of the burning wood. For instance, smoke and gases could make up the apparently missing mass.

Exercise 6: Radioactive Decay, Fission, and Fusion

1. A
2. A
3. C
4. B
5. D

Exercise 7: Balanced and Unbalanced Forces

1. C
2. According to Newton's first law, an object in motion will continue in motion until an unbalanced force acts on it. If the passengers are not seat-belted in the car, the passengers would stay in motion at the speed that the car was going before the collision with the stationary object, until they collide with objects such as the steering wheel, dashboard, windshield, and the like.

EXERCISE ANSWER KEY

Exercise 8: Force, Mass, and Acceleration

1. speed / direction
2. **B**

Exercise 9: Graphing Motion

1. **A**
2. **D**

Exercise 10: Momentum

1. When the carts stuck together, the mass of the first cart effectively doubled. If momentum is conserved, the formula $p = mv$ suggests that if m doubles, v must be cut in half to maintain a constant p.

Exercise 11: Strength of Noncontact Forces

1. **A**

Exercise 12: Electricity and Magnetism

1. The magnetic field around the magnet exerts a non-contact force on the electrons in the wire, thus creating the electric current.

Exercise 13: Electromagnets

1. wire, core
2. Wrapping a coil of wire around an iron core and creating an electric current in the coil produces an electromagnet. Increasing the current or the number of turns of the coil increases the strength of the magnetic field.

Exercise 14: Materials Engineering

1. Extended responses may mention one of these ideas: Steel is stronger and more flexible than iron. Concrete does not rot like wood. Steel and concrete are less expensive than cut stone. Glass is harder than plastic, will not scratch as windows, etc.

Exercise 15: Conservation of Energy

1. **D**
2. **C**
3. **A**

Exercise 16: Thermodynamics

1. **A**
2. **B**
3. **D**

Exercise 17: Electrostatic Forces

1. **B**
2. **A**
3. equal / opposite

Exercise 18: Mechanical Waves

1. medium

2. transverse

3. 2 m/s

4. frequency / velocity (or speed)

Exercise 19: Advantages of Digital Information Systems

1. **B**

2. **A**

3. **B**

4. *Answers will vary.* Copies can be made indefinitely; moderate corruption can be ignored; digital data is easy to manipulate.

Exercise 20: Disadvantages of Digital Information Systems

Any three of the following:

1. sampling error

2. need for greater bandwidth

3. data easily lost

4. need for synchronization

Exercise 21: Electromagnetic Radiation—Waves or Particles?

1. photon

2. particle

3. The photoelectric effect occurs when a photon of light shines on a metal surface and electrons are emitted from the metal. When a photon of light with enough energy strikes the surface of the right type of metal and hits an electron in an atom, it knocks the electron away from the atom.

Exercise 22: Effects of Electromagnetic Radiation

1. **D**

2. **C**

3. Shorter wavelength radiation has more energy and greater ionizing ability.

Social Studies

Chapter 1: Civics and Government

Exercise 1: Foundations of American Democracy

1. **D** In a direct democracy, citizens make decisions without the mediation of representatives.

2. **A** The Petition of Right was created to protect citizens from unlawful or arbitrary actions by government.

Exercise 2: The Influence of the Enlightenment

1. **C** John Locke

2. **D** William Blackstone

3. **A** Jean-Jacques Rousseau

4. **B** Baron de Montesquieu

5. Social contract theory asserts that an organized society forms a compact with its ruler or government, promising obedience in return for safety and justice. When the government no longer honors that compact, the people have a right to change their government. The idea of natural rights asserts that all people are entitled to certain liberties and freedoms that no government can take away.

Exercise 3: Creating a New Government

The Articles of Confederation   vs.   The U.S. Constitution

• No president
• Only states have power to tax
• Unicameral legislature

• Outlines powers and duties of Congress

• Bicameral legislature
• Bill of Rights
• President
• Outlines three-branch federal government

Intersection Area

EXERCISE ANSWER KEY

Exercise 4: The Six Basic Principles

1. Judicial review is the principle that a court has the power to examine and annul any acts by a legislature or governing executive that the court deems unconstitutional. It is part of the United States government's system of checks and balances.

2. Popular sovereignty is the principle that citizens have the final say on issues. Limited government is the principle that a government has only the authority that the people grant to it. The two principles work together to ensure that a nation's citizens are the final source of governmental authority.

3. A government that features a checks-and-balances system is

one in which the authority of each branch of government acts as a limit to the authority of the other branches of government.

Exercise 5: The Three Branches of the Federal Government

1. **D** Cabinet members are appointed by the president and are part of the executive branch.

2. **D** The president has the power to nominate Supreme Court justices, but the nominees must be approved by the Senate.

3. **B** The Constitution grants the Senate the right to approve the president's cabinet appointments.

Exercise 6: Federalism and the Concurrent Powers

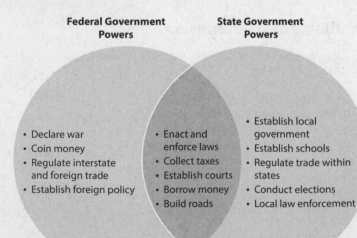

Federal Government Powers

- Declare war
- Coin money
- Regulate interstate and foreign trade
- Establish foreign policy

Shared Powers

- Enact and enforce laws
- Collect taxes
- Establish courts
- Borrow money
- Build roads

State Government Powers

- Establish local government
- Establish schools
- Regulate trade within states
- Conduct elections
- Local law enforcement

Exercise 7: The Bill of Rights and Civil Liberties

1. **C**   The Constitution gives the government a specific list of powers. Amendments are necessary to allow the government to meet the changing needs and beliefs of society. One example would be the extension of suffrage to African Americans after the Civil War.

2. **A**   The First Amendment of the Constitution specifically provides for the freedom to practice any religion.

3. **D**   The Fourth Amendment specifically limits the government's power to intervene in a citizen's private life or seize a citizen's property.

Exercise 8: The Expansion of Rights

1. **B**   The Fourteenth Amendment requires the states to provide equal protection under the law to all persons within their jurisdictions.

2. **C**   The Warren Court played an active role in setting out new guidelines for the legal protection of individuals.

3. **A**   The Supreme Court in recent times has extended rights and protections to groups that previously had lacked them.

Exercise 9: Political Parties and the Two-Party System

1. **C**   Political parties are organized for the purpose of nominating candidates for public office and campaigning for them.

2. **B**   Both parties continue to influence the American political system more than any other political group, as evidenced by the fact that relatively few third-party or independent candidates have won important elections in the United States in recent times.

Exercise 10: The Election Process

1. caucus—a group of party members meeting to select delegates who support particular electoral candidates

2. primary—an election in which voters for a particular party cast ballots for delegates who support particular electoral candidates; the candidate receiving the most delegate votes becomes the party's candidate in the election.

3. Electoral College—the group of people, chosen by each state and the District of Columbia, who formally elect the president

4. candidate—an individual chosen to run for public office on behalf of a political party

5. delegate—a person who represents his or her political party at the party's national convention

Exercise 11: Government Agencies

1. **A** The purpose of most federal agencies is to carry out laws. That makes them part of the executive branch, which is charged by the Constitution with carrying out the laws.

2. **A** One of the legislative powers of a government agency is to enforce laws that are subject to that agency's authority, so the best example is the Federal Trade Commission enforcing a consumer protection law.

Exercise 12: Interest Groups

1. **C** *Amicus curiae* briefs are legal arguments written by a person or group who is not party to a lawsuit but who shows support because the court's decision is likely to affect that person or group

2. Public opinion can help interest groups put political pressure on government officials to act or vote in the way the interest group wants.

3. Lobbying is a positive force when used to bring attention to issues that can benefit large sections of the American public, such as public health issues or consumer safety issues. Lobbying is a negative force when it is used to gain influence in Congress to unfairly advance the interests of a few against the interests of others.

Chapter 2: United States History

Exercise 1: The Making of a New World

1. **A** Based on the map, the Spanish traveled the furthest into North America.

2 **B** The map shows the voyages of discovery to the Americas.

Exercise 2: The 13 Colonies

D The map shows that after the end of the French and Indian War, Great Britain controlled not only the 13 colonies on the Atlantic seaboard, but also the territory west to the Mississippi River, including the area surrounding the Great Lakes.

2. **A** Native Americans would have benefited most because the proclamation banned settlement by American colonists in the area west of the Appalachian Mountains. which was still populated by Native Americans.

Exercise 13: The New Deal and Trouble in Europe

1. **C** The governments of both the communist Soviet Union and fascist Nazi Germany drastically restricted the liberties of their citizens.

2. **C** The New Deal was a set of policies with a common goal of helping the United States recover from the Great Depression.

Exercise 14: The Cold War Era

1. **A** The satellite countries that bordered the Soviet Union had been occupied by the Soviet army at the end of World War II. They were nominally independent but were in fact controlled by the Soviets.

2. **B** The Soviet Union was a casualty of the Cold War in that the cost of building and maintaining armaments and nuclear weapons proved economically ruinous.

Exercise 15: America in the Twenty-First Century

1. **A** After the end of the Cold War, the United States no longer faced a military threat from the Soviet Union. However, it encountered new problems in politically unstable regions throughout the world, as well as threats from various terrorist organizations.

Chapter 3: Economics

Exercise 1: Factors of Production

1. Natural resource
2. Entrepreneurship
3. Capital
4. Labor
5. Natural resource
6. Labor
7. Natural resource
8. Capital
9. Entrepreneurship
10. Capital

Exercise 2: Markets: Supply, Demand, and Prices

1. **B**
2. **A**

Exercise 3: Gross Domestic Product (GDP)

1. **C**

2. The graph indicates that manufacturing is a smaller share of overall economic activity today than it was in 1970 in all of the countries shown except China.

Exercise 4: Fiscal and Monetary Policy

1. The government can lower taxes and increase employment and the money supply by spending more on programs like education and infrastructure projects.

2. **D**

Exercise 5: Consumer Economics

1. **C**

2. **B**

Exercise 6: Political and Economic Freedom

1. **C**

2. People are protected from discrimination because markets encourage democratic governments with greater freedom of expression and operate according to impersonal forces of supply and demand.

Chapter 4: Geography and the World

Exercise 1: The Tools and Skills of Geography

1. **C**

2. **B**

Exercise 2: Place and Region

1. Africa: continent (or landform)

2. Rocky Mountains: landform

3. Mississippi River: body of water

4. the West in the United States: region

Exercise 3: Population Trends and Issues

1. birthrate: the average number of births per 1000 people

2. death rate: the average number of deaths per 1000 people

3. population density: the average number of people living in a square mile or kilometer

4. zero population growth: population stasis, occurring when birth and death rates are equal

Exercise 4: Human Settlement

1. A settlement is a temporary or permanent location where people live.

2. Urbanization is the process by which settlements grow into towns and cities as population increases and infrastructure such as buildings and streets is developed.

3. People move to cities to seek jobs. They also move to cities to improve their standard of living.

Exercise 5: Population Movement

1. **D** Immigration is the movement of people into a nation from another place.

2. **A** Free health care would be a powerful incentive to attract immigrants, and thus an important pull factor.

3. **C** A famine that makes it difficult to survive would be a powerful incentive to leave a place, and thus an important push factor.

Exercise 6: Elements of Culture

1. language—the system of words or signs that allows members of a group to communicate their ideas and beliefs to one another

2. cultural diversity—many different cultures existing in the same place

3. command economy—an economy in which the means of production are publicly owned; decisions about what is produced and how goods and services are distributed are made by a central authority

4. autocracy—a system of government in which a nation is ruled by a single leader

5. traditional economy—an economy in which long-established customs, habits, and beliefs determine what goods and services are produced and how they are distributed

6. social groups—groupings of people who share similar characteristics and have a sense of unity; groups may be further distinguished by social classes